Writing Great Fiction:
Storytelling Tips and Techniques

James Hynes, M.F.A.

THE
GREAT
COURSES

PUBLISHED BY:

THE GREAT COURSES
Corporate Headquarters
4840 Westfields Boulevard, Suite 500
Chantilly, Virginia 20151-2299
Phone: 1-800-832-2412
Fax: 703-378-3819
www.thegreatcourses.com

Copyright © The Teaching Company, 2014

Printed in the United States of America

This book is in copyright. All rights reserved.

Without limiting the rights under copyright reserved above,
no part of this publication may be reproduced, stored in
or introduced into a retrieval system, or transmitted,
in any form, or by any means
(electronic, mechanical, photocopying, recording, or otherwise),
without the prior written permission of
The Teaching Company.

James Hynes, M.F.A.
Novelist and Writing Instructor

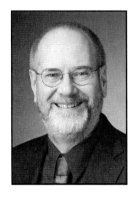

Professor James Hynes is a working novelist who has taught creative writing as a visiting professor at the University of Iowa Writers' Workshop, the University of Michigan, The University of Texas, Miami University, and Grinnell College. He earned a Bachelor of Arts degree in Philosophy from the University of Michigan in 1977 and a Master of Fine Arts degree from the Iowa Writers' Workshop in 1989.

Professor Hynes is the author of four novels: *Next*, which received the 2011 Believer Book Award from *Believer* magazine; *Kings of Infinite Space*, a *Washington Post* best book for 2004; *The Lecturer's Tale*; and *The Wild Colonial Boy*, which received the Adult Literature Award from the Friends of American Writers and was a *New York Times* Notable Book for 1990. His novella collection *Publish and Perish: Three Tales of Tenure and Terror* was a *Publishers Weekly* Best Book of 1997 and appeared on several critics' best-of-the-year lists.

Professor Hynes has received numerous literary grants and teaching fellowships. He received a James Michener Fellowship from the University of Iowa (1989–1990), and he was a member of the Michigan Society of Fellows at the University of Michigan (1991–1994). He received a Teaching-Writing Fellowship from the Iowa Writers' Workshop at the University of Iowa (1988–1999) and a Michigan Council for the Arts writer's grant (1984). As an undergraduate, he received the Hopwood Short Fiction Award from the University of Michigan (1976).

Professor Hynes is also a media and literary critic. He is a former television critic for *Mother Jones*, *The Michigan Voice*, and *In These Times*. His book reviews and literary essays have appeared in *The New York Times*, *The Washington Post*, *Boston Review*, *Salon*, and other publications.

Professor Hynes lives in Austin, Texas, the main setting of his novel *Next*, and is currently working on a new novel. ∎

Table of Contents

Table of Contents

Table of Contents

Writing Great Fiction:
Storytelling Tips and Techniques

Scope:

We all think we have a novel in us, and in this course of 24 lectures, a professional novelist will guide you through a survey of the most important concepts and techniques behind the creation of contemporary prose fiction, using examples from a wide range of classic novels and stories, as well as some demonstrations of his own process. By taking you step by step through such topics as creating characters, composing dialogue, crafting plots, and using different points of view, this course will help you get that book out of your head and heart and into the hands of readers.

Lecture 1 considers how to prepare yourself, both logistically and emotionally, for beginning to write a piece of fiction, and Lecture 2 explores the concept of evocation, or the art of making fictional characters in a fictional world come alive, which is fundamental to most fiction.

The next four lectures provide an introduction to the creation of fictional characters. In Lecture 3, we explore the differences between fictional characters and real people and consider how a "person" who is only a few thousand words on a page can come to life in the mind of the reader. Lecture 4 shows how you can create credible and interesting characters by combining your imagination with observations of real people. Lecture 5 looks at several ways of introducing a character into a narrative for the first time, and Lecture 6 examines different types of characters, such as round and flat characters and major and minor characters, and explores how they work together in a story or novel.

The next two lectures are about writing dialogue. Lecture 7 explains the mechanics and grammar of dialogue, including tips on when and when not to use dialogue tags and adverbs. Lecture 8 is about using dialogue to evoke character and tell a story and about integrating dialogue seamlessly into the rest of the narrative.

Next comes the longest block of lectures in the course, six lectures about plot. Lecture 9 introduces the subject by discussing the difference between a story and a plot and by showing three ways to structure a traditional plot. Lecture 10 demonstrates how traditional plots can usually be diagrammed with the well-known Freytag pyramid, while Lecture 11 suggests ways you can rearrange or adapt the individual pieces of a traditional chronology to make your plot more complex and intriguing. Lecture 12 covers how to structure a narrative when you're not interested in using a traditional plot; Lecture 13 introduces techniques for getting a plot started; and Lecture 14 explores ways to bring a plot to a satisfying conclusion.

© Sasaloi/iStock/Thinkstock.

The next three lectures discuss the concept of point of view in fiction. Lecture 15 surveys the range of points of view, from the godlike, omniscient third person to the intimacy of the first person. Lecture 16 looks at the various ways you can use the first-person point of view, and Lecture 17 runs through the many varieties of the third person.

The remaining seven lectures look at a variety of individual topics of importance to fiction writers. Lecture 18 discusses the various ways setting and place can be used in fiction, while Lecture 19 explores pacing and the need to pace different types of narratives in different ways. Lecture 20 considers how to craft an individual scene, which is one of the basic building blocks of fiction, and Lecture 21 looks at the advantages and disadvantages of composing manuscripts in complete drafts. In Lecture 22, we'll take a look at the essential process of revision and rewriting, while Lecture

23 considers two approaches to doing research for a work of fiction. The final lecture touches on the changing nature of the publishing business and offers personal insights into the challenges and joys of making a life as a fiction writer. ∎

Starting the Writing Process
Lecture 1

Whether you're a beginner starting your first story ever or a professional with many publications behind you, few things make a writer more anxious than facing a blank page. One approach to overcoming this obstacle is to think about what the opening of a story is supposed to do: draw readers in and capture their curiosity. The beginning should also suggest something important about the story—the main characters, the tone, or the setting. But even if you know the story you want to tell, how do you decide what the first paragraph or sentence should be? In this lecture, we'll look at some ways to make the beginning seem less foreboding.

Three Questions

- One way to sneak up on the start of your story is to break the question "How shall I begin?" into three separate questions: the artistic question, the logistical question, and the psychological question.

- Simply put, the artistic question is: What is this story about? What's the idea you want to explore? You may have an entire plot worked out in your head already, or you may have only a character or a situation in mind. Whatever it is, something has motivated you to write.

- The logistical question relates to the technical aspects of starting a story, the basic decisions you have to make at the start even if you don't know everything about your story. This is actually a number of questions combined, such as: Who's telling the story? What verb tense will you use? What voice is the story in? These early choices can be daunting because every decision you make will have consequences later on, many of which you can't foresee.

- Finally, the psychological question relates to how you gear up—emotionally—to begin. Even published writers become anxious about starting something new. Trying to leap that psychological hurdle involves being able to answer the first two questions, at least in part. That, in turn, ratchets up the anxiety, because there's so much you could worry about in advance that it's a wonder anyone ever starts at all.

The Five Ws

- Another way to approach starting a work of fiction is by using the old-fashioned five Ws of journalism: who, what, where, when, and why. Assuming you have a rough idea of what you want to write about, try to give a brief answer to each of these questions pertaining to the story you want to tell.

- The first question to address is: Who are your characters, and how are they related to each other? The who question also encompasses the choice of point of view, that is: Who is your protagonist, and who is your narrator? Sometimes these two are the same person, but that's not always the case. Often, the story is told by a third-person narrator, who can vary from the godlike, seeing into each character's thoughts, to one who is more like a surveillance camera, relating what the characters do without revealing their inner lives.

- The answer to the who question determines, in large part, how you answer the next question: What happens in the story? Another interpretation of this question is: What is your story about? Do you have some larger theme you want to get across, or are you just telling a good tale? Even if it's the latter, you still have to think about another version of the what question: What effect do you want the story to have on the reader?

- The where question seems relatively simple at first glance: Where is the story set? But this question leads to a more complex one: How important is the setting of the story to the story itself? In answering the where question, you decide whether your story is tied to a specific geographical and historical context and whether it is, in part, about that place and time or whether it is more archetypal and timeless.

- The question of when the story takes place is also more complex than it seems at first. It can identify the historical time of the story or the time it takes place in the lives of the characters. It also asks: When is the story being told in relation to when it happened? Is it being narrated in the present tense or in the past tense by a present-day narrator? If you tell a story in the past tense, you gain the benefit of hindsight, but if you tell it in the present tense, what you lose in hindsight you may gain in immediacy and suspense.

- o Other aspects of the when question include: At what point in the story does the plot begin, and how do you order the events of the plot? Do you tell the story chronologically, backward, or moving backward and forward in time?

- o Answering this question is at the heart of learning how to construct a plot, because you come to realize that the same series of chronological events can be told in many different ways. By deciding what to reveal and when, you're choosing the most important moments in the plot.

- Finally, the why question asks: Why do the characters do what they do? What do the characters want, and why are they in the situation of the story? Is it a situation of their own making, or is it a situation that has been thrust upon them? Of course, asking why the characters do what they do is both the hardest and the most essential question you must answer. Indeed, for many writers, trying to answer this question is the reason they write novels or stories to begin with.

A Simple Story?
- To illustrate how the answers to these questions might help you get started, let's take a simple story as an example. Let's say we have a married couple, Sarah and Brad. One Friday night, they decide to take in a baseball game, but during the middle of the game, Sarah tells Brad that she's unhappy in the marriage and wants a divorce.

- On the face of it, this seems to be a simple story; we started with two characters and a specific setting, and we told what happened in chronological order. But as soon as Sarah says that she wants a divorce, the story becomes more complicated than it seemed at first. It turns out to have started before the "beginning," and it sets up a complex dynamic between the two characters.

- A couple of lessons can be learned from this example. One is that a story is not mere chronology. In fact, we might say that most stores are not chronologies but rely on backstories. In his famous series of lectures about fiction writing, *Aspects of the Novel*, the British novelist E. M. Forster made a distinction between story and plot. Story, according to Forster, is the chronological listing of events; plot is the story plus causality and motivation.

- Another way of looking at this idea is to consider that all stories begin *in medias res*, "in the middle of things." Even stories that seem to begin at the very beginning, such as the opening of the book of Genesis, actually begin in the middle. Although it may seem as if we can't get much closer to the beginning than "in the beginning," even this opening presumes a previously existing character—God.

- This leads to a larger philosophical point about fiction: Literature is the creation of order out chaos and the creation of meaning out of meaninglessness. Stories may feel natural, but they don't occur in nature. As writers, we imagine a series of events or we borrow them from life, we order them in a certain way, we choose to highlight some facts and ignore others, and we bring these events and characters to a conclusion or a resolution.

- The fact that even a simple-seeming story can suddenly turn complicated brings us back to the difficulty of deciding where to begin. We know the basic facts about Sarah and Brad, but to explore this situation, we must start making choices—about what's important to tell, what's not, whose point of view to tell it from, and when in the story to begin.

- Even if you've decided on the answers to the five Ws, you still have to think of the first words of the story. Do you open with a description that sets the scene, an exchange of dialogue, an interior monologue, some action, or a combination of these? One possible solution is to outline the story in advance, but many writers prefer to improvise as they work.

This approach allows you to discover the story in much the same way that a reader does.

Psychological Question Revisited

- It's clear that starting a story involves making a number of choices, and that, in turn, can ratchet up a writer's anxiety. Let's return, then, to the psychological question mentioned earlier: How do you gear up—emotionally—to begin? One way to sneak up on this question is to remind yourself of what you don't need to do or know to start a story.

- First of all, writing a story is not necessarily linear; you don't have to write it the way the reader will read it. Writing can be more like putting a puzzle together: You can start anywhere in the story; then, when the larger picture gets clearer, you can craft a beginning.

A whole novel might be developed by answering the five Ws about a couple at a baseball game, working backward and forward in the characters' lives.

- You also don't have to know how the story ends. Sometimes knowing the ending is a good thing because it gives you a point to aim at, but sometimes not knowing can allow you to discover where the story itself wants to go along the way.

- Further, you don't have to have an outline, and even if you do, you don't have to stick to it. Be prepared for happy accidents.

- Your story doesn't even have to be good to begin with. As a writer, you have the luxury of being able to do as many drafts of a story as it takes to get it right, or you can revise as you go along. Don't be afraid to start over or go back and fix something, no matter where you are in the process.

© Stockbyte/Thinkstock.

- Finally, keep in mind that creative writing isn't a science. The only rule in this endeavor is: Whatever works. Throughout these lectures, we'll look at many choices for presenting stories; the best way you can use the lectures is to adapt the possibilities in these choices to your own work, taking whatever is useful and ignoring the rest.

Suggested Reading

Forster, *Aspects of the Novel*.

Writing Exercise

1. Without thinking too hard about it, try to recall a vivid image you may have seen recently, in real life or on television, and see if you can imagine a story to explain it. You can start with the Faulkner technique: Simply describe the image, such as a mother yelling at her child in the supermarket, then branch off from there, explaining why the mother is so exasperated or why the child is being so difficult. Then try Fitzgerald's technique with the same image: Outline the life of the mother so far— her girlhood, her courtship, the birth of her child—and work up to the moment in the supermarket. See which approach works best for you.

Starting the Writing Process
Lecture 1—Transcript

Few things make a writer more anxious than facing a blank page. It doesn't matter if you're a beginner starting your first story ever, or if you're a battle-scarred old professional with many publications behind you—having to fill that blank space with words is almost always a very intimidating prospect.

Like any worker faced with a difficult task, a writer can find all sorts of ways to allay that anxiety. These include petty rituals of procrastination, like, say, alphabetizing your bookshelf, experimenting with different fonts on your computer, or sharpening all your pencils to just the right length. Some writers go further, indulging in such self-destructive practices as using alcohol or drugs to numb their anxiety.

And ever since the advent of the Internet, there's been a vast middle ground between these two extremes, now that a writer is able to kill almost all his writing time by checking his e-mail, making wisecracks on Twitter, or watching adorable kittens on YouTube and calling it "research."

A more fruitful approach is to stop and think about what the opening of a story is supposed to do, and that's pretty simple: The beginning of a story is supposed to make the reader want to keep reading. It's supposed to draw readers in, capture their curiosity, make them want to find out more.

The beginning should also suggest something important about the story—who the main characters are, what the tone is, where the story is set, anything, as long as it hooks the reader and turns out to be important later on. The opening, in other words, should be evocative of the rest of the story as a whole.

But even knowing this doesn't necessarily allay the writer's anxiety. Even if you know the story that you want to tell, how do you know where to enter into it? How do you take that first step? How do you decide what that first paragraph, that first sentence, that first word should be?

Let me suggest some ways to make the beginning seem less foreboding. Or, to put it another way, let me show you how to sneak up on the beginning. One way to do this is to break the question of "How shall I begin?" into three separate questions. I'll call these the artistic question, the logistical question, and the psychological question.

The artistic question is, simply, what is my story about? What's the idea, the seed, the itch I want to scratch for the next few weeks or months, if you're writing a short story, or for the next year or two (or three), if you're writing a novel. This is the *sine qua non* of artistic creation: You wouldn't even be facing a blank page if you didn't have an idea you wanted to express.

But this doesn't mean you know everything about your story yet—you may not know who all the characters are, or what happens to them, or how it ends—but at least you know the ineffable thing you wanted to write a story about in the first place. You might have an entire plot worked out in your head already, or you might have only a character, or a situation, or even just an image you want to explore, but at the very least you have *something* that has put you face to face, so to speak, with the blank page.

The next question, then, is the logistical question. This question is about the technical aspects of starting a story, the nuts and bolts stuff, all the basic decisions you have to make right at the start even if you don't know everything about your story. And this question is actually a lot of questions all rolled up together.

Answering these questions, at least in part, involves making specific technical choices right off the bat, such as deciding who's telling the story, what verb tense to use, what voice the story is in, and so on. Even if you already have a clear idea of what your story is, these early choices can be daunting, because every decision you make will turn out to have consequences later on, many of which you can't foresee.

Then, finally, there's the psychological question, or, to put it another way, the question of how you gear up—emotionally—to begin. Even those of us who have written before get anxious about starting—maybe even *especially* those of us who have done it before, because we already know what a long, arduous, taxing, sometimes exhilarating, but often nerve-shredding process writing can be.

All three of these questions, of course, are inextricably intertwined, and trying to leap that psychological hurdle involves being able to answer the first two questions, at least in part. And that, in turn, ratchets up the anxiety, because there's so much stuff you could worry about in advance that it's a wonder anybody ever starts at all. As William Faulkner once famously said, writing a novel is like a one-armed man trying to hammer together a chicken coop in a hurricane.

The first two questions, the artistic and the logistical, are *especially* intertwined, so let's talk about them together. So what *do* you need to know about a story before you start? Some people start with a more or less fully formed plot in their heads. In one edition of *The Last Tycoon*, the unfinished novel that F. Scott Fitzgerald left behind him when he died, the last portion of the book is made up of Fitzgerald's detailed outline for the plot, in which he not only indicated how many chapters the book would have and what happens in each chapter, but how many words each chapter was going to be—all of this worked out before he even started writing.

At the other extreme, some writers start with only an image or a character and then just wing it for 100,000 words. To invoke William Faulkner again, he once said that when he started work on his greatest novel, *The Sound and the Fury*, all he had was an image of a little girl wearing muddy underpants hiding in a tree. Yet out of that image, through the process of figuring out who that little girl was, how she dirtied her drawers, and what she was doing up a tree, he created a work as rich, complex, and profound as any novel in American literature.

Another way to approach starting a work of fiction is by using the good, old-fashioned Five Ws of journalism: who, what, where, when, and why. This technique is very old, dating back to the rhetoricians and philosophers of the ancient and medieval world, who used a Latin version of the Five Ws (*quis, quid, ubi, quando, cur*) to help frame an argument or structure the exegesis of a text.

Most of us recall them from high school or from a college journalism class, where the Five Ws are used to structure a simple newspaper story: [Who] is the story about? What happened? Where did it take place? When did it take place? Why did it happen?

Let's adapt the Five Ws to thinking about a piece of fiction, turning them into the questions a writer might ask him or herself before embarking upon a new project. Assuming you have a rough idea of what you want to write about, this is another simple but powerful exercise that you might find helpful in getting started: Take out your notebook or your laptop and open to a blank page, and just write down who, what, where, when, and why, and, again, without thinking too hard about it, answer each question as it pertains to the story you want to tell.

Here are a few things to think about before you begin. The first question is, who are your characters, and how are they related to each other? The who question also encompasses the choice of point of view, that is, who is your protagonist, or main character, and who is your narrator? Sometimes the narrator and the protagonist are the same person. For example, Jane Eyre is both the narrator and the protagonist of the Charlotte Brontë novel that bears her name.

But sometimes the protagonist and the narrator are not necessarily the same person—in Herman Melville's *Moby-Dick*, the protagonist is Captain Ahab, the obsessed whaling captain who wants to kill the great white whale that bit off his leg, but the book is narrated by Ishmael, who is a member of Ahab's crew.

And, of course, in many cases a story is not narrated by any of the characters *in* the story, but is told by a third-person narrator, who can vary from the godlike, seeing into each character's thoughts the way George Eliot does in *Middlemarch*, to a narrator who is more like a surveillance camera, merely relating what the characters do, without revealing their inner lives, the way Dashiell Hammett does in *The Maltese Falcon*.

This is a tricky choice, but also an important one, because *who* tells your story determines in large part how you answer the next question, which is, what happens in the story? What do your characters do over the course of the story?

Another, larger interpretation of the what question is, what is your story about? Do you have some larger idea or theme you want to get across, or are you just telling a ripping yarn with no deeper meaning? Even if it's only the latter, you still have to think about another version of the what question, namely, what effect do you want the story to have on the reader? Do you want to make the reader laugh, cry, be afraid, get angry, or all of the above?

The where question seems relatively simple at first glance—where is the story set?—but it leads to a more complex question: How important is the *setting* to the story? Some stories are very specifically related to a particular time and place. For example, Virginia Woolf's novel *Mrs. Dalloway* is uniquely tied to the city of London in the years right after World War I. But in some cases, it's possible to transfer the plot of a great novel from one setting to another and still have it tell recognizably the same story.

The plot and characters of Jane Austen's novel *Emma*, for example, were successfully transferred from England in the early 19th century to Los Angeles in the late 20th century in the film comedy, *Clueless*. And Homer's *Odyssey*, one of the defining stories of Western civilization, has been retold many times, in many settings, from James Joyce's great modernist novel *Ulysses*, set in Dublin on a single day in 1904, to the Coen brothers' film, *O Brother, Where Art Thou?*, set in the American South during the Great Depression.

So when you answer the question, "Where is the story set?" you have to decide if your story is tied to a specific geographical and historical context, and if it is in part about that place and time, or if it is more archetypical and timeless.

The next question—when does the story take place?—is likewise more complex than it seems at first. "When" can mean something as simple as "When in history does the story take place?" In other words, does it take place in the present day, or two hundred years ago, or two hundred years in the future? More importantly, though, is the question, when does the story take place in the lives of the characters? Are they young, middle-aged, or old?

And, *most* importantly, when is the story being told in relation to when it took place? In other words, is it being narrated in the present tense, as it happens, or is it being narrated in the past tense, by a present-day narrator who is remembering something that happened in the past? A strong present-tense narration, as in many of the short stories of Raymond Carver, lends a story immediacy, but more often you have a first-person narrator remembering something that happened in the past.

In Harper Lee's *To Kill a Mockingbird*, for example, the story is told by the main character, Scout, in the past tense, with the implication that she is now a grown woman remembering events that happened decades before, when she was a girl. Among other things, this allows the author to show the events from the point of view of a child, while at the same time allowing the narrator to present things from an adult perspective, allowing her to explain things now that she wouldn't have understood when they were actually happening.

If you tell a story in the past tense, you gain the benefit of hindsight, since it's told by someone who already knows how the story turns out. But if you decide to tell it in the present tense, what you lose in hindsight you might gain in immediacy and suspense.

Another aspect of the when question is, at what point in the story does the plot begin? How do you order the events of the plot? Do you tell the story chronologically, as most conventional stories and novels do? Or do you tell it backwards? In the play *Betrayal*, the British writer Harold Pinter tells the story of an adulterous affair by starting with the bitter end of the relationship and then working back through the course of the affair, scene by scene, until he ends with the first meeting of the lovers.

Or do you jump all over the place chronologically, the way Joseph Conrad does in his novel *Lord Jim*, interspersing the "present day" of the story with flashbacks from various stages in the lives of his characters?

Answering this question is at the heart of learning how to construct a plot, because you come to realize that the same series of chronological events can be told in a surprisingly large number of different ways. By deciding what to reveal and when, you're deciding what the most important moments in the plot are.

Finally, we have the why question: Why do the characters do what they do? What does each character want? As actors say, what are their motivations? And why are they in the situation they're in? Is it a situation of their own making, as in a lot of American middleclass novels of middleclass life?

Or is the characters' situation thrust upon them or out of their control, forcing them to deal with it with as best they can? Many of the great realist novels of the 19th and 20th centuries, by such writers as the Frenchman Emile Zola and the American Edith Wharton, are about characters caught in the coils of social or economic circumstance, struggling to survive in a world they can't control.

Of course, asking why the characters do what they do is both the hardest and the most essential question that you have to answer, and it's not going too far to say that for a lot of writers, maybe even for most of them, answering this question is why they write the novel or story to begin with.

To illustrate how the answers to all of these questions might help you get started, let's take a simple story as an example. Let's say we have two characters, Sarah and Brad, who are married to each other. One Friday night, they decide to take in a baseball game. Because I'm a native Michigander, let's say this takes place in Detroit. So they go to see the Tigers play, and during the middle of the seventh inning stretch, Sarah turns to Brad and says, "I'm really unhappy."

Now up until this point, Brad has been having a good time, so he's a little surprised. But it's late in the game, so he says, "Relax, there are only a couple more innings." And that's when Sarah says, "No, you don't understand. I'm *really* unhappy. I want a divorce."

Now, this seems, on the face of it, to be a simple story—you start with two characters and a specific setting, and you tell what happened, in chronological order. But then, the climax is a surprise. As soon as Sarah says that she wants a divorce, the story turns out to be more complicated that it seemed at first. Not only that, but the story turns out to have started before the "beginning"—Sarah's wanted to leave Brad for a long time, but she was afraid to tell him, so she waited until they were at the game, when she knew he'd be happy, or at least groggy with beer and hot dogs, before she lowered the boom.

So right away we understand something about the complex dynamic of the two characters—that Sarah is either afraid of Brad, or manipulative, or both, and that Brad is possibly insensitive or has been deliberately ignoring Sarah's unhappiness. And we learn all this before we get into the longstanding reasons why Sarah is unhappy.

There are a couple of lessons to be learned from this example. One is that a story is not mere chronology. Some stories are chronological, but many are not. You might even say that most are not, that most stories rely on backstory.

In his famous series of lectures about fiction writing, *Aspects of the Novel*, the British novelist E. M. Forster made a distinction between story and plot. Story, according to Forster, is just the chronological listing of events. His example of a story is, the king died, and then the queen died. A plot, on the other hand, according to Forster, is the story plus causality and motivation—the king died, and then the queen died of grief.

Another way of looking at this is to consider that all stories begin *in medias res*, which is a Latin phrase that means "in the middle of things." Even stories that seem to begin at the very beginning, begin *in medias res*, the most famous example being the opening of the book of Genesis—"In the beginning, God created the heavens and the earth." This may not seem like it begins *in media res*—you can't get much more in the beginning than "in the beginning"—but if you think about it, you realize that even Genesis begins *in media res* because it presumes a previously existing character, namely God.

This leads to a larger philosophical point about fiction. As my ninth grade English teacher, Mrs. Giltner, liked to tell us, literature is the creation of order out chaos, and the creation of meaning out of meaninglessness. Stories may feel natural, but stories do not occur in nature. Real life does not happen in stories. Stories are arbitrary.

As writers, we imagine a series of events or we take them out of our life or somebody else's, we order them in a certain way, we choose to highlight some facts and ignore others, and we bring these events and characters to a conclusion or a resolution. The crudest kind of resolution is some sort of victory or defeat, while the more subtle variety leads to a character's deeper understanding of him or herself, or to the reader's deeper understanding of the character, often in a moment that James Joyce called an epiphany.

The fact that even a very simple-seeming story can turn suddenly sticky, complicated, and messy in a matter of a few words brings us right back to the difficultly of deciding where to begin.

We know the basic facts of Sarah and Brad—they've been married for a while, she's been unhappy, he didn't notice it or chose to ignore it, she's decided to tell him in a public setting. But now, in order to explore this situation, we have to start making choices, about what's important to tell, what's not, whose point of view to tell it from, and where in the story (which is to say *when* in the story) to begin.

So, let's go back to the Five Ws and see if can apply them usefully to Sarah and Brad, in the way I suggested in the exercise above.

Who: Sarah and Brad, who are married to each other.

What: They are attending a Tigers baseball game, and one of them wants to get divorced, while the other one doesn't know it yet. A whole novel could easily be developed from answering this question, working backwards and forwards through their lives.

Where: A crowded baseball stadium in Detroit, Michigan.

When: The present day, but also some years into a marriage that one of them thinks is less successful than the other one does. Also (for the sake of argument), let's say they're in their late 30s.

Why: Sarah wants out. That's the main motivating factor in the story—so far as we know. It may change later on, as we learn more about the characters and their situation.

Then the next question becomes, whose story is it, which is another way of asking, from whose point of view are we seeing the story? Is it Sarah's story, or Brad's, or both, alternating between the two? Or do we go all godlike and 19th century, looking with perfect understanding on both of our characters from above, the way George Eliot does in *Middlemarch*?

Now, even if you've decided on your five Ws, you still have to break the ice, you still have to think of those very first words, the very beginning of the story.

Do you open with a description that sets the scene? The lights of Tiger Stadium were glowing against the night sky…

Or do you open with an exchange of dialogue? "Let's see if we can get closer to the dugout," said Brad. "Do we have to?" said Sarah.

Do you open with interior monologue? He looks so happy, thought Sarah. But I'd rather be anywhere but here.

Or do you begin with action? Clutching Sarah's hand, Brad dragged her down the stadium steps, closer to the dugout.

Or do you open with a combination of all of the above? The scoreboard of Tiger Stadium was brilliant against the black sky over the backfield fence. Brad clutched Sarah's hand and dragged her down the stadium steps, closer to the dugout. "You're hurting me," said Sarah, squeezing between two huge guys who were already drunk. "Sorry," said Brad over his shoulder. He relaxed his grip without letting her go. He looks so happy, Sarah thought, but I'd rather be anywhere but here.

How do you pick between all these choices? How do you decide without hamstringing yourself, knowing that every choice you make will have consequences later on?

One possible solution is to outline the whole story in advance. You could sit down before you start writing and map out the entire thing. Writing the story then just becomes a process of filling in the blanks. Some people work very fruitfully this way. It's sort of how I wrote my novel *Kings of Infinite Space.* I never had an actual written outline, but I mulled over the book in my head for a couple of years before I ever wrote a word, and then I wrote it very quickly, in eight months, because I already knew everything that happened in it.

But on the whole (just using myself as an example here), I prefer to work without an outline, as in my novel *Next.* When I started writing that book, I only knew a couple of things to begin with, and then just improvised, making everything up as I went along.

This suggests a different way of starting than what I've been talking about so far: Rather than letting the rest of the book determine the beginning, let the beginning determine the rest of the book. Then the book becomes more of an exploration, and the experience of writing it becomes more like the experience of reading it. You discover the story the same way a reader does.

Most books, I suspect, fall somewhere between these two poles, tending one way or the other, but still not entirely one or the other.

At any rate, it's clear that starting a story involves making a lot of choices, and that in turn can ratchet up your anxiety, which brings us at last to the third question I mentioned at the start, the psychological question. And rather than sharpening our pencils or administering a liberal dose of Jack Daniel's or Xanax (or both), let's sneak up on this last question the way we snuck up on the first two. Rather than dwelling on all the things you *do* need to worry about, let's consider what you *don't* need to do, or what you don't need to know, when you're starting a story:

First of all, you don't have to start at the beginning. Writing a story is not necessarily linear: you don't have to write it the way the reader is going read it. It can be more like putting a puzzle together: You can start anywhere, and then, when the larger picture gets clearer, you can craft a beginning to it.

Second, as a corollary to this, you don't have to know how the story ends. Sometimes you do, and sometimes you don't. Sometimes knowing is a good thing, because it gives you a point to aim at. But sometimes it isn't, because you discover along the way that the story doesn't want to go where you want it to go.

Third, you don't have to have an outline, and even if you do, you don't have to stick to it. Be prepared for happy accidents. As I said earlier, for me, writing a novel is a process of exploration. Part of the reason I write is to figure out what I think about something—though of course many fine writers already know what they think when they start, and they write to make a point.

Fourth, it doesn't have to be good to begin with. One of the mottos I've shared with students over the years comes from the rock-and-roll musician Nick Lowe. Early in his career, Lowe also worked as a producer for other artists, and he worked so quickly in the studio that someone gave him the nickname "Basher," because his motto for making recordings was "Bash it out now, and tart it up later."

As a writer, you have the luxury of being able to do as many drafts of a story or a novel as it takes to get it right, or, if you don't do drafts, and some writers don't, you can revise as you go along. Don't be afraid to start over or to go back and fix something, no matter where you are in the process.

Now the best teachers, of course, are the ones who teach by example, and in this opening lecture, I have been practicing what I've been preaching. At the beginning of this lecture, I said that a good opening should suggest what the rest of the story is about, or at least hint at what might be important later on. And for the past 25 minutes, I've done more than just hint at what's coming: I've essentially fast-forwarded through the entire course, hitting most, if not all, of the main topics I want to talk about in more detail in the next 23 lectures.

In the lecture after this one, I want to talk about the concept of evocation, which I think is at the heart of all fiction. The next 15 lectures will be divided into four blocks: the first one will be about what a fictional character is, how characters work in fiction, and some strategies for creating them. Next will come two lectures about the technical and artistic aspects of writing dialogue. Then I'll talk for six lectures about the various types of plot and how to create them, and after that, I'll devote three lectures to the different points of view available to the writer.

Each of the last seven lectures will be devoted to a special topic, including how to create and use setting, how to pace a narrative, and how to develop a scene. We'll also be talking about what a draft is, how to approach revision, and how to incorporate research into a story or novel.

Finally, I'll end this particular long narrative with a talk about what it means to live and work as a writer. In that last lecture, I will be half evangelist and half drill sergeant, striking a balance between inspiration and realism.

One last word before we embark on this journey together: Having invoked evangelism just now, I want to stress that nothing that I've already said or that I'm going to say is gospel. Creative writing isn't a science, where there are rules and right or wrong answers. The only rule in creative writing is: Whatever works.

A different teacher will tell you different things about all the topics I'm going to explore, and if you caught. me on a different occasion, I might say different things about them myself. What I'll be offering you throughout is a set of choices, and the best way you can you can use these lectures is to think about the various choices I'll present—about creating character, developing a plot, or building a scene—and then adapt those possibilities to your own work, taking whatever is useful and ignoring the rest.

In the next lecture, I'll be talking about the concept of evocation, which is the fancy Latinate word behind what creative writing teachers mean when they say "Show, don't tell." We'll be looking at examples of both showing and telling from the work of Stephen King and the French novelist Irène Némirovsky.

In the meantime, here's an exercise where you can compare using an outline, the way F. Scott Fitzgerald did, with starting with just an image and winging it, the way William Faulkner did. Without thinking too hard about it, try to recall a vivid image you may have seen recently, in your real life or on television, and see if you can imagine a story to explain it.

You can start with the Faulkner technique, by simply describing the image—say you saw a mother yelling at her child in the supermarket—and then branching off from there, by explaining why the mother is so exasperated, or why the child is being so difficult.

Or you could use Fitzgerald's technique with the same image, by outlining the life of the mother so far—her girlhood, her courtship, the birth of her child—and work up to the moment in the supermarket.

Try them both and see which one works best for you, and I'll see you next time!

Building Fictional Worlds through Evocation
Lecture 2

One of the most venerable tropes in the teaching of creative writing is this: Show, don't tell. But what exactly does this dictum mean? When teachers of creative writing invoke it, they often mean that a scene or story was under-dramatized or that the writing trafficked in vague generalities. For example, a writer might tell us something that is generally true about a character without fixing that trait or action in a specific moment or situation. In this lecture, we'll see how showing rather than telling can make your writing more immediate, vivid, detailed, and visceral. We'll see how it invites readers to identify with your characters and participate in the story, if only in their imaginations.

Telling versus Showing

- Let's consider two versions of a scene, one that gets the facts across and one that puts the reader in the scene with the characters. Here's the first version:

> I was driving home from work this afternoon when some jerk came out of a side street and cut right in front of me. I was angry about something my boss had said that afternoon, so instead of just letting it go, I sounded my horn and tailgated the guy for half a mile. He pulled over, and we nearly got into a fight.

- Now let's look at an excerpt from what a fiction writer might do with this same scene:

> Naturally, as I was just about to cross the river, a guy in a Jeep Cherokee with enormous tires shot out right in front of me and cut me off. Worse yet, he was a young guy, with big redneck sideburns and a feed cap, and when I honked my horn, he gave me the finger and a big nasty grin. Worst of all, he had out-of-

state plates and an NRA bumper sticker, and all of these, along with my rage at my boss, made me erupt.

- Note that the outline of the two versions is the same, but the second version has much more detail. Instead of "a guy shot out in front of me," it's a young guy with sideburns and a baseball cap. He not only cuts the narrator off, but he seems to enjoy it. It's essentially the same story, but the second version is fleshed out with many more details about the two characters and the setting. The reader is much closer to being in the mind of the narrator.

- When creative writing teachers say, "Show, don't tell," they mean: Give us more detail, make it dramatic, and put the reader in the scene.
    - Writing fiction by showing rather than telling means bypassing the logical, analytical mind and going for the gut, engaging the readers' senses, not just their minds. More important, you're engaging the readers' imaginations and allowing them to fill in the gaps by drawing on their own experience.

    - What you're doing, in fact, is evoking the experience for the reader. The idea of evocation is at the heart of all fiction; it's the thing that allows a fictional story and imaginary characters to lodge themselves ineradicably in the minds of readers.

Defining *Evocation*
- The variants of the word *evoke* come from the Latin *evocare*, which means "to call out" in several different senses: to summon the spirits of the dead, to call forth a deity, or simply to summon another person. In English, when talking specifically about art and literature, the dictionary definition of *evocative* is "tending by artistic imaginative means to *re-create* ... especially in such a manner as to produce a compelling impression of reality."

- In English, *evoke*, *evocative*, and *evocation* can also mean "calling out or calling forth," "summoning a spirit by incantation," "calling up an emotional response," or "calling up memories, recollections, or associations." All these meanings apply when it comes to writing fiction because all these definitions have in common the idea of drawing something out of a reader's imagination, not just putting something into it.

- When you tell readers something, you appeal mainly to the rational, analytical mind, not to the senses. But when you show readers something, you draw out something that is already present—memories or imaginings—even if your readers don't know it. In other words, when you tell readers something, you make them witnesses, but when you show them something, you make them participants.

- Evocation is both a subtle and a powerful technique. It entails both the writer and the reader using their imaginations.
    o Writers use their skill with words to call forth scenes from their imaginations in enough detail that readers, without really thinking about it, use their own imaginations and memories to fill in the gaps. In the process, memories, emotions, and sensory impressions are evoked.

    o One of the benefits of evocation is that even though readers are doing half the work, they don't realize it, and they actually enjoy the experience. The feeling of being in the scene with the characters and being engaged by the narrative is one of the great pleasures of reading fiction. A phrase that brilliantly captures this effect comes from the American novelist and creative writing teacher John Gardner, who once defined fiction as the creation of "a vivid and continuous dream."

    o In her book *Writing Fiction*, another creative writing teacher, Janet Burroway, said that reading fiction allows us to feel strong emotions "without paying for them." This is what evocation is all about. When you get the reader to laugh, you're evoking merriment; when you get the reader to sweat and turn on all the lights, you're evoking fear. You don't just allow readers to visualize themselves in certain situations, but you prompt them to engage with the situation emotionally in the same way they would if they were actually experiencing it in real life.

The Balance of Detail and Economy

- Stephen King's *'Salem's Lot* is one of the best horror novels ever written. Here's a passage from it in which King evokes the arrival of spring in New England:

> By mid-May, the sun rises out of the morning's haze with authority and potency, and standing on your top step at seven in the morning with your dinner bucket in your hand, you know that the dew will be melted off the grass by eight and that the dust on the back roads will hang depthless and still in the hot air for five minutes after a car's passage; and that by one in the afternoon it will be up to ninety-five on the third floor of the mill and the sweat will roll off your arms like oil and stick your shirt to your back in a widening patch and it might as well be July. (pp. 192–193)

By evoking memories we all have of heat and dust, an author can draw us out of our own lives and into the life of a laborer in another time and place.

- This passage is a wonderful example of how evocation works because it gives us a nice balance between detail and economy. As we've said, evocative writing provides significant detail, but it doesn't overwhelm the reader. The point is to draw something out of your readers, which you can't do if you pour too much in.

- This is a tricky balance to get right, and beginning writers often have the most difficulty with it. Just as one common error among young writers is not providing enough detail, another common error is to overcompensate by telling too much. Often, inexperienced writers will go on for several paragraphs about the appearance of a character or a place when a few well-chosen sentences or words would have done just as well.

- What are the right details to include? One way to answer that question is to include too much detail in your early drafts. Write much more than you need, then pare it back later.
    - o You can also ask yourself some questions about the details you provide: Does this detail tell something that the reader didn't already know? Does it advance the story? Does it say something about the character that is specific to this scene?

    - o Think about whether your details are concrete and appeal directly to the senses. Don't just write, "He was in love with her"; instead, write, "He felt his face get hot when she came into the room."

- Another issue to consider in making a passage evocative is the language itself. There are no rules in creative writing, but on the whole, evocation works best when you use active, specific verbs and avoid adverbs unless they're absolutely necessary.
    - o Inexperienced writers often write such sentences as "She hurried quickly across the room" or "He pounded the table angrily." In these examples, the adverbs are unnecessary; it's clear from the verbs that she's moving quickly or that he is angry.

    - o In most cases, use the strongest verbs you can think of. "It was raining" is not as evocative as "The rain hammered the roof and spattered the windows like buckshot." Instead of starting with the bland pronoun *it* and the even blander verb *was*, the second sentence makes the rain itself the subject; the strong verb *hammered* evokes not only an image but a sound and renders any adverbs superfluous.

Telling, Not Showing

- Despite the importance of evocation in fiction, it's also sometimes acceptable—even preferable—to tell a story rather than to show it. Many of the great books of the 18th and 19th centuries used telling as their default mode, as do many philosophical and satirical novels.

- In most conventional narratives, where much of the story is shown or evoked, there are also long passages in which the writer or narrator simply addresses the readers, telling them what they need to know. Just as a composer might vary the tempo of a piece of music to maintain the listener's interest, the fiction writer should provide variety among intensely evocative scenes, passages of pure exposition, and scenes that combine the two.

- In science fiction and fantasy, for example, there is often a passage or even an entire chapter early in the narrative known as the *info dump*, whereby the author takes a few pages to simply explain the world of the story before the action starts. Many fine literary novels and dramatic popular novels also have passages in which the author simply tells readers about the action or the characters.

- Another excellent example of a careful balance between telling and showing is Irène Némirovsky's *Suite Française*, a novel about the Nazi occupation of France during World War II. The book effectively combines exquisitely evocative passages with straightforward expository descriptions, making a point to present characters only as vividly as the reader needs to see them to advance the story.

Suggested Reading

Burroway, *Writing Fiction.*

Gardner, *The Art of Fiction.*

King, *'Salem's Lot.*

Némirovsky, *Suite Française.*

1. Try this exercise from John Gardner's *The Art of Fiction*: Write a passage describing a building, a landscape, or an object, but imagine that you're writing from the point of view of a parent whose child has just died. Describe the object without mentioning the child or death. The idea is to see if you can evoke a feeling of loss and grief in the reader without mentioning the emotions themselves.

Building Fictional Worlds through Evocation
Lecture 2—Transcript

One of the most venerable tropes in the teaching of creative writing, or perhaps one of the hoariest, is the old saying, "Show, don't tell." If you've ever taken a creative writing class, you've heard it, and if you've ever taught a creative writing class, you've said it. In fact, there have been times when I've considered getting a stamp made up, just to save myself the trouble of having to write it out so often when I was reading student work. I could just bang it in the margin of a story: "Show, don't tell," "Show, don't tell," "Show, don't tell." Not only would this have saved me a lot of time, it would have been pretty satisfying.

But "Show, don't tell" is used so often that most writers cringe when they hear it, and most teachers cringe when they have to say it. It's become such a cliché that even talking about how it's a cliché, as I'm doing right now, has become a cliché in itself.

So, what exactly do we mean when we say, "Show, don't tell"? In the case of those student stories, what I usually meant was that the scene or story was *under-dramatized*, or that the writer trafficked in vague generalities rather than specific details.

For example, the writer would tell us something that was generally true about a character, without associating that trait or action with a specific moment or situation. So the writer might say, "She fixed herself a drink," which evokes nothing in particular, even if you already know something about the character. What I would suggest in a case like this was that the writer show us the character in a specific setting at a specific time: "After dining out that night at a nearby Italian restaurant, she knelt in the light of the open mini-fridge in her hotel room, pulled out a little bottle of gin and a little bottle of tonic, and made herself a drink in a plastic cup."

Both of these sentences convey the same essential information, but the second one is more immediate, vivid, detailed, sensuous, and visceral. In the first version, the writer is merely *telling* us what the character did, but in the second, the writer is *showing* us the character in action, putting her within a specific setting and showing us specifically what she did. In the second version, we are as readers invited to see and feel what the character is doing, which allows us to identify with the character. In other words, showing rather than telling blurs the boundary between the character and the reader, which allows us as readers (and this is the important part) to *participate* in the scene, if only in our imagination.

Let's take a look at a longer example. Here's a barebones version of a scene, one that is told rather than shown:

> I was driving home from work this afternoon when some jerk came out of a side street and cut right in front of me. I was angry about something my boss had said, so instead of letting it go, I sounded my horn and tailgated the guy for half a mile. He pulled over and we nearly got into a fight.

Now, there's nothing wrong with that. It's brisk, it's concise, it gets the facts across, it even has a bit of psychology, namely the fact that the narrator let his anger over something else affect his behavior behind the wheel of his car. But by the standards of modern prose fiction, it's woefully under-dramatized: The reader has no idea from the storyteller what it was like to be there, in that particular setting, at that particular time.

What showing does, that telling doesn't, is put the reader *in the scene* with the characters.

Taking that same set of events, here's what a fiction writer might do with it:

> That afternoon, I left work angry. Just before I'd switched off my computer, my boss had come into my office with a file I'd just given her—a file I was pretty proud of, if you want to know the truth—and told me six things I needed to do over. I like my boss, but at times like this, she talks to me like I'm six years old. And I responded like I was six, crossing my arms and pushing out my lower lip, and saying, "Yes. Yes. Yes," so insincerely I was surprised she didn't send me to my room without supper.

When I finally left, I was radiating rage in the stairwell and letting it ricochet off the concrete beams of the parking structure. It's a wonder I didn't set off every car alarm in the place. And of course, I fumed all the way home, riding the accelerator with a foot as heavy as a diving boot, switching from lane to lane, rushing yellow lights, scowling at the speed limit signs as if they were another admonition from my boss.

So, naturally, as I was just about to cross the river, a guy in a Jeep Cherokee with enormous tires shot out right in front of me and cut me off. Worse yet, he was a young guy, with big redneck sideburns and a feed cap, and when I honked my horn, he gave me the finger and big, nasty grin. All of this, along with my rage at my boss, made me erupt. Even then there was a little part of my brain, a little Jiminy Cricket sitting just behind me and to the left, saying, "What on earth are you doing?" I rammed my horn with the heel of my hand and kept it there all the way across the bridge, and even more surprising, I rode right up behind the guy's dented rear bumper. Of course, it's hard to be intimidating when you're in a Honda Civic tailgating a Jeep Cherokee, but at the moment, I didn't care, and I told Jiminy Cricket to go to hell.

Then, of course, at the end of the bridge, where the traffic was piled up at the light, and I was hemmed in by cars on one side and by the railing of the bridge on the other, Mr. Jeep Cherokee slammed on his brakes and got out of his car, all six-foot-three, bench-pressing, denim-clad inch of him. Then, and only then, did Jiminy Cricket get the upper hand, and I heard myself say out loud, "Maybe this wasn't such a good idea."

Now, you'll note that the outline of the two versions is the same, but the second version has a lot more detail. Instead of "a guy shot out in front of me," it's a young guy with sideburns and a baseball cap who's driving an SUV with a dented rear bumper. And he not only cuts the narrator off, he seems to enjoy it. And we can tell from the voice of the narrator that he's a different social class than the young guy, that he's an office worker driving an economy car. It's essentially the same story, but I've fleshed it out with many more details about the two characters, about the narrator's mood—namely, exactly why he's ticked off on his way home from work—and about the setting. You're in the head of the narrator. You're seeing the scene as if you're there.

So this is what creative writing teachers mean when they say "show, don't tell." They mean: 1) give us more detail, 2) make it more dramatic, and 3) put the reader in the scene. Writing fiction by showing rather than telling means bypassing the logical, analytical mind and going for the gut, engaging the reader's senses, not just her mind.

More importantly, you're engaging the reader's imagination and allowing her to fill in the gaps by drawing on her own experience.

What you should be doing, in fact—and here's the word I've been sneaking up on for the last 10 minutes—what you should be doing is *evoking* the experience for the reader. That's a word I want you to remember all throughout this course: *evocation*, and its verb, to *evoke*, and its adjective, *evocative*. For me, the idea of evocation is at the heart of all fiction, it's the thing that makes it work, that makes it memorable, that allows a fictional story and imaginary characters to lodge themselves ineradicably in a reader's head.

And it's a word I want to take a few minutes to explain. The variants of the word *evoke* come from the Latin word *evocare*, which means "to call out," in several different senses: to summon the spirits of the dead, to call forth a deity, or simply to summon another person. In English, when talking specifically about art and literature, the dictionary definition of *evocative* is "tending by artistic imaginative means to recreate (as a mood, time, place, or personality), especially in such a manner as to produce a compelling impression of reality"—that's from Webster's 3rd International dictionary.

But there's more to it than that: In English as in Latin, *evoke*, *evocative*, and *evocation* can also mean "calling out or calling forth," "summoning a spirit by incantation," "calling up an emotional response," or "calling up memories, recollections, or associations." You can *evoke* a response from someone, you can *evoke* fear or love in someone, you can *evoke* in someone a vivid memory from time gone by.

All of these meanings apply when it comes to writing fiction, because all of these definitions have in common the idea of *drawing something out* of a reader's imagination, and not just putting something new into it.

This is so important that I want to say it again: When the writer is *evoking* something for the reader, she is drawing it out of the reader, not simply telling the reader something. She is engaging the reader's imagination and reminding the reader of something from his or her own life.

This is the fundamental difference between "telling" and "showing." When you are *telling* a reader something, you're not engaging him as deeply; you're appealing mainly to the rational, analytical mind and not to the senses. On the other hand, when you are *showing* the reader something, or, more precisely, when you are *evoking* something for the reader, you are drawing something out of that reader that was already there, even if she didn't know it, namely memories and imaginings of her own that can fill in the gaps of what the writer is merely suggesting.

In other words, when you simply tell a reader something, you're making her a witness, but when you show her something, you're making her a participant. You're putting her in the story with the characters. So you can see that evocation is both a subtle and a very powerful technique. As its etymology suggests, it works both ways: it's not just the author planting images in the reader's mind, images that the reader receives in the passive way a viewer watches a movie or a TV show, it's about drawing those images (in part) out of the reader's memory and imagination.

Evocation depends on the reader meeting the author halfway. It means that both the writer and the reader are using their imaginations. The writer uses his skill with words to call forth a scene from his own imagination, in enough detail that the reader, without really thinking about it, uses his own imagination and memories to fill in the gaps. And, in so doing, memories are evoked, emotions are evoked, sensory impressions are evoked.

Evocation as it pertains to creative writing even has something of the spiritual about it, in the sense of evoking the spirit of a scene or a character, drawing it out of the reader. Now here's the great thing about evocation: The reader may be doing half the work, but he doesn't know it. In fact, not only doesn't he know he's working, he's enjoying it. This feeling of being *in* a scene with the characters, of being engaged by the narrative and not just watching it, is one of the greatest pleasures in reading fiction, perhaps even *the* greatest pleasure.

The American novelist and creative writing teacher John Gardner once defined fiction as the creation of "a vivid and continuous dream," and I think that phrase brilliantly captures the effect that great fiction has on the reader. We feel as if we are living in someone else's life for a few hours; we feel as we are seeing the world through their eyes. As Gardner himself put it, in his book *The Art of Fiction*:

> In great fiction, the dream engages us heart and soul; we not only respond to imaginary things—sights, sounds, smells—as though they were real, we respond to fictional problems as though they were real: We sympathize, think, and judge. We act out, vicariously, the trials … and successes of particular modes of action, particular attitudes, opinions, assertions, and beliefs exactly as we learn from life. (p. 31)

Another great creative writing teacher, Janet Burroway, puts it even more succinctly in her book *Writing Fiction*, when she says that reading fiction allows us to feel strong emotions "without paying for them."

This is what evocation is all about. When you get the reader to laugh, you're evoking her joy; when you get the reader to sweat and turn the light up a notch, you're evoking his fear; when you get the reader aroused, you're evoking her desire. You're not just getting the reader to visualize him or herself in a certain situation, you're getting them to feel something about it, to engage with it emotionally in the same way they would as if they were actually experiencing it in real life.

And if you don't believe me, or John Gardner, or Janet Burroway, consider this: In recent years, neuroscientists have discovered that the same parts of a person's brain that light up on a CAT scan when he is merely thinking of playing chess, for example, are the same parts of his brain that light up when he's actually playing chess. In the same way, experiments have shown that a scary story can make us feel real fear without actually putting us in danger, or make us sad without forcing us to experience a genuine loss.

So, since we're speaking of scary stories, let's take an example from one of the best horror stories ever written, Stephen King's vampire novel, *'Salem's Lot*. Here's a passage in which King is *evoking* the arrival of spring in New England:

> By mid-May, the sun rises out of the morning's haze with authority and potency, and standing on your top step at seven in the morning with your dinner bucket in your hand, you know that the dew will be melted off the grass by eight and that the dust on the back roads will hang depthless and still in the hot air for five minutes after a car's passage; and that by one in the afternoon it will be up to ninety-five on the third floor of the mill and the sweat will roll off your arms like oil and stick your shirt to your back in a widening patch and it might as well be July. (pp. 192–193)

This is wonderfully evocative, not only of the growing heat and stillness of a spring day, but of a working class way of life, and even if you've never carried a lunch bucket or worked in a mill, you can feel what that third floor feels like, you can feel that sweat roll off your arms, you can feel that shirt stick to your back—all because you are supplying the details from your own experience. By evoking memories we all have of heat and dew and dust, King is able to draw us out of our own lives into the life of a man who works in a mill. You're doing half of Stephen King's work for him in this passage, but you don't even have to break a (real) sweat doing it.

This passage is a wonderful example of how evocation works, because there's a nice balance in the paragraph between detail and economy. I've already stressed that one of the signature features of evocative writing— perhaps *the* signature feature—is the prolific use of detail, but the other requirement of evocative writing is that it be economical: An evocative piece of writing does not try to set the scene by brute force, it does not overwhelm the reader with too much detail.

In other words, as I've already said, what makes a passage or a sentence evocative is when it draws something out of the reader. And you can't draw anything out of the reader if you're pouring too much in. By putting in just the right amount of detail—the sun rising through the haze, the dew burning off the grass, the sweat-soaked shirt sticking to the skin—and then leaving it to the reader to fill in the rest of the picture in her mind, you're engaging the reader in a much more subtle and effective way.

Now, this is a tricky balance to get right, even for the most experienced writer, but beginning writers often have the most difficulty with it. Just as one common error among young writers is not showing us nearly enough detail, another common error is to overcompensate by telling us too much. Often an inexperienced writer will go on and on and on for paragraph after paragraph about the appearance of a character or a place, when only a few well-chosen sentences, or even just a few well-chosen words, would have done.

But what, you may ask, are the right details to include? How do you know which words to choose? Well, having just said that it's a rookie mistake to include too much detail, I'm going to backtrack a bit and say this instead: It may be a rookie mistake to include too much detail in the finished product, but it is *not* a mistake to use too much detail in your early drafts. I can't speak for every writer, of course, and perhaps there are writers who have never wasted a word, even in an early draft. But I'm guessing that most writers, especially in their early drafts, write much more than they need, and then pare it back later on, on the principle that it's easier to cut what you don't need than to go back into a passage which has already fixed itself in your head and wedge more stuff in.

This is how I work, anyway, and while it's certainly inefficient, it's very effective. Say I'm describing a place which is important to the story (and that's another trick to the art of evocation—you don't waste time on details that aren't important to the larger narrative): I often write twice as much stuff as I need, putting in every detail I can think of. Then, later, when the shape of the scene and how it fits into the larger story are clearer to me, I return to that mass of details and keep the ones I need and get rid of the ones I can do without. Indeed, sometimes in revising a scene for maximum evocative effect, I make a little game out of it, trying to see how many words I can delete from a passage without diminishing its effect.

Deciding which details to keep and which to discard isn't purely intuitive, though with practice, it can become so. There are logical rules you can apply to every moment in a story, though what these rules are will depend on the individual story you're writing. But some examples might be: Does this detail tell us something we didn't already know? Does it advance the story? Does it say something about the character that's specific to this scene?

The rules I most often use have to do with the nature of the details themselves, especially, are they visceral? Are they concrete? Do they appeal directly to the senses? For example, don't just say, "He was in love with her," but say something like "He felt his face get hot when she came into the room." Don't just say, "She found the noise grating," but say, "The noise made her grit her teeth and dig her fingernails into her palms," and so on.

Another thing to consider in making a passage evocative is the language itself. There are no rules in creative writing, but on the whole, evocation works best when you use active, specific verbs, and avoid adverbs unless they're absolutely necessary.

This is another rookie mistake you often find in inexperienced writers. They write something like "She hurried quickly across the room" or "He pounded the table angrily." In these examples, it's already clear from the verb "hurry" that she's being quick, and the fact that he's pounding the table makes it pretty obvious that he's angry.

And remember to bear down on the language and use the strongest verbs you can think of. "It was raining" is not very evocative. "It was raining hard" is slightly better but not by much, while "The rain hammered the roof and spattered the windows like buckshot" is much better. Instead of starting with the bland pronoun *it* and the even blander verb *was*, we start with the rain itself, making it the subject of the sentence, and with the strong verb *hammered* we evoke not only an image, but a sound, and we render any adverbs superfluous. You wouldn't need to say, "The rain hammered hard," for example, because "hammered" already implies that the rain is coming down hard. The second half of the sentence evokes the wind without actually mentioning the wind, because saying that the rain "spattered the windows like buckshot" implies a strong wind, evoking an image and a sound all in one go.

Now, having spent the last 20 minutes or so stressing the importance of evocation to fiction, I'm going to spend the last few minutes taking it back a little bit. As much as writing students hate to hear "Show, don't tell," writing teachers hate saying it even more, and that's because, sometimes, it's perfectly okay, and sometimes even preferable, to *tell* a story rather than *show* it.

Many of the great books of the 18th and early 19th centuries used telling as their default mode. In her novels, Jane Austen often simply tells us what a character is thinking, or simply summarizes an action. There's also a long tradition in European literature of narratives that privilege telling over showing, especially in philosophical novels or novels of ideas such as Milan Kundera's *The Unbearable Lightness of Being*.

There is also a long tradition of a certain sort of short story writer, especially those influenced by the great Russian short story writer and playwright, Anton Chekhov, who tell more than they show. A fine example, in fact, is Anton Chekhov's own great story "The Darling," which has little intense bursts of drama that serve mainly as seasoning for the main meal of the story, which is told rather than shown.

Another genre that often relies heavily on telling rather than showing is satire. Much of *Catch-22*, Joseph Heller's great antiwar novel about World War II, is told rather than shown, as Heller summarizes characters and situations with his scathing wit. But even in a more conventional narrative, where much of the story is shown or evoked, there are going to be long passages in which the writer or the narrator simply addresses the reader and tells her what she needs to know. Just as a composer might vary the tempo of a piece of music to maintain the listener's interest, or a chef might provide diners with a variety of courses that each hit the palate in a different place, the fiction writer needs to vary between intensely evocative scenes, passages of pure exposition, and even scenes that are a little bit of both.

In other words, "Show, don't tell"—unless, of course, you just need to tell the reader something.

There are any number of ways of doing this. In some varieties of popular fiction, science fiction and fantasy in particular, there is often a passage or even an entire chapter early in the narrative known as the *info dump*, whereby the author takes a few pages to simply explain the world of the story, before he even introduces a character or starts the narrative. Many great literary novels have long passages of simply telling: George Eliot's *Middlemarch*, one of the greatest novels ever written, opens with a straightforward description of one of its main characters, Dorothea Brooke, that is not tied to any particular setting or specific moment, and it goes on for four solid pages before we get an actual scene with action and dialogue.

Even in a highly dramatic popular novel like the aforementioned *'Salem's Lot*, there are passages between the dramatic scenes where Stephen King simply tells us what's going on, and what's up with the characters.

Another excellent example of a careful balance between telling and showing, between evocation and exposition, is Irène Némirovsky's novel *Suite Française*, which, despite being tragically incomplete (the author died in Auschwitz before she could finish it), is one of the greatest works of literature to have come out of World War II. It's about the Nazi occupation of France from the point of view of a variety of French characters, and some of it is exquisitely evocative, like this passage from the point of view of a French woman who has fallen in love with the German officer who has been billeted in her house as she waits for him to come home:

> Finally the sound of his horse neighing on the road, the clanking of weapons, orders given to the groom who walks away with the horse. The sound of spurs on the doorstep. Then the night, the stormy night, with its great gusts of wind in the lime trees and the thunder

rumbling in the distance. She would tell him. Oh, she was no hypocrite, she would tell him in clear, simple French—that the prey he so desired was his. "And then what? Then what?" she murmured; a mischievous, bold, sensual smile suddenly transformed her expression, just as the reflection of a flame illuminating a face can alter it. Lit up by fire, the softest features can look demonic; they can both repel and attract. (p. 324)

This is showing rather than telling, because what we get vividly from this passage is that the woman is passionately in love with the German officer, that she desires him, but nowhere in the passage does Némirovsky say (or "tell" us) that she's in love. Instead, her intense longing is evoked by vivid and specific sights and sounds: the sound of his spurs, the gusts of wind in the lime trees, the rumble of thunder in the distance, and the demonic look of desire on her face, as if lit by fire.

Contrast this with another passage from the book, a straightforward, expository description of a different German officer:

Like many young men subjected to strict discipline from childhood, he had acquired the habit of bolstering his ego with outward arrogance and stiffness. He believed that any man worthy of the name should be made of steel. And he had behaved accordingly during the war, in Poland and France, and during the occupation. But far more than any principles, he obeyed the impulsiveness of youth. … He behaved kindly or cruelly depending on how people and things struck him. If he took a dislike to someone, he made sure he hurt them as much as possible. … On the other hand he would behave with infinite kindness and sympathy towards certain prisoners who seemed likeable to him. (p. 230)

This is also vivid in its way, and we certainly get a clear idea of the officer, but we aren't drawn into this passage the way we are drawn into the scene with the woman in love, or the way we would be if Némirovsky had taken a moment to dramatize some of this officer's acts of cruelty or kindness. The adjectives and metaphors used to describe him are definitive but generic: He's arrogant, stiff, and made of steel, qualities that could describe countless officers in the German army at the time. He isn't really singled out as an individual.

But then—and here's my point—we don't need to see him as vividly as we see the woman, because he's not as important to the story as she is. He is, in other words, a secondary character, whose main function in the plot is to get killed by a jealous French husband later on. And, to be sure, we do see him in action in several scenes, but under the circumstances, on our first meeting with him, it makes perfect sense for the author to simply present him to us, fully formed.

As it happens, I'm going to be talking about creating characters for the next four lectures, and I'll come back to how evocation applies to character development. In my first lecture about character, however, I'll be talking about how fictional characters are different from real people, and we'll be taking a look at three characters in particular, from Virginia Woolf's *Mrs. Dalloway*, Fitzgerald's *The Great Gatsby*, and Dashiell Hammett's *The Maltese Falcon*.

In the meantime, here's an exercise in evocation you might try. It's one of the exercises from John Gardner's *The Art of Fiction*: write a passage describing a building, a landscape, or an object, but imagine you're writing from the point of view of a parent whose child has just died.

The interesting part of the exercise is that all you're allowed to do is describe the object, without mentioning the parent, the child, or death. The idea is to see if you can evoke the feeling of loss and grief in the reader without mentioning either, the way Némirovsky evokes love and desire without mentioning either of them in the passage I quoted earlier. It sounds daunting, but give it a try. You might surprise yourself!

How Characters Are Different from People
Lecture 3

One of the curious facts about the emotional life of human beings is that some of the most memorable and influential people in our lives have never existed at all. Odysseus, King Arthur, Jane Eyre, Mrs. Dalloway, Holden Caulfield—these imaginary people have become part of the common cultural currency of humankind; further, they are the very foundation of the craft of fiction. We often hear people talk about the difference between character-driven stories and plot-driven stories, but the fact is that every narrative begins with its characters. In this lecture, we'll explore the fundamental differences between the imaginary characters of fiction and the people we know in real life.

Characters in Fiction and Life

- Writers love to talk about how complex and layered their characters are—and they often are—but one major difference between fictional characters and real people is that characters are simpler.

  - A fictional character is constructed out of a few thousand words by a single writer, whereas a real person, even an uncomplicated one, is the product of millennia of heredity, centuries of culture, and a lifetime of experience. The best a fictional character can do is suggest a real person, not replicate one. They have only the illusion of complexity.

  - Indeed, their very simplicity is what makes fictional characters so vivid, because we can, by the end of a book or a play, see a fictional character whole in a way that we can't with most real people, even the ones we know intimately. But again, this wholeness is an illusion. In *Hamlet*, for example, we see only a few days in Hamlet's life, and even in larger-scale works, we never see as much of a character as we could a real person.

- Another difference between fictional characters and real people is that characters are made up of only the most dramatic or the most representative moments of their lives. We all live through moments of drama that might make for good stories, but the vast majority of our lives is made up of an endless chain of ordinary moments. Such moments are of no interest to anyone else and sometimes not even to us.

- o When we write stories, however, we leave out all the ordinary, boring parts. The story of Hamlet starts when he learns, from his father's ghost, that his father was murdered by his uncle and his mother so that his uncle could be king. The rest of the play is about how Hamlet deals with this information, and by the final scene, he's managed to kill, or cause to be killed, everyone he thinks has wronged him.

- o By contrast, a version of *Hamlet* that reproduced every single moment of his life would be both impractical and tedious. The life of a real person goes on and on, with no scene breaks or dramatic structure, but in a narrative, we see only the significant moments.

- o Of course, some books try to reproduce the minute-by-minute progression of everyday life. The high-modernist novels *Ulysses* and *Mrs. Dalloway* both take place over a single day—and not a particularly dramatic one—in the lives of the main characters. But even with these seemingly all-inclusive narratives, we see only a few hours of the characters' lives, not a complete record of every moment from dawn to dusk.

- We know the people in our lives by what they look like, what they say, what they do, and what other people tell us about them—that is, by report. When we add this fourth way of knowing, we can expand our experience of real people beyond personal relationships to include all the real people we've ever heard about, from a friend of a friend to a movie star to a figure from history.

- o Both the people we know personally and those we know about by report are equally real, and because of that, people in both groups share a certain impenetrable mystery: We can't know what they're thinking. We have no direct access to the consciousness of other living people.

o   To understand this idea, consider the fleeting and digressive nature of your own inner life. Then, consider how impossible it would be to express that inner life to another person. Remember, too, that every other person in the world is experiencing the same kind of inner life, all the time. You quickly realize that each of us is alone in the universe inside our heads, surrounded by many other universes with which we can communicate only indirectly.

o   Thus, the most important difference between fictional characters and real people is that the author can, if he or she chooses, let us know exactly what a fictional character is thinking or feeling. We can know fictional characters in the way we know ourselves. In fiction, we have direct access to the consciousness of other human beings in a way we cannot in real life.

Qualifications and a Paradox

*   We must note three significant qualifications about this unusual intimacy we share with fictional characters, starting with the fact that it is an illusion. It's not real intimacy because the character sharing his or her innermost thoughts with us isn't a real person. The second qualification is that what feels like direct access to another consciousness isn't direct at all but is mediated through the talent, craft, and imagination of the writer.

*   Taken together, these two qualifications leave us with a paradox: We know fictional characters only by report, yet through the genius of certain authors, we feel as if we know some characters even better than we know those with whom we have intimate relationships.

Through the special relationship that fiction can have with its characters, we as readers can have the sort of intimacy with these fictional people that we otherwise have only with ourselves.

- o Even though your brother, for example, is real and infinitely more complex than such a character as Virginia Woolf's Mrs. Dalloway, if you were asked at any given moment what your brother might be thinking, you could only guess. But you can know with absolute certainty what Clarissa Dalloway is thinking at any given point in the novel.

- o This paradox is at the core of the power of fiction to thrill and move us. In reading a book, all we really get are the imaginary thoughts of an imaginary person, but we feel as if we get something real and immediate, something we would never otherwise see: namely, the world through someone else's eyes, unmediated.

- o The intimacy we share with fictional characters is only an illusion of intimacy, but it's such a powerful illusion that, at its best and most sublime, the book in our hands disappears, the voice of the author disappears, the world around us disappears, and we become fully engaged in the fictional world—at one with the character.

- The third qualification is this: Even though all writers could put us in the heads of their characters, not all of them do. The amount of access a writer allows us to have to the mind of a character varies on a continuum from complete intimacy to no intimacy at all. Most fiction falls somewhere in the middle, where most of what we learn about a character is through action and dialogue, with occasional access to his or her thoughts.

The Continuum of Intimacy
- Let's look at three examples of different points on the continuum of intimacy, beginning with *Mrs. Dalloway* on the most intimate end. This novel gives us one day in the life of Clarissa Dalloway, an upper-middle-class woman living in London in the years right after the end of World War I.

- o Published in 1925, *Mrs. Dalloway* is written in a style called *stream of consciousness*. With this technique, the narration keeps close to the consciousness of its characters, shifting among perceptions, thoughts, and memories effortlessly and with lightning speed in an attempt to evoke the quicksilver nature of human consciousness.

- o The novel relates the thoughts of Mrs. Dalloway at the very moment she thinks them in a way that's simply not possible for an outside observer to do in real life. Even if we knew Mrs. Dalloway and could ask what she was thinking, the mere act of translating her thoughts into speech would change what was happening; she would no longer be alone in her own mind but talking to another person.

- Another remarkable book published in 1925 is F. Scott Fitzgerald's *The Great Gatsby*. This book is narrated in the first person by Nick Carraway, but even though Nick speaks directly to the reader in his own voice, the narration here is less intimate than it is in *Mrs. Dalloway*.
  - o We learn about Nick's history and his moral character through his narration, but we get the impression that he is holding certain things back.

  - o Nick stands somewhere in the middle of the literary continuum between complete intimacy and no intimacy. We learn only what he chooses to tell us, which means that we learn no more about him than we might learn from him in real life.

- A third example is *The Maltese Falcon*, Dashiell Hammett's classic detective story, published in 1930. Hammett's main character, the private detective Sam Spade, appears in every scene in the book, and we see the entire story from Spade's point of view.
  - o We get detailed descriptions of Spade's appearance, gestures, and actions; we also get a great deal of dialogue, in much of which Spade isn't necessarily telling the truth. But what we never get in the novel is direct access to what Spade is thinking,

and because *The Maltese Falcon* is written in the third person, Spade does not directly address us. Everything we know about Sam Spade we learn from observing him move and listening to him talk, the same way we would in real life.

o   At the end of the book, Spade must decide what do with Brigid O'Shaughnessy, the femme fatale who murdered his partner, but with whom Spade may or may not have fallen in love. It's an extreme situation, but Hammett doesn't plunge us into Spade's thoughts or allow his character to speak directly to us; instead, he lets us listen to a scene in which Spade thinks out loud about his feelings for Brigid and the choice he must make.

o   The scene is a vivid portrayal of a man wrestling with a bad situation. Although we don't have access to Spade's thoughts, we do have access to the dark world in which he lives. Hammett may not choose to show us every fleeting shift of Spade's consciousness, but he understands Spade and his moral universe every bit as deeply as Woolf understands Clarissa Dalloway's or as Fitzgerald understands Nick's.

Suggested Reading

Fitzgerald, *The Great Gatsby*.

Forster, *Aspects of the Novel*.

Hammett, *The Maltese Falcon*.

Woolf, *Mrs. Dalloway*.

1. Try to rewrite the scene of Mrs. Dalloway walking down Bond Street in the first-person style of *The Great Gatsby* or, perhaps, in the terse and more literal-minded approach of Dashiell Hammett. In other words, see if it's possible to evoke Mrs. Dalloway by having her tell us what she's thinking directly or by simply describing what she does or says as she moves through the scene. Conversely, see if it's possible to apply Virginia Woolf's stream-of-consciousness technique to Sam Spade's hard-boiled world and still keep the scene tense, energetic, and suspenseful.

How Characters Are Different from People
Lecture 3—Transcript

One of the curious facts about the emotional life of human beings is that some of the most vivid, memorable, and influential people in our lives have never existed at all.

I'm talking, of course, about fictional characters, and the funny thing about them is that many of the people who are most familiar to us, in fact many of the people who may be the most *important* to us are imaginary, from Odysseus to King Arthur to Jane Eyre to Mrs. Dalloway to Holden Caulfield to Tyrion Lannister.

These characters are often more vivid and more comprehensible to us than some of the people we know in real life, and occasionally even more appealing to us than our own loved ones.

Anyone who enjoys storytelling, from tales told round a campfire, to novels and short stories, to movies and television, willingly consents to a shared illusion: We understand that the characters we read or watch are not real, but we allow ourselves to react to them as if they were. The best-known characters, in fact, are instantly recognizable to millions of people all over the world. The names Sherlock Holmes, Dracula, James Bond, Buffy the Vampire Slayer, and Lisbeth Salander are so widely known that the mere mention of each one instantly puts an image in your head, even if you've never read any of the books or seen of the movies in which they appear. These characters are an essential part of the common cultural currency of humankind.

Most importantly for our purposes, though, these imaginary people are the very foundation of the craft of fiction. You often hear people talk about the difference between character-driven stories and plot-driven stories, with the implication that the people in character-driven stories are richer, more complex, and more realistic than the people in plot-driven stories, and while that's sometimes true, it isn't always.

From the simplest and most accessible pop fiction to the most challenging and ambitious literary fiction, every narrative begins with its characters. To put it simply, you can have a character without a story, but you can't have a story without characters. We might even say, with apologies to George Orwell, that *all* fiction is character-driven, but that some fiction is more character-driven than others.

Every story or novel is about the psychology and/or behavior of people, or, in the case of fantasy, science fiction, and children's literature, about characters who may not actually be human beings—hobbits, aliens, little engines that could—but who are basically substitutes for people. But for all their vividness and appeal, fictional characters are fundamentally different from real people, and not just because characters are imaginary and real people are, well, real. It seems to me there are three fundamental differences between real people and the characters in fiction. I'd like to talk about each one in turn, because I think it will help you think about how to create your own characters.

The first reason characters are different from real people is that they are simpler than real people. Writers love to talk about how complex and layered and mysterious their characters are, and it's true, they often can be. It's pretty much a critical commonplace that you can never quite get to the bottom of Hamlet, for example, that there are countless different interpretations of Hamlet's thoughts and behavior in the Shakespeare play that bears his name.

And there are certainly many, many other examples of rich, layered characters: the everyman Leopold Bloom in James Joyce's *Ulysses*, the idealistic young Dorothea Brooke in George Eliot's *Middlemarch*, the title character in Virginia Woolf's *Mrs. Dalloway*.

But even these characters, as great as they are, are still necessarily simpler than the least interesting real person you have ever met. A fictional character is constructed out of a few thousand words by a single writer, whereas a real person, even an uncomplicated one, is the product of millennia of heredity, centuries of culture, and a lifetime of experience. The best a fictional character can do is *suggest* a real person, not replicate one. They only have the illusion of complexity.

Indeed, their very simplicity is what makes them so vivid, because we can, by the end of a story or a book or a play, see a fictional character whole in way that we can't with most real people, even the ones we know intimately. But again, this wholeness is an illusion. In *Hamlet*, for example, we only see a few days of his life, and even in larger scale works, we never see as much of a character as we could a real person. Take, for example, John Updike's epic quartet of novels about Harry "Rabbit" Angstrom, a mid-20th century, white middleclass American everyman. Through four novels, *Rabbit Run*, *Rabbit Redux*, *Rabbit Is Rich*, and *Rabbit at Rest*, we see Rabbit in enormous detail, from the age of 26 to his death in his early 50s, but even so, each novel only shows a slice of Rabbit's life lasting a few months, while whole years of his life go unrecorded, or only hinted at in flashbacks.

By the end of the last novel, when Rabbit is dying in a hospital bed, we feel like we know everything there is to know about him, and that powerful illusion is partly the result of the fact that he is, in the end, even after all those pages, simpler than a real man.

And yet that illusion, that uncanny vividness, that feeling we get with a great story or a great book that we're meeting someone real and not imaginary, remains very powerful. And that brings me to the second reason fictional characters are not like real people: namely that fictional characters are made up only of the most dramatic and/or the most representative moments of their lives.

This is part of what I mean when I say that fictional characters are simpler than real people, and that even a complex character can only suggest a real person, not replicate one. We all live through moments of drama that might make for good stories, but the vast majority of our lives is made up of an endless chain of ordinary moments laid out one after the other. These moments are of no interest to anyone else, and sometimes not even to us. When we write stories, however, we leave out all the ordinary, boring parts. The story of Hamlet starts when he learns, from his father's ghost, that his father was murdered by his uncle and his mother so that his uncle could be king. You can't have a more dramatic set-up than that.

The rest of the play is about how Hamlet deals with this information, and though of course he rather famously spends much of the play dithering at great length, the fact remains that by the final scene, he's managed to kill, or cause to be killed, everyone he thinks has wronged him, and even a few people who haven't.

By contrast, a version of *Hamlet* that reproduced every single moment of his life would be both impractical and tedious. Impractical, by virtue of the fact that such a story would take as long to read as it did to live. Nobody would sit through a play that lasted 30 years; indeed, you can't even get some people to sit through the four hours the play usually takes. We wouldn't want to watch Hamlet sleeping for eight hours, or reading, or eating, or doing his laundry. The life of a real person goes on and on and on without stopping, with no scene breaks or dramatic structure, but in a narrative, you only want to see the moments where Hamlet confronts his uncle or his mother or the other people he holds responsible for his father's death.

Not all narratives are like this, of course. There are some books and stories that actually do try to reproduce the minute-by-minute progression of everyday life, and try to make it interesting. This is why I said that in fiction we see either the most dramatic or the most representative moments of a character's life. The high modernist novels *Ulysses* and *Mrs. Dalloway* each take place over a single day, and not especially dramatic days at that. Instead, we watch Leopold Bloom in *Ulysses* and Mrs. Dalloway from moment to moment throughout their day, paying close attention to their point of view, with occasional flashbacks to important moments in their past. There is a death in *Mrs. Dalloway*, but it doesn't happen to her or to anyone she knows, and what we see of her is pretty ordinary. But even with a seemingly all-inclusive narrative such as this, we only see a few hours of Mrs. Dalloway's day, not a complete record of every moment from dawn to dusk, just enough to give us a vivid picture of her world and how she sees it, so that by the end we feel as if we really know her.

Even when a writer is focusing on representative moments and not the more dramatic moments of a character's life, she is still selecting only those moments that will tell us the most about the character.

But there's another, deeper reason why fictional characters are different from real people, and to explain this third reason, I want you to think about how you know people in real life. Start with the people you know most intimately: How do you know your spouse, your children, your parents, your friends? The question is simple, and so is the answer: You know your family and friends by what they look like, by what they say, and by what they do. To these three ways of knowing them directly, let's add a fourth, less direct way: You also know the people in your lives by report, that is, you know them by what other people tell you about them.

And when we add this fourth way of knowing, knowledge by report, we can expand our experience of real people beyond our personal relationships to include all the real people we have ever heard about—from the friend of a friend who made a fool of herself at a New Year's Eve party, to the movie star whose love life is endlessly chronicled on the Internet, to the Roman emperor Claudius, whose stuttering speech we learn about from history books.

Obviously, the further a person is from us personally, the less intimate our knowledge is and the more it depends on the report of others. I know my brother Tom pretty well, because I've spent a lot of time in his company, whereas I know the actress Meryl Streep only because I've seen her in movies or interviews. Clearly I know Tom better than I know Meryl Streep, because I've had direct access to him, while my experience of Ms. Streep has been mediated by filmmakers and journalists.

Now, this may be the only moment in the whole history of the universe when my brother Tom and Meryl Streep are mentioned in the same paragraph, but the fact remains that they are both (so far as I know) equally real, and because they're both real, they still have something in common with each other, and with every other real person in the world, that sets them apart from every fictional character ever created.

As improbable as it may sound, especially if you know my brother Tom, he and Meryl Streep share a certain impenetrable mystery, and that mystery is this: I don't know what they're thinking. In fact, I *can't* know what they're thinking.

In other words, to put it in slightly more hifalutin language, I can have no direct access to the consciousness of any other living person. None of us can. Not to get all bleak and existentialist on you, but each of us is trapped inside his or her own head, and we can only *infer* what other people are thinking and feeling from—as I've already said—what they look like, what they say and do, and what other people tell us about them.

You don't need an undergraduate degree in philosophy like mine to understand this—all you have to do is consider your own inner life in those moments when you're alone or not communicating with anyone else. Think of how quick and fleeting and digressive your inner life is, shifting from perception to perception, from thought to thought, from memory to memory, effortlessly and with lightning speed. Then consider how impossible it would be not only to express all that to another person, but even just to remember all of it yourself five minutes later.

Then consider that every other person in the world is doing the same thing, all the time, and you realize that each of us is alone in the teeming little universe inside our head, surrounded by a lot of other little universes with which we can communicate only indirectly.

So, just when you thought I was never going to get around to it, the most important difference between fictional characters and real people turns out to be that the author can, if he or she chooses, let us know *exactly* what a fictional character is really thinking or feeling. We can know a fictional character the way the fictional character knows him or herself. In fact, we can know a fictional character as well as we can know *ourselves*.

In fiction we can have direct access to the consciousness of another human being in a way that we simply cannot in real life. In his book *Aspects of the Novel*, the great English novelist E. M. Forster puts it succinctly: Fictional characters "are people whose secret lives are visible," whereas we (by which he means real human beings) "are people whose secret lives are invisible." (p. 64) We can know things about a fictional character that in real life we can only know about ourselves, the things we never tell other people: We can know a character's deepest secrets, her most private longings, his wildest ambitions, her worst fears.

Right away, of course, I have to point out three whopping qualifications about this unusual intimacy we share with fictional characters, and the most whopping qualification of all is that this intimacy is an illusion. It's not real intimacy, obviously, because the character sharing his or her innermost thoughts with us isn't really a person. As I said earlier, fictional characters are just words on a page: Not only can't they have innermost thoughts, they can't have any thoughts at all.

The second qualification is that what feels like direct access to another consciousness isn't direct at all, but is mediated through the talent, craft, and imagination of the writer. Taken together, these two qualifications leave us with a paradox. Because fictional characters are presented to us by a writer who is a real person, we know fictional characters only by report, the way we know the real people who are the most distant from us—the way I "know" Meryl Streep, for example. And yet through the genius of Virginia Woolf, I feel like I know the character Clarissa Dalloway not only better than I could ever know Meryl Streep, but perhaps ever better than I know my brother Tom. But even though my brother Tom is real and, all appearances notwithstanding, infinitely more complex than Mrs. Dalloway, whose existence consists only of a few thousand extremely well-chosen words in a book, the fact remains that if you ask me at any given moment in Tom's life what he might be thinking, I can only guess. I can never be sure. But I *can* tell you with absolute certainty what Clarissa Dalloway is thinking at any given point in the novel that bears her name.

This paradox is at the heart of the power of fiction to thrill and move us. All we're *really* getting are the imaginary thoughts of an imaginary person, as invented and reported to us by the writer, but we *feel* as if we're getting not only something real and immediate, but something we would never otherwise see—namely, the world through someone else's eyes, unmediated. It's one of the reasons that the act of reading fiction can feel so private and intimate, even illicit, because we feel like we're getting a look backstage, behind the curtain, where normally we're not allowed to go.

As Forster puts it, "It is the function of the novelist to reveal the hidden life at its source." (p. 45) It's only an illusion of intimacy, but it's such a powerful illusion that, at its best and most sublime, the book in our hands disappears, the voice of the author disappears, the world around us disappears, and we are fully engaged in the fictional world, and at one with the character.

But here's the third and final qualification: Even though every writer could, if he or she wanted, put us in the heads of their characters, not all of them do. The amount of access a writer allows us to have with the mind of a character varies on a continuum from complete intimacy at one end to no intimacy at all. At one end, we're like mind readers, but at the other, we're like a surveillance camera, learning no more about a character than we would learn about them from real life. Most fiction, in fact, falls somewhere in the middle, where most of what we learn about a character is through action and dialogue, but with occasional access to their thoughts.

Let's take a look at three different examples at three different spots on this continuum, from three books published within a few years of each other. At the most intimate end of the continuum is *Mrs. Dalloway*, which gives us one day in the life of Clarissa Dalloway, an upper-middle-class woman living in London in the years after the end of World War I. Published in 1925, *Mrs. Dalloway* is written in the style we call stream of consciousness, by which the narration keeps very close to the consciousness of its characters, shifting from perception to perception, from thought to thought, and from memory to memory, effortlessly and with lightning speed, attempting to evoke, if not actually reproduce, the quicksilver nature of human consciousness.

Here's Mrs. Dalloway walking up Bond Street in London on a summer's day shortly after World War I, going out to buy flowers for a party she's hosting that evening:

> Bond Street fascinated her; Bond Street early in the morning in the season; its flags flying; its shops; no splash; no glitter, one roll of tweed in the shop where her father had bought his suits for fifty years; a few pearls; salmon on an iceblock.

> "That is all," she said, looking at the fishmonger's. "That is all," she repeated, pausing for a moment at the window of a glove shop where before the War, you could buy almost perfect gloves. And her old Uncle William used to say a lady is known by her shoes and

her gloves. He had turned on his bed one morning in the middle of the War. He had said, "I have had enough." Gloves and shoes, she had a passion for gloves; but her own daughter, her Elizabeth, cared not a straw for either of them. (Virginia Woolf, *Mrs. Dalloway*, pp. 9–10)

There are a lot things I could say about this brilliant passage, but mainly I want you to notice that, even on a first reading, you can see how the prose relates the thoughts of Mrs. Dalloway at the very moment she thinks them, in a way that's simply not possible for an outside observer to do in real life.

If you were standing next to a real Mrs. Dalloway on that London street in 1921, all you would see would be a middle-aged woman of aristocratic bearing, gazing absently at items in a shop window. Even if you knew her and could ask her what she was thinking, the mere translation of her thoughts into speech would change what was happening, in the literary version of Heisenberg's uncertainty principle: The very act of asking the question would change the result, because she would no longer be alone in her own head, but talking to another person. You could never know the real woman the way you know Mrs. Dalloway through Virginia Woolf's prose, when you are eavesdropping on her private thoughts.

Now, let's take a look at another remarkable book published in 1925, F. Scott Fitzgerald's *The Great Gatsby*. This book is narrated in the first person by Nick Carraway, who introduces himself in the book's famous opening passage:

In my younger and more vulnerable years my father gave me some advice that I've been turning over in my mind ever since.

"Whenever you feel like criticizing any one," he told me, "just remember that all the people in this world haven't had the advantages that you've had."

He didn't say any more, but we've always been unusually communicative in a reserved way, and I understood that he meant a great deal more than that. In consequence, I'm inclined to reserve all judgments, a habit that has opened up many curious natures to me and also made me the victim of not a few veteran bores. The abnormal mind is quick to detect and attach itself to this quality when it appears in a normal person, and so it came about that in college I was unjustly accused of being a politician, because I was privy to the secret griefs of wild, unknown men. Most of the confidences were unsought—frequently I have feigned sleep, preoccupation, or a hostile levity when I realized by some unmistakable sign that an intimate revelation was quivering on the horizon; for the intimate revelations of young men, or at least the terms in which they express them, are usually plagiaristic and marred by obvious suppressions. Reserving judgments is a matter of infinite hope. I am still a little afraid of missing something if I forget that, as my father snobbishly suggested, and I snobbishly repeat, a sense of the fundamental decencies is parceled out unequally at birth.

When we compare this with *Mrs. Dalloway*, we discover a curious thing about this passage: Even though Nick Carraway is speaking in the first person, directly to the reader in his own voice, this passage is less intimate than the passage from *Mrs. Dalloway*, where we had direct access to Clarissa Dalloway's every thought during a particular moment. We learn something about Nick's history in this passage, we learn something about his moral character, but because of the lapidary elegance with which this passage is written, we get the impression that he is holding a great deal back. For one thing, he's summarizing rather than evoking a particular moment, and for another, he leads away from the particular—the specific advice his father gave him once—to the general.

In other words, Nick Carraway stands somewhere in the middle of the literary continuum between complete intimacy on the one hand and no intimacy on the other. We learn only what he chooses to tell us, which means we learn no more about him than we might learn from him in real life. I'll talk much more about point of view and voice in later lectures, but for now I just want to emphasize that the sort of intimacy with a character that I'm talking about, that direct access to a character's thoughts, does not necessarily depend on what voice or point of view the author adopts. The first person can be less intimate than the third.

My third example comes from a book that was published in 1930, only five years after *Mrs. Dalloway* and *The Great Gatsby*, namely Dashiell Hammett's classic detective story, *The Maltese Falcon*. Hammett's main character, the private detective Sam Spade, appears in every scene in the book, and we see the entire story from Spade's point of view. We get a very detailed physical description of Spade, who we're told looks "rather pleasantly like a blond satan" (p. 391); we also get very detailed descriptions of his physical gestures and actions, including a whole paragraph on how he rolls a cigarette; and we get lots and lots of dialogue, in much of which he isn't necessarily telling the truth.

But what we never get, not once in the whole novel, is direct access to what he's thinking, the way we do with Clarissa Dalloway. And because *The Maltese Falcon* is in the third person, Spade does not directly address to the reader, the way Nick Carraway does. Everything we know about Sam Spade, we learn from observing him move and listening to him talk, the same way we would in real life.

At the end of the book, Spade has to decide what do with Brigid O'Shaughnessy, the femme fatale who murdered his partner, but with whom Spade may or may not have fallen in love. It's an extreme situation, the very stuff of melodrama—do I rat my lover out to the cops?—and Spade's thoughts must be racing even faster than Mrs. Dalloway's. But instead of plunging deep into his thoughts, the way Woolf does with Mrs. Dalloway, or letting Spade speak directly to the reader, the way Fitzgerald does with Nick Carraway, Hammett lets us listen instead to a sweaty-palmed climactic scene in which Spade thinks out loud on the fly, trying to square his love for a deceitful, murderous, but seductive woman with his sense of self-preservation.

After listing all the reasons for turning her in, he gives her the only reason he can think of not to:

> "Now on the other side we've got what? All we've got is the fact that maybe you love me and maybe I love you."

> "You know," she whispered, "whether you do or not."

"I don't. It's easy enough to be nuts about you." He looked hungrily from her hair to her feet and up to her eyes again. "But I don't know what that amounts to. Does anybody ever? But suppose I do? What of it? Maybe next month I won't. I've been through it before— when it lasted that long. Then what? Then I'll think I played the sap. And if I did it and got sent over then I'd be sure I was the sap. Well, if I send you over I'll be sorry as hell—I'll have some rotten nights—but that'll pass." (*The Maltese Falcon*, pp. 582–583, Library of America edition)

Now this may not have the complexity or depth of *Mrs. Dalloway*, and the prose isn't nearly as elegant as Fitzgerald's, but it's still a vivid portrayal of a man wrestling with a bad situation. It also vividly evokes the moral universe of Sam Spade, where love is primarily erotic and never lasts long, and where the worst humiliation he can think of is being played for a sap by a conniving woman.

We may not have access to Spade's thoughts, but we have direct access to the dark and morally labyrinthine world in which he lives. Hammett may not choose to show us every fleeting shift of Spade's consciousness the way we follow the flickerings of Mrs. Dalloway's thoughts on Bond Street, but Hammett understands Spade and his moral universe every bit as deeply as Woolf understands Clarissa Dalloway's, or as deeply as Fitzgerald understands Nick's.

With these three examples, I think you get an idea of the range of possibilities for getting into a character's head, from complete intimacy to complete opacity. The fact that Nick Carraway withholds something of himself and that Sam Spade's thoughts are completely blocked off from the reader may seem to contradict what I said earlier, about how fictional characters are different because we can tell what they're thinking, but I contend that it still holds true, because even if the author chooses not to show us what a character's thinking, he could if he wanted to.

Even in novels that do not reveal the consciousness of their characters, that impossible intimacy with people who never really existed is always present underneath the narrative, even if the writer chooses not to show it to us at every point, or even at all. Dashiell Hammett and F. Scott Fitzgerald know the hearts of Sam Spade and Nick Carraway every bit as intimately as Virginia Woolf knows Mrs. Dalloway's, but because they are writing different sorts of books than Virginia Woolf was, they choose to withhold that information. And yet that intimate understanding is there even if the reader never sees it, holding up the characters like the unseen superstructure of a building. To quote E. M. Forster one more time, we know a character in a book is real "when the novelist knows everything about it." (p.63)

Here's an exercise to help you get some firsthand experience with some of the issues I talked about in this lecture. Think of it as the literary version of that old body-swapping comedy, *Freaky Friday*: Try to rewrite the scene of Mrs. Dalloway walking down Bond Street in the first-person style of *The Great Gatsby*, or perhaps in the terse and more literal-minded approach of Dashiell Hammett. In other words, see if it's possible to evoke Mrs. Dalloway by having her tell us what she's thinking directly, or by simply describing what she does or says as she moves through the scene. And conversely, see if it's possible to apply Virginia Woolf's stream-of-consciousness technique to Sam Spade's hardboiled world and still keep the scene tense, energetic, and suspenseful.

None of these approaches may turn out to work, but it might be a lot of fun to try. At the very least, you will learn something about the limits and possibilities of each approach.

In the next lecture, I'll be talking about how you can use both imagination and observation to create characters, and we'll look at examples from Jane Austen, Charlotte Brontë, and yours truly.

Through the special relationship that fiction and only fiction can have with its characters, we can have the sort of intimacy with other people, albeit fictional ones, that we otherwise only have with ourselves. Even if we take into account the wide variety of ways that writers of different backgrounds and temperaments use characters, fiction allows us what Forster calls the "illusion of perspicacity and of power," and broadens our understanding of what it means to be human.

Fictional Characters, Imagined and Observed
Lecture 4

A ll writers draw, both consciously and unconsciously, on behaviors and traits we have seen in ourselves or others, with the result that all the characters you create combine to form a portrait of your view of human nature. But although the roots of any character lie in your observations of yourself and of other people, those observations are refracted through your imagination. In the last lecture, we talked about the continuum between complete intimacy with a character and no intimacy at all, and in this lecture, we'll look at three other continuums: between observation and imagination, between exterior and interior approaches, and between psychology and circumstances in creating characters.

The Continuum of Imagination

- Some writers hew more closely to observation than to imagination, basing their characters almost entirely on people they know. Others write convincingly about characters or experiences they've never had themselves. Some writers even create characters who are a different gender, age, background, ethnicity, or temperament from themselves.

- Of course, there many variations along this continuum between pure observation and pure imagination. In historical novels, for example, the novelist may combine a real figure from history with both real and imaginary characters from the same period.

- Whichever pole a writer tends toward—observation or imagination—no writer relies purely on one or the other. Although some writers may base their characters on real historical figures or close family and friends, all must exercise their imaginations to the extent of seeing the world through the eyes of these characters and relating how the characters behave in fictional situations in which their real-life models may never have found themselves.

The Exterior-Interior Continuum

- The exterior-interior continuum relates to creating a character from the outside in versus creating a character from the inside out.
    - As mentioned in the last lecture, one of the defining features of fiction is that authors can give us direct access to the thoughts of their characters, even if they sometimes choose not to. But even for those characters whose thoughts we do have access to, there are many different ways to express them.

    - If you think of the continuum between observation and imagination as one axis, consider that there is another axis at right angles to this one, and the poles of that axis are the exterior approach and the interior approach.

- To help understand this idea, consider the difference between the British and American styles of acting as they were practiced during the 1950s and 1960s.
    - During this time, the method style of acting became popular among young American actors; this approach required the actor to identify with the character he or she was playing, to analyze that character's psychology in depth, and to use elements from the actor's own memories to evoke the emotions the character felt. In contrast, British actors at the time were trained to build characters out of small physical details and bits of behavior: an accent, a gesture, a prosthetic nose.

    - In this analogy, the American actor is using the interior method, building a character from the inside out, while the British actor is using the exterior method, building the character from the outside in. Fiction writers often use similar exterior or interior approaches.

Comparing *Emma* and *Jane Eyre*

- In the opening pages of her great comic novel *Emma*, Jane Austen lays the title character bare simply by telling us point blank almost everything we need to know about her: "Emma Woodhouse, handsome, clever, and rich, with a comfortable home and happy disposition, seemed to unite some of the best blessings of existence; and had lived nearly twenty-one years in the world with very little to vex or distress her."

  o After two paragraphs that explain Emma's family situation, Austen then tells us: "The real evils indeed of Emma's situation were the power of having rather too much her own way, and a disposition to think a little too well of herself; these were the disadvantages which threatened to alloy her many enjoyments. The danger, however, was at present so unperceived, that they did not by any means rank as misfortunes with her."

  o The rest of the novel is essentially a gloss on the first two pages, showing Emma's impetuosity, vanity, and cluelessness as she tries to manage the love lives of everyone around her without recognizing her own true love. There's no need for any *Mrs. Dalloway*–style intimacy with Emma's stream of consciousness, and there's no watching her slowly reveal herself through her speech and behavior. Austen simply tells us about Emma's character right from the start, then launches into her story.

  o Austen's description of Emma is frank, to the point, and unironic in the sense that Austen never has Emma do anything later in the book that undercuts her original description. Thus, with Emma fixed firmly in our imaginations as a vain, beautiful, meddlesome girl after reading only the first two pages, we are free to enjoy her effect on the lives of the people around her.

  o This approach works especially well with comic fiction, which often depends on types rather than fully developed characters or at least on characters who never really change our first impression of them.

• We can compare Austen's approach with a more indirect, interior one from the opening paragraphs of Charlotte Brontë's *Jane Eyre*. Again, in just a few paragraphs, we meet an adult, first-person narrator who is looking back with bitter irony on her unhappy childhood. We learn that she grew up in a household where she was considered an outsider, but she knew how to stick up for herself.

- o The difference between *Jane Eyre* and *Emma* is that we don't learn everything we need to know about Jane in the first few paragraphs. Instead, we are drawn only gradually into the story while being given hints of her struggles to come.

- o This technique works better than Austen's would in this instance because *Jane Eyre* is a darker, more serious book. There's more at stake here than romances and marriages among the idle rich; in the first few paragraphs of Brontë's book, we get the first hint of Jane's struggle to survive in a world in which she has no money, no connections, and no prospects.

- How you decide to configure characters—from the outside in or the inside out—has a profound effect on the sort of story you end up writing; the cause and effect here are inextricably intertwined.

- o A comedy, for example, often announces itself right from the start by being funny and staying funny, which requires characters who can be quickly and easily identified. In contrast, a drama often draws the reader in with an intriguing situation, the distinctive voice of a strong character, and the suggestion of more trouble to come.

- o Jane Eyre's world is more complex and more unpredictable than Emma's, and this extra complexity requires a more subtle and complex main character. Although Emma eventually grows up and learns not to meddle in the affairs of others, she doesn't do much to surprise us. But Jane, having shown us that she's smart and judgmental from the first page, turns out to be surprisingly wrong in her judgments of some of the other characters, particularly Mr. Rochester.

- Another way to look at the difference between these two approaches is to consider how much you want the reader to identify with the character. By writing in the third person and by telling readers directly of Emma's vanity, Austen invites readers to detach themselves from the character.

But Brontë has Jane Eyre address readers directly, inviting us to view the world through her eyes and to endorse her judgments.

The Psychology-Circumstances Continuum

- To understand the exterior-interior continuum from a slightly different angle, think about the difference between a character who is defined by psychology versus one who is defined by circumstances.

  o We're tempted to think that Emma is determined by her circumstances, but notice that it's the way her particular psychology butts up against the people and the world around her that makes the book funny.

  o In *Jane Eyre*, even though we have instant access to Jane's mind from the first sentence, it's the circumstances of her life that largely determine the course of the novel, even though we see that struggle mainly through its effect on her thoughts and feelings.

© Valueline/Hulton Collection/Thinkstock.

The books of American realist writers tend to be large-scale portraits of a whole city or class of people, emphasizing the social world through which the characters move rather than their individuality.

- Another tempting generalization is that character-driven narratives, such as *Mrs. Dalloway*, rely more on psychology than plot-driven narratives, such as *The Maltese Falcon*, but that's not entirely true either. Even though we don't have direct access to Sam Spade's mind and even though *The Maltese Falcon* is packed with dramatic incidents, the narrative mainly works as a record of his decisions. Underlying all his actions are thoughts that drive those actions, even if they are not directly expressed to the reader.

- Among the characters who are largely determined by their circumstances we might include many of the characters in Dickens, as well as those in the works of realist American writers, such as Theodore Dreiser, Edith Wharton, and Sinclair Lewis. Even though we have direct access to the thoughts of many of these characters, their thoughts are not as determinative of their conduct as their circumstances are.

- There is an intimate relationship between the sort of characters you create and the sort of narrative you write. In fact, they may be inseparable. You could just as easily say that the sort of characters you decide to use determines the kind of story you write as you could say that the kind of story you decide to write determines the sort of characters you use. You can't really make up your mind about one without making up your mind about the other.

- As we've said, however, these are continuums, not either/or decisions, and the same writer will try different sorts of stories and characters at different times.

- For some writers, choosing to work from the outside in or the inside out is purely instinctive: You just sit down at the keyboard and start to write in the first person or the third person. Even so, sometimes it turns out that what comes naturally doesn't work, and you may have to go back and do it a different way.

- You can also be more self-conscious and deliberate about your choices, thinking about what's more important to your story: that the characters are reflective of the larger world they inhabit or that the story is more intimate, told from inside one consciousness. How you answer that question will tell you how to create your character.

Suggested Reading

Austen, *Emma.*

Bernays and Painter, *What If?*

Brontë, *Jane Eyre.*

Hynes, *The Wild Colonial Boy.*

——, *The Lecturer's Tale.*

——, *Next.*

Writing Exercise

1. This exercise is drawn from an excellent book called *What If? Writing Exercises for Fiction Writers* by Anne Bernays and Pamela Painter: Pick a character from a story or novel that has already been written, either by you or by someone else, and make a list of everything you know or can infer about that character. Include basic features, such as the character's name, age, gender, appearance, relationship status, and so on, but also include such attributes as the character's fears, obsessions, and politics, even if they aren't explicitly mentioned in the text. Depending on the sort of narrative you're working with, you may not be able to get a complete list for any character. Such a list for Elizabeth Bennet from *Pride and Prejudice*, for example, would include a great deal about her opinions and personality but nothing about her appearance. In contrast, you can detail Sam Spade's physical appearance, but you can't find much about his opinions on anything. This exercise reinforces the idea that different sorts of stories require different types of characters.

Fictional Characters, Imagined and Observed
Lecture 4—Transcript

No fictional character is created out of nothing. All writers draw, both consciously and unconsciously, on behaviors, traits, and actions we have seen in ourselves or in others. As a result, all the characters you create combine to form a portrait of your view of human nature. But although the roots of any character lie in your observations of yourself and of other people, those observations are refracted through your imagination.

In the last lecture, I talked about the continuum between complete intimacy with a character and no intimacy at all. In this lecture I want to start by talking about another continuum, between *observation* on the one hand and *imagination* on the other.

Some writers hew more closely to observation than to imagination. They base their characters almost entirely on people they know, writing thinly disguised versions of their family or friends, and sometimes sharply etched versions of people they want to get back at. Woe betide the family that has a writer in it. The British novelist Edward St. Aubyn has written a series of five novels about a character named Patrick Melrose whose harrowing family history is based on St. Aubyn's. And it's not just limited to families: The American writer Anne Beattie once said that she had learned to throw very nice dinner parties for her friends, by way of apology for the thinly disguised versions of themselves that appear in her stories.

On the other hand, many writers write very convincingly about characters who are unlike the people they know, or about experiences they've never had themselves. *The Red Badge of Courage* is perhaps the most vivid fictional account of combat during the American Civil War, but its author, Stephen Crane, wasn't even born until six years after the war ended, and he had not yet personally seen a battle when he wrote the book.

Other writers venture even further afield, not only writing about experiences they haven't had themselves, but creating characters who are a different gender, age, background, ethnicity, or temperament from the author. The first three books by the British novelist Pat Barker stay close to her own experience of having grown up as a woman in the north of England. But later in her career, she went on to write three superb novels about World War I, *Regeneration*, *The Eye in the Door*, and *The Ghost Road*, in which she created a wide variety of vivid and believable male characters who have experienced at least two things Barker herself has never experienced, namely being in combat and simply being a man.

And of course there are all sorts of variations along the continuum between pure observation and pure imagination. Take the case of historical novels, such as Marguerite Yourcenar's *The Memoirs of Hadrian*, in which the novelist combines a real figure from history with both real and imaginary characters from the same period in order to evoke the life and times of the title character, the Roman emperor Hadrian. In Yourcenar's novel, we hear directly from the emperor himself in the form of a fictional memoir. Yourcenar takes what is actually known about the real Hadrian and uses her imagination to inhabit the emperor's consciousness. She treats Hadrian the way she would treat a wholly imaginary character while also trying to stay faithful to the historical record.

But whichever pole a writer tends towards, observation or imagination, no writer relies purely on one or the other. Yourcenar may base her character on a real Roman emperor, and Edward St. Aubyn may base his characters closely on his family and friends, but both writers still have to exercise their imaginations in order to see the world through the eyes of these characters, and to show how the characters would behave in a fictional situation in which their real life models may never have found themselves.

Yourcenar, for example, doesn't write only about Hadrian's public life, but also about the sort of private, intimate scenes that are never recorded by history, imagining actions and thoughts that would only have been known to Hadrian himself. And while much of St. Aubyn's saga of family dysfunction is told from the point of view of Patrick Melrose, the character based on himself, much of it is told from the point of view of the other people in Melrose's life. This means that St. Aubyn needed to imagine his way into the minds of the people around him. Conversely, while Pat Barker's evocation of the inner lives of men is a brilliant act of the imagination, no doubt she did her homework as well, talking to veterans or reading memoirs and histories by men who actually *had* been in the trenches, and then filtering this information *through* her imagination.

But whether you're drawing your characters from life in every detail, or you're making them up entirely out of whole cloth, you have to start somewhere. To help you think about that, I'm going to introduce yet another continuum—I'm very big on continuums—to go along with the one between imagination and observation. This new one is the difference between creating a character from the outside in versus creating a character from the inside out.

As I said in the last lecture, one of the defining features of fiction is that an author can give us direct access to the thoughts of her characters, even if she sometimes chooses not to. And even for those characters whose thoughts we *do* have access to, there are many different ways to express them. If you think of the continuum between observation and imagination as one axis, consider that there is another axis at right angles to this one, and the poles of that axis are the exterior approach and the interior approach.

To help you understand what I mean by this, consider the difference between the British style of stage and film acting and the American style of acting, at least as these two styles were practiced during the 1950s and '60s. During this time, the Method style of acting became popular among young American actors such as Marlon Brando and Shelly Winters. This method required the actor to identify with the character he or she was playing, to analyze that character's psychology in depth, and to use elements from the actor's own memories to evoke the emotion the character was feeling. In other words, to oversimplify, the actor was encouraged, as much as possible, to become the character.

On the other hand, the British actor was trained to build a character out of little physical details and bits of behavior: an accent, a gesture, a prosthetic nose. The actor Charles Laughton told the director Alfred Hitchcock that he didn't really get the character he was playing in their film *Jamaica Inn* until he got the character's walk just right. And many great actors such as Alec Guinness and Laurence Olivier devoted a great deal of care to a character's appearance, taking special pride in wearing false teeth or elaborate hairpieces. In fact, Olivier is reputed to have given another actor a piece of advice: "Let the wig do the work."

In this analogy, the American actor is using the interior method, building a character from the inside out, using the character's psychology to dictate his or her behavior. Meanwhile, the British actor is using the exterior method, building the character from the outside in, using external details to evoke the character's personality.

Fiction writers often use similar approaches, working from the outside in or from the inside out. Let's take a look at how several writers have used these different methods in practice. In the opening pages of her great comic novel, *Emma*, Jane Austen lays the title character bare simply by telling us point blank almost everything we need to know about her. Austen does this very quickly and economically in the first paragraph of the novel:

> Emma Woodhouse, handsome, clever, and rich, with a comfortable home and happy disposition, seemed to unite some of the best blessings of existence; and had lived nearly twenty-one years in the world with very little to distress or vex her.

Then, after two paragraphs that explain Emma's family situation—her mother is dead, her older sister has married and moved away, and her best friend is her governess, Miss Taylor—Austen tells us this:

> The real evils indeed of Emma's situation were the power of having rather too much her own way, and a disposition to think a little too well of herself; these were the disadvantages which threatened to alloy her many enjoyments. The danger, however, was at present so unperceived, that they did not by any means rank as misfortunes with her.

Taken together, these two paragraphs are exactly 100 words, and the rest of the novel is essentially a gloss on those first two pages. For the rest of the book, we observe Emma's impetuosity, vanity, and cluelessness as she tries to manage the love lives of everyone around her, without recognizing her own true love—until the last pages, of course. This is a Jane Austen novel, after all.

There's no need for any *Mrs. Dalloway*-style intimacy with Emma's stream of consciousness (though that might have been interesting), and, at least to start with, there's no standing back and watching her slowly reveal herself through her speech and her behavior, the way we learn about Sam Spade. No, Jane Austen simply tells us right from the start what's what with Emma and then launches into her story. And then we get plenty of Emma's speech and behavior, but only after we've already been told what she's like.

Austen's description of Emma is frank, to the point, and unironic. Jane Austen never has Emma do anything later on in the book that undercuts her original description. And so with Emma fixed firmly in our imaginations as a vain, beautiful, meddlesome girl after reading only the first two pages, we are free to enjoy her effect on the people around her for the rest of the story.

This approach works especially well with comic fiction, which often depends on types rather than fully developed characters, or at least on characters who never really change your first impression of them. Think of the Duke and the Dauphin, the two conniving swindlers in *Huckleberry Finn*, or nearly all the characters in Evelyn Waugh's first few novels, or pretty much everybody in Joseph Heller's great antiwar comedy, *Catch-22*. We learn everything we need to know about these characters the first time we meet them. Then, in each instance, the author just turns them loose to wreak havoc on each other or on themselves.

Now compare this with a more indirect, interior approach, one that works from the inside out, and one that feels more modern. Here are the opening paragraphs of Charlotte Brontë's *Jane Eyre*:

> There was no possibility of taking a walk that day. We had been wandering, indeed, in the leafless shrubbery an hour in the morning; but since dinner (Mrs. Reed, when there was no company, dined early) the cold winter wind had brought with it clouds so somber, and a rain so penetrating, that further out-door exercise was now out of the question.

I was glad of it: I never liked long walks, especially on chilly afternoons: dreadful to me was the coming home in the raw twilight, with nipped fingers and toes, and a heart saddened by the chidings of Bessie, the nurse, and humbled by the consciousness of my physical inferiority to Eliza, John, and Georgiana Reed.

The said Eliza, John, and Georgiana were now clustered round their mama in the drawing-room: she lay reclined on a sofa by the fireside, and with her darlings about her (for the time neither quarrelling nor crying) looked perfectly happy. Me, she had dispensed from joining the group; saying, "She regretted to be under the necessity of keeping me at a distance; but that until she heard from Bessie, and could discover by her own observation, that I was endeavouring in good earnest to acquire a more sociable and childlike disposition, a more attractive and sprightly manner— something lighter, franker, more natural, as it were—she really must exclude me from privileges intended only for contented, happy, little children."

"What does Bessie say I have done?" I asked.

This is only 246 words, and yet it feels longer, because it is packed with detail. In that brief space, we learn that we have an adult, first-person narrator who is looking back with bitter irony on her unhappy life as a child. We learn that she grew up with a family to whom she was not related by blood. And we learn that in that household were three other quarrelsome children, their haughty mother, and a judgmental nurse. More importantly, we learn that Jane was considered to be an unwelcome outsider by this unpleasant family. And most importantly, we learn that even as a girl, Jane Eyre knew how to stick up for herself, that she is every bit as determined and headstrong as Emma Woodhouse.

But the difference between Jane Eyre and Emma is that we don't learn everything about Jane in those first few paragraphs. Instead, we are drawn only gradually into the story while being given hints of her struggles to come. In that unwelcoming household on that dreary, cold day, the coming conflict of the book—namely, the irresistible force of Jane Eyre against the immovable object of the world—is only suggested.

This technique works better than Jane Austen's would in this instance, because *Jane Eyre* is a darker, more serious book. There's more at stake here than romances and marriages among the idle rich. In those first few paragraphs we get a foreshadowing of Jane's struggle to survive in a world in which she has no money, no connections, and no prospects.

In other words, how you decide to configure your characters—from the outside in or the inside out—has a profound effect on the sort of story you're going to end up writing. Whether the characters determine the story, or the story determines the character, is up to you, of course. But even so, the characters and story are so inextricably intertwined, you probably won't be able to tell which is the cause and which is the effect.

A comedy, for example, often announces itself right from the start by being funny and staying funny. This depends on characters who can be quickly and easily identified. A drama, on the other hand, often draws you in with an intriguing situation, the distinctive voice of a strong character, and the suggestion of more trouble to come.

Jane Eyre's world is more complex and unpredictable than Emma Woodhouse's, and this extra complexity requires a more subtle and complex main character. While Emma eventually grows up and learns not to meddle in the affairs of others, she doesn't do much to surprise us. Jane Eyre, on the other hand, having shown us that she's smart and judgmental from the first page, turns out to be surprisingly wrong in her judgments of some of the other characters, particularly about Mr. Rochester, the brooding master of the household where she ends up as a governess.

Another way to look at the difference between these two approaches to is consider just how much you want the reader to identify with the character. By writing in the third person, and by telling the reader directly of Emma's vanity and stubborn self-regard in the first few pages, Austen invites the reader to detach herself from Emma and to view her, as Austen does, from a remove, with a bemused and slightly condescending affection.

Charlotte Brontë, on the other hand, has Jane Eyre herself address the reader directly, in the first person. This forceful voice invites the reader to view the world through Jane's eyes and to endorse Jane's judgments of the other people in it. It would take a heartless reader, or at least a stubbornly contrarian one, to read those opening paragraphs of *Jane Eyre* and find himself taking the side of Mrs. Reed and her awful children against Jane. And since this is a continuum and not an either/or choice, I want to emphasize that there are all sorts of variations in between.

Using the first person, for example, is not automatically a sign that the author is writing from the inside out or that he is inviting us to identify with the character. Let's hope that there aren't many readers who identify with the pedophile Humbert Humbert, who narrates Nabokov's novel *Lolita* in the first person. And it's certainly not a hard and fast rule that comic narratives require the reader to be put at a distance. The British novelist Nick Hornby writes very funny and sneakily profound books such as *About a Boy* (which is in the third person) and *How to Be Good* (which is in the first), and in both of these books, he invites us to regard his characters warmly, no matter how foolishly they're behaving, and to see ourselves in their foolishness. Indeed, you might even say Hornby's books fall spang dab in the middle of the range, regarding their characters with great affection, but also without any illusions.

To look at this continuum from a slightly different angle, think about the difference between a character who is defined by her psychology versus a character who is defined by her circumstances. This is close to being the same thing as the split between working from the outside in and working from the inside out, but it's not exactly the same. To use our earlier examples, we're tempted to think that Emma Woodhouse is determined by her circumstances and not by her psychology. But you can actually look at it the other way around: What makes the book funny is the way that Emma's particular psychology butts up against the people and the world around her. And in *Jane Eyre*, even though we have instant access to Jane's mind from the first sentence, it's the circumstances of her life that largely determine the course of the novel, though we see that struggle mainly through its effect on her thoughts and feelings.

Another tempting generalization is that character-driven narratives, such as *Mrs. Dalloway*, rely more on psychology than plot-driven narratives, such as *The Maltese Falcon*. I'm not sure that's entirely true, either. Even though we don't have access to Sam Spade's mind the way we have access to Mrs. Dalloway's, and even though *The Maltese Falcon* is packed with dramatic incident, including violence and the threat of violence, the narrative mainly works as a record of Sam Spade's decisions at every moment.

These decisions are often a mystery to the reader, because the motivation for some of the things he does are unclear until the end of the book. But the fact remains that Sam Spade's thoughts and feelings drive all his actions, even though his thoughts and feelings are never directly expressed to the reader. In its own, oblique way, *The Maltese Falcon* is a very psychological book.

Among the characters who are largely determined by their circumstances you might include many of the characters in Dickens, as well as many of the characters of realist American writers such as Theodore Dreiser, Edith Wharton, and Sinclair Lewis. Even though we have direct access to the thoughts of many of the characters in the works of these authors, the fact remains that their thoughts do not determine their conduct as much as their circumstances do.

Oliver Twist, for example, is defined by the fact that he's a homeless orphan while the title character of Theodore Dreiser's novel *Sister Carrie* is defined by her journey from the rural Wisconsin to the opportunities and temptations of Chicago.

What all these writers have in common is that the their books tend, on the whole, to be large-scale portraits of a whole city or a whole class of people. The emphasis is on the social world of the characters and not so much on their individual choices.

You find a similar effect in large-scale fantasy novels, the sort that create a richly detailed world for the reader to inhabit. In George R. R. Martin's *Song of Ice and Fire* series, the characters are vivid and complex, and sometimes etched with real psychological insight, but for the most part they exist to illuminate the social world in which they move, not the other way around.

Which is not to say they don't have a psychology: The evil young king Joffrey, for example, is clearly a heartless psychopath, but his pathology is not dwelt upon for its own sake, but rather serves as the reason for his extremely capricious and violent behavior within the complex and detailed world of Martin's fantasy.

In other words, there's an intimate relationship between the sort of characters you create and the sort of narrative you write. In fact, they may be inseparable. You could just as easily say that the sort of characters you decide to use determines the kind of story you write as you could say that the kind of story you decide to write determines the sort of characters you use. You can't really make up your mind about one without making up your mind about the other.

And, as I keep stressing, these are continuums I'm talking about, not either/or decisions. John Updike, in his novels about the middle-class everyman Harry "Rabbit" Angstrom, was writing, on one level, the same kind of social realist novel that Sinclair Lewis and Theodore Dreiser were, with very careful attention to getting the social milieu just right.

But at the same time, he was writing an acutely psychological portrait of Rabbit Angstrom, lavishing as much attention on Rabbit's thoughts and feelings as Virginia Woolf ever did with Mrs. Dalloway.

And, of course, the same writer at different times will try different sorts of stories, with different sorts of characters. My own first novel, *The Wild Colonial Boy*, was a political thriller set in Northern Ireland during the 1980s. It tells the story of a callow young Irish American who helps some members of the Irish Republican Army carry out a terrorist bombing in London. The book is told in the third person, but each section is narrated from the point of view of one of four different characters.

While I was certainly concerned to get the psychology of each character right, it was a plot-driven novel, in which the characters mainly react to circumstances. The book is also a kind of tragedy, in which the lives of each of these four characters is shattered (and in one case, ended), and tragedy often requires a kind of inevitability.

There's an implicit view of the world in a narrative like this, one that assumes that people don't really understand their own motives and desires, and though they think they're making rational decisions, they're being driven by circumstances and their own weakness.

This was certainly true of my main character, Brian, who ends up helping to perpetrate an atrocity, a bombing in an art museum, out of a dilettante-ish idealism, a misplaced desire for adventure, and an inability to say no to someone else with a stronger personality.

And yet, though their psychology may not have been as important as their circumstances, Brian and the other three major characters are mainly pure products of my imagination, and they were created from the inside out, as I evoked each chapter or individual scene from each character's point of view. The plot rattled right along, if I do say so myself, and you never saw it from a distance, but from above, and at any given moment, only through the eyes of one of its participants.

Ten years later, I published a very different novel called *The Lecturer's Tale*, a satire of academia. It was a much longer book, with a much wilder plot and a lot more characters. My intent was to make fun of certain tendencies and ideologies in academic literary criticism, with the result that the characters were much less complex than the characters in *The Wild Colonial Boy*. They were drawn more from life than from my imagination.

Some were based on, or composites of, real academics I'd read about, with their particular personalities and characteristics heightened for satiric effect. These characters were created from the outside in. Like Laurence Olivier putting on a hump and a prosthetic nose to play Richard III, I created them out of their appearances, their funny ways of speaking, and their often outrageous beliefs and actions.

The novel's point-of-view character, a hapless, mediocre young professor named Nelson, was a bit more complex than the other people in the book, but not by much. A lot of the characters were like Dickens's characters, in fact, with one or two instantly vivid, recognizable characteristics, and no real psychology to speak of. The book was meant to be a comedy of ideas, and the characters were just complex enough to get my point across.

Then, in my most recent novel, *Next*, I attempted to do something different yet again. I wanted to try my hand at one of those novels like *Mrs. Dalloway* that looks at one character's life over the course of a single day. I'm not even remotely in the same league as Virginia Woolf, of course, but I thought it might be fun to write a book that was more or less plotless and see if I could create a character by following the lightning shifts of his consciousness, moment by moment over the course of a few hours. This way I could reveal much of his history and personality to the reader—much like *Mrs. Dalloway*, in fact, only with more jokes, and not nearly as good.

To align him along the continuums I've been using in this lecture, my main character, Kevin, was created completely from the inside out; there's not a single moment in the book that doesn't come from his point of view. And my evocation of him is, obviously, intensely psychological, shifting from paragraph to paragraph and even from sentence to sentence, from what's right in front of him at a given moment to his remotest memories, from the comic to the serious, from the trivial to the profound.

For some writers, choosing whether to work from the outside in or the inside out is purely instinctive: You just sit down at the keyboard and you start to write in the first person or the third person, as the case may be. Even so, sometimes it turns out that what comes naturally doesn't work, and you may have to go back and do it a different way.

You can also be more self-conscious and deliberate about it, by thinking long and hard about what's more important to your story: Do you want the characters to be reflective of the larger world they inhabit, or do you want to write a more intimate story, from inside one consciousness?

How you answer that question will tell you how to create your character. With *Next*, for example, I had to be quite self-conscious about how I created Kevin, because on the one hand, I wanted the reader to be in his head the whole time, but on the other hand, for certain structural reasons, I couldn't let him speak for himself in the first person. So I created a character from the inside out, but written in the third person. There's no one way to do it, so you may have to find your own way by trial and error.

Let's sum up where we are. In the last lecture, I talked about how characters are different from real people, namely that they're simpler, they're made up of the most dramatic and/or representative moments, and that we can hear what they're thinking (sometimes).

In this lecture, I talked about three different approaches to creating character, by using observation and imagination, by working from the inside out or the outside in, and by determining a character from his or her psychology or his or her circumstances.

In the next lecture, I'm going to talk about the things that all characters have in common (well, the things that most of them do, anyway), and I'm going to talk about how all characters are created out of evocative detail.

And in the lecture after that, I'm going to talk about the different types of character and how you can use them in the same narrative.

In the next lecture, we're going to talk about introducing characters, with examples from Joseph Conrad's *Lord Jim*, Eva Figes's *Light*, Kate Christensen's *The Epicure's Lament*, and William Faulkner's "A Rose for Emily." And in the lecture after that, I'm going to talk about major and minor characters and also about E. M. Forster's famous distinction between round and flat characters, with examples from such writers as Mark Twain, F. Scott Fitzgerald, Leo Tolstoy, and Denise Mina.

In the meantime, here's an exercise from an excellent book called *What If? Writing Exercises for Fiction Writers* by Anne Bernays and Pamela Painter. Pick a character from a story or novel that has already been written, either by you or someone else, and make a list of everything you know or can infer about the character. Include basic features such as the character's name, age, gender, appearance, relationship status, and so on, but also include such things as the character's fears, obsessions, and politics, even if they aren't mentioned explicitly in the text.

You'll find, I think, that depending on the sort of narrative it is, you may not be able to get a complete list for any character. Such a list for Elizabeth Bennett from *Pride and Prejudice*, for example, would include a great deal about her opinions and personality, but nothing about her appearance. On the other hand, you can detail Sam Spade's physical appearance, but you can't find much about his opinions on anything.

You're going to find in this exercise that different types of stories require different types of characters.

Call Me Ishmael—Introducing a Character
Lecture 5

In our first two lectures about character, we talked in general about how characters are different from real people and from each other, but in this lecture, we'll talk about what all characters have in common—primarily, that they are all constructed out of specific details. Further, both the writer and the reader are most aware of those specific details in the moment they meet a character. In this lecture, we'll look at how you make that first impression by exploring five ways to introduce characters: (1) through straightforward description, (2) by showing the character in action, (3) through first-person narration, (4) through report by other characters, and (5) by placing the character in a specific time and place.

Straightforward Description

- Perhaps the most straightforward way to introduce a character is to simply describe him or her. For example, here are the first few lines from Joseph Conrad's *Lord Jim*:

  > He was an inch, perhaps two, under six feet, powerfully built, and he advanced straight at you with a slight stoop of the shoulders, head forward, and a fixed from-under stare which made you think of a charging bull. His voice was deep, loud, and his manner displayed a kind of dogged self-assertion which had nothing aggressive in it. ... He was spotlessly neat, appareled in immaculate white from shoes to hat, and in the various Eastern ports where he got his living as a ship-chandler's water-clerk he was very popular. (p. 1)

- Here, the main character comes right off the page at the reader; we see him vividly and whole. This introduction is compelling and intriguing: Here's an attractive character who also has a bit of mystery about him. In addition, the introduction sums up the main character in a nutshell: He has something to prove to himself, and the rest of the book shows why that's so and how he goes about it.

- Conrad's introduction is also economical. Rather than lingering over details, it merely suggests physical attributes that evoke awkwardness—the slight stoop of the shoulders; the deep, loud voice—and adds a few conjectures about Jim's character—that his manner was assertive but not aggressive. Jim is shown to us here, not told; he is evoked.

- Notice that although this description is detailed and specific, it's not tied to a specific moment in Jim's life. Note, too, that this is an example of a character being introduced to us from the outside in: We're seeing how he appears to other people, not how he seems to himself.

A Character in Action
- A character who is introduced to us through a specific action comes from the book *Light* by Eva Figes:

  > The sky was still dark when he opened his eyes and saw it through the uncurtained window. He was upright within seconds, out of the bed and had opened the window to study the signs. It looked good to him, the dark just beginning to fade slightly, midnight blueblack growing grey and misty, through which he could make out the last light of a dying star. It looked good to him, a calm pre-dawn hush without a breath of wind, and not a shadow of cloud in the high clear sky. He took a deep breath of air, heavy with night scents and dew on earth and foliage. His appetite for the day thoroughly aroused, his elated mood turned to energy, and he was into his dressing room, into the cold bath which set his skin tingling, humming an unknown tune under his breath. (pp. 1–2)

- This opening is dynamic in a way that the opening of *Lord Jim* is not. The character is in action, with all his senses awake, right from the first sentence. And, unlike the opening of *Lord Jim*, where we can only surmise what Jim is thinking from his appearance, Figes gives us direct access to the character's thoughts. Although we don't know it yet, this is the French artist Claude Monet, and he's just decided that this will be a good day to paint.

- Again, unlike the opening of *Lord Jim*, this opening tells us nothing of the man's physical appearance and very little about his psychology. In *Lord Jim*, it's the hint of complexity in the character that invites us to keep reading, but in this case, it's the character's energy and our curiosity to discover why he's so engaged with the natural world that propel us forward.

Direct Address to the Reader

- Another way to introduce a main character is to have him or her directly address the reader. Three of the books that are often cited as the great American novel open this way: *Moby-Dick*, *The Great Gatsby*, and *The Adventures of Huckleberry Finn*.

- A modern example of a novel whose narrator addresses the reader on the opening page is Kate Christensen's *The Epicure's Lament*:

  > October 9, 2001—All the lonely people indeed. Whoever they are, I've never been one of them. The lack of other people is a balm. It's the absence of strain and stress. I understand monks and hermits, anyone who takes a vow of silence or lives in a far-flung cave. And I thought—I hoped, rather—that I would live this way for the rest of my life, whatever time is left to me. (p. 3)

- In the subsequent paragraphs, we get some more information about this narrator, Hugo Whittier, but mainly what this opening does is draw the reader in with a specific and intriguing voice. We see immediately that the character is literate and erudite; that he not only prefers his own company, but he harbors an active hostility to other people; and that he's something of a fatalist, who doesn't expect to live much longer.

- With these types of introductions, the paragraphs that follow the opening lines start to fill in details about the character's history and current situation, but what draws us in is the fact that we're hearing individual people tell us their stories in a way that only they can. Even if we don't know what they look like or see them in action right away, we know we're hearing from a unique individual.

Introduction by Report

- Another way to introduce a character is through the eyes of other characters. Jim in *Lord Jim* is one character introduced in this way. William Faulkner also introduces Miss Emily in this way in his story "A Rose for Emily":

    When Miss Emily Grierson died, our whole town went to her funeral: the men through a sort of respectful affection for a fallen monument, the women mostly out of curiosity to see the inside of her house, which no one save an old man-servant—a combined gardener and cook—had seen in at least ten years. (*Collected Stories*, p. 119)

- Notice that the unnamed first-person narrator speaks on behalf of a town. After a few paragraphs that describe Miss Emily's history and her standoffish relationship with the town, we get a physical description of her. Interestingly, this description is also given from the point of view of the entire community; this is important in the story because Miss Emily has become an object of fascination to the townspeople.

- Faulkner deploys vivid, even pungent details to describe Miss Emily, comparing her appearance to that of a bloated corpse submerged in water. This physical description foreshadows a great deal about the character and her story without being explicit, while leaving the reader with an extremely vivid—perhaps repulsive—visual impression.

Introduction through Time or Place

- One last way of introducing a character is by the technique of situating him or her in a specific time or place. We see this approach in the opening paragraph of Robert Stone's *A Flag for Sunrise*:

    Father Egan left off writing, rose from his chair and made his way—a little unsteadily—to the bottle of Flor de Cana which he had placed across the room from his desk. The study in which he worked was lit by a Coleman lamp; he had turned the mission generators off to save kerosene. The shutters were open to receive the sea breeze and the room was cool and pleasant. At Freddy's Chicken Shack up the road a wedding party was in progress and the revelers were singing along with the radio form Puerto Alvarado, marking the reggae beat with their own steel drums and crockery. (p. 3)

- This introduction relies almost entirely on the character's circumstances and a little bit of action rather than a description or direct access to his thoughts. We get no physical description of Father Egan, but we know from the first sentence that he's a bit of a scholar and that he's been drinking.

- The rest of the paragraph says nothing about Father Egan specifically but, with great economy and expert handling of detail, shows us that he lives at a mission near the sea in a Third World country. We get a compelling portrait of a lonely, drunken priest—cut off from any intellectual stimulation and far from home—that simultaneously uses the setting to show us the character and the character's point of view to show us the setting.

Approaches to Creating Characters

- Each of these examples is constructed with specific, evocative details, and more important, each introduction tells us at least one thing about the character that turns out to be important later on. This leads us to the question: How much does the writer have to know about a character before he or she starts writing?

- As we've said, you don't need to write a story or a novel in the same order as it will be read. You can craft the meatier parts of the character's story first, then go back and write the opening in such a way as to foreshadow what you've already written.

© creativecoopmedia/iStock/Thinkstock.

Character introductions rarely rely solely on one technique but often combine several: introduction by report, by physical description, and by showing the character in action.

- Another method is to work out all of a character's physical details, history, and context in advance. Some writers even create dossiers or journals for their major characters, crafting detailed histories and compiling idiosyncrasies before they ever put the characters in a story. This method may make it easier to decide what the characters are likely to do in various situations as the plot develops.

- Many writers follow a more indirect, exploratory, and improvisatory process. They may start with only a little bit of information about a character—perhaps even a single trait—rather than a full portrait, then gradually add details as the character develops. This method enables the writer to learn about the character in the same way that the reader will—a little at a time, through a process of discovery.

Suggested Reading

Burroway, *Writing Fiction*.

Christensen, *The Epicure's Lament*.

Conrad, *Lord Jim*.

Faulkner, "A Rose for Emily."

Figes, *Light*.

Hynes, *The Wild Colonial Boy*.

Stone, *A Flag for Sunrise*.

Writing Exercise

1. Choose someone, either in your personal life or in the public eye, about whom you know a great deal; write a paragraph about this person as if you were introducing him or her for the first time as a fictional character. Bear in mind as you write that your imaginary reader is meeting this character for the first time; thus, you should think about what sort of first impression your character makes: how he or she looks, acts, and speaks.

If you're writing about someone famous, write it as if that person isn't famous yet. If you're writing about someone you know personally, write as if that person will never read it—and don't share your results.

Call Me Ishmael—Introducing a Character
Lecture 5—Transcript

So far, in my first two lectures about character, I've been talking in general about how characters are different from real people and from each other. But in this lecture I want to talk about what all characters have in common, and to suggest a variety of techniques for introducing a character. In my next and final lecture about character, we'll talk about developing a character and about deploying different types of characters in the same narrative.

Now, while there are no rules in creative writing, I want to lay out two general propositions that should help you in creating character. One is that fiction is all about the particular rather than the universal. Even if you have a large, overarching theme you're trying to get across, and even if you mean your characters to be representative of types of people, fiction is about individual people in a specific situation. That's one thing all characters have in common: They're constructed out of specific details.

The other proposition, and the other thing that all fictional characters have in common, is that each character, no matter whether they're simple or complex, no matter whether they're round or flat, no matter whether they're the leading character or a minor character, each character has a purpose in the narrative. Each one almost always has something he or she wants, or something at stake. We'll talk more about this in the next lecture, as we talk about developing a character through the course of a narrative, but it's something you need to be thinking about when you're introducing a character.

Whether you're imagining your characters from the inside out or from the outside in, whether you're imagining them based on their psychology or their circumstances, all characters are constructed out of specific, vivid, visceral, sensuous, evocative details. And both the writer and the reader are never more aware of those specific details than they are in the moment when they meet a character. In other words, meeting a fictional character is a lot like meeting someone in real life.

Think about the first moment you met someone important to you—a spouse or a friend or even an enemy—and the chances are very good that what you remember most vividly is something very specific about them: a physical feature, or something they were wearing, or some gesture they made, or something specific they said, or the particular circumstances in which you met them.

We have a very similar experience with fictional characters. First impressions are very important, and we know within a page or two if we find a character appealing, interesting, or annoying. Think about the stories or books where you've fallen in love with a character on first sight, or even the books where you've given up after the first few pages, because you realized quickly that you didn't want to spend any more time with this person. In real life, it's considered rude to turn your back on someone you've just been introduced to, but with a story or a book you can shut it and walk away and no one's feelings are hurt.

To help you think about making that all-important first impression, let's take a look at five different ways we can be introduced to a new character: 1) through a straightforward description of the character, 2) by seeing the character in action, 3) through direct address in the first person from the character, 4) through report by other characters, and 5) by placing the character in a specific time and place.

As I go through the various examples of each technique, I especially want you to notice how each technique uses details and specifics, and how the introduction to the character reveals or at least hints at what the character wants.

Perhaps the most straightforward way to introduce a character is simply to describe him or her. Here's the very first paragraph of one of my favorite novels, Joseph Conrad's *Lord Jim*:

> He was an inch, perhaps two, under six feet, powerfully built, and
> he advanced straight at you with a slight stoop of the shoulders,
> head forward, and a fixed from-under stare which made you think of
> a charging bull. His voice was deep, loud, and his manner displayed

a kind of dogged self-assertion which had nothing aggressive in it. It seemed a necessity, and it was directed apparently as much at himself as at anybody else. He was spotlessly neat, appareled in immaculate white from shoes to hat, and in the various Eastern ports where he got his living as a ship-chandler's water-clerk he was very popular. (p. 1)

Here's your main character, coming right off the page at the reader. We see him vividly and whole, from his "fixed from-under stare" to his immaculate white shoes. This introduction is compelling and intriguing, which is what the opening of a novel should be. Here's a rather attractive character who already has a bit of mystery about him. Think about that "dogged self-assertion" that is "directed apparently as much at himself as at anybody else." Without giving anything away, that's the main character of *Lord Jim* in a nutshell: He's a man who has something to prove to himself, and the rest of the book shows why that's the case, and how he goes about it.

The introduction is also economical. It's not the sort of description that lingers over every detail of a character's appearance and his clothing, but merely suggests physical attributes that evoke awkwardness—the slight stoop of the shoulders, the deep, loud voice—and adds a few conjectures about his character—that his manner was assertive but not aggressive—and allows the reader to fill in the rest.

This is not to say that giving an elaborate description of the character is necessarily a bad thing. Lots of books and stories introduce the physical appearance of a character in great detail. As always, it depends on the book and on what you're trying to do.

At any rate, the point is that Jim is shown to us, not told. He is evoked. We know that he is muscular, that he is fastidious about his appearance, that he has a direct, blunt, but not intimidating manner, and that he is concerned with proving something to himself. After little more than 100 words, we have a very intriguing (though not comprehensive) view of the main character.

I also want you to notice that although this description is very detailed and specific, it's not tied to a specific moment in Jim's life. We're not getting a scene, per se. And I also want you to notice that this is an example of a character being introduced to us from the outside in. We're seeing how he appears to other people, not how he seems to himself. And just to reiterate what I said in the last lecture, defining a character from the outside in is not the same as defining him by his circumstances, just as defining a character from the inside out is not the same as defining him by his psychology. Although we hear Jim speaking later in the book, we're never really inside his head, and yet *Lord Jim* is fundamentally a psychological portrait of an idealistic young man trying to live down a moment of cowardice.

Now let's take a look at a character who is introduced to the reader in a specific moment, through a specific action. It comes from another favorite novel of mine, a very slim book called *Light*, by the English writer Eva Figes. Here's the opening of the book:

> The sky was still dark when he opened his eyes and saw it through the uncurtained window. He was upright within seconds, out of the bed and had opened the window to study the signs. It looked good to him, the dark just beginning to fade slightly, midnight blueblack growing grey and misty, through which he could make out the last light of a dying star. It looked good to him, a calm pre-dawn hush without a breath of wind, and not a shadow of cloud in the high clear sky. He took a deep breath of air, heavy with night scents and dew on earth and foliage. His appetite for the day thoroughly aroused, his elated mood turned to energy, and he was into his dressing room, into the cold bath which set his skin tingling, humming an unknown tune under his breath. (pp. 1–2)

This is also a very intriguing opening, though in a different way. It's dynamic in a way that the opening of *Lord Jim* is not. The character is in action, with all his senses awake, right from the first sentence, and he looks at the view outside his window with a gaze that is both practiced and eager. Moments later, he's in a cold bath, his senses tingling. And, unlike the opening of *Lord Jim*, where we can only surmise what Jim is thinking from his appearance, Figes gives us direct access to the character's thoughts.

Although we don't know it yet, this is the French artist Claude Monet, and he's just decided that this will be a very good day to paint. But even before we realize who the man is, we get a vivid and attractive first impression of a man who pays keen attention to the natural world and is eager to engage with it, though we don't know why or how till a few pages further on.

And yet, unlike the opening of *Lord Jim*, it tells us nothing of his physical appearance and not much more about his psychology than the simple fact that he's enthusiastic about starting his day. But whereas in *Lord Jim* it's the hint of complexity in the character that keeps us reading, in this case it's the character's energy, and our curiosity to discover why he's so engaged with the natural world. So even though we don't learn as much about Monet in this opening paragraph as we do about Jim in his opening paragraph, the opening of *Light* is just as compelling.

There's another tried and true way of introducing a character, one that seems somehow uniquely American, though I'm sure there are plenty of similar examples in the literature of other countries. This is by having the main character, or at least the first-person narrator, directly address the reader.

Three of the novels that are often cited as the Great American Novel open this way. *Moby-Dick* begins with its narrator inviting the reader to "Call me Ishmael." *The Great Gatsby* opens with Nick Carraway, who isn't the main character, but who is the predominant voice in that book, speaking directly to the reader. And, of course, there's the opening of Mark Twain's *Adventures of Huckleberry Finn*: "You don't know about me without you have read a book by the name of *The Adventures of Tom Sawyer*, but that ain't no matter."

Over the years, there have been any number of great American novels whose narrators address the reader on the opening page. Saul Bellow's *The Adventures of Augie March*, the title of which deliberately echoes Twain, opens with a declamatory sentence that evokes Melville: "I am an American, Chicago born—Chicago, that somber city—and go at things as I have taught myself, free-style, and will make the record in my own way: first to knock, first admitted; sometimes an innocent knock, sometimes not so innocent."

The narrator of Marilynne Robinson's novel *Housekeeping* also evokes Melville by announcing in the first sentence "My name is Ruth," and then echoes Twain by immediately summarizing the story so far, the way Huck Finn does in the first few paragraphs of his novel.

Here's a more recent example, by the novelist Kate Christensen, from her book *The Epicure's Lament*:

> October 9, 2001—All the lonely people indeed. Whoever they are, I've never been one of them. The lack of other people is a balm. It's the absence of strain and stress. I understand monks and hermits, anyone who takes a vow of silence or lives in a far-flung cave. And I thought—I hoped, rather—that I would live this way for the rest of my life, whatever time is left to me. (p. 3)

In the subsequent paragraphs, this narrator, Hugo Whittier, gives us some specific details of his morning, as well as some hints of his backstory. But mainly what this opening gives us—and what it has in common with all those other first person openings I just listed—is that it draws the reader in with a very specific and intriguing voice. In this example, we can see right away that the character is literate and erudite, that he not only prefers his own company, but that he harbors an active hostility to other people, and that he's a something of a fatalist, who doesn't expect to live much longer.

In all these examples, the paragraphs immediately following the opening line or paragraph start to fill in details about the character's history and current situation. But what draws us in is the fact that we're hearing an individual person telling us his or her story in a way that only he or she could tell it to us. So even if we don't know what they look like right off the bat, or don't see them in action right away—and in most of the books I've just mentioned, we don't get action for a few pages yet—we know we're hearing from a unique and specific individual.

Another way to introduce the character is by report. Now, obviously, if you want to be nitpicking about it, all fictional characters are introduced to us by report, through the intermediary of the writer. But, as I say, in fiction we often have the illusion of direct access. But some characters are presented to us only through the eyes of other characters.

Jim in *Lord Jim* is one such character, since we never get inside his head and mainly learn his story through other characters. Another example is Jay Gatsby, whose story is told to us by the first-person narrator, Nick Carraway.

The example I want to quote from, though, is from William Faulkner's famous story, "A Rose for Emily." Here's the first paragraph:

> When Miss Emily Grierson died, our whole town went to her funeral: the men through a sort of respectful affection for a fallen monument, the women mostly out of curiosity to see the inside of her house, which no one save an old man-servant—a combined gardener and cook—had seen in at least ten years. (*Collected Stories*, p. 119)

Right away, you notice that it's an unnamed first-person narrator, speaking on behalf of his or her entire town. Then, after four paragraphs that describe Miss Emily's house, her family history, and her standoffish relationship with the town, we get a very detailed physical description as part of a brief flashback describing the day that the town's alderman paid a visit to her, hoping to persuade her to pay her taxes:

> They rose when she entered—a small, fat woman in black, with a thin gold chain descending to her waist and vanishing into her belt, leaning on an ebony cane with a tarnished gold head. Her skeleton was small and spare; perhaps that was why what would have been merely plumpness in another was obesity in her. She looked bloated, like a body long submerged in motionless water, and of that pallid hue. Her eyes, lost in the fatty ridges of her face, looked like two small pieces of coal pressed into a lump of dough as they moved from one face to another while the visitors stated their errand. (*Collected Stories*, p. 121)

This is perhaps the most vivid of the introductions I've cited so far, and mainly what I want you to notice about it is that we're not seeing Miss

Emily from a remote, third-person point of view, as in the opening of *Lord Jim* or the opening of *Light*. And we're not hearing from her directly in her own voice, as in *The Epicure's Lament*. But rather, we're hearing about her from the communal point of view of an entire community. That's important, especially in this story.

A character is being revealed to us as an object of fascination to an entire town. Because Emily has withdrawn herself from the life of the community, the people of the town have spun all sorts of legends and theories around her, all of which have the rug yanked out from under them at the end of the story, which is one of the creepiest endings in American literature.

As always, I want you to notice the very vivid, even pungent details Faulkner deploys to describe Miss Emily, especially that wonderfully disturbing comparison of her elderly, fat body to that of a bloated corpse submerged in water—and not just any water, but motionless water. Again, without giving the ending away, this single paragraph foreshadows a great deal about the character and her story, without being explicit. And at the same time, it provides the reader with an extremely vivid, one might almost say repulsive, visual impression of her.

The four ways I've suggested so far of introducing a character certainly aren't exhaustive, and I also want to make it clear that very, very rarely does any introduction of a character rely solely on one technique. The last example, from "A Rose for Emily," combines several techniques at once: introduction by report, introduction by physical description, and, in the paragraphs immediately following the paragraph I quoted, introduction by showing the character in action, speaking dismissively to the men who've come to see her.

Let's take a look at one more way of introducing character, namely the technique of introducing a character by situating him or her in a very specific time or place. This is the opening paragraph of Robert Stone's novel *A Flag for Sunrise*:

> Father Egan left off writing, rose from his chair and made his way—a little unsteadily—to the bottle of Flor de Cana which he

had placed across the room from his desk. The study in which he worked was lit by a Coleman lamp; he had turned the mission generators off to save kerosene. The shutters were open to receive the sea breeze and the room was cool and pleasant. At Freddy's Chicken Shack up the road a wedding party was in progress and the revelers were singing along with the radio from Puerto Alvarado, marking the reggae beat with their own steel drums and crockery. (p. 3)

Again, as in "A Rose for Emily," this is a very pungent introduction to a character, but one which relies almost entirely on his circumstances and a little bit of action rather than a description or direct access to his thoughts. We get no physical description of Father Egan, but we know from the very first sentence that he's a bit of a scholar, because he's been writing. We also know that he's been drinking, because he's unsteady on his feet, and that he's self-conscious about his drinking, because he has deliberately placed the bottle across the room from his desk, so that he has to get up each time he wants another drink.

The rest of the paragraph says nothing about him specifically, but with great economy and expertly deployed detail shows us that he's living at a mission in a Third World country where money is scarce, that it's near the sea, and that the local residents are probably impoverished, celebrating a wedding noisily at a place called Freddy's Chicken Shack.

The rest of the chapter tells us a great deal more about Father Egan's situation and history, and about the perilous political situation in a fictional Latin American country during the 1970s. But that opening paragraph gives us a very vivid and compelling portrait of a lonely, drunken priest, cut off from any intellectual stimulation, far from home, simultaneously using the setting to show us the character, and the character's point of view to show us the setting.

Let's pause for a moment here and sum up the lessons of the previous examples, specifically what they all have in common. Each one is constructed of specific, evocative details: of Jim's physical appearance in *Lord Jim*, of Claude Monet's energetic actions in *Light*, of Hugo's comic bitterness in *The*

Epicure's Lament, of Emily's appearance and imperious manner in "A Rose for Emily," and of Father Egan's physical setting in *A Flag for Sunrise*.

More importantly, each introduction tells us at least one thing about the character that turns out to be important later on, and at least hints at what the character has at stake. Right from the start, we know that Jim has something to prove to himself; that Claude Monet is passionately engaged with the natural world; that Hugo loathes the company of other people; that Emily has withdrawn from the world for some reason; and that Father Egan has isolated himself in a remote village in a distant country.

Given that what each of these characters wants or has at stake is at least hinted at from our very first meeting with them, how much does the writer have to know about the character before he or she even starts writing?

Well, for one thing, as I mentioned in my first lecture, you don't need to write a story or a novel in the same order as the reader is going to read it. You can craft the meatier parts of the character's story first, and then go back and write the opening in such a way as to foreshadow what you've already written.

Another method is to work out all of a character's physical details, history, and context in advance. You might call this the Iceberg Theory of Character Creation. On the principle that most of an iceberg is out of sight below the water line, keeping the visible part afloat, some writers concoct whole backstories for their characters, even if they don't use all or even most of it in the finished story.

Some writers even create a dossier or a journal for each major character in a story, crafting a detailed history of each character, and compiling every quirk and idiosyncrasy before they ever put them in a story.

The novelist and teacher Janet Burroway compares this technique to the famous method used by actors, one of the features of which is that actors are required to write biographies of their characters, coming up with details that even the playwright or screenwriter hadn't thought of.

This method has a lot to recommend it since it means that even before you start to worry about plot, you have a fully formed character fixed firmly in your head, making it easier to decide what he or she is likely to do at any given moment as the plot develops.

As I said in the opening lecture of this course, there is no right or wrong way to do things in fiction writing, so if this works for you, have at it. That said, my own experience of creating characters is a more indirect, exploratory, and improvisatory process, and I suspect that's the case with many other writers. Writers who work this way start with only a little bit of information about a character: the way a person looks, perhaps, or even a simple character trait like a nervous tic, or even just the way they wear a hat. We don't start with a full portrait of a character, but with a glimpse just intriguing enough to make us want to follow that character through scene after scene, to see how the character develops, or simply to see what he does next.

The Iceberg Method is perhaps like that of a classical composer, who composes detailed sketches of themes and movements before embarking on the entire symphony, while my method is perhaps more like jazz, where a musician takes a scrap of melody and sees what he can spin out of it for 20 minutes at a stretch. Please bear in mind that I'm not necessarily endorsing my way of doing things—which is kind of a weird thing to say, actually— but let me explain how it has worked for me in the past, and why I still create characters that way—on the fly, as it were.

When I was writing my first novel, *The Wild Colonial Boy*, one of my main characters was a terrorist, a member of the Irish Republican Army named Jimmy Coogan. All I knew about him to begin with was that he was disgruntled with the leadership of the IRA and that he wanted to embarrass them by setting off an unauthorized bomb in central London. But that's all I had—a Northern Irish Catholic in his late 20s or early 30s, who hated the British but who hated certain members of his own organization even more. I didn't know what he looked like. I didn't know what he sounded like. I didn't know how he thought.

I could have invented a complicated backstory for him, or filled a notebook with a dossier detailing everything I could think of about him. But instead

I simply started writing the novel, putting him in a car with 10 pounds of plastic explosive, on his way to a meeting with a confederate. It was only as I wrote that I started accumulating details. He wasn't just driving a car, he was driving a rented Ford Escort that smelled of cigarette smoke. And he wasn't just carrying the explosives, he was carrying them in a leather Adidas sports bag. And he wasn't just going anywhere for the meeting, but to Giant's Causeway, a tourist destination on the northern coast of Ulster, away from the prying eyes of British soldiers and policemen.

As I accumulated these details, I began to sense not only his wariness, but also his self-consciousness about being wary, which made him uncomfortable. I also took care of some exposition, by having him mull over why he was breaking ranks with the leadership of the IRA. But even then, he didn't really come alive to me until I gave him a particular item of clothing, namely a brand new raincoat, the kind with big lapels and a belted waist. It was the sort of coat, in fact, that an IRA man of the late 1970s or early 1980s would never have been caught dead in. Real Irish terrorists of the era were a pretty scruffy lot, working class guys from very rough neighborhoods in Belfast. So when I had my scruffy, working class character steal an expensive Burberry raincoat from a posh men's store in London, he suddenly snapped into focus and became an individual, a living person.

The theft not only symbolized his break with the puritanism and caution of the IRA leadership, who certainly didn't want their operatives drawing attention to themselves with flashy trench coats, but more importantly, it symbolized Jimmy's own self-mythologizing romanticism and vanity. Here was a character who not only had decided to break with the discipline and orthodoxy of a radical movement, he wanted to look good while he was doing it. So by giving him this incongruous coat, I began to learn what Jimmy Coogan looked like, what he sounded like, how he carried himself when he walked down the street.

It's entirely possible I would have arrived at the same point if I had used the Iceberg Method and painstakingly constructed a dossier for Jimmy in advance. It's possible I might even have come up with the raincoat, but I kind of doubt it. I had to launch myself sink or swim into the story, by putting a guy I barely knew into a complicated situation. And, by the steady accumulation of detail—the Ford Escort, the Adidas bag, Giant's Causeway—stumbling onto the one detail that gave me the key to his character, that showed me that not only was he a True Believer who refused to compromise his revolutionary ideology, but also that he was vain, cocky, and rash. By writing my way into Jimmy Coogan, I was also telling myself the story, learning about Jimmy bit by bit the same way the reader eventually would.

But here is where the Iceberg Method and mine come together. By time I finished the book, I knew Jimmy Coogan intimately. You could have asked me anything about him—what did he like to drink? What was his favorite movie? What was his mother like?—and I could have told you, perhaps not instantly, but after a moment or two of reflection. If you'd asked me what he was like before I started writing, I couldn't have told you much about him at all. It was only by the actual process of writing him that he became clear to me. Even though I could answer hardly any questions about him when I started, by time I finished the book I could have told you things about him that I'd never consciously considered. Even though I didn't use the Iceberg Method, I ended up with an iceberg.

In other words, creating character is usually, and most productively, a process of exploration. By discovering a character as you go, you are learning about the character the same way that the reader will, a bit at a time. And, when you think about it, the Iceberg Method works pretty much on the same principle. It's just that you do all the hard graft of imagining the character independently of creating the plot. You're still working by trial and error, trying out bits in your character journal and rejecting them, making the character clearer and clearer with each step.

I'm just saying that, for me, the process works better if I'm telling the story at the same time, because the story reveals the character even as the character determines the story. I'm not saying my way is easier, or even more efficient. In fact, it's probably less efficient. You will wander into blind alleys and dead ends, and you may find yourself tearing up whole chapters and starting them over, the way I have, many times.

But you might also say that those blind alleys and dead ends are signs that the process is working. If you write a scene that feels flat or seems like something the character wouldn't do, that means that the character has started to live an independent existence in your imagination, digging in his heels, or standing up on her hind legs and saying, "I won't do that. That's not me." And that's a very good sign, because then your character is beginning to behave like a real person, with a will and an inner life of his own, and he or she will come alive on the page.

So, whichever method you prefer—creating the character independently of the story or making him up as you go along—the point is that while you don't have to know a character completely when you start, if things go the way they're supposed to, you'll know him by the end as well as you know yourself, and maybe even better.

In the meantime, here's an exercise to help you think about introducing a character. Take someone you know a lot about, either in your personal life, or someone famous, and write a paragraph about them as if you were introducing them for the first time as a fictional character. Bear in mind as you write it that your imaginary reader is meeting these people for the first time, so you're going to have to think hard about what sort of first impression they make: how they look, how they act, how they speak.

If you're writing about someone famous, write it as if that person isn't famous, and we're meeting her for the first time.

If you're writing about someone you know personally, write it as if they're never going to read it—and then, for heaven's sake, don't show it to them. This is meant to be a writing exercise, one that focuses your attention on distilling a whole person into a few hundred words.

In the next lecture, we'll be talking about how to use different types of characters—round and flat characters, major and minor characters—in the same narrative. We'll be looking at examples from the work of Twain, Dickens, Fitzgerald, and the Scottish mystery writer Denise Mina.

Characters—Round and Flat, Major and Minor
Lecture 6

A s we've said, characters are constructed in different ways for different stories, and part of the reason for this is that they fulfill different functions. In some narratives, writers provide as much detail as possible about leading characters because they are the main focus of the story. In other narratives, the cast of characters is quite large, with no single dominant character. This kind of story requires the writer to sketch characters in quick, powerful strokes. Narratives also have minor characters, who often simply introduce a plot point before they disappear. These characters need to be useful and vivid and not much more. In this lecture, we'll discuss character development and the uses of different types of characters.

Flat Characters

- The distinction between round and flat characters was formulated by the English novelist E. M. Forster in his book *Aspects of the Novel*. According to Forster, flat characters are sometimes called humorous types or caricatures; their chief distinguishing feature is that they have only one chief distinguishing feature. As Forster puts it, "They are constructed round a single idea or quality."

- In *The Adventures of Huckleberry Finn*, Huck himself is round, but he is surrounded by characters of varying degrees of flatness. A good example might be Huck's father, Pap Finn, who can be summed up in a single sentence: He's a mean drunk. Pap exists mainly to further the plot: When Huck can no longer stand Pap's abuse, he fakes his own death and takes off down the Mississippi River with the slave Jim.

- The works of Charles Dickens are famously full of flat characters: the conniving and oily Uriah Heep in *David Copperfield*; the brutal criminal Bill Sikes in *Oliver Twist*; and Miss Havisham in *Great Expectations*, who was abandoned at the altar on her wedding day and has set herself apart from the rest of the world ever since.

- We might even think of such characters as the sort of people found in sitcoms: the clueless dad, the wacky neighbor, the gay best friend, the wisecracking child. Such characters are often just machines for delivering or setting up jokes, and the moment they appear on screen, we know exactly what to expect. Indeed, it's that quick identification and the sudden anticipation of something funny that often makes such characters so popular. They may be simple and predictable, but they are also reliably satisfying.

- The same is true of flat characters in fiction. "The great advantage of flat characters," says Forster, "is that they are easily recognized whenever they come in—recognized by the reader's emotional eye." This ease of recognition is important; one of the most significant traits of flat characters is that we get the whole effect of them the minute they reappear. Whenever Bill Sikes reappears in *Oliver Twist*, we immediately know that something bad will happen.

- Forster also notes a second advantage of flat characters: "that they are easily remembered by the readers afterwards." He goes on to say, "It is a convenience for an author when he can strike with his full force at once, and flat characters are very useful to him, since they never need reintroducing, never run away, have not to be watched for development, and provide their own atmosphere."

- It's important to note that a flat character must be both simple and vivid. Characters who are simple but not memorable don't really serve a purpose, and characters who are vivid but not simple are not flat characters.

- Keep in mind, too, that a flat character is not the same thing as a minor character. Even minor characters can be round. George Wilson, the working-class garage owner in *The Great Gatsby*, appears in only a few scenes, but late in the story, his grief after a tragic accident is one of the most moving scenes in the novel. Someone who was just a caricature up to that point—the clueless cuckolded husband—becomes, for a page or two, a real human being.

- o It's also true that flat characters can be important to a story. Miss Havisham is one of the most distinctive and influential characters in *Great Expectations*, yet she never develops or changes.

- o It's possible to have a story or a novel that is peopled entirely with flat characters. Sherlock Holmes is the major character in Arthur Conan Doyle's stories, but he is usually flat, producing the same effect nearly every time he appears. Holmes is also proof that flat characters are not necessarily simple or sketchy but can be quite detailed.

Round Characters

- The closest Forster comes to defining round characters is to say, "The test of a round character is whether it is capable of surprising in a convincing way. If it never surprises, it is flat. If it does not convince, it is a flat pretending to be round." The very nature of round characters is encapsulated in the metaphor we use to describe them: They curve up and away from the flat page into three dimensions. They have different sides and aspects, unlike flat characters, who appear the same from every angle.

- Round characters are also richer, deeper, more mysterious, and more unpredictable than flat characters. They can do all the things a flat character can do—come vividly to life, be memorable and instantly recognizable, and be engaging and entertaining—but they can also surprise, delight, and disappoint us in the same way as real people. Further, as Forster notes, they don't just surprise us, but they surprise us in a convincing way.

  - o Flat characters can be surprising, but they provide the sort of mechanical surprise we find in a mystery or a spy novel, where a trustworthy character suddenly turns out to be the murderer or the double agent. Although this kind of a surprise can be effective, it also sometimes comes across as a kind of cheating, and our response can sometimes be a groan or a roll of the eyes.

○ In contrast, the kind of surprise we get from a round character should evoke both shock and the strong feeling of inevitability. The reader thinks, "Of course! I should have seen that coming." When a round character surprises us, we're delighted or moved in ways that flat characters can't manage—by sudden acts of kindness or cruelty that we didn't expect but that we believe the moment we see them. Round characters can also break our hearts in ways that flat characters can't, by disappointing us in a lifelike way.

○ Round characters should be both surprising and inevitable so that whatever happens to them is probably the only way things could have turned out—not because of circumstance necessarily, but because their own complex, flawed natures drove them to it.

• As mentioned in an earlier lecture, fictional people are different from real people because we can know what they're thinking, which is perhaps another definition of roundness. This is the case even if the writer never actually shows us what the character is thinking, as long as the potential for the writer to show us is present. By the same token, characters may be round as long as they have the potential to change, even if they never actually do. Some of the most heartbreaking people in fiction are rounded characters who, for whatever reason, lose their nerve or are defeated by circumstance.

• The complexity or roundness of a character isn't necessarily defined entirely by psychology but can be defined by circumstances, as well. Mrs. Dalloway is round because we are inside her mind at every moment, listening to her private thoughts. In a series of detective novels by Denise Mina, we see inside the mind of the main character, Paddy Meehan, but much of the richness of that character comes from her circumstances—from Mina's skillful evocation of the dank, melancholy world of working-class Glasgow in the 1970s and 1980s.

Characters and Conflict

- Perhaps the most important distinction between flat and round characters has to do with the idea of conflict in fiction. A useful generalization here is that all characters want something or are driven by something; all characters have something at stake in the narrative.

- Flat characters want only one simple thing: Sherlock Holmes wants to solve a mystery; Miss Havisham wants revenge against men. Round characters, in contrast, want something complicated, ineffable, or ambiguous. They may be conflicted about what they want, often to the point that they have no clear idea what they're actually looking for.

- With Anna Karenina, for example, not only is it hard for the reader to pin down what's driving her, but Anna herself can't articulate exactly what's lacking in her life. She wants her lover, Count Vronsky, yet having him doesn't satisfy her. Her desperation grows as the costs of leaving her husband and losing her child mount up. There's something unreachable in Anna that makes her frustrating, poignant, and supremely human.

© Szepy/iStock/Thinkstock.

By including a bit of description for flat characters—"a sour waiter brought her a cup of coffee"—you hint at the possibility of a richer, fuller world in your work.

Character Development

- Distinctions between major and minor characters offer us a number of insights into character development. First of all, minor characters receive less space and attention in a narrative than major characters do. You don't need a complicated backstory for a waiter to bring your main character a cup of coffee, although you may want to add a hint of description to give that waiter a bit of substance.

- As for the distinction between round and flat, you may not notice which a character is until after you've created him or her, but at some point, you should think deliberately about the function of each character, major or minor, flat or round, in your narrative.

  o Whether you construct characters in advance or let them develop organically as you write the narrative, at some point, you will come to a visceral understanding of how your characters figure in the story and how simple or complex their desires are.

  o You may discover that a character you originally conceived of as round and complex actually functions only to move the plot along. In that case, you have a flat character, and you can draft or revise your story to ensure that he or she is memorable but without constructing a detailed backstory.

  o You may also discover that a character you meant to be minor turns out to be rounder and more important than you originally thought. If that's the case, you can make the introduction of that character a little fuller so that his or her reappearance in the story seems believable.

Suggested Reading

Dickens, *Great Expectations*.

Fitzgerald, *The Great Gatsby*.

Forster, *Aspects of the Novel*.

Mina, *Field of Blood*.

Twain, *The Adventures of Huckleberry Finn*.

1. Using a story you like or a completed draft of one of your own stories, list all the characters and describe what each character wants as briefly as possible. Using only what the story itself says about the character, you should be able to determine quickly who is flat versus round and who is major versus minor. Sherlock Holmes's entry might say, "He wants to solve the crime and impress everyone with his brilliance." Anna Karenina's entry might say, "She wants the sort of passion from another man that she's never had from her husband, but in truth, she doesn't really know what she wants." If you find yourself pausing over one of your own characters and wondering what he or she wants to do, you may discover that you have some additional work to do in character development.

Characters—Round and Flat, Major and Minor
Lecture 6—Transcript

Not all characters are created equal. In fact, some characters are decidedly more equal than others. There are major characters and minor characters, with all sorts of varieties in between. There are narratives that have only one character, or only one dominant character. There are also narratives that have ensembles, in which no one character takes the lead. George R. R. Martin's *A Song of Ice and Fire* has so many characters that the author needs to provide a list of them at the back of each volume. The list at the back of *A Clash of Kings*, the second volume in the series, goes on for 30 pages.

As I've said several times already, different sorts of stories require different sorts of characters. Elizabeth Bennett in Jane Austen's *Pride and Prejudice* is one of the most vividly evoked and beloved characters in literature. She's smart, sharp-tongued, judgmental, and fiercely loyal to her sisters, even when they don't deserve it—but we never get a description of what she looks like. And we don't need to, because what's important about Elizabeth Bennett is her quicksilver wit and her place in the social order.

On the other hand, Dashiell Hammett gives us a very specific physical description of Sam Spade on the first page of *The Maltese Falcon*. Hammett shows us the detective's gestures and physical movements in great detail, because Spade is a man of action caught in a fluid and fast-moving situation, and it's important for us to see exactly how he moves through his world. Elizabeth Bennett and Sam Spade are two very different characters from two very different worlds in two very different books, so it makes sense that they would be constructed very differently.

But you can also have different types of characters in the same story, because they fulfill different functions. Take your typical episode of *Star Trek* as an example. There are the leading players (Kirk and Spock), there are the secondary characters (Scotty and Uhura), and then there are the minor players, the famous Red Shirts, each of whom says a line or two, if he's lucky, and then gets killed before the opening credits. A Red Shirt's chief function is to lie face down in the dirt so that Dr. McCoy can kneel over him and say, "He's dead, Jim."

Your leading characters are the main focus of the story, so you want to know as much detail about them as possible. But minor characters such as Red Shirts, or what they call in the theater the spear carriers, exist only to deliver a line or a plot point.

In Margaret Mitchell's *Gone with the Wind*, the main reason you keep reading is to find out if Scarlett O'Hara and Rhett Butler are ever going to get together and then, when they do, if they are going to stay together. You don't read to find out what happens to the Tarleton brothers, the two boys who are wooing Scarlett in the opening pages. In a big, expansive novel like *Gone with the Wind*, with lots of characters who pop on, do their bit, and disappear again forever, the minor characters only need to be useful, and efficient, and not much more. You're not going to lavish as much attention on a minor character as you do on your major characters.

There are also narratives, such as *A Song of Ice and Fire*, where no one character dominates, and the world being evoked is the main reason for reading the story. In a narrative like this, you may not have the luxury of long descriptions of each character, or subtle evocations of their psychology. Even the major characters in this sort of narrative need to be sketched in quick, vivid strokes, because there are so many of them, and there is so much story to tell.

But it's important to remember that even the minor characters in a novel or a story, even characters who exist to deliver a single line or just keel over dead, still have something at stake. Part of what I mean is that all characters fulfill a purpose in the narrative, even if it's only to do one thing and then disappear. But I also mean that even characters who only appear once and do one thing have at least the potential to be major characters in a different version of the same story.

In a well-imagined, vividly evoked fictional world, you want to create even your minor characters with enough attention to detail and with enough respect for their potential inner life that they could step up and act like major characters if required. Remember what I said in my very first lecture: a plot is only one particular way of looking at a story. The same set of circumstances could be told in countless different ways, from the point of view of any one of the characters in it. All characters potentially have an inner life as rich as that of your main characters, and in that sense, all characters *are* created equal.

This potentiality adds to the richness of the fictional world, giving the reader the feeling that the world the writer is evoking is larger and more comprehensive than the story he's chosen to tell. In an imaginary world that has this potential, the reader has the feeling that she could take a left turn away from the main story and just keep going.

In fact, over the past half century, a whole subgenre of revisionist literature has grown up in which famous stories are told from a different character's point of view. John Gardner's *Grendel*, for example, tells *Beowulf* from the monster's point of view. In *The Wind Done Gone*, Alice Randall retells the story of *Gone with the Wind* from the point of view of a slave. And Valerie Martin's novel *Mary Reilly* retells the story of *Dr. Jekyll and Mr. Hyde* from the point of view of one of Dr. Jekyll's servants.

That said, in most narratives you can't treat all the characters equally—it would read like a transcript of a surveillance tape. Even important characters can be divided into types, not only between different kinds of books (as between *Pride and Prejudice* and *The Maltese Falcon*), but sometimes even between characters in the same story.

One of these differences is the distinction between round characters and flat characters. This distinction is one of the most famous tropes in the teaching of creative writing, and it was formulated by the English novelist E. M. Forster in his book, *Aspects of the Novel*. The terms have become so famous that you probably have already heard of round and flat characters even if you've never read Forster's book, or even heard of E. M. Forster.

Let's take a moment to review what he actually said. Flat characters, according to Forster, have sometimes been called humorous types or caricatures. Their chief distinguishing feature is that they have, well, one chief distinguishing feature. Or, as Forster puts it, "In their purest form, they are constructed round a single idea or quality: when there is more than one factor in them, we get the beginning of the curve towards the round. The really flat character can be expressed in one sentence." (pp. 67–68) Here, Forster gives some examples which may not be readily recognizable to a 21st-century reader, so I'll provide some examples of my own.

In *The Adventures of Huckleberry Finn*, Huck himself is round, but he is surrounded by characters of varying degrees of flatness. A good example of a flat character is Huck's rotten father, "Pap" Finn, who can be summed up, as Forster suggests, in a single sentence: To wit, Huck's father is a mean drunk. That's all you really need to know about him—that he drinks, that he's basically good for nothing, and that he treats Huck very badly.

Like the poor, neglected Tarleton brothers in *Gone with the Wind*, Pap exists mainly to further the plot. When Huck can't stand Pap's abuse anymore, he fakes his own death and takes off down the Mississippi River with the slave Jim. After that, Pap's only other function in the story is to turn up dead later on, thus freeing Huck from any family obligations.

The works of Charles Dickens are famously full of flat characters. You have Uriah Heep in *David Copperfield*, who is conniving and oily. You have Bill Sikes in *Oliver Twist*, who is a brutal criminal. You have Miss Havisham in *Great Expectations*, who was abandoned at the altar on her wedding day as a young woman and has set herself apart from the rest of the world ever since.

You might even think of such characters as the sort of people you'd find in a sitcom: the clueless dad, the wacky neighbor, the gay best friend, the wisecracking child. Sitcom characters of this sort are often just machines for delivering or setting up jokes, and the moment they appear on screen, you know exactly what to expect. Indeed, it's that quick identification and the sudden anticipation of something funny, if not necessarily surprising, that often makes such characters so popular. They may be simple, they may be predictable, but they are also reliably satisfying.

It's the same with flat characters in fiction. "One great advantage of flat characters," says Forster, "is that they are easily recognized whenever they come in—recognized by the reader's emotional eye, not by the visual eye, which merely notes the recurrence of a proper name." (p. 68)

That part—the ease of recognition—is crucial. The most important trait of a flat character is the fact that, the minute he or she reappears, you get the whole effect of them right away. Whenever Bill Sikes turns up in *Oliver Twist*, we immediately know that something bad is going to happen. He does the same sort of thing, or threatens to, every time he appears. So although Bill may be a very bad man from the point of view of the other characters in *Oliver Twist*, he is, from the point of view of the writer and the reader, very reliable and satisfyingly frightening. The fact that he produces the same effect every time does not really diminish the satisfaction of the effect. This, in fact, is what Forster calls the flat character's second advantage: "that they are easily remembered by the readers afterwards."

Says Forster, "It is a convenience for an author when he can strike with his full force at once, and flat characters are very useful to him, since they never need reintroducing, never run away, have not to be watched for development, and provide their own atmosphere."

It's also important to note that a flat character needs to be both simple and vivid. If a character is just simple but not memorable, then the character doesn't really serve its purpose. And if he's vivid but not simple, then he's not a flat character. Now, please bear in mind that a flat character is not the same thing as a minor character. For one thing, a minor character can be round. Take George Wilson, for example, who is the working class garage owner in F. Scott Fitzgerald's *The Great Gatsby*. He only appears in a few scenes, but late in the story, his grief after a tragic accident is one of the most moving scenes in the novel. Someone who was just a caricature up to that point—the clueless cuckolded husband—becomes for a page or two a real human being.

For another thing, a flat character can be very important to a story. Miss Havisham is one of the most memorable and influential characters in Charles Dickens's *Great Expectations*. She never develops or changes, and she is essentially the same character in her final scene as she was in her first, but if you took her out of the book, you'd lose one of the major plotlines of the novel. In fact, it's possible to have a story or a novel that is peopled entirely with flat characters. Forster himself claims that all of the characters in Dickens are flat, even the leading ones like Pip in *Great Expectations* or the title character in *David Copperfield*.

And consider Sherlock Holmes. Not only is he the major character in Conan Doyle's stories, he's the main reason we read them at all. And while, very occasionally, Holmes "makes the curve towards the round," as Forster puts it, he is usually triumphantly flat. He produces the same effect in nearly every scene in every story, every single time he appears. Indeed, most readers would be pretty badly disappointed if Holmes suddenly burst into tears, or fell in love, or exhibited a passion for anything other than the art of deduction. He is clearly flat by Forster's definition, because he never really develops and because you almost always get the full effect of him every time he appears.

He's also proof that flat characters are not necessarily simple or sketchy, and that they can be very detailed. Indeed, Sherlock Holmes is one of the *most* detailed characters in popular fiction, from Conan Doyle's very specific description of his physical appearance, to his distinctive mannerisms, to the elaborately evoked rooms he shares with Dr. Watson on Baker Street.

Let's look now at round characters. Forster himself does not offer a formal definition of roundness the way he does for flatness, but he shows us what a round character is by giving us examples. The closest that he comes to defining a round character is when he says that, "The test of a round character is whether it is capable of surprising in a convincing way. If it never surprises, it is flat. If it does not convince, it is a flat pretending to be round."

The very nature of round characters is encapsulated in the metaphor we use to describe them. Round characters curve up and away from the flat page into three dimensions. They have different sides and aspects, unlike flat characters, who appear the same from every angle.

Round characters are also richer, deeper, and more mysterious and unpredictable than flat characters. They can do all the things a flat character can do. They can come vividly to life, they can be memorable and instantly recognizable, they can be just as engaging and delightful and entertaining.

But they can also surprise us, delight us, and disappoint us, the way real people can and flat characters cannot.

As Forster puts it, round characters don't just surprise us, they surprise us in a convincing way. This part is important: Flat characters can be surprising, too, but flat characters provide only the sort of mechanical surprise you get from a mystery or a spy novel, when a trustworthy character suddenly turns out to be the murderer or the double agent. While this kind of a surprise can be effective, it can also come across as cheating, as if the writer hasn't been playing by the rules. Our response to this kind of surprise is often a groan or a roll of the eyes.

On the other hand, the kind of surprise we get from a round character should evoke not just shock, but, at the same moment, the strong feeling of inevitability. You should be thinking, "Of course! I should have seen that coming." When a round character surprises us, we're delighted or moved in ways that flat characters can't manage, by actions that we didn't expect, but which we believe the moment we see them.

Round characters can also break our hearts in ways that flat characters can't. They can disappoint us in a lifelike way, the way loved ones or friends can sometimes disappoint us.

The actions of round characters should be both surprising and inevitable. Whatever happens to a round character is probably the only way things could have turned out for them—not because of her circumstances, necessarily, but because her own flawed, complex nature drove her to it.

Take the most famous adulterous wife in 19th-century literature, Anna Karenina, from Leo Tolstoy's novel. You don't have to be clairvoyant to guess early on that Anna's story is not going to end well. And yet, her ending breaks your heart, because you have become so intimately acquainted with every aspect of Anna through Tolstoy's ceaselessly detailed evocation of her character.

In my first lecture on character, I pointed out that fictional people are different from real people because we can know what they're thinking, which is perhaps another definition of roundness. This is true even if the writer never actually shows us what the character is thinking, as long as the potential is there for the writer to show the character's thoughts. By the same token, a character may be considered round as long as he or she has the potential to change, even if they never actually do. Some of the most heartbreaking people in fiction are rounded characters who, for whatever reason, lose their nerve or are defeated by circumstance.

One of my favorite short stories is Anton Chekhov's "The Kiss. " In this story, a dull little man is offered a chance for passion early in the story, does not take it, and then spends the rest of the story thinking uselessly about that lost opportunity. He's the same person at the end of the story as he is at the beginning, but by the end, even though nothing changes, we as readers have a deeper understanding of what he's lost, and just how tragic that loss is, even if the character himself doesn't see it.

I also want to stress, as I did in the previous lecture, that the complexity or roundness of a character isn't necessarily defined entirely by psychology. It can be defined by their circumstances as well. Both kinds of characters can aspire to roundness. Our old friend Mrs. Dalloway is round because we are inside her head at every moment, listening to her private thoughts.

On the other hand, consider Paddy Meehan, a young Scottish journalist who is the main character of a series of gritty detective novels by the Scottish writer Denise Mina. We see these stories from Paddy's point of view, and we are given direct access to her thoughts. But much of the richness of her character comes from her circumstances, from Mina's skillful evocation (through Paddy's eyes) of the dank, melancholy world of working class Glasgow in the 1970s and '80s. Certainly Paddy is a psychologically rich character, but her psychology has been formed largely by her reaction to the world in which she lives. She has been shaped specifically by her oppressive Catholic family, her drippy boyfriend, and the overtly macho atmosphere of the newspaper where she works, not to mention by her social class and the times in which she lives, both of which Mina evokes in great detail.

So, to oversimplify a bit, we can say that flatness and roundness in fictional characters each depend on holding two potentially contradictory values in balance. Flat characters should be both simple and vivid, and round characters should be both surprising and convincing. A flat character is instantly recognizable, and we view him from a slight remove. The author tends not to invite us to see the world from a flat character's point of view. On the other hand, a round character takes more time to get to know, and often, though not always, we are invited to see the world through her eyes.

But please note that I am not saying that all characters need to be likable. Most writers and readers don't have a problem with flat, unlikable characters, because we don't have as much invested in flat characters. But somehow the expectation has grown up among some readers and writers that that round characters, or at least main characters, should be likable. This is a pet peeve of mine. As a novelist whose principal characters are universally unlikable (or so I'm told), I take particular exception to the belief that a character needs to be likable in order to be worth reading about.

I'm not saying that great characters have to be unlikable: certainly Huck Finn and Jay Gatsby and Dr. Watson, not to mention countless people in Dickens, are very attractive people. But think of all the great characters throughout the history of literature who are not only unlikable, but downright unpleasant. Achilles in the *Iliad* is vain and arrogant and vengeful; Captain Ahab in *Moby-Dick* is a heartless obsessive; Mrs. Dalloway is a shocking snob; Lady Macbeth is murderously ambitious; Humbert Humbert in *Lolita* is a manipulative pedophile, and so on. These are all great characters, but in real life, we'd probably want to have nothing to do with any of them.

One of the great things about literature is that we're able to broaden our experience of human nature through reading, with no real risk to our safety or our morals. Reading about Lady Macbeth is a bracing experience, but hearing her story doesn't necessarily make us want to murder our spouse's boss.

This brings me to perhaps the most important distinction between flat and round characters, or at least important as it seems to me, since Forster himself doesn't mention it. This has to do with the idea of conflict in fiction, which we will discuss again when we talk about plotting. But for now, I want to make a generalization which may not always apply, but applies often enough that I think it's useful. All characters want something or are driven by something. Or, as I put it a few minutes ago, all characters have something at stake in the narrative.

Flat characters only want one, simple thing. Sherlock Holmes only wants to solve a mystery, to the point of driving every other consideration out of his head. Miss Havisham only wants revenge against men. Round characters, on the other hand, want something complicated or ineffable or ambiguous. Another way to put it is to say that they are conflicted about what they want, often to the point where they have no clear idea what they're actually looking for.

Take Anna Karenina, for example. Not only is it hard for the reader to pin down what's driving her, Anna herself can't articulate precisely what's lacking in her life. She wants her lover Count Vronsky, but for much of the book, (spoiler alert!) she has him, and yet having him does not satisfy her, for all sorts of reasons. Her desperation grows as the costs of leaving her husband and losing her child mount up. There's something unreachable in Anna, something even she can't reach, that makes her supremely human, frustrating, and poignant. Miss Havisham in *Great Expectations* is unlucky in love, too, and (another spoiler alert) she also comes to a bad end. But while Miss Havisham's death is lurid and dramatically satisfying, it isn't as heartbreaking as the death of Anna Karenina. Miss Havisham's death is the ironic comeuppance of a flat character, but Anna's death is the last resort of a confused, desperate, passionate, and utterly lifelike human being.

So, how do these distinctions between major and minor characters, or between round and flat characters, figure into the process of creating them? With the first distinction, it's pretty simple. Minor characters get less space and attention in a narrative than the major characters do. You don't need a great deal of description or a complicated backstory for a waiter who is simply providing your main character with a cup of coffee.

But even here, you might want to expend a bit more effort than just saying, "The waiter brought her a cup a coffee." You might want to add an adjective or a clause or two in order to give that waiter a bit more substance than just a coffee-delivery mechanism. Even if you say something as simple as "a sour old waiter brought her a cup of coffee" or a "nervous young waiter brought her a cup of coffee," you're not only adding a little evocative texture to the scene. You're also suggesting that the world you're creating is so complex and rich that, if you wanted to, you could follow that waiter home and find out why he's sour or nervous. Now, no matter whether a character is major or minor or flat or round, at some point, you need to think self-consciously about his or her function in your narrative.

In my last lecture, I talked about two different techniques for creating character. You can either construct a character in advance, or let the character develop organically as you write the narrative. Either way, you're going to come at some point to a visceral understanding of how that character figures in the story. Not only, is she major or minor, but what does she want and how simple or complex is that desire? Sometimes this means that a character you thought was round is really flat, or vice versa.

A character you thought was round and complex may actually turn out to do nothing more than move the plot along. In the opening chapters of Conan Doyle's *The Hound of the Baskervilles*, for example, we meet a character named Dr. Mortimer, who gets a lot of screen time, as it were, explaining the set-up of the mystery to Sherlock Holmes. But in the end, Dr. Mortimer turns out to be pretty uninteresting and unimportant. Having served his purpose, there really isn't much more for him to do, and on a second reading of the novel, you might wonder, as I did, why Conan Doyle included him at all.

On the other hand, you may discover that a character you meant to be a minor character turns out to be rounder and more important than you thought. Early in my novel *Next*, my main character, Kevin, a middle-aged man who has come to Austin, Texas, for a job interview, meets a middle-aged businesswoman in a coffee shop and is inadvertently rude to her. When I was writing the scene in which she first appeared, this woman didn't even have a name or a backstory. She was just there for me to show that Kevin was the sort of callow middle-aged guy who would ignore an attractive woman his own age because he thinks he still has a shot with a younger woman. Then, without my intending her to show up again or even be referred to, she turned up, much to my own surprise, under very different circumstances at the end of the book. Suddenly she was round and complicated, with a name—Melody—and an inner life and a fate all her own, independent of her encounter with Kevin earlier in the book.

As a result of this happy accident, I went back and slightly reworked her first scene to make her a little more memorable, so that when she turned up again at the end, her return felt more organic and believable, and not like some plot trick on my part. In other words, in the course of constructing the novel, I had to think self-consciously about what sort of character Melody was, just as I did with every other character, even those whose function or fate didn't change.

In the next two lectures, I'll be talking about writing dialogue. The first lecture is about the mechanics of writing dialogue, and the second lecture is about using dialogue to evoke character and tell a story. It's also about integrating the dialogue into the rest of the narrative.

In the meantime, here's an exercise to help you think about how different sorts of characters can function in a narrative. Take a story you like, or use a completed draft of one of your own stories. List all the characters (this won't work if you're George R. R. Martin), and leave a little space after each name. Then describe what each character wants, as briefly as possible, and using only what the story itself says about the character.

I think you'll learn pretty quickly who is flat and who is round, and who is major and who is minor. Sherlock Holmes's entry might say, "He wants to solve the crime and impress everyone with his brilliance." Anna Karenina's entry might say, "She wants the sort of passion from another man that she's never had from her husband, but in truth she doesn't really know what she wants." These two are pretty obvious, but if you find yourself pausing over that waiter and wondering what else he wants to do besides deliver that cup of coffee, you may discover that you have some work to do.

A final word about character: All writers, whether we have thought about it consciously or not, have a theory or at least a strong opinion about what human beings are like—whether people are fundamentally good, fundamentally self-interested, or fundamentally amoral. We express that theory or opinion through the depiction of the characters in our work. In other words, when we create fictional characters, we reveal what we think about real people, even if the characters are wholly imaginary.

The greatest writers have a rich and expansive view of humanity. Shakespeare's menagerie of memorable characters encompasses every sort of person, from the most venal and conniving, such as Iago in *Othello*, to the comic and endearing, such as the Nurse in *Romeo and Juliet*, to the most conflicted and complex, such as Hamlet.

Other writers are not as warm or all-inclusive as Shakespeare. Dashiell Hammett had a much narrower view of human nature in *The Maltese Falcon*, where every character, from Sam Spade to the femme fatale Brigid O'Shaughnessy, is cynical and self-interested. But while Hammett's view of human nature may not be as nuanced or humane as Shakespeare's, it's still distinctive and recognizably his own.

Whether we're creating characters with the power and complexity of Shakespeare's, or with the focused, visceral force of Hammett's, every detail, quirk, and foible of a character is like a dab of paint in a pointillist portrait of our personal view of human nature. And not just of human nature in the abstract. As the great Argentinian writer Jorge Luis Borges put it, "A man sets himself the task of portraying the world. Through the years he peoples a space with images of provinces, kingdoms, mountains, bays, ships, islands, fishes, rooms, instruments, stars, horses, and people. Shortly before his death, he discovers that the patient labyrinth of lines traces the image of his face."

The Mechanics of Writing Dialogue
Lecture 7

A s we saw in an earlier lecture, fictional people are often more memorable than real people because they are less complicated and more vivid. By the same token, dialogue in fiction can be more vivid and memorable than real speech because it is more focused and coherent than real speech. Further, in fiction, dialogue has a purpose—usually to evoke character, advance the plot, or provide exposition—while real-life dialogue is often rambling, incoherent, or dull. In this first lecture on dialogue, we'll talk about the mechanics of writing dialogue and some basic techniques for using dialogue tags and for mixing speech, action, and exposition.

Rules of Dialogue

- The mechanical rules of dialogue, including frequent paragraph breaks and the use of quotation marks, serve two fundamental purposes: to separate direct quotations by the characters from the rest of the narrative and to clarify for the reader just who is speaking at any given time. Some excellent writers have ignored these conventions in writing dialogue, but in most cases, using nonstandard formats or punctuation for dialogue is not worth the extra effort it requires from the reader to interpret the text.

- The first rule for writing dialogue is that all direct quotations should be set apart from the rest of the text by quotation marks, and the second rule is that every time a new character speaks or the speaker changes, that first line of dialogue should be set apart with a paragraph break. Also, the beginning of a direct quotation should always begin with a capital letter.

- In its most basic form, a *dialogue tag* is simply the name of a character or a pronoun standing in for the name, plus some variation of the verb *say*: "He said," "Bob exclaimed," and so on. The rules for punctuating dialogue tags can be a little tricky.

- Because the dialogue tag is not part of the actual quotation, it should never be included within the quotation marks.

- Sometimes a dialogue tag comes in the middle of the quoted sentence; when that happens, the first half of the quotation is set off by a comma and a quotation mark, the dialogue tag is followed with a comma, and the second half of the sentence begins with a quotation mark and a lowercase letter.

- If a dialogue tag appears between two complete sentences, then the dialogue tag ends with a period, and the second sentence starts with a capital letter.

Reasons for Dialogue Tags

- In general, dialogue tags are necessary for three reasons: (1) to introduce a character who is speaking for the first time, (2) to identify the speakers when two or more people are speaking, or (3) to get across necessary information or a bit context that isn't clear from the dialogue itself, such as exactly how someone is saying something. Let's look at these three reasons in turn.

- A dialogue tag is used when you're introducing a character for the first time or returning to a character at the beginning of a new chapter or scene. However, a dialogue tag may be unnecessary in some situations, such as a scene with a single character who is calling for help. A dialogue tag may also be deferred for dramatic effect, although there's usually the expectation that the speaker will be identified fairly quickly.

- The second reason for using dialogue tags is to identify speakers when two or more people are talking. The usual practice here is to identify each speaker with his or her first line of dialogue, though again, there can be exceptions. If you have more than two speakers in a scene, you will have to use more dialogue tags to keep them straight for the reader.

- The third use of dialogue tags requires more judgment and skill than the first two but is just as essential: using tags to provide some context or nuance that isn't conveyed by the dialogue itself or to clear up an ambiguity.

- o Consider this simple example: "'I love you,' she said." In most cases, the context for this statement is likely to be clear from the narrative, but it is easy to imagine situations in which that statement could be spoken in multiple ways by a character or understood in multiple ways by the reader.

- o If you don't want the declaration to be ambiguous, you can clarify it by adding a more descriptive verb or an adverb: "'I love you,' she sobbed"; "'I love you,' she said casually." Instead of altering the dialogue tag, you might also italicize one or more of the words in the dialogue to show the speaker's emphasis: "'*I* love you,' she said"; "'I *love* you,' she said."

If you have a conversation between two characters that goes on for less than a page, you can probably get away with identifying the speakers at the beginning, then not mentioning them again.

Using Dialogue Tags

- Another rule of thumb for dialogue tags is to use them sparingly and keep them as simple as possible. The more you can rely on the speech of the characters to convey the emotion and reveal who's saying what, the better. In fact, in general, you should use dialogue tags only when it would otherwise be impossible to tell who is speaking or when the context needs clarification.

- Keep in mind, however, that you shouldn't be too sparing with dialogue tags. On the one hand, you don't want to be obtrusive or redundant, but on the other hand, you don't want the reader to get confused. You want to strike a balance between letting the characters' actual words carry the weight of the conversation and risking that the reader will lose track of who's saying what.

- Even if only two people are talking, a dialogue tag may be necessary later in the conversation, especially if it goes on for a long time and isn't broken up with much action or exposition.
  - o Crime stories, for example, often feature long conversations in which an investigator asks a suspect or witness a long series of questions. Some writers introduce the two characters at the start, then dispense with dialogue tags entirely, assuming that it's clear from the dialogue who's asking questions and who's answering them.

  - o However, even if the writer is careful to distinguish between the two speakers at the start of a long exchange, at times, readers can get confused about who's speaking. In these cases, it's helpful for the writer to include a dialogue tag every few lines as a signpost for readers.

- Again, when you use dialogue tags, keep them as simple as possible, avoiding excessive description or explanation. It may be helpful to use a stronger verb or an adverb in some instances, but in general, the dialogue itself should carry as much of the meaning as possible, without unnecessary help. "'You're a clumsy idiot,' said the coach" is probably clear enough without any extra emphasis; "'You're a clumsy idiot,' said the coach disparagingly" is unnecessary, given that the coach is obviously disparaging his listener.

Interweaving Dialogue Tags with Narrative
- The most graceful way to write dialogue is not to separate it from the rest of the narrative but to interweave the two. In real life, people don't always stop what they're doing to talk to each other but carry on conversations while doing other things. Further, each participant in real-

life conversations takes note of the other person's facial expressions, gestures, and body language. Dialogue usually works best when it is an integral part of a scene that combines the thoughts, actions, and speech of the characters.

- Consider a dialogue passage from the novel *Next*, in which the main character, Kevin, an academic editor, is meeting with Eileen, the professor who has just become his new boss. In the following bare bones version of this passage, with just the speech and no action or description, it's obvious that Eileen is being imperious and condescending, while Kevin is nervous and defensive.

"I've seen you at the gym," Eileen said.

"Yes," Kevin said.

"I assume that's your lunch hour?"

"Yeah, I play a pickup game with some guys two, three days a week."

"So the game itself lasts, what, forty-five minutes?"

"Maybe a little less."

"So by the time you walk over there, change your clothes, warm up, play the game, shower and walk back to your office, that's what? An hour and a quarter? An hour and a half?"

"Come on, Eileen, I see you at the gym all the time."

"I'm not on the clock. May I call you Kevin?"

"Of course."

"Kevin, you're not salaried like I'm salaried. Do we understand each other?"

"Perfectly."

"I'll look over your budget, and we'll have a talk about it, soon," said Eileen.

- In a more fleshed-out version of the same passage, the dialogue is integrated with the setting, the physical presence of the two characters, and Kevin's thoughts as Eileen dresses him down. Again, the exchange begins as follows:

    "I've seen you at the gym," she said, still standing.

    "Yes." Kevin brightened—she remembers me!

- With just a bit more description of the action and a glimpse into Kevin's thoughts, even these two lines give us subtle cues that the conversation won't end well: The fact that Eileen remains standing should be a warning sign for Kevin, but he misreads her mood and "brightens," thinking that she remembers him from the gym. He obviously didn't expect her to remember him but thinks the fact that they both use the gym might serve as common ground between them.

- As the second version progresses, we learn, through some simple details, that Eileen can be cold, at least with a subordinate: She speaks with "icy politesse," and she looks at Kevin with "glacially blue eyes." We also infer that she has little respect for Kevin from the fact that she continues to sort through the carpet swatches for her new office while she talks to him. Indeed, her gestures act as a counterpoint to the dialogue, showing her physically judging something as she verbally judges Kevin.

- We learn more about Kevin in the second version. Because the novel is told from his point of view, we have access to Kevin's thoughts, and as the dialogue progresses, we don't have to infer his growing anxiety about his meeting with his new boss, but we can see it happening in real time. The dialogue and Kevin's internal monologue reinforce each other.

- In the first version, with the dialogue alone, we are witnessing a conversation, but in the second version, we are participating in it, at least from Kevin's point of view. We feel that he starts to feel smaller under Eileen's icy gaze, and we feel him vibrating with repressed rage as he leaves the office. That effect is the result of interweaving the dialogue with visual cues, physical sensations, and access to at least one character's thoughts.

Suggested Reading

Faulkner, *The Sound and the Fury*.

Hynes, *Next*.

McCarthy, *Blood Meridian*.

————, *The Road*.

Writing Exercise

1. Write out a dialogue, perhaps half a page or a page, between two people who are at cross purposes to each other: one is in love and the other isn't, for example, or one wants something that the other doesn't want to give up. In the first version, write the dialogue like a play, with no dialogue tags or even the names of the characters—just the dialogue itself. Then, add layers to that initial dialogue. Try a version with basic dialogue tags, then a version with slightly more descriptive dialogue tags, then a version with some action and physical description, then a version with access to the characters' thoughts, and so on. Each version will likely have a very different effect. Depending on what effect you prefer, choose the version that you think is best.

The Mechanics of Writing Dialogue
Lecture 7—Transcript

Just as people do in real life, people in fiction talk to each other. And like real people, fictional characters have all sorts of reasons for talking to each other: to convey information, to persuade, to dissuade, to inspire, to manipulate, to tell the truth, to lie, to seduce, to enrage, to comfort, to amuse. But, as with everything else in fiction, it isn't enough just to reproduce the way that real people talk.

In my first lecture about character, I talked about how fictional people are often more memorable than real people, because they are less complicated and more vivid. By the same token, dialogue in fiction can be more vivid and memorable than real speech, and for many of the same reasons that characters are more vivid than real people.

In real life, speech and conversation can be rambling, ungrammatical, incoherent, ambiguous, repetitive, inconclusive, and dull. Fiction writers often mimic these effects to make characters sound more lifelike, but in the end, fictional speech can only suggest real speech, not reproduce it.

If you've ever read a transcript of a real conversation, you'll have noticed that it didn't read anything like the speech we see in fiction. If you compare the speech of the real conspirators in the Watergate tapes, for example, with the conspirators in a Shakespeare history play like *Julius Caesar*, you'll find that Shakespeare's characters sound much more interesting and complex than Richard Nixon's staff. If people in fiction talked the way people do in real life, nobody would read it or believe it.

Instead, fictional speech is more focused and coherent than real speech, just as fictional characters are more immediately comprehensible than real people. Even if fictional speech is ungrammatical and rambling, it still has to be ungrammatical and rambling in an interesting and purposeful way.

I want to emphasize that second word: purposeful. In real life, sometimes we talk just to pass the time, or because we're nervous, or just to keep from being bored or rude. But in fiction, dialogue has to have a purpose, usually to evoke character, to advance the plot, or to provide exposition. Sometimes it does all three at once. This does not mean that dialogue is purely utilitarian or that it can't be entertaining for its own sake. And the fact that dialogue is purposeful doesn't require that characters always say what they mean. Some of the best dialogue, especially the dialogue that evokes character or the relationship between two characters, can be wonderfully oblique. Sometimes what a character isn't saying is more meaningful than what he or she is saying. I'll talk more about that in the next lecture.

Meanwhile, in this first lecture about dialogue, I want to talk first, very briefly, about the mechanics of writing dialogue. Then I want to talk about some basic techniques for using dialogue tags, for mixing speech and action, speech and exposition, and so on. Along the way, as painlessly as possible, I'm going to sneak in some actual grammar and punctuation. It's been my experience that even very good writers are sometimes unclear on the actual rules for writing dialogue.

Unless you're writing some sort of postmodernist narrative where you're trying to call the reader's attention to the mechanics of the text, you want dialogue to be seamlessly integrated into the rest of the text, and that's more easily accomplished if you have mastered the rules and stick to them.

If you glance at a page of fiction from a slight distance, close enough to see the paragraphs but too far away to read the words, it's impossible to tell if the text you're looking at is exposition or action or character description. From a distance, these different sorts of passages all look the same. Action and exposition are differentiated from each other only through context and by internal cues in the text itself.

But even from across the room, you can identify a passage of dialogue by the choppy paragraph breaks, and, if you look closer, by the use of quotation marks and some special rules of punctuation. These special rules for dialogue serve two fundamental purposes: to separate direct quotations from the rest of the narrative, and to make it clear for the reader just who is speaking at any given time.

The vast majority of fiction published since the 18th century has followed these rules, with some variations. But from time to time, you'll come across some very good writers and some very good books where dialogue is punctuated in a non-standard way. In some books each line of dialogue is marked with a dash at the beginning of each line instead of by quotation marks. Sometimes dialogue doesn't use quotation marks at all. Instead, it is set off from the rest of the narrative only by a paragraph break. And sometimes the dialogue isn't even set off by paragraphing. Instead, it's buried right in the middle of a passage, in which case you have to guess that it's dialogue from the context.

As I say, there are some very good writers who have written dialogue in an unconventional way. There are long sections of dialogue in William Faulkner's *The Sound and the Fury*, for example, that don't use quotation marks, and *The Sound and the Fury* is one of the greatest American novels ever written. Another great writer who tends not to use quotation marks is Cormac McCarthy, the author of *Blood Meridian* and *The Road*.

But great writers don't always make good role models. And on the whole, and with very few exceptions, writing dialogue without quotation marks or paragraph breaks is usually pretentious and often annoying. Think of it in terms of a cost/benefit analysis, and ask yourself the following question: Is what you're gaining by not using standard punctuation for dialogue worth the extra effort you're making for the reader? On the one hand, in the case of *The Sound and the Fury*, the lack of quotation marks helps evoke the mental disability of the character Benjy, in the passages that are told from his point of view. On the other hand, even though I yield to no one in my admiration of Cormac McCarthy's *Blood Meridian*, I don't really think that the book would have been diminished if he'd used quotation marks.

Most of what you need to know about the mechanics of writing dialogue can be summed up in a few rules. For examples of all these, pick up the nearest work of fiction you have to hand—at least, the nearest one that isn't written by William Faulkner or Cormac McCarthy. Find a few pages that are made up mostly of dialogue. You should be able to find most of the kinds of sentences I'm about to describe.

The first rule is that all direct quotations, namely the exact words of a character, should be set apart from the rest of the text by quotation marks. The second rule is that every time a new character speaks, or the speaker changes, his or her first line of dialogue should be set apart with a paragraph break. Also, the very beginning of a direct quotation should always begin with a capital letter.

Now, remember that I said that the rules of punctuation serve two purposes: to set dialogue apart from the rest of the narrative, and to identify who is speaking at any given time. The first purpose is served by quotation marks and the paragraph breaks. The second purpose is served by identifying each speaker with something called a *dialogue tag*. In its most basic form, a dialogue tag is simply the name of the character or a pronoun standing in for the name, plus some variation on the verb *said*: "he said," "she said," "Bob exclaimed," "Elaine whispered," and so on.

The rules of punctuating dialogue tags get a little tricky, but I'll lay them out quickly. The first rule is that the dialogue tag is not part of the actual quotation, so it should never be included within the quotation marks. But sometimes a dialogue tag comes in the middle of the quoted sentence. And when that happens, the first half of the quotation is set off by a comma and a quotation mark, the dialogue tag is followed with a comma, and the second half of the sentence begins with a quotation mark and a lower case letter. However, if a dialogue tag appears between two complete sentences, then the dialogue tag ends with a period, and the second sentence starts with a capital letter.

That was quick and, I hope, relatively painless. If any of it is confusing, any good grammar guide will explain the rules of punctuating dialogue in more detail than I can here. An even better way to learn them is simply to model what you do after what your favorite writer does—assuming your favorite writer isn't Cormac McCarthy.

Okay, now that we've got that out of the way, let's talk about when to use dialogue tags, what sort of dialogue tags you should use, and how to mix dialogue with action and exposition. Unlike the rules of punctuation I just talked about, these are just tips, not rules. None of what I'm about to say is set in stone or is absolute. Other writers or writing teachers might disagree with them. And there are always exceptions and complications. These represent the rules of thumb that I use when I'm writing dialogue, and I think they represent more or less standard practice for most modern fiction writers.

The first rule of thumb is that dialogue tags are necessary for three reasons: 1) to introduce a character who is speaking for the first time, 2) to identify the speakers when two or more people are speaking, or 3) to get across necessary information or a bit of context that isn't clear from the dialogue itself.

Let's take these three reasons one at a time, starting with introducing a character with a dialogue tag. You use a dialogue tag when you're introducing a character for the first time, or when you're returning to a character at the beginning of a new chapter or scene. This is the most self-evident use of a dialogue tag; you want to tell the reader who's speaking. But even in this case, there can be exceptions. Say, for example, you open a scene with a single character walking alone into a setting—a woman coming ashore on a desert island after a shipwreck, say. You might write a paragraph or two about her struggling through the surf and struggling onto the beach. Given that she's the only person in sight, the first thing she says—"Is anybody here?" for example, or "Thank God I'm alive"—would not necessarily need a dialogue tag, because she's the only person present.

Another instance when you might not need a dialogue tag at the very beginning of a scene would be if you were trying for a dramatic effect, like this:

"Look out!"

The detective turned just in time to see a large guy behind him swinging a baseball bat in his direction.

That's a little crude, but you get the idea. The intent of this opening gambit is to immerse the reader right away in a dangerous and suspenseful situation. As a result, you don't need to know immediately who yelled "Look out!"— though this kind of opening sets up the expectation that the speaker will soon be identified. So perhaps this isn't so much an example of a dialogue without a tag, as it is an example of dialogue with a deferred tag.

Let's move to the second reason for deploying dialogue tags, which is to use them when you're writing a scene that has two or more speakers in it. The usual practice in this case is to identify each speaker with his or her first line of dialogue. Again, however, there can be exceptions. And if you've got more than two speakers in a scene, then you're going to have to use more dialogue tags just to keep them straight.

Simply identifying the speaker or keeping several speakers straight are the most mechanical uses of dialogue tags. But now we come to my third reason for using dialogue tags—namely, to provide some context or nuance that isn't conveyed by the dialogue itself, or to clear up an ambiguity. This use requires more judgment and skill, but it is just as essential. Let's take a very simple example:

"I love you," she said.

In most cases, the context for this simple but emotional statement is likely to be clear from whatever comes before or after it in the narrative. But it is easy to imagine a number of different ways that statement could be said by the speaker, or heard by the character at whom it's directed—not to mention a number of ways it could be understood by the reader.

Assuming you don't want the declaration to be ambiguous, there are simple ways of using the dialogue tag to make the statement clear. For example:

"I love you," she laughed.

"I love you," she sobbed.

"I love you," she said casually.

Or, instead of altering the dialogue tag, you could italicize one of the words in the dialogue itself, to show the speaker's emphasis. Each one of the following versions is subtly different from the others:

"*I* love you," she said.

"I *love* you," she said.

"I love *you*," she said.

These examples should make clear that how and when you use a dialogue tag, and what sort of dialogue tag you use, depends almost entirely on the context of the scene. A little bit later in this lecture, I'll explore that idea in more detail.

But first, having talked about when dialogue tags are necessary, let's talk about when they're not. My next rule of thumb about dialogue tags is that you should use them sparingly, and that you should keep them as simple as possible. How you define "sparingly" varies from writer to writer, from story to story, and even from scene to scene within a story. But on the whole, the more you can rely on the actual speech of the characters to relay information or convey emotion, the better. In fact, on the whole, you should only use dialogue tags when it would otherwise be impossible to tell who is speaking, or, as I was just saying, when the context needs clarification.

But when I say, "Use dialogue tags sparingly," I don't mean too sparingly. On the one hand, you don't want to be obtrusive and redundant, hammering the reader with superfluous "he saids" or "she saids," or "he sobbed" or "she whispered," but on the other hand, you don't want the reader to get confused. You want to strike a balance between two goals: On the one hand, you want the characters' actual words to carry the weight of the conversation as much as possible. On the other hand, you don't want the reader lose track of who's saying what.

If you have a conversation between two characters that goes on for less than a page, you can probably get away with identifying the speakers at the beginning and then, not mentioning them again. Here's an example:

"Are you going to Miriam's party?" Mary asked.

"I don't know," said Glen. "I haven't made up my mind."

"Oh, for heaven's sake, are you still mad at her?"

"I guess. A little."

"You're being silly. Get over it."

In this case, it's easy not to use too many dialogue tags for two reasons: One is that it's a short exchange. The other is that it's reasonably clear from what the characters are saying just who is speaking at every moment, because one character, Mary, is taking the opposite position from the other character, Glen.

But even if only two people are talking, a dialogue tag is often necessary later in the conversation. This is especially the case if the conversation goes on for a long time, and it isn't broken up with a lot of action or exposition. Detective stories, for example, often feature long conversations between an investigator and a suspect or a witness. The investigator asks the suspect a long series of questions, and the suspect answers.

Some writers introduce the two characters at the start and then dispense with dialogue tags entirely. They're acting on the assumption that it's clear from the dialogue itself who is speaking, simply by virtue of the fact that the detective is usually asking questions and the other character is usually answering them. And this often works pretty well, especially if the internal cues in each line of dialogue are clear. Sometimes the detective comes from a different social class than the suspect. And in that case, you can tell the difference because the detective speaks in one dialect and the suspect speaks in a different dialect—though the use of dialect raises issues of its own that I'll talk about in the next lecture.

But even if the writer is careful to distinguish between the two speakers, sometimes a reader can get confused about just who is saying what, especially during a long exchange. I've certainly had this experience, and I'm sure you have, too. There have been times when I've had to go back to the first moment where the speakers were identified and count forward by twos (or however many characters there were). In cases like this, it might have helped if the writer had thrown in a dialogue tag every few lines, like a signpost, so we didn't have to keep track on our fingers.

Another thing to remember about dialogue tags is that when you do use them, you want to keep them as simple as possible, and to avoid over-explaining them. Again, some other writers might say differently, but it's my feeling that you want to avoid verbs that are too descriptive. As I've already said, you want the speech itself to carry as much of the meaning as possible, without unnecessary help from a dialogue tag.

In my example about the simple sentence "I love you" a few moments ago, I suggested that you could clear up the ambiguity of such a statement with a stronger verb than a simple "she said." You might say "she sobbed" instead, which gives you a more definitive impression of the speaker's emotion and intent.

Or you might add an adverb to the dialogue tag, for the same reason. Again,

"I love you," she said casually.

is clearer and less ambiguous that simply

"I love you," she said.

But if you have a piece of dialogue where the meaning itself is sharper and more definitive, you might not need the stronger verb or the adverb at all. For example,

"You're a clumsy idiot," said the coach.

is probably clear enough without any extra emphasis, depending on what else going on in the narrative. Another example,

"You're a clumsy idiot," snarled the coach.

seems to me to remain within the bounds of necessity, since it tells us something about the coach's vehemence and anger that we might not have gotten from the first example. However,

"You're a clumsy idiot," said the coach disparagingly.

is simply unnecessary. It's already clear from what the coach said that he's disparaging whomever he's talking to. We don't need the dialogue tag to tell us the coach is being disparaging; we can hear it for ourselves. And the sentence

"You're a clumsy idiot," snarled the coach disparagingly.

is just over the top. Any one of these examples (except maybe the last one) could still be permissible, depending on the context. But you need to walk a fine line between leaving the dialogue too ambiguous on the one hand, and over-explaining it, on the other. When using dialogue tags, less is more.

I'll say it again: You want the actual words the character is speaking to carry as much of the dialogue's meaning as possible. Now here's my final rule of thumb: The most graceful and evocative way to write dialogue is not to separate it out from the rest of the narrative, but to interweave it with the narrative as much as possible. In real life, people don't necessarily stop whatever else they're doing to talk to each other, but they carry on conversations while they're doing all sorts of things. And even if they do stop and concentrate on their conversation, each participant in that conversation is taking note of the other person's facial expression, gestures, and body language. Dialogue usually works best when it is an integral part of a scene that combines the thoughts, actions, and speech of your characters.

To show you what I mean, here's a passage of dialogue from my novel *Next*, in which my main character, Kevin, who is an academic editor, is having a meeting with Eileen, the professor who has just become his new boss. Kevin is trying to present the budget for the publication program he manages, while Eileen is standing behind her desk looking at carpet swatches for her new office.

Here's the barebones of the dialogue, just the direct quotations themselves, with the bare minimum of dialogue tags.

"I've seen you at the gym," Eileen said.

"Yes," Kevin said.

"I assume that's your lunch hour?"

"Yeah, I play a pickup game with some guys two, three days a week."

"So the game itself lasts, what, forty-five minutes?"

"Maybe a little less."

"So by time you walk over there, change your clothes, warm up, play the game, shower and walk back to your office, that's what? An hour and a quarter? An hour and a half?"

"Come on, Eileen, I see you at the gym all the time."

"I'm not on the clock. May I call you Kevin?"

"Of course."

"Kevin, you're not salaried like I'm salaried. Do we understand each other?"

"Perfectly."

"I'll look over your budget, and we'll have a talk about it, soon," said Eileen.

Now, even with just the speech and nothing else, this is a reasonably clear passage of dialogue. It's obvious what's happening: Eileen is being imperious and condescending, and Kevin is being nervous and defensive.

Even without any description of their actions or gestures or thoughts, it gets the point across. And even without being told anything else about them, you get a pretty vivid idea of what sort of people Kevin and Eileen are.

Now here's the scene as it appeared in the book. In this version, we have a bit more description of what Kevin and Eileen are actually doing as they speak. More importantly, because the novel is told entirely from Kevin's point of view, we have access to Kevin's thoughts. I'm also including a bit of the paragraph just before the exchange, to show how the dialogue arises out of this particular situation.

Eileen continued to stand and sort through swatches while Kevin delivered his little State of the Pubs Program address, complete with a spreadsheet printed out that morning from Excel …

"I've seen you at the gym," she said, still standing.

"Yes." Kevin brightened—she remembers me!

"I assume that's your lunch hour?" Still she wouldn't meet his eye, but instead glanced from a wine-red swatch in her left hand to a blue one in her right.

"Yeah," he said casually. "I play a pickup game with some guys two, three days a week."

"So," she said, laying down the blue swatch and picking up a bluer one, "the game itself lasts, what, forty-five minutes?"

"Maybe a little less." Uh oh.

"So by time you walk over there, change your clothes, warm up, play the game, shower—"

And sauna, thought Kevin, but he knew better than to say so.

"—and walk back to your office, that's what? An hour and a quarter? An hour and a half?" Still she wasn't looking at him.

"Come on, Eileen," Kevin said, collegially. "I see you at the gym all the time."

"I'm not on the clock." She let both swatches fall from her hands in disgust, and then said, with icy politesse, "May I call you Kevin?"

"Of course." He could feel himself dwindling in the chair.

"Kevin." Eileen fixed him with glacially blue eyes. "You're not salaried like I'm salaried."

His feet dangled above the carpet, his head shrank into his collar.

"Do we understand each other?" Eileen said.

"Perfectly," said Kevin, the Incredible Shrinking Man.

The meeting was over. "I'll look over your budget," she said as he walked, vibrating with rage, across the crummy old carpet to the door, "and we'll have a talk about it, soon."

Now, the second version is not necessarily better than the first. But it does have the advantage of being more complete, more evocative, and more complex. The first version is shorter and sharper, but it doesn't give you any visual cues about the setting or the character. Even though you can infer each character's state of mind from what he or she says, you can't know it for sure. The first version leaves a lot for the reader to fill in. On the other hand, the second version integrates the dialogue with the setting, with the physical presence of Kevin and Eileen, and with Kevin's thoughts.

Take their very first exchange, for example. In the first version, Eileen simply says, "I've seen you at the gym," and Kevin simply replies, "Yes." It's direct and clear, but it tells you very little about each character. It isn't until we get further into that version of the dialogue that we start to understand how it's going to go badly for Kevin. Now look at the second version again:

"I've seen you at the gym," she said, still standing.

"Yes." Kevin brightened—she remembers me!

This second version is only five words longer than the first version, but already we're getting very subtle, almost subliminal cues that this conversation won't end well. The fact that Eileen remains standing should be a warning sign for Kevin. Instead he misreads her mood, and he "brightens," thinking that she remembers him from the gym. This implies that he didn't expect her to remember seeing him there, and it further implies that he expects the fact that they both use the gym to be common ground between them. We don't get any of this from the first version, or at least we only get the barest hint of it.

Then, as the second version progresses, we learn along the way, through some very simple details, that Eileen can be cold, at least with a subordinate. She speaks with "icy politesse" and she looks at Kevin with "glacially blue eyes." We can also infer that she has little respect for Kevin from the fact that she does not give him her full attention, but continues to sort through the carpet swatches while she talks to him.

But this isn't just busy work in order to show the character doing something. These particular gestures act in counterpoint to her actual dialogue. They show her physically judging something as she starts to verbally judge Kevin, until, at the moment she lowers the boom on him, she lets "both swatches fall from her hands in disgust." Her gesture reinforces her disapproval of Kevin's long lunch hours.

And, by the same token, we learn much more about Kevin in the second version. Since the novel is told from his point of view, we have access to his thoughts. And, as the dialogue progresses, we don't have to infer his anxiety, the way we do in the first version of the passage. Instead, we can actually see it happening in real time. We can hear his attempts to keep it light, such as when he speaks "casually" or "collegially." We can see how his anxiety is expressed at first in little silent asides like "uh oh" or "he knew better than to say so." And finally we can see his anxiety expressed as comic hyperbole, such as when he starts to feel himself diminish under her gaze, becoming the Incredible Shrinking Man. The dialogue and his silent, internal monologue reinforce each other. His attempt to keep it light only heightens his anxiety, and his anxiety makes his excuses seem even more feeble.

In the first version, with the dialogue alone, we are witnessing a conversation, but in the second version, we are participating in it, at least from Kevin's point of view. We feel how he starts to feel smaller under Eileen's icy gaze, and we feel him vibrating with repressed rage as he leaves her office. And that effect is the result of *interweaving* the dialogue with visual cues and physical sensations, and by giving the reader access to at least one of the character's thoughts. It would be easy to take the same exchange and write it from Eileen's point of view, showing us what Kevin looks like to her, cringing in his chair, and we'll talk more about that in the lectures about point of view.

In my second lecture on dialogue, we'll be looking at examples from a wide variety of novels and stories, including *David Copperfield*, *The Maltese Falcon*, and *Anna Karenina*, as well as Toni Morrison's *Beloved*, Elmore Leonard's *Cuba Libre*, and Alice Munro's story "Walker Brothers Cowboy."

In the meantime, here's an exercise you can use to help you think about writing dialogue and incorporating it into the rest of the narrative. It's very simple: Just write out a dialogue, say half a page or a page, between two people who are at cross purposes to each other—one is in love and the other isn't for example, or one wants something that the other doesn't want to give up.

In the first version, write it like a play, with no dialogue tags or even the names of the characters, just the dialogue itself. Then take that dialogue and start layering in more stuff. Do a version with basic dialogue tags, then a version with slightly more descriptive dialogue tags, then a version with a little bit of action and physical description, then a version with access to the characters' thoughts, and so on. I think you'll find that each different version has a very different effect. Depending on what effect you prefer, you may find that the simplest version is the best, or you might find that one of the more complicated versions is. Which one you choose depends on what purpose the dialogue has in the larger narrative, and that is what I'm going to talk about in the next lecture.

Integrating Dialogue into a Narrative
Lecture 8

In our first lecture about dialogue, we said that speech in fiction, no matter how rambling, digressive, elaborate, or colorful, must serve a purpose, and that, generally speaking, we can categorize those purposes as evoking character, telling the story, and providing exposition. In this lecture, we'll talk in more detail about how dialogue can serve those purposes and about finding the balance between dialogue and other parts of the narrative. Some stories and novels are made up almost entirely of dialogue, while some stories use it only as a seasoning. Deciding just how much, how often, and how effectively your characters speak will also help you decide just what sort of story you're writing.

Dialogue to Evoke Character

- Character is evoked by a variety of techniques used together or in close succession, including description, action, dialogue, interior monologue, and so on. Although dialogue doesn't always bear the brunt of characterization, it's not unusual for individual characters to speak in distinctive ways. Dickens, for example, is known for his colorful secondary characters, who often use catchphrases or speak in a particular dialect. George R. R. Martin, who has proven to be a sort of a latter-day Dickens, also uses this technique with the characters in his fantasy series *A Song of Ice and Fire*.

- It's perhaps more common for a character to have a distinctive pattern of speech than an oft-repeated catchphrase. The perpetually debt-ridden Mr. Micawber in Dickens's *David Copperfield*, for example, is distinguished by his comically elaborate way of expressing himself. This technique works well in narratives where the characters are a bit more extreme than they might be in a more realistic narrative.

- In the 19th century, many writers used dialect, with the result that much 19th-century fiction is now unreadable. In *Dracula*, for example, there's a long, almost incomprehensible passage in which Bram Stoker tries to reproduce the accent of an old sailor from Yorkshire. The use of dialect, as in Mark Twain's *Huckleberry Finn* or Zora Neale Hurston's *Their Eyes Were Watching God*, can also come across as offensive or stereotypical.

- o The problem with dialect, then, is twofold: It's often difficult to follow, and unless the entire work is written in dialect (as *Huckleberry Finn* is, for example), dialect can set certain speakers apart as "not normal," with the result that it's difficult for readers to think of them as fully human.

- o Today, most writers evoke dialect in a more subtle fashion, relying on word choice and variations in grammar and syntax to suggest regional speech or social class, rather than trying to reproduce it in every detail. Consider Toni Morrison's *Beloved*, a novel about an African American family in the aftermath of the Civil War. The characters speak a straightforward, conversational, modern English, with just an occasional hint of slang or nonstandard syntax or grammar to suggest their race, social class, and era.

- As mentioned earlier, people in fiction generally have something at stake or something they want, and the best way to evoke character with dialogue is to have them express what they want, though not necessarily directly. In other words, creating effective dialogue for a character involves inhabiting that character's point of view, not necessarily reproducing an accent or a particular pattern of speech.

© Comstock Images/Stockbyte/Thinkstock.

- It's also true that characters sometimes just talk—not about what they want or about the situation they're in—but about something tangential or even

Creating a character's speech is less about reproducing a real-life dialect and more about who that character is and how his or her speech might reflect the immediate situation; a nervous character, for example, may stammer or ramble.

completely unrelated, and the sound of their voices serves to evoke the speaker and the milieu.

Dialogue to Tell the Story

- George V. Higgins's *The Friends of Eddie Coyle* tells the story of an armed robbery and its aftermath mainly through a series of monologues and conversations, some of which read almost like a play by Samuel Beckett. Many crime narratives or detective stories are told almost entirely through dialogue; the modern master of this are Elmore Leonard, the author of *Get Shorty* and many other books.

- Mystery narratives often consist of two stories told in tandem, namely, the story of the investigation, which is usually chronological, and the story of the events leading up to the crime, which the reader usually gets in bits and pieces from dialogue as the detective listens to statements from witnesses or suspects. Many, if not most, of the Sherlock Holmes stories are structured this way, as is *The Maltese Falcon*, which consists almost entirely of scenes in which characters argue, plead, and negotiate with each other.

- However, it isn't just crime fiction that uses dialogue to move the plot along. Another dialogue-filled novel is Jane Austen's *Pride and Prejudice*, in which many of the most important encounters and incidents take place in conversation. In one scene at a ball, the novel's heroine, Elizabeth Bennet, finds herself dancing against her will with Mr. Darcy, the novel's haughty leading man, and the two verbally spar with each other for three pages.

- It's important to note that not every conversation in fiction is a competition or argument. As we've said, people in fiction speak to each other for all the reasons people in real life do, and people in fiction are just as capable of misdirection, confusion, and reticence as real people are. Some of the greatest scenes in literature feature characters who are not actually talking about what's at stake in the scene but about something else entirely. Dialogue can hide a character's intent as well as show it, and often, the meaning of a dialogue is more present in what the characters don't say rather than in what they do.

- A wonderful example is from part 6 of Tolstoy's *Anna Karenina*, at the start of chapter 5, in which two minor characters, a middle-aged man named Sergei Ivanovich and a middle-aged woman named Varenka, are picking mushrooms in the forest. Each is in love with the other, and not only is Sergei working up his nerve to ask for Varenka's hand, but Varenka is expecting him to propose at any moment.

- At the crucial moment, Sergei loses his nerve. Instead of proposing to Varenka, he asks her the difference between two types of mushrooms. With that question and Varenka's response, both characters realize that the marriage will never take place. Perhaps the most heartbreaking feature of the scene is the fact that the dialogue has nothing to do with what's really on the characters' minds. They're thinking about love, but they're talking about mushrooms.

- Even though the dialogue itself does not actually address the matter at hand or directly express any of the repressed emotion, it's crucial to the devastating effect of the scene. In fact, the scene would not work without it. What makes the scene work is that the intensity of the characters' private emotions is immediately juxtaposed on the page with their banal statements about mushrooms.

- Such oblique use of dialogue has become even more subtle in contemporary short fiction. An expert practitioner of this technique is the Nobel Prize–winning Canadian writer Alice Munro. Her story "Walker Brothers Cowboy" is about a married salesman named Ben who takes his two children with him one day into rural Ontario, where he stops at the house of a woman named Nora whom he hasn't seen in years.
  - The story is narrated in the present tense by the man's daughter, but the voice is clearly that of an adult looking back on a situation she didn't understand when it took place. Near the end of the story, Nora plays a phonograph record and makes the narrator, Ben's unnamed daughter, dance with her. Nora then stands in front of Ben and asks him to dance.

○ Munro's narrator never directly says, "This woman was an old flame of my father's, and now she wants him back," but instead, Munro allows us to experience the situation as the narrator did, picking up the cues from what she hears and observes: the way Nora begs Ben to dance with her and the way he refuses, the way Nora's arms hang "loose and hopeful" and her face shines with delight.

○ Unlike the more direct and instrumental dialogue in *The Maltese Falcon* or *Pride and Prejudice*, where characters speak directly to the matter at hand, and unlike the scene in *Anna Karenina*, where Tolstoy makes the subtext explicit by telling us what the characters are thinking, Munro's dialogue is oblique, carrying a great deal of emotion but stopping just short of addressing its root cause.

Dialogue to Provide Exposition

• The most mechanical use to which dialogue can be put is to provide exposition, that is, to have one character explain the backstory or impart some necessary information, ostensibly to another character but, in reality, to the reader. When it's done stylishly and evokes character at the same time, this technique can be quite entertaining.

• One expert practitioner of expository dialogue is the novelist Elmore Leonard. His novel *Cuba Libre* is about an American who gets caught up in the Spanish-American War in 1898. In the first chapter of the novel, two of the major characters, a couple of cowboys who are planning to ship some horses to Cuba, talk about the deal. In the course of the dialogue, they fill in their own backstories and provide a quick-and-dirty history of the war in Cuba.

• Leonard's approach in the scene is relatively painless, but it's not as seamless or engrossing as the rest of the book. In fact, we've all read books or seen movies in which an especially flat minor character appears to explain the backstory, then disappears, never to be heard from again. The sole function of Dr. Mortimer in Conan Doyle's *The Hound of the Baskervilles*, for example, is to appear from time to time and explain things.

- There are three alternative methods to trying to shoehorn exposition into dialogue.
  - The simplest of these is to violate the "show, don't tell" rule and provide the information directly to the reader in the narration itself. Some authors write a dramatic opening chapter or two to draw the reader in, then put the main narrative on hold to fill in the background on the main character.

  - If your story is told in the first person and the narrator is privy to the information you need to get across, you can have him or her fill in the background directly.

  - If the information must come from a particular character at a particular moment in the story, you might use *indirect dialogue*, which is a summary of what a character has said, without using his or her exact words.

Suggested Reading

Austen, *Pride and Prejudice.*

Dickens, *David Copperfield.*

Hammett, *The Maltese Falcon.*

Higgins, *The Friends of Eddie Coyle.*

Leonard, *Cuba Libre.*

Morrison, *Beloved.*

Munro, "Walker Brothers Cowboy."

Tolstoy, *Anna Karenina.*

1. Without invading the participants' privacy, take a fragment of real-life conversation—one you may have been party to or a brief exchange you may have overheard—and try to construct a more lengthy and detailed dialogue out of it. The conversation could be something as banal as one person asking, "Is this seat taken?" and the other replying, "No, it isn't," or it could be freighted with significance, such as one woman saying to another, "So what did you tell him?" and the other woman saying, "I told him no." Whatever fragment you use, start by figuring out what the next line would be, then try to spin as much out of it as you can, incorporating a variety of the uses to which dialogue can be put. In other words, starting with just two overheard lines, use dialogue to create a couple of characters and tell a story.

Integrating Dialogue into a Narrative
Lecture 8—Transcript

In my first lecture about dialogue, I said that speech in fiction has to serve a purpose, no matter how rambling, digressive, elaborate, or colorful it is. I also said that, generally speaking, dialogue is used to evoke character, advance the story, and provide exposition.

In this lecture, I want to talk in more detail about how you can use dialogue to serve those purposes, and I also want to talk about how you can find the balance between dialogue and the other parts of the narrative.

Some stories and novels are made up almost entirely of dialogue, while some stories use it only as a seasoning, so to speak. Deciding just how much, how often, and how effectively your characters speak will also help you decide just what sort of story you're writing.

Let's start with using dialogue to evoke character. As I said in my earlier lectures, character is usually evoked through a variety of techniques, all at once or in close succession. These include description, action, dialogue, interior monologue, and so on. While dialogue doesn't always bear the brunt of characterization, it's certainly not unusual for individual characters to talk in a distinctive way. Charles Dickens is especially known for his colorful secondary characters, who often use catch phrases or speak in a particular dialect.

In *David Copperfield*, for example, there are a number of characters who are memorable using repeated phrases or words. The oily Uriah Heep, who is one of the villains of the book, frequently mentions how "'umble" he is. The perpetually debt-ridden Mr. Micawber is always counting on the fact that "something will turn up." His loyal wife Mrs. Micawber, who is forced to make do because of his financial ineptitude, constantly swears that she will "never desert Micawber!"

George R. R. Martin, who has proven to be a sort of a latter-day Dickens in the scope, variety, and detail of his many colorful characters, also uses this technique with the characters in his fantasy series *A Song of Ice and*

Fire. The noble Eddard Stark is always repeating the motto of his house, "Winter is coming," and the wilding warrior Ygritte is always telling her lover, "You know nothing, Jon Snow." And the members of the villainous Lannister family love to repeat their ominous slogan, "A Lannister always pays his debts."

It's more common, however, for a character to have a distinctive pattern of speech which makes him or her instantly recognizable, rather than an oft-repeated catchphrase. The aforementioned Mr. Micawber, for example, is especially distinguished by his comically elaborate way of expressing himself. It's probably the most memorable thing about him.

Here he is, saying goodbye to his friends David Copperfield and Tommy Traddles, as he prepares to move his family to a new job in another city:

> "My dear Copperfield," said Mr. Micawber, rising with one of his thumbs in each of his waistcoat pockets, "the companion of my youth: if I may be allowed the expression—and my esteemed friend Traddles: if I may be permitted to call him so—will allow me, on the part of Mrs. Micawber, myself, and our offspring, to thank them in the warmest and most uncompromising terms for their good wishes. It may be expected that on the eve of a migration which will consign us to a perfectly new existence," Mr. Micawber spoke as if they were going five hundred thousand miles, "I should offer a few valedictory remarks to two such friends as I see before me."

This goes on for another four paragraphs, and it's a lot of fun to read, but by modern standards it does rather hit the same nail over and over again.

A somewhat more modern example is the erudite and rather jolly criminal Caspar Gutman from *The Maltese Falcon*. Gutman has something of Micawber's pomposity, but is a much cleverer and more menacing man. Here he is, taking his leave of Sam Spade at the end of the book:

> "Now, sir, we will say good-bye to you, unless"—the fat puffs around his eyes crinkled—"you care to undertake the Constantinople expedition with us. You don't? Well, sir, frankly I'd like to have you

along. You're a man to my liking, a man of many resources and nice judgment. Because we know you're a man of nice judgment we know we can say good-bye with every assurance that you'll hold the details of our little enterprise in confidence. We know we can count on you to appreciate the fact that, as the situation now stands, any legal difficulties that come to us in connection with these last few days would likewise and equally come to you and the charming Miss O'Shaughnessy. You're too shrewd not to recognize that, sir, I'm sure."

This sort of speech works well in stories where the characters are a bit more extreme than they might be in a more realistic narrative. Micawber is a comic character in a Dickens melodrama, while Caspar Gutman is a charismatic villain in a noir thriller. When creating more complex characters in less outrageous circumstances, you probably want to tone it down a bit.

I want to say a few words here about using dialect in fiction. In the 19th century, lots of writers used it, with the result that a lot of 19th-century fiction is now unreadable. In *Dracula*, for example, there's a long passage in which Bram Stoker tries to reproduce the accent of an old sailor from Yorkshire, and it's almost incomprehensible. Most readers just skip it.

More controversially, dialect can often come across as offensive or stereotypical. In *Huckleberry Finn*, Mark Twain reproduced the African American dialect of the runaway slave, Jim. Fifty years later, Zora Neale Hurston had her African American characters speak in dialect in her novel *Their Eyes Were Watching God*. Both Twain and Hurston were recreating patterns of speech they knew from personal experience. In Hurston's case, she was African American herself, as well as an anthropologist and folklorist who had done extensive field work across the American South and the Caribbean. But even these two great American writers have been criticized for perpetuating what some critics consider to be a racist stereotype.

The problem with dialect is two-fold: with its dropped g's, bristling apostrophes, and phonetic spellings, it's often hard to follow. The other problem is that unless the entire work is written in dialect (as *Huckleberry Finn* is, for example), using dialect while the rest of the narrative is in standard English can have the effect of setting its speakers apart as "other" and not normal. As a result, it's difficult for the reader to think of them as fully human.

Today, most writers evoke dialect in a more subtle fashion. They rely on word choice and variations in grammar and syntax to suggest regional speech or social class, instead of trying to reproduce it in every detail. Consider *Beloved*, the great novel by Toni Morrison about an African American family coping with the aftermath of slavery in the years after the Civil War. The characters speak a straightforward, conversational, modern English. Now and then, they use just a bit of slang or nonstandard syntax or grammar to suggest their race, social class, and the era.

Here's a scene in which the main character, Sethe, a pregnant slave who is making a run for her freedom, has gone into labor in a field of wild onions. She has just been discovered by a poor young white girl named Amy:

Picking her way through the brush [Amy] hollered back to Sethe, "What you gonna do, just lay there and foal?"

"I can't get up from here," said Sethe.

"What?" She stopped and turned to hear.

"I said I can't get up."

Amy drew her arm across her nose and came slowly back to where Sethe lay. "It's a house back yonder," she said.

"A house?"

"Mmmmm. I passed it. Ain't no regular house with people in it though. A lean-to, kinda."

"How far?"

"Make a difference, does it? You stay the night here snake get you."

"Well he may as well come on. I can't stand up let alone walk and God help me, miss, I can't crawl."

"Sure you can. Come on," said Amy.

This is as close to dialect as Morrison gets in the book. She has Amy use a few slang expressions like "gonna" and "kinda," some nonstandard usage like "ain't," and some nonstandard constructions, like saying "It's a house back yonder" instead of "There's a house back there." It suggests a time and place without the kind of slavish and often off-putting verisimilitude that Twain and Huston deployed. What it loses in exactitude, it gains in immediacy and intimacy, by giving us characters that any reader, of any background, can identify with.

Another author who makes subtle and effective use of dialect is the Scottish mystery writer Denise Mina, whose novels are often set in working-class Glasgow. Instead of troweling on the Scottish dialect, she drops in the occasional turn of phrase or regional slang—using "aye" for yes, for example, or "bairn" for child. In this way she conveys a sense of place, and of the economic status of each character, without making them sound like Groundskeeper Willie from *The Simpsons*.

As I said in my lectures about character, people in fiction generally have something at stake, or something that they want. The best way to use dialogue to evoke character is to have them express what they want, though not necessarily directly. In other words, creating effective dialogue for a character involves inhabiting that character's point of view, and not necessarily reproducing an accent or a particular pattern of speech.

Reviews of fiction often talk about what a great ear a writer has, but creating a character's speech is less about reproducing a dialect or a speech mannerism and more about thinking hard about who that character is, where she comes from, and how her speech might reflect her situation at a given moment. A terse character is going to talk in short bursts; an angry character is going to bluster or speak through clenched teeth; a nervous character is to stammer or ramble on and on. A domineering character might not say much of anything at all, but keep her thoughts to herself, forcing everyone around her to fill in the silence. Or she might rage, overwhelming the people around her. Sometimes characters don't talk about what they want or about the situation they're in. Instead, they might talk about something tangential or even completely unrelated, and their style of speech serves to evoke both the speaker and the milieu.

One of the masters of evoking character almost entirely through speech was the crime novelist and former Boston prosecutor, George V. Higgins. Here's part of a monologue from the first chapter of his novel *The Friends of Eddie Coyle*. In this excerpt, the title character, a small-time Boston criminal, is talking about the time two thugs broke his hand:

"What made it hurt more," the stocky man said, "what made it hurt worse was knowing what they were going to do to you, you know? There you are and they tell you very matter of fact that you made somebody mad, you made a big mistake and now there's somebody doing time for it, and it isn't anything personal, you understand, but it just has to be done. Now get your hand out there. You think about not doing it, you know? I was in Sunday School when I was a kid and this nun says to me, stick out your hand, and the first few times I do it she whacks me right across the knuckles with a steel-edged ruler. It was just like that. So one day I says, when she tells me, 'Put out your hand,' I say, 'No.' And she whaps me right across the face with that ruler. Same thing. Except these guys weren't mad, they aren't mad at you, you know? Guys you see all the time, maybe guys you didn't like, maybe guys you did, had some drinks with, maybe looked out for the girls. 'Hey look, Paulie, nothing personal, you know? You made a mistake. The hand. I don't wanna have to *shoot* you, you know.' So you stick out the hand and—you get to put out the hand you want—I take the left because I'm right-handed and I know what's going to happen, like I say, and they put your fingers in a drawer and then one of them kicks it shut. Ever hear bones breaking? Just like a man snapping a shingle. Hurts like a bastard."

In its own way, this is as beautiful as a Puccini aria: It's got rhythm, it's got music, and it tells a little self-contained story. Best of all, it gives you Eddie Coyle, his history, his world, in his own voice, in less than 300 words.

It also intrigues the reader and prepares the way for the story to come, and that's a good segue to my next topic: using dialogue to tell the story. *The Friends of Eddie Coyle* tells a story about an armed robbery and its aftermath mainly through a series of monologues and conversations. Some of these almost read like a play by Samuel Beckett, if Beckett had been an assistant U.S. attorney.

The use of dialogue in crime narratives and detective stories is especially interesting, because a mystery often consists of two stories told in tandem with each other. One is the story of the investigation, which is usually chronological, and the other is the story of the events that led up to the crime. This second story is revealed to the reader in bits and pieces, not necessarily in chronological order. This backstory is often told entirely in dialogue, as the detective questions suspects or listens to long statements from witnesses. For example, large sections of the Sherlock Holmes stories are told through dialogue. Characters tell Holmes what they saw, heard, or did, and at the end Holmes himself gives a long speech that reveals to Watson what actually happened.

Another example is our old friend *The Maltese Falcon*. This novel is almost entirely made up of scenes in which the characters argue, plead, negotiate, and bully each other in offices, apartments, and hotel rooms around San Francisco. There are a few scenes of violent action, but most of the violence, in particular two shootings and a fire on a freighter, takes place offstage, so to speak. The most important elements of the plot involve what the characters say to each other as they fight for advantage, betray each other, and reveal their true natures, all in dialogue.

But it isn't just crime fiction that uses dialogue to move the plot along. Another talky novel is Jane Austen's *Pride and Prejudice*. Many of the most important encounters and incidents take place in conversation. During a scene at a ball in chapter 18, the novel's proud heroine, Elizabeth Bennett, finds herself dancing against her will with the novel's haughty leading man,

Mr. Darcy, and the two verbally spar with each other for three pages. It's too long to quote here, but it's one of the great romantic duels in literature, and it's one of the models for every scene since in which two lovers spend the first meeting loathing each other.

Another one of the novel's most famous scenes is another verbal jousting match near the end of the book. This one is between Elizabeth and the imperious Lady Catherine de Bourgh, who tries to bully Elizabeth into giving up any hopes of marrying her nephew, Mr. Darcy. Again, it's too long to quote, but you can find it in chapter 56 of *Pride and Prejudice*. It's one of the great smackdowns in literature, and it's conducted almost entirely in dialogue.

But this is not to say that every conversation in fiction is a kind of competition or argument. As I said at the start, people in fiction speak to each other for all the reasons people in real life do, and people in fiction are just as capable of misdirection, confusion, and reticence as real people are. Some of the greatest scenes in literature feature characters who are not actually talking about what's at stake in the scene, but about something else entirely. Characters talk past each other, they lie, they manipulate, they are inarticulate. Sometimes they don't even realize what they're saying or not saying.

Dialogue can hide a character's intent as well as show it. Often the meaning of a dialogue is more evident in what the characters *don't* say than in what they *do*. A wonderful example is from Part 6 of Tolstoy's *Anna Karenina*, at the start of chapter 5. In this scene, two minor characters, a middle-aged man named Sergei Ivanovich and a middle-aged woman named Varenka, are picking mushrooms in the forest. Each is in love with the other, and they both sort of know it. Not only is Sergei working up his nerve to ask for Varenka's hand in marriage, but Varenka is expecting him to propose at any moment.

Here's the crucial moment, when Tolstoy, in the godlike way of the great 19th century novelists, puts us inside both characters' heads simultaneously:

And now it was to be decided. She was frightened. Frightened that he would speak, and that he would not.

He had to declare himself now or never, Sergei Ivanovich felt it, too. Everything in Varenka's gaze, colour, lowered eyes, showed painful expectation. Sergei Ivanovich saw it and pitied her. He even felt that to say nothing now would be to insult her. In his mind he quickly repeated all the arguments in favour of his decision. He also repeated to himself the words in which he wished to express his proposal; but instead of those words, by some unexpected consideration that occurred to him, he suddenly asked:

"And what is the difference between a white boletus and a birch boletus?"

Varenka's lips trembled as she answered:

"There's hardly any difference in the caps, but in the feet."

And as soon as these words were spoken, both he and she understood that the matter was ended, and that what was to have been said would not be said, and their excitement, which had reached its highest point just before then, began to subside.

"In the birch boletus, the foot resembles a two-day growth of beard on a dark-haired man," Sergei Ivanovich said, calmly now.

"Yes, that's true," Varenka replied, smiling, and the direction of their walk changed inadvertently.

This is one of the most heartbreaking passages I have ever read, two people coming this close to happiness and mutually losing their nerve. It's the kind of utterly human misunderstanding that has been played for laughs in countless romantic comedies, but Tolstoy allows the inherent tragedy at the heart of this exchange to come to full flower. The most heartbreaking feature of it is the fact that the dialogue in the scene has nothing to do with what's really on the characters' minds. They're thinking about love, but they're talking about mushrooms. And yet, even though the dialogue itself does not actually address the matter at hand or directly express any of the repressed emotion, this seemingly pointless dialogue is crucial to the devastating effect of the scene. In fact, the scene would not work without it.

The intensity of their private emotions is juxtaposed on the page with their banal statements about mushrooms. Sergei Ivanovich agonizes for 88 words, pitying Varenka, worrying that he might insult her. In his head, at lightning speed, he reviews one more time all the reasons he should propose to her. Then, when the moment comes, he asks her a useless question about two different types of boletus mushroom. Varenka's lips tremble before she gives him an equally banal answer. They both know what's going on, but neither of them will say it aloud. The banality of their speech is the necessary counterpoint to the depth of their feelings. This counterpoint shows us that the one thing Varenka really wants to hear is the one thing Sergei Ivanovich can't bring himself to say.

This oblique use of dialogue has become even more subtle in contemporary short fiction. Under the influence of the great short fiction writers of the late 19th and early 20th centuries, such as Anton Chekhov, James Joyce, and Katherine Mansfield, many contemporary short story writers often create powerful scenes in which the dialogue acts in counterpoint to what is actually going on.

An expert practitioner of this technique is the great Nobel Prize–winning Canadian writer Alice Munro. In "Walker Brothers Cowboy," the very first story of her first collection, *Dance of the Happy Shades*, she was already a master of the technique. The story is about a married salesman named Ben who takes his two children with him one day into rural Ontario, where he stops at the house of a woman named Nora whom he hasn't seen in years. The story is narrated in the present tense by Ben's daughter, but the voice is that of an adult looking back on a situation that she didn't understand at the time. The story is set in the 1930s, and near the end of it, Nora plays a phonograph record and makes the narrator, Ben's daughter, dance with her. As you listen to this excerpt, note how few dialogue tags Munro uses:

She whirls me around in front of my father—causing me to stumble, for I am by no means so swift a pupil as she pretends—and lets me go, breathless.

"Dance with me, Ben."

"I'm the world's worst dancer, Nora, and you know it."

"I certainly never thought so."

"You would now."

She stands in front of him, arms hanging loose and hopeful, her breasts, which a moment ago embarrassed me with their warmth and bulk, rising and falling under her loose flowered dress, her face shining with the exercise, and delight.

"Ben."

My father drops his head and says quietly, "Not me, Nora."

This is almost as heartbreaking as the scene from *Anna Karenina*, but it has a more subtle effect than that scene did, for a number of reasons. One reason is that Munro only tells us what her narrator is thinking, unlike Tolstoy, who tells us exactly what both Sergei Ivanovich and Varenka are thinking. We have no direct access to the thoughts of the Ben and Nora. We have to infer their emotions from what they say and do, and we can only guess, along with the narrator, what happened between them years ago. Munro's narrator never comes right out and says, "This woman was an old flame of my father's and now she wants him back." Instead, she allows us to experience the situation as the narrator did, picking up the cues from what she hears and observes: from the way Nora begs him to dance with her and the way he refuses, from the way her arms hang "loose and hopeful" and her face shines with delight, from the way he drops his head and says, "Not me, Nora."

Now, in *The Maltese Falcon* and *Pride and Prejudice*, the dialogue is more direct and instrumental, with the characters speaking directly to the matter at hand. And in *Anna Karenina*, Tolstoy makes the subtext explicit by telling us what the characters are thinking. But Alice Munro's dialogue is oblique. It carries a lot of emotion, but stops just short of addressing the root cause of the emotion.

Finally, the most mechanical use of dialogue is to provide exposition. This is the use of dialogue to have one character explain the backstory or impart some necessary information, ostensibly to another character, but in reality, to the reader. When it's done stylishly and evokes character at the same time, it can be a lot of fun.

One expert practitioner of expository dialogue was the great American crime novelist, Elmore Leonard. Sometimes Leonard also wrote Westerns and historical fiction, and his novel *Cuba Libre* is about an American who gets caught up in Spanish-American War in 1898.

The first chapter of the novel provides an excellent example of using dialogue for exposition. In this chapter, two of the novel's major characters, a couple of cowboys who are planning to ship some horses to Cuba, sit with their feet up on the railing of a hotel in Texas and talk about their deal. During this conversation they fill in their own backstories and, at the same time, provide the reader with a quick and dirty history of the war in Cuba. It goes on for several pages, but here's just a taste of it:

> Tyler said, "What about the war going on down there? It was in the paper the whole time I was at Yuma, the Cubans fighting for their independence."
>
> They were getting to it now.
>
> "It isn't like a real war," Charlie Burke said. "The two sides line up and shoot at each other. It's more like a hit and run. The Cuban insurgents blow up railroad tracks, raid the big estates, burn down sugar mills, and the Spanish army, the dons, chase after 'em. You understand that's what gives us our market, replacing the stock they run off or kill. Once I'd made a few trips for a Texas outfit ships cattle down there, it dawned on me, hell, I can run this kind

of business. No time at all I'm living in railroad hotels and drinking red wine with my supper."

This is very economically and charmingly done. It tells us what we need to know about the politics of the situation they're getting themselves into, or at least enough to start with. At the same time, it still sounds like a couple of guys sitting around and talking.

But even in this expertly written passage, we never quite lose sight of the fact that Elmore Leonard is sneaking a little history past us. It's painlessly done, and he introduces us to two important characters at the same time, but it's not as seamless or engrossing as the rest of the book. Even for a great writer like Elmore Leonard, working in the exposition can be tricky.

We've all read books in which an especially flat minor character is wheeled on to explain the backstory and then wheeled off, never to be heard from again. Take the second chapter of Conan Doyle's *The Hound of the Baskervilles*, for example. A character named Dr. Mortimer introduces the necessary background of the case by reading aloud from a couple of documents and then telling Holmes and Watson what he himself witnessed. Mortimer is thinly characterized as a practical-minded country doctor, but his main function in the story is to turn up from time to time and explain things. After delivering that backstory in the introductory chapter, Mortimer could disappear, and the book would be essentially the same without him.

So, instead of trying to shoehorn exposition into dialogue, I would suggest three alternate methods. The simplest way is just to flat out violate the old "show, don't tell" rule, and provide the information directly to the reader in the narration itself. This is what I usually do. In two of my novels, *The Lecturer's Tale* and *Kings of Infinite Space*, I have a dramatic opening chapter or two to draw the reader into the story. Then I put the main narrative on hold while I fill in the background of the main character for a whole chapter. If your story is told in the first person, and that narrator is privy to the information you need to get across, you could have him or her do the same thing.

Or, if the information absolutely has to come from a particular character, at a particular moment in the story, you should consider using what's known as indirect dialogue, which is a summary of what a character has said, without using his or her exact words.

For example, you could distill Eddie Coyle's speech about getting his fingers broken into indirect dialogue, like this:

> Eddie explained that getting your fingers broken was like having the nuns slap your hand with a ruler back in Sunday school. They'd tell you to hold out your hand, and knowing what was going to happen only made the pain worse. The difference, Eddie said, was that the guys who broke your fingers weren't mad at you. They made you choose a hand and put your fingers in a drawer, then they'd kick the drawer shut. Eddie said it hurt like a bastard.

This doesn't have the poetry of the original, but it gets across the same information more quickly.

In the next lecture, I'll be starting a block of six lectures about plot. In the introductory lecture, I'll be comparing three different types of plot, using as examples Joseph Conrad's novel *Lord Jim*, George R. R. Martin's *A Song of Ice and Fire*, and the Bruce Willis movie *Die Hard*.

Meanwhile, here's another dialogue exercise. Without invading anybody's privacy, take a fragment of real life conversation, one you may have been party to, or a brief exchange between two people you may have overheard in a public place—and try to construct a more lengthy and detailed dialogue out of it. It could be something as banal as one person asking, "Is this seat taken?" and the other replying, "No, it isn't." Or it could be freighted with significance, such as one person saying to another, "So what did you tell him?" and the other person saying, "I told him no." Whatever fragment you use, start by figuring out what the next line would be, and try to spin as much out of it as you can, incorporating as many of the uses to which dialogue can be put as you can.

In other words, starting with just two overheard lines, use dialogue to create a couple of characters and tell a little story. It may sound daunting, and it may be a bit tough to get started, depending on what two sentences you start with, but once you get going, I think you can have fun with it. The point of the exercise is to reinforce what I've been saying in these two lectures: namely that dialogue is not a separate beast from the rest of fiction writing, but an integral part of storytelling that can bear the weight of almost everything fiction can do.

And Then—Turning a Story into a Plot
Lecture 9

A s noted earlier in the course, literature is the creation of order out of chaos—the creation of meaning and structure out of reality, which is otherwise meaningless and without structure. We've already seen several ways in which fiction imposes order on chaos: When we evoke a person, a scene, or a situation, we select the details that best get across what we want the reader to see and understand. When we write dialogue, we suggest real speech without actually reproducing it, thus imposing purpose on speech. But perhaps the most obvious way that fiction imposes order on chaos is through the creation of stories and plots, which will be the subject of this and the next five lectures.

Introduction to Plot

- Given the prevalence of stories in all human cultures and in our own personal lives, it's easy to think that stories occur naturally in the world, like fruit hanging from a tree, and that all a writer has to do is pluck them. But the reality is more complicated than that.

- If literature is the creation of order out of chaos, it follows that all fiction has a structure. Even for narrative works that don't have plots, all fiction can be broken down into a few fundamental components: a situation or context, at least one character, a conflict of some sort, and a resolution to that conflict. All these elements are inextricably linked in every work of fiction, and if you're missing one of them, your narrative won't work.

- The initial situation needs to be dramatically productive, that is, it needs to be a situation that will produce a conflict, and the character or characters need to have some sort of relationship to that situation. The conflict can be external to the character, or it can be an internal conflict within the character, and the resolution must resolve that conflict in some believable and dramatically satisfying way, though not necessarily happily or pleasantly.

- All fiction must also possess a quality that the writer and teacher John Gardner called "profluence," which he defined as the feeling you have when you're reading a novel or short story that you're getting someplace. Another way to think of this quality is as forward momentum.
    - Whether it's a highly plotted, complicated story, such as *Game of Thrones*, or a modernist, plotless masterpiece, such as *Mrs. Dalloway*, a book or story needs to give the reader a reason to keep turning pages.

    - Profluence doesn't necessarily mean that a story has a plot per se; there are other reasons besides plot to keep reading. Sometimes, you read to gain a deeper understanding of the central character, as is the case in Anton Chekhov's plotless story "The Kiss." Or you might read simply to inhabit a strange and richly detailed world or to enjoy an author's writing style.

Defining *Plot*

- Although our culture is dominated by the traditional narrative structure, some writers remain uneasy with the idea of plot. John Gardner, in his book *The Art of Fiction*, called plotting "the hardest job a writer has." E. M. Forster wrote that a story "can only have one merit: that of making the audience want to know what happens next. And conversely, it can only have one fault: that of making the audience not want to know what happens next." As we'll see, however, creating an engrossing plot is one of the most satisfying things a writer can do and no more arbitrary an act than creating characters.

- Think back to the story we concocted in our first lecture about Sarah and Brad, the couple at the baseball game whose marriage was on the rocks. We could take that same situation and tell it from any number of different points of view—Sarah's, Brad's, a mutual friend's, even from a godlike, omniscient point of view. We could also play with the order of events, telling the story in a strictly chronological fashion or starting from the moment when Sarah tells Brad she's unhappy, then showing their previous relationship in flashbacks.

- Done well, each version of Sarah and Brad's story could be satisfying and meaningful, yet each would be completely different from all the others. Plotting is an incredibly powerful tool, but like any powerful tool, it's difficult to handle. If you don't take enough control over it, your plot will seem loose and formless, with no forward momentum—a series of events that has no particular importance or obvious meaning. But if you use narrative too forcefully, you could end up with something melodramatic, mechanical, contrived, and unbelievable.

- How do we create stories out of formless events and create an order that seems both satisfying and lifelike? Let's return to Forster again, who clarified this problem by making a distinction between stories and plots. In a famous passage in *Aspects of the Novel*, he defines a story as simply a series of events linked by their chronology, but he defines a plot as a series of events linked by cause and effect.

The Story-Plot Continuum

- We might think of the same distinction between stories and plots as opposite ends of a continuum, with the most basic, chronological story at one end of the continuum and the most subtle plot at the other.

The fact that children insist on hearing the same story told in exactly the same way reinforces the idea that with a good story, it's not just how it turns out that counts but how you get there.

- The simplest and often the most addictive stories are the ones that simply answer the question "And then?" These are the stories we like best as children, the ones that we beg our parents to finish for us because we can't stand not knowing how they turn out. As we get older, the desire to learn the answer to "And then?" never really leaves us. Much of the pleasure we derive from even a mediocre Hollywood blockbuster comes from watching the story unfold one plot point at a time—even if the story is predictable.

- Closer to the middle of the continuum between story and plot are such blockbuster series as the Harry Potter books by J. K. Rowling or the epic fantasy series *A Song of Ice and Fire* by George R. R. Martin, better known in its HBO version as *Game of Thrones*. The overarching story of each of these series of novels moves relentlessly forward chronologically, yet each is more complicated than a simple chronology.

  o Much of the narrative momentum of Harry Potter involves Harry figuring out what happened between his parents and the villain Voldemort before he was born. We get this information in flashbacks, stories from other characters, mysterious documents, and magic visions, all of which Rowling uses to mix up the chronology of the backstory. Each of these nonchronological additions moves the Harry Potter books away from Forster's simple chronological "tapeworm"—what will happen to Harry next?—and toward his idea of a plot—why is Harry so important?

  o The construction of *A Song of Ice and Fire* is even more complicated. The fictional world of Westeros has a long, convoluted history that precedes the events of the first book, and the story is told from the point of view of many characters, sometimes returning to earlier events told from a different point of view. The books have tremendous forward momentum, but still, much of the pleasure in reading them comes from elements other than the plot. We want to know the answer to "And then?" but there is much to savor that doesn't relate to that question.

The Literary End of the Continuum

- At the literary end of the story-plot continuum is Joseph Conrad's novel *Lord Jim*. This book has one of the most complex plots in modern literature, yet the basic events of the story are fairly simple.

  o Jim, a romantic young Englishman, seeks his fortune as a sailor in the seas of South and Southeast Asia in the late 19th century. Even before his career at sea has properly gotten started, he becomes the first mate of a rusting old freighter carrying Muslim pilgrims across the Indian Ocean to Mecca. When the freighter, called the *Patna*, collides with some unseen object in the water and threatens to sink, the rest of the crew prepares to abandon ship, leaving the pilgrims to die. At the last minute, Jim betrays his own sense of honor by jumping into the lifeboat along with the other crew members.

o   After Jim and the rest of the crew are rescued and arrive in port, they learn that the *Patna* didn't sink. The rest of the crew disappears, but Jim turns himself in to accept responsibility for what happened. At a tribunal of sea captains, he is stripped of his seaman's license, and his career and reputation are ruined.

o   After the trial, Jim drifts from job to job across Southeast Asia until he decides to accept a dangerous job far upriver on a remote island, where he helps a village defeat an oppressive warlord and win its freedom. By the end of the story, it looks as though Jim has found peace and redemption at last when, in a final series of incidents, his past returns to destroy him.

- Told chronologically, *Lord Jim* sounds like an action-packed adventure story, but the complexity of its plotting makes it into something richer and more melancholy. In telling the story, Conrad not only jumbles the chronology, but he also tells the story through several layers of point of view.

- If *Lord Jim* is told chronologically, it's a simple tale about a young man who makes a bad mistake and tries to redeem himself. But told by Conrad, through various narrators, with the story starting in the middle and looping backward and forward, *Lord Jim* becomes an intimate and intense psychological study of a character who is destroyed by his idealistic conception of honor rather than redeemed by it.

- Despite the complexity of Conrad's plot, *Lord Jim* may be the most realistic of all the narratives discussed in this lecture. Chronological narratives seem lifelike because we experience our own lives in chronological order. Conrad's method doesn't mimic the way Jim's life happens, but it does mimic, in a very lifelike way, the manner in which most of us learn about other people in our lives. The result is a much more intense and intimate experience of the character because it forces readers to assemble the chronology of Jim's life, leading to greater understanding and compassion.

- It isn't true that simple storytelling is inferior, and complex, nonchronological, modernist plotting is superior. But it is true that the two approaches reach different regions of a reader's heart and brain and serve different functions for the writer.

Suggested Reading

Conrad, *Lord Jim*.

Eliot, *Middlemarch*.

Forster, *Aspects of the Novel*.

Gardner, *The Art of Fiction*.

Martin, *A Song of Ice and Fire*.

Rowling, *Harry Potter and the Sorcerer's Stone*.

Writing Exercise

1. List all the major plot points of a story you admire or a story of your own, but write them out on index cards, one plot point to a card, in the order they actually appear in the story. If the story is a narrative that is told out of chronological order, try putting the cards in chronological order and see how that sequence changes the effect of the narrative. If the story is a narrative that already moves chronologically, lay the cards out and see what happens if you start rearranging them. If you want to be especially bold, shuffle the cards and try retelling the story in whatever order they end up in. Deciding how to arrange or shuffle the events of a narrative is a large part of deciding what you want the reader to take away from it.

And Then—Turning a Story into a Plot
Lecture 9—Transcript

In this first of six lectures about plot, I want to take as scripture something that my freshman English teacher at Big Rapids High School told me, before I was 14 years old. Even at that age, I already knew that I wanted to be a writer, and my English teacher, Mrs. Nancy Giltner, saw at least enough promise in me to offer me the following insight, and to trust that I would understand it: Literature, Mrs. Giltner said, is the creation of order out of chaos. It is the creation of meaning and structure out of a reality that is otherwise meaningless and without structure. Another way to put this insight is to say that real life does not happen in stories.

It's true that our lives have beginnings, middles, and ends. But unlike a story, where the writer chooses which events are important and arranges them in a meaningful way, real life happens in a seamless, irresistible flow that does not break itself into discrete, well-rounded scenes. We do not speak in carefully crafted sentences; our lives don't necessarily have clear conflicts; and our lives do not necessarily resolve neatly, the way lives resolve in stories. We are carried from the birth canal to the grave in a relentless stream of experience, surrounded by countless other people who are experiencing the same thing.

While some of our experiences are more important than others, it's only because we choose to impose meaning upon them—often, in fact, by telling stories. Stories, in other words, are not natural. They are created in an arbitrary process through which the writer picks and chooses from a nearly infinite set of possibilities and makes something orderly and significant out of it. Stories are often what make our lives meaningful, bearable, and even joyful. But we impose stories on real life, and not the other way around.

At this point in these lectures, this should not be news to you. We've already looked at several ways that fiction imposes order on chaos. When we evoke a scene or a situation, we pick and choose the details that best get across what we want the reader to see and understand. When we create character, we pretend to get inside the heads of other people, and we pick and choose traits to make a lifelike individual out of a handful of details. And when we write dialogue, we suggest real speech without actually reproducing it. We impose purpose on speech that, in real life, can be messy, halting, and digressive.

But perhaps the most important way fiction imposes order on chaos is through the creation of stories and plots. Often people will look at a real life situation and say something like, "Boy, that would make a great novel." Writers get this all the time. Sometimes, after I've told a friend of something that happened to me in real life, that friend will say to me, "Well, there's your next book." Stories are so prevalent in human cultures and in our own personal lives that it's easy to think that they occur naturally in the world. We sometimes think that stories are like fruit hanging from a tree, and that all a writer has to do is pluck them.

But it's more complicated than that. Taking what Mrs. Giltner told me as scripture, it becomes axiomatic that all fiction has a structure. Even for narrative works that don't have plots, all fiction can be broken down into a few fundamental components. Specifically, all stories have a situation or a context, at least one character, a conflict of some sort, and a resolution to that conflict.

All these elements are inextricably linked in every work of fiction, and if you're missing one of them, it won't work. The initial situation needs to be dramatically productive. In other words, the initial situation needs to produce a conflict. Furthermore, the character or characters need to have some sort of relationship to that situation. The conflict can be external to the characters or it can be an internal conflict within a character. And the resolution must resolve that conflict in some believable and dramatically satisfying way, though not necessarily happily or pleasantly. Sometimes, in fact, the resolution of the conflict is the fact that it doesn't get resolved. We'll look at that paradox in a later lecture, when I talk about narratives that don't use an ordinary plot.

And let me add just one more thing: all fiction must possess a quality that the writer and teacher John Gardner called "profluence." He defined profluence as the feeling you have when you're reading a novel or short story that you're getting someplace. Another way to think of this quality is to simply call it forward momentum. Whether you're writing a highly plotted, complicated story like *Game of Thrones* or Harry Potter, or a modernist, plotless masterpiece like *Mrs. Dalloway* or Thomas Pynchon's epic novel *Gravity's Rainbow*, you need to give the reader a reason to keep turning the pages.

Profluence doesn't necessarily mean that a story has a plot, per se: In a conventional narrative, you read to find out what happens next, but there are other reasons to keep reading. Sometimes, as in a plotless story like Anton Chekhov's story "The Kiss," you read to gain a deeper understanding of the central character, even if that character, as in "The Kiss," never comes to understand himself.

Or you might read just to inhabit a strange and richly detailed world, or to enjoy the author's writing style. For example, plot is secondary in Mervyn Peake's Gormenghast trilogy of fantasy novels, but they are still tremendous fun to read. The profluence in those books comes from their evocative detail, their wonderfully strange characters, and the author's gorgeous prose. We're going to talk about nontraditional structures in a later lecture. But in this lecture and the next two lectures, I'm going to talk about the old-fashioned, traditional plot, which is still by far the most common structure for fiction.

I think it's safe to say that our culture is dominated by the traditional plot, and not just in prose fiction. If you've ever, as I have, devoted an entire weekend to devouring all the episodes of a single season of *The Wire*, *Battlestar Galactica*, or *Breaking Bad*, you'll know what exactly I'm talking about. All three of these shows are superb feats of long form storytelling, and they offer many other riches besides simply a gripping plot. But on a first viewing, they turn the question "What happens next?" into something as addictive as Walter White's blue meth.

And yet some fiction writers remain uneasy with the idea of plot. In his book *The Art of Fiction*, John Gardner called plotting "the hardest job a writer has." And from among the writers of my own acquaintance, I've heard that plotting is the part of the job that usually gives them the most anxiety. Some writers even think of plot as slightly disreputable. All the elements of fiction are fundamentally arbitrary impositions of order on the formless chaos of reality, and yet plotting is somehow seen as even more arbitrary than the rest.

Probably no one has expressed this uneasiness as productively as our old friend, E. M. Forster, in *Aspects of the Novel*. At the beginning of his second chapter, he imagines three types of reader and asks the question, "What does a novel do?"

The first reader seems a bit puzzled, as if he'd never considered this before, and he says, "Well, a novel tells a story, I suppose."

The next reader, who's a bit of a blowhard, says, "Why, a novel tells a story, of course, and I've got no use for it if it doesn't."

The third reader is Forster himself, who says, "in a sort of drooping regretful voice, 'Yes—oh, dear, yes—the novel tells a story.' "

He then says that he wishes this were not so, and he calls storytelling a "low, atavistic form." He then goes on to compare a story to a tapeworm, calling it a series of simple, linked segments laid out in chronological order. A story, he says, "can only have one merit: that of making the audience want to know what happens next. And conversely, it can only have one fault: that of making the audience not want to know what happens next."

I'll confess that I sometimes share this ambivalence. You may recall that, in my first lecture about character, I defended talking about character before anything else by making the argument that you can write about characters without a plot, but you can't create a plot without characters. I even said that all fiction is character driven, but that some fiction is more character driven than others.

Well, I'm not taking any of that back, but I want to take what Forster said about the one merit and the one fault of storytelling, and I want to apply it to all fiction, not just storytelling. Here's my version. A work of fiction can only have one merit: that of making the reader want to keep reading. And it can only have one fault: that of making the reader not want to keep reading. Note that my version takes Gardner's idea of profluence into account. In other words, we may want to keep reading for other reasons than plot, and not just to find out what happens next.

In fact, there are all sorts of ways of generating profluence that don't necessarily put storytelling up front. In a later lecture, I'll talk about other ways to structure fiction and to give it forward momentum in order to keep that hypothetical reader turning the pages. But right now I want to make the case that creating a good, engrossing, and, yes, entertaining plot is one of the most satisfying things a writer can do. I also want to make the case that creating a plot is no more arbitrary than creating characters.

Think back to the story I concocted in my very first lecture, about Sarah and Brad, the couple at the baseball game whose marriage was on the rocks. You could take the same series of events and tell it from several different points of view—from Sarah's, from Brad's, from a mutual friend's, even from the godlike, omniscient point of view of a narrator. You could also play with the order of events in all sorts of ways. You could tell the story strictly chronologically, starting from Sarah and Brad's first meeting and ending with their divorce. Or you could start from the moment where Sarah tells Brad she's unhappy and then show their previous relationship in flashback. Or you could even tell the whole story backwards, the way Julia Alvarez tells the story of a Dominican-American family in her novel *How the Garcia Girls Lost Their Accents*, or the way Harold Pinter tells the story of an adulterous love affair in his play *Betrayal*.

Done well, each version of Sarah and Brad's story could be equally satisfying and meaningful. Yet each would be very different from all the others. Each starts with the same series of events, but depending on how you order those events, and whose point of view you tell them from, the same situation could amount to a completely different story in each version.

Plotting is an incredibly powerful tool, but like any powerful tool, it's difficult to handle. If you don't take enough control over it, your plot will seem loose and formless, with no forward momentum. You'll end up with a series of events that have no particular importance or obvious meaning—too much like real life, in other words. But if you use narrative too forcefully, you could end up with something melodramatic, mechanical, contrived, and unbelievable. We've all read books where the characters appear to be little more than puppets of the author. Even if the characters are fully rounded, they are often required to do unbelievable things in order for a plot to come out a certain way.

So, how do we avoid contrivance? How do we create stories out of formless events and create an order that seems both satisfying and lifelike?

Let's return to E. M. Forster again. He clarified this problem by making a distinction between stories and plots. In a very famous passage in *Aspects of the Novel*, he defines a story as simply a series of events linked by their chronology, but he defines a plot as a series of events linked by cause and effect. Here's Forster, in his own words:

> "The king died and then the queen died" is a story. "The king died, and then the queen died of grief" is a plot. The time-sequence is preserved, but the sense of causality overshadows it. Or again: "The queen died, no one knew why, until it was discovered that it was through grief at the death of the king." This is a plot with a mystery in it, a form capable of high development. It suspends the time-sequence, it moves as far away from the story as its limitations will allow. If it is in a story we say "and then?" If it is in a plot we ask "why?"

Just like Forster's distinction between flat and round characters, this is one of the most famous tropes in creative writing. And like a lot of famous pronouncements, it's easy to oversimplify it. I still love placing things on a continuum, so perhaps it might help if we think of stories and plots being at opposite ends of the same continuum, with the most basic, chronological story at one end of the continuum and the most subtle plot at the other.

Let's look at some examples. Often the most addictive stories are the ones that simply answer the question, as Forster puts it, "And then?" These are the stories we like best as children, the ones that we beg our parents to read over and over again. On a first reading, children can't stand not knowing how the story turns out, but they insist on repeat readings, because they take comfort in revisiting the same steps the story took in getting to the end. And children also often insist on hearing the story told in exactly the same way, and they become frustrated and disappointed if you vary the details even slightly. This reinforces the idea that, with a good story, it's not just the destination, it's the journey.

And as we get older, that desire to learn the answer to "And then?" never really leaves us. When you're gobbling down episodes of *Breaking Bad* and neglecting the rest of your life, you're watching the story in the same way you used to lose yourself in a book as a child.

Much of the pleasure we derive from even a mediocre Hollywood blockbuster comes from watching the story unfold one plot point at a time— and we still derive that pleasure even if the story is predictable, as many blockbusters are.

Take one of my favorite action pictures, for example: *Die Hard*, in which a tough New York City cop named John McClane takes on a bunch of terrorists in a Los Angeles skyscraper. Even watching that film for the very first time, back in 1988, I pretty much knew how it was going to end. (Spoiler alert! The terrorists lose!) But the predictability of the plot didn't diminish my pleasure in watching the story twist and turn, step by step, to reach the inevitable triumph of Bruce Willis. And knowing exactly how it ends hasn't diminished my pleasure in watching it at least half a dozen times since. Because it's a clever story, with vivid if not especially complicated characters, the film works as an unusually seductive sequence of "And then's," with each sequence being a little more over the top than the last.

Closer to the middle of the continuum between story at one end and plot at the other are such blockbuster literary series as the Harry Potter books by J. K. Rowling or the epic fantasy series *A Song of Ice and Fire* by George R. R. Martin, better known in its HBO version as *Game of Thrones*. The overarching story of each of these series of novels moves relentlessly forward chronologically. The Harry Potter books start with Harry Potter being chosen to attend the wizard's school at Hogwarts, and they end years later with an epic battle at the school between good and evil. *A Song of Ice and Fire* starts just before the start of an all-out war between several aristocratic houses which will determine who is going to be the ruler of Martin's imaginary medieval world of Westeros.

Each of these series are tremendous feats of old-fashioned storytelling—just ask any of the countless readers who have stood in line at a bookstore on publication day and then raced home to do nothing for the next 24 hours but read the latest installment.

But these narratives are more complicated than *Die Hard*. Whereas *Die Hard* moves forward chronologically with no flashbacks and only a few references, in dialogue, to previous events, most of the narrative momentum of Harry Potter involves Harry figuring out what happened between his parents and the villain Voldemort before he was born. We get this information in flashbacks, stories from other characters, mysterious documents, and magic visions. Rowling very skillfully mixes up the chronology of the backstory and give us all sorts of information out of order, even as the main story moves unstoppably forward.

Each of these non-chronological additions moves the Harry Potter books away from Forster's simple, chronological tapeworm—what will happen to Harry next?—and towards Forster's idea of a plot—why is Harry so important? It's a plot, in other words, not just a story.

The construction of *A Song of Ice and Fire* is even more complicated. For one thing, the fictional world of Westeros has a long, convoluted history that precedes the events of the first book. And that previous history largely determines the existing relationships of the various aristocratic houses and the individual characters in them.

For another thing, Martin's use of point of view is more complex than Rowling's. Whereas the Harry Potter books take place almost entirely from the point of view of Harry himself, *A Song of Ice and Fire* is told from the points of view of many characters, varying chapter by chapter. This also makes the chronology of *A Song of Ice and Fire* more complex. Especially in the later books, the same period of time is told from several different points of view, which means that the plot occasionally loops back on itself.

And even though the books have a tremendous forward momentum, much of the pleasure in reading them comes from elements other than the plot. These other elements include the rich evocation of a fantasy world and access to the thoughts of some really interesting characters. In the end, of course, we want to know who wins the struggle for Westeros, and we want to know who lives and who dies. But along the way, there is much to savor that has little to do with simply answering the question, "And then?"

Now, moving to the literary end of the story/plot continuum, let's consider a book I talked about in my lectures about character, Joseph Conrad's great novel, *Lord Jim*. This book has one of the most complex plots in modern literature, yet the basic events of the *story* are pretty simple. Bear with me as I go into a bit of detail.

In the late 19th century, a romantic young Englishman whom we know only as Jim seeks his fortune as a sailor in the seas of South and Southeast Asia. Even before his career as a sailor has properly gotten started, he becomes the first mate of a rusting old freighter carrying Muslim pilgrims across the Indian Ocean to Mecca. When the freighter, called the *Patna*, collides with some unseen object in the water and threatens to sink, the rest of the crew prepares to abandon the ship, leaving the pilgrims to die. Jim considers himself superior to the other members of the crew, but at the last minute he jumps into the lifeboat along with them. With this impulsive act, he instantly betrays his own sense of honor and shatters his naïve conception of himself as heroic.

After Jim and the rest of the crew are rescued and arrive in port, however, they learn that the *Patna* didn't sink after all. The rest of the crew disappear, but Jim deliberately turns himself in to the authorities, in order to accept responsibility for what happened. At a tribunal of sea captains, he is stripped of his seaman's license, and his career and his reputation are ruined.

After that he drifts from job to job across Southeast Asia. Finally he accepts a dangerous job far upriver on a remote island, and he helps a village defeat an oppressive warlord and win its freedom. By the end of the story, it looks as though Jim has found peace and redemption at last. But in a final series of incidents which I won't give away, his past returns to destroy him.

Told this way, chronologically, this sounds like a pretty straightforward story. It's an action-packed one at that, featuring storms at sea, dramatic courtroom encounters, and battles in the jungle. And it is exciting: I read it for the first time at the age of 10, after seeing the movie version starring Peter O'Toole, and as a child, I read it strictly as an adventure story.

What I didn't recognize at that age, however, was how complex the plotting was. And I couldn't understand how the complexity of that plotting made it into something richer and more melancholy than a mere adventure story. Bear with me again for a few moments as I compare the chronological version—Forster's idea of "story"—with the way Conrad actually tells it—Forster's idea of "plot."

As you may recall from my lecture on character, *Lord Jim* opens with a description of Jim, marching straight off the page at the reader. As it happens, that moment actually comes about halfway through the chronological version of the story, several years after Jim's disgrace at the trial, but before he goes upriver into the jungle. After that introduction, Conrad then jumps back to Jim's upbringing in Britain, and then works forward chronologically to the moment when the *Patna* runs over something in the water.

At that point, without saying what happens to the ship, Conrad jumps to Jim in the witness box at the trial a month later. Up till now, the novel has been narrated in the third person, but now the story is picked up by a first-person narrator named Marlow. This narrator is talking to some acquaintances on a hotel veranda long after the trial, but before the final events of the book.

Marlow tells them about attending the trial, and then he jumps back a few weeks to tell how he witnessed the arrival in port of the rescued crew of the *Patna*, before it was discovered that the *Patna* hadn't actually sunk. Marlow then returns to the trial, with a long digression about one of the members of the tribunal, Captain Brierly, who committed suicide not long after the verdict. Then Marlow tells of meeting Jim in the street shortly after the verdict and of inviting him to dinner at his hotel. At this point, over the course of the next several chapters, Jim tells Marlow what really happened that fateful night on the *Patna*.

And that is only the first quarter of the book. The rest of the book is equally complex. I want you to note that not only does Conrad jumble the chronology, he also tells the story through several layers of point of view. There's the unnamed third-person narrator who starts the book. Then, within that narration, there is Marlow speaking in the first person, within quotation marks. And within Marlow's first-person account, there is Jim's account of what happened on the *Patna*, which is told in the third person by Marlow with occasional snatches of Jim's actual words, in the first person. Got all that?

We're a long way from *Die Hard* here. In fact, we're even a long way from *Game of Thrones*. If you tell *Lord Jim* chronologically, it's a fairly straightforward tale about a young man who makes a bad mistake and then tries to redeem himself. But told the way Conrad does, through various narrators, with the story starting in the middle and looping backwards and forwards, it becomes an intimate and intense psychological study of a character who is not redeemed by his idealistic conception of honor but in the end, destroyed by it.

Now think back to what Forster said about the difference between a story and a plot: A story answers the question, "And then?" and a plot answers the question, "Why?" A simple story like *Die Hard* has a binary resolution: Does Bruce Willis defeat the terrorists or doesn't he? Harry Potter is a bit more complicated, because we learn a lot of backstory along the way. Also, the world of Harry Potter is more complex than the world of *Die Hard*, but in the end, the story comes down to another binary resolution: Does Harry Potter defeat Voldemort, or doesn't he?

Game of Thrones is more complicated still, with more points of view, a more complex imaginary world, and a much darker view of human nature. Book by book there are winners and losers, but the author complicates things by sometimes letting the people we hate win and letting the people we love lose, and even die on occasion. *Game of Thrones* is a richer experience because it answers both questions. Readers rip through the books to find out what happens next, but what makes reading them so satisfying is that each volume also answers the question "Why are these things happening?" Each of the leading characters becomes more complex and rounded as the plot progress. Characters we thought were old-fashioned heroes to begin to show weakness, bad judgment, and even cruelty, while characters we hated from the start turn out to show flashes of tenderness and compassion.

Conrad's plot in *Lord Jim* is the most complex of all of these examples. And yet, oddly enough, it may be the most realistic of all of them. Chronological narratives seem lifelike because we seem to experience our lives in chronological order, without knowing what's going to happen next. But while Conrad's method may not mimic the way Jim's life happens, it does mimic, in a very lifelike way, the manner in which most of us learn about the other people in our lives.

Think about someone you've met as an adult and have gotten to know really well—your spouse perhaps, or a good friend—and then think about how you learned about them. Chances are, that person didn't sit down with you on your first meeting and tell you his or her whole life story in chronological order from birth. Rather, you got a vivid first impression, and then, over days or weeks or years, the rest of that person's life was revealed to you, in bits and pieces and out of chronological order.

This is how the plot in *Lord Jim* works, and it results in a much more intense and intimate experience of the character. The reader is given the basic information about Jim's life and then expected to assemble it in chronological order without any help from Jim or, for that matter, the author. Some readers, of course, won't want to put in the effort, and that's fine. But for those of us who do, we come to know the character of Jim as intimately as we would one of our best friends.

The conclusion of *Lord Jim* is very powerful. Even though I've read it at least as many times as I've seen *Die Hard*, it never fails to shake me up. The final effect is not just, "Oh, so that's how that turned out," or "Take that, Voldemort," but a profound understanding of how a person's best qualities can sometimes lead to his ruin.

Before I wrap this lecture up, I want to make clear that I'm not saying that simple storytelling is inferior, and that complex, non-chronological, modernist plotting is superior. One of my other favorite books, and one of the greatest novels ever written, is George Eliot's massive Victorian novel,

Middlemarch. This book has a wonderful, complex plot with many strands, but it moves forward just as chronologically as *Die Hard* or *Game of Thrones*, only with a lot fewer explosions and beheadings.

And I really, really love *Die Hard*; it's just that narratives like *Die Hard*'s and narratives like *Lord Jim*'s reach different regions of a reader's heart and brain, and they serve different functions for the writer.

Now here's an exercise to help you explore the difference between a story and a plot. List all the major plot points of a story you admire, or a story of your own, but write them out on index cards, one plot point to a card, in the order in which they actually appear in the story.

If it's a narrative which is told out of chronological order, try putting the cards in chronological order and see how it changes the effect of the narrative.

If it's a narrative that already moves chronologically, lay the cards out and see what happens if you start rearranging them.

And if you want to be especially bold, just shuffle the cards and try retelling the story in whatever order they end up in. Deciding how to arrange the events of a narrative helps to determine what you want the reader to take away from it.

In the next lecture, I'll explain the famous Freytag pyramid by using *The Wizard of Oz* as an example. And in the subsequent lectures about plot, I'll look at different types and techniques of plotting, and give you some suggestions for making choices about just what kind of story you want to tell.

Plotting with the Freytag Pyramid
Lecture 10

The basic structure of a traditional plot—situation, conflict, resolution—was first codified by Aristotle in the *Poetics*, in which he defines the elements that make up a tragic drama. Aristotle was the first to state that a story should have a beginning, a middle, and an end; that the events of the plot should be causally connected and self-contained; and that the ending of the plot—particularly the plot of a tragedy—should provide both closure and catharsis. More commonly referenced today than Aristotle is Freytag's pyramid, a diagram of dramatic structure based on Aristotle's theory. In this lecture, we'll look at the pyramid, using the film version of *The Wizard of Oz* as an example.

The Wizard of Oz and Freytag's Pyramid

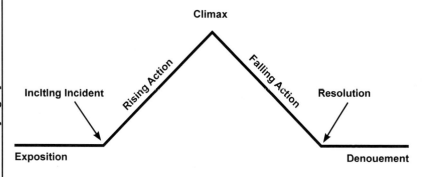

- According to Freytag's pyramid, the exposition stage of a story sets the scene and introduces the characters. In *The Wizard of Oz*, the exposition is everything that happens from the beginning of the film to the tornado: We meet all the major characters; Dorothy runs away with Toto and meets Professor Marvel; and on her way back to the farm, Dorothy is overtaken by the storm.

- Next comes the inciting action, which is the event that introduces conflict into the story. This bit is tricky with *The Wizard of Oz* because there are two elements in the story that might be called the conflict.
    - One is the conflict between Dorothy and Miss Gulch because Miss Gulch wants Dorothy's dog put to sleep. This is what causes Dorothy to run away from home, leading to the blow to the head she receives during the tornado. In that sense, we might consider Miss Gulch's threat the inciting moment.

    - But this conflict becomes more complicated when the tornado transports Dorothy to the Land of Oz. There, Dorothy's house lands on the Wicked Witch of the East and kills her, and the Wicked Witch of the West threatens to kill Dorothy in revenge. However, this is actually the same as the first conflict because the Wicked Witch of the West is Miss Gulch in her Oz incarnation, and in both incarnations, she wants to harm Dorothy.

    - There's also another potential conflict that arises after Dorothy lands in Oz: the fact that she wants to go home, but nobody knows how to send her back to Kansas. The two conflicts—Dorothy versus the Wicked Witch and Dorothy's quest to go home—are linked and become even more explicitly linked later on.

- The rising action is the part where the plot becomes more complicated and exciting, building tension. In *The Wizard of Oz*, the rising action includes Dorothy's departure from Munchkinland; her meetings with the Scarecrow, the Tin Man, and the Cowardly Lion; her arrival in Emerald City; her first audience with the wizard; and her capture by the witch.
    - During this party of the story, small obstacles are thrown in the path of Dorothy and her companions, and the two conflicts mentioned earlier are reemphasized. Once Dorothy and her companions arrive in Oz, the witch spells out "Surrender Dorothy" in the sky, and Dorothy, trembling before the flaming head of the wizard, asks for his help in returning home. The

two conflicts are then explicitly linked when the wizard tells Dorothy that he'll help her get back to Kansas if she brings him the witch's broomstick.

- o Dorothy and her companions then face their most difficult challenge, with Dorothy getting carried away by the flying monkeys and her companions breaking into the witch's castle to rescue her.

- The climax is the most dramatic and exciting event in a story. In *The Wizard of Oz*, the climax comes when Dorothy and her friends are trapped in the witch's castle, and Dorothy kills the witch by dousing her with a bucket of water. At that moment, much of the film's tension is released because at least one of the conflicts, the one between Dorothy and the witch, is ended, and the plot begins its descent down the other side of the pyramid.

- The next element is the falling action, which is made up of the events that result directly from the moment of climax. The element after that is called the resolution, where the character's conflict is resolved.
  - o After Dorothy has killed the witch, she takes the broomstick back to the wizard. He solves the problems of the Scarecrow, the Tin Man, and the Cowardly Lion and agrees to take Dorothy back to Kansas himself. This is the falling action: It shows the results of the death of the witch, but it doesn't resolve Dorothy's second conflict, the fact that she wants to go home to Kansas.

  - o The resolution comes when the wizard accidentally takes off in his balloon without Dorothy, and Dorothy learns from Glinda the Good Witch that she could have taken herself back to Kansas at any time by using the ruby slippers. At this point, Dorothy's conflict is finally resolved—the threat from the witch is liquidated, and she realizes that she always had the power to go home.

- The denouement is the ending of the story, when order is restored. At this stage, we are often shown the characters one more time so that we can see what happened to them. In *The Wizard of Oz*, it's the final scene in Dorothy's bedroom, where she is reunited with Aunt Em and Uncle Henry and the now-familiar farmhands.
    - In some stories, the denouement simply shows that order has been restored, and the world is now back the way it was. But this isn't usually the case, and it's certainly not the case in *The Wizard of Oz*.

    - Dorothy is back home, but everything is not back to the way it was before she went to Oz. Dorothy's understanding of herself and her place in the world have profoundly changed.

Pros and Cons of Traditional Structure

- The structure outlined by Freytag's pyramid is sturdy, reliable, and ubiquitous, but it can, at times, seem like a straightjacket. With many conventionally plotted novels, we can guess the ending after the first few pages or even from the jacket copy. Sometimes we feel both reassured and annoyed at the same story: You may guess during the first 10 pages that the sparring lovers will eventually get together, but you might be irritated if, at the end, they don't really like each other and wind up with other people. The predictable can be both seductive and disappointing at the same time.

- Even so, this particular narrative structure has proved to be surprisingly adaptable, especially considering that it was originally conceived to apply to stage tragedies. The plays Aristotle was familiar with usually focused on the fate of a single central character, such as Oedipus or Medea, not novels that incorporate numerous characters. Yet this structure can be applied to everything from comedy to tragedy, thrillers to love stories, and *Hamlet* to *Star Wars*.

- For writers who are just starting out, this narrative structure can be a useful set of training wheels, especially if you're uneasy about plotting. It's so common in our culture, in fact, than many writers adopt it instinctively, without even thinking about it.

Complicating Traditional Plots

- Perhaps the Freytag pyramid seems so instinctive because, in its simplest form, it is often the foundation for a *binary plot*, that is, one in which an either/or question is posed near the start of the narrative and answered at the climax or resolution. Who is the murderer? Will the two lovers get together? Will Dorothy ever get back to Kansas?
    - o In later lectures, we'll explore many ways to complicate the answers to those questions, but for now, it's important to emphasize that there are ways to complicate this kind of plot long before you get to the end. A binary plot structured according to the Freytag pyramid doesn't have to be a simplistic or unsophisticated one.

    - o You can scale up the story to encompass more time and more characters by weaving together several binary plots or Freytag pyramids into one larger narrative. In George Eliot's novel *Middlemarch*, for example, the central story is about a love triangle, but there are also two other major romantic relationships in the book, in addition to several other subplots, each of which follows its own Freytag pyramid.

- Using a *fractal plot* is another way to complicate a traditional narrative structure. A fractal is a kind of self-similar mathematical pattern, meaning that it looks the same at a distance as it does up close.
    - o Trees are an excellent example: The limbs of a tree coming off the trunk make the same basic pattern as the branches coming off each limb; the twigs make the same pattern coming off each branch; and so on.

    - o You can create the same effect with large-scale narratives, such as novels that run in a series but come to a final conclusion. George R. R. Martin's *A Song of Ice and Fire* poses a single binary question: Who will sit on the Iron Throne and be the king or queen of Westeros? In Martin's work, however, this larger binary plot is made up of a vast number of smaller but no less compelling binary plots at nearly every level.

- Another way to vary the Freytag pyramid is to create *leapfrogging* or a *contrapuntal narrative*.
  - The first variation of this approach tells a single story from the point of view of multiple characters. One famous example is William Faulkner's *As I Lay Dying*, which is narrated from the point of view of 15 different characters, each speaking in the first person.

  - Another variation of leapfrogging is one that tells several equally important stories that remain separate for much of the book but come together at the end for a single climax. J. R. R. Tolkien used this approach in *The Fellowship of the Ring*. At the end of this book, the overarching story of the quest to destroy the Ring of Power splits into three equally important strands that are then followed to the climax of *The Return of the King*.

  - Still another variation of contrapuntal narrative is commonly used by modern historical novelists. Here, two main stories that are linked, one from the past and one from the present, are woven together. An excellent example is A. S. Byatt's novel *Possession*, in which the outcome of the historical plot determines the outcome of the modern one.

  - Finally, the basic murder mystery is usually a contrapuntal story. It's the most basic kind of binary plot there is—who killed the victim?—but the answer is often found through a combination of the present-day story and the story of the recent past.

Suggested Reading

Aristotle, *Poetics*.

Byatt, *Possession*.

Eliot, *Middlemarch*.

Faulkner, *As I Lay Dying*.

Martin, *A Song of Ice and Fire*.

Tolkien, *The Lord of the Rings*.

Writing Exercise

1. Try to graph some of your favorite books, movies, or television shows on Freytag's pyramid. Notice how common this structure is but also how often it is a complicated tangle of many pyramids rather than a single pyramid. If you don't want a traditionally structured plot to become a straightjacket, you need to walk a fine line between being too predictable, on the one hand, and disappointing the reader, on the other. You want readers to be satisfied and not feel betrayed by your climax, but you don't want them to see it coming. This exercise will help you begin to think about meeting that challenge.

Plotting with the Freytag Pyramid
Lecture 10—Transcript

Everybody thinks they know how to tell a joke. What that usually means in practice is that most of us understand, at least intuitively, the basic structure of the typical joke: You introduce a situation with a twist in it; the joke exploits the twist to build tension; and then the tension is released as a punchline, which usually involves a reversal of expectations.

There are countless jokes that follow this structure, and depending on the content of the joke and delivery of the joke teller, the amazing thing is that most people still find this sort of joke funny. It doesn't matter that the structure is simple and predictable, it doesn't matter that we know instinctively that the joke's going to end in a reversal. The fact is, when most of us hear the phrase, "A guy walks into a bar," our ears perk up. We know exactly what to expect—situation, twist, punchline. You'd think this would prevent us from being surprised, and yet we also expect to laugh at the end of it. It's a very reliable, almost reflexive response.

In fiction, the structure of the traditional plot works in much the same way, especially in popular fiction, and very often in literary fiction as well. When we start reading a certain type of story—a mystery story, say, or a romance novel—we're given a particular situation we've seen many times before: A detective is called to the scene of a murder, or a young couple have a cute meeting.

Then a conflict or complication arises: The murdered body was found alone in a room that was locked from the inside, or the couple dislike each other intensely on first sight.

Then the story or novel proceeds to work its way through the conflict: The detective searches for clues, interviews witnesses, and finds herself threatened by the murderer or by someone who is protecting the murderer. The lovers circle each other warily as the rest of the plot revolves around them.

Finally the detective catches the murderer, or at least learns the murderer's identity. And the sparring lovers come to their senses, fall into each other's arms, and live happily ever after, as we always knew they would.

This basic structure—situation, conflict, resolution—was first codified by the Greek philosopher Aristotle in his work the *Poetics*, in which he names and defines the various elements that make up a tragic drama. To this day, 2,300 years after his death, people still talk about a narrative having an Aristotelian structure.

It's beyond the scope of this lecture for me to explain Aristotle's theory in detail, but suffice it to say that he was the first to state explicitly that a story should have a beginning, a middle, and an end. He was also the first to say that the events of the plot should be both causally connected and self-contained, and that the ending of the plot—and remember that he's talking specifically about tragedy here—should provide both closure and catharsis. Aristotle also introduces the concepts of the protagonist and the antagonist, or the two major characters who are in conflict with each other.

But when we're talking about prose fiction these days, Freytag's Pyramid is more commonly referred to than Aristotle. Freytag's Pyramid is a graph of dramatic structure based on Aristotle's theory and created by an otherwise obscure 19th-century German novelist and playwright named Gustav Freytag. This distinctive sketch of a pyramid, which is actually more of a triangle, has been a staple of literature and creative writing classes for years, and depending on who's explaining it, Freytag's Pyramid is made up of either five, six, or seven elements. For the sake of completeness, I'm going to explain the seven-element version.

As the name suggests, these elements are usually graphed in the shape of a pyramid. Starting at ground level on the left-hand side of the pyramid and rising toward the top, the first three elements are the exposition, the inciting incident, and the rising action. At the peak of the pyramid is the climax, which is the moment of greatest emotion or drama. Then the pyramid descends on the right-hand side in the falling action and the resolution, and it ends at ground level again on the other side with the denouement. In order to show the pyramid in practice, I'm going to use a story everybody knows, namely, the plot of the film version of *The Wizard of Oz*.

The exposition stage of a story sets the scene and introduces the characters. In *The Wizard of Oz*, the exposition is everything that happens from the beginning of the film all the way up to the tornado. During this section, we meet Dorothy Gale, who lives on a farm in Kansas with her Aunt Em and Uncle Henry as well as the farmhands Hunk, Zeke, and Hickory. We also meet their mean neighbor, Miss Gulch, who has been bitten by Dorothy's dog, Toto, and who wants to have Toto put to sleep. As a result of this threat, Dorothy runs away with Toto and meets the medicine show pitchman Professor Marvel. He sends her back to her family, but on her way back to the farm, Dorothy is overtaken by a storm. By time we get to the tornado at the end of the exposition, all the major characters have been introduced.

Next comes the inciting action, which is the event that introduces conflict into the story. The inciting action of *The Wizard of Oz* is a bit ambiguous, because there are two different elements in the story that might be called the conflict. One is the conflict between Dorothy on the one hand and Miss Gulch on the other, because Miss Gulch wants Dorothy's dog put to death. This is what causes Dorothy to run away from home, leading directly to her getting conked on the head during the tornado. In that sense, you might consider Miss Gulch's threat the inciting moment, but then this conflict becomes more complicated a few minutes later, when the tornado transports Dorothy to the Land of Oz.

There, Dorothy's house lands on the Wicked Witch of the East and kills her, and the witch's sister, the Wicked Witch of the West, threatens to kill Dorothy in revenge. However, this is really just the same conflict, because the Wicked Witch of the West is actually just Miss Gulch in her Oz incarnation, and in both incarnations, she wants harm to Dorothy. In fact, using Aristotle's terminology, we now have a protagonist, Dorothy, and an antagonist, Miss Gulch, a.k.a. the Wicked Witch.

But there's another conflict that arises after Dorothy lands in Oz, and that's the fact that she wants to go home, and nobody knows how to send her back to Kansas. These two conflicts—Dorothy versus the Wicked Witch, and

Dorothy's quest to go home—are linked, of course, and they get linked even more explicitly later on. Let's just say that by time Dorothy starts down the Yellow Brick Road, the inciting incident has already happened.

The rising action is the part where the plot gets more complicated and exciting, building tension along the way. Here's where you get twists and obstacles and digressions. As a result of these obstacles, in most stories, the rising action makes up the majority of the plot.

In *The Wizard of Oz*, the rising action includes Dorothy's departure from Munchkinland and her meetings with the Scarecrow, the Tin Man, and the Cowardly Lion (whom we've already met in the exposition, as Hunk, Zeke, and Hickory). The rising action also includes her arrival in the Emerald City, her first audience with the Wizard of Oz (who is really, of course, Professor Marvel), and her capture by the Wicked Witch of the West.

Along the way, obstacles are thrown in the path of Dorothy and her companions. During the scene where she and the Scarecrow discover the Tin Man, they are attacked by the talking trees, and the witch turns up to threaten them with a fireball. Then Dorothy, the Scarecrow, and the Tin Man tame the Cowardly Lion after he attacks them, and after that, they survive the witch's attempt to put them all to sleep in the poppy field.

During this part of the story the two conflicts I mentioned earlier are reemphasized. Once Dorothy and her companions arrive in the Emerald City, the Wicked Witch's rage at Dorothy is spelled out in the sky, when she writes the words "Surrender Dorothy" in smoke with her broomstick. Then Dorothy, trembling before the big, flaming head of the Wizard, asks for his help in sending her home. The two conflicts are then explicitly linked, when the Wizard tells Dorothy he'll help her get back to Kansas if she brings him the Witch's broomstick.

Dorothy and her companions then face their most difficult challenge, with Dorothy getting carried away by the flying monkeys in the haunted forest, and her companions breaking into the witch's castle to rescue her. All of these scenes, from Dorothy's arrival in Oz to the final showdown in the witch's castle, constitute the story's rising action, and they make up much of the running time of *The Wizard of Oz*.

This brings us to the climax, which is the most dramatic and exciting event in the story. The climax of *The Wizard of Oz* comes when Dorothy and her friends are trapped in the witch's castle, and she kills the Wicked Witch by dousing her with a bucket of water. It's without a doubt the most heart-stopping moment in the film, no matter how many times you've seen it. And at that moment, much of the film's tension is released, because at least one of the conflicts, the one between Dorothy and the Witch, is ended, and the plot begins its descent down the other side of the pyramid.

The next element is called the falling action, which is made up of the events that result directly from the moment of climax, and the element after that is called the resolution, where the main character's conflict is resolved.

In a detective story, catching or revealing the killer is often the climax, after which there isn't much else to relate. In a romance, the lovers usually declare their love for each other only a few pages before the end of the novel, and, just like in the detective story, not much happens after the climax.

In *The Wizard of Oz*, after Dorothy has killed the Wicked Witch, she takes the witch's broomstick back to the Wizard. Then the Wizard, after a little persuading, solves the problems of the Scarecrow, the Tin Man, and the Cowardly Lion with something for each of them out of his big black bag. As for Dorothy, he agrees to take her back to Kansas himself. That's the falling action: It shows the results of the death of the witch, but it still hasn't resolved Dorothy's second conflict, the fact that she wants to go home to Kansas. That moment, the resolution, comes when the Wizard accidentally takes off in his balloon without Dorothy, and Dorothy learns from the Glinda the Good Witch that she could have taken herself back to Kansas at any time by using the ruby slippers.

At this point, Dorothy's conflict is finally resolved—the threat from the Witch is liquidated, so to speak, and she realizes she always had the power to go home.

The denouement is the ending of the story, when order is restored. The word denouement is the French word for untying, which frankly seems a little counterintuitive to me—we usually talk about tying up the loose threads of a plot, but if you think of it as referring to untying the knot of the conflict, I suppose it makes sense. But at any rate, during the denouement we are often shown all the major characters one more time, so we can see what happened to them. In *The Wizard of Oz*, it's the final scene in Dorothy's bedroom, where she is reunited with Aunt Em and Uncle Henry, and also with the now suspiciously familiar farmhands. Even the Wizard of Oz himself returns in the final moments, in the form of Professor Marvel. Miss Gulch is nowhere to be seen, because, of course, she has been killed off in her incarnation as the Wicked Witch.

In this final scene, both Dorothy and the narrative are literally returned home, back to where they both began. In some stories, this simply means that order has been restored, and the world is now back to the way it was. But this isn't always the case, and it's certainly not the case in *The Wizard of Oz*. Dorothy is back home, where she wanted to be, but this is not to say that everything is back to the way it was before she went to Oz. Dorothy's understanding of herself and her place in the world has profoundly changed. After the strangeness and violence she experienced in Oz, order has been restored, but she is a wiser and stronger person.

Now, I've gone into so much detail about this particular structure because it's the sturdy, reliable, ubiquitous, and often predictable structure of countless books, stories, plays, movies, and television series. And predictability is not necessarily a bad thing. Predictability can be enormously reassuring and satisfying. I've seen *The Wizard of Oz* probably at least once a year for the last 50 years. The tornado never fails to thrill me, the witch never fails to terrify me, and Dorothy saying goodbye to the Scarecrow never fails to make me cry.

The appeal of this simple, sturdy structure runs deep. Some people even think there's something instinctual about it, something hardwired in our consciousness that makes us want to see the world ordered into stories like these. The disadvantage of this traditional structure, however, is that it can also be a one-size-fits-all straightjacket. Think of the countless bestselling novels or blockbuster movies that are pretty much cut to the same pattern. With too many conventionally plotted novels, you can not only guess the ending after the first few pages, you can often guess it from the jacket copy, before you even open the book. The publishing industry and Hollywood don't exactly help the situation by turning out books and movies that are carbon copies of earlier books and movies that have done well. But we as readers bear some of the blame, by rewarding the predictable and the reassuring, and by making it harder for more offbeat forms of storytelling to succeed.

Sometimes you feel both reassured and annoyed at the same story. You may have guessed during the first 10 pages that the sparring lovers are eventually going to get together. But imagine how disappointed and annoyed you would be if it turns out at the end that they really don't like each other after all, and they wind up with other people. Or worse, they wind up alone. The predictable can be both disappointing and seductive at the same time.

Even so, this particular narrative structure has proved to be surprisingly adaptable, considering that when first Aristotle and then, centuries later, Gustav Freytag outlined it, they were thinking only of stage tragedies.

Plays, obviously, have a limited running time and, because of that limited running time, a limited number of scenes and characters. The plays Aristotle was familiar with, in fact, usually focused on the fate of a single central character, such as Oedipus or Medea or some other character from Greek history or mythology. He had never seen a novel, and certainly not a novel that works on an epic scale and incorporates lots of characters—more characters than you can fit into most plays. And yet the Aristotelian structure can be applied to everything from comedy to tragedy, from thrillers to love stories, from *Hamlet* to *The X-Men*.

And for writers who are just starting out, Freytag's Pyramid can serve as a set of training wheels, especially if you're uneasy about plotting. It's so common in our culture, in fact, than many writers adopt it instinctively, without really thinking about it. My own first novel, *The Wild Colonial Boy*, can easily be graphed on Freytag's Pyramid. And yet at the time I was writing it, I had never heard of Freytag's Pyramid. I was just feeling my way through the story organically, or so I thought. The fact that my book can easily be plotted along the pyramid is just proof of how deeply ingrained in our culture it is, as if it actually were something natural and instinctive.

Freytag's Pyramid seems so instinctive and ubiquitous because, in its simplest form, it is often the foundation for what I'm going to call a binary plot. I'm going to talk in more detail about binary plots in Lectures 13 and 14 when I talk about how to start and how to end a narrative. But for now, I'll just say that a binary plot is one in which an either/or question is posed near the start of the narrative and then answered at the climax or resolution of the narrative. Who is the murderer? Will the two lovers ever get together? Will Dorothy ever get back to Kansas?

There are all sorts of ways to complicate the answers to those questions which I'll explore in the later lectures. But while we're talking about the traditional plot as a whole, I want to emphasize that there are ways to complicate this kind of plot long before you ever get to the end. A binary plot structured according to Freytag's Pyramid doesn't have to be a simplistic or unsophisticated one.

For one thing, you can scale up the story to take in a lot more time and many more characters than Aristotle or Freytag had in mind. You can do this by weaving together several binary plots or Freytag Pyramids into one larger narrative.

Take the great 19th-century novel *Middlemarch* for example, by the writer Mary Ann Evans, who wrote under the pen name George Eliot. It does have a main character: Dorothea Brooke is a beautiful, intellectual, and naïvely idealistic young woman. And it has a central plotline: Dorothea enters into a marriage with a much older religious scholar named Casaubon, because she admires his intellect and his moral character.

The marriage, predictably, is a disaster, because Casaubon is a mediocre scholar and a passionless husband. It also fails because Dorothea is attracted to an intense young man her own age, named Will Ladislaw. This love triangle is the central story of *Middlemarch*, but it takes up no more than a third of the book. There are two other major romantic relationships in the book. These include another unhappy marriage, between an ambitious young doctor named Lydgate and a beautiful but shallow young woman named Rosamond, and a budding romance between Rosamond's charming but unreliable brother Fred and an earnest young woman named Mary.

There's nothing unconventional or avant-garde about *Middlemarch*. Instead, it convincingly demonstrates that a conventionally plotted novel can still be sophisticated and true to life. Dorothea's story is plainly the narrative spine of the book, with a clearly defined beginning, middle, and end, but her story is enriched and complicated by all the other plotlines, each of which has a similar structure. Apart from a few flashbacks, all these plotlines move forward chronologically, but they are threaded together and interlinked, and in many cases, the events in one plotline have an effect on the others.

The result is that it would be impossible to plot all of *Middlemarch* on only one Freytag's Pyramid. Instead of one main story, we have several, all woven together, each one with its own conflict, rising action, and resolution.

There's another way you can complicate a traditional plot, which I'm going to call the fractal plot. A fractal is a kind of mathematical pattern which is self-similar, which means that the pattern as a whole looks the same at a distance as it does up close, in detail. Fractals often appear in nature. Trees are an excellent example: the limbs of a tree coming off the trunk make the same basic pattern as the branches coming off each limb, and the twigs make the same pattern coming off each branch, and so on. You can even take it down to the level of individual leaves, where the veins spread across each leaf like the pattern of branches. The point is, no matter whether you look at the tree from across a field or peer very close up at a single leaf, you're always going to see essentially the same branching pattern. That's a fractal.

You can create the same effect with large-scale narratives, in novels that run in a series such as George R. R. Martin's *A Song of Ice and Fire*. There's a single binary question posed by Martin's books: Who will sit on the Iron Throne and be the king or queen of Westeros? But because the books involve so many rival factions and so many individual characters, this larger binary plot is made up of a huge number of smaller but no less compelling binary plots, at nearly every level.

Just below the level of the main binary question are several largish questions: Will the Starks defeat the Lannisters? Will the Night's Watch keep the White Walkers north of the Wall? Will Daenerys Targaryen bring her dragons back to Westeros? These separate plotlines play out over the course of several books.

Below that level are binary questions that play out over the course of a single book. For example, will Brienne of Tarth deliver Jaime Lannister to King's Landing? These single volume plotlines usually involve the fate of a single character or a pair of characters.

Within each book, each individual chapter can also be plotted out as a little Freytag Pyramid. In each chapter, the point-of-view character, whether it's Tyrion Lannister or Arya Stark or Daenerys Targaryen, is usually faced with a problem at the beginning of the chapter which is resolved or complicated by the end of the chapter.

Obviously, these little pyramids are not as complex or detailed as the overarching one that describes the whole narrative. For example, with many of the chapters, you already know the characters and the setting, so Martin can dispense with exposition. But even so, Martin's narrative uses a traditional narrative pyramid—situation, conflict, climax, resolution—at every level. There's one overarching pyramid that governs the whole story, but it's made up of lots of smaller pyramids. The plot of *A Song of Ice and Fire* is a fractal, in other words. You can see the same pattern at every level, whether it's the whole series, an individual book, or an individual chapter. It's pyramids all the way down.

If you've ever wondered, as I have, how Martin keeps all these plotlines and characters and all that backstory straight, I think this structure might be the key to it. By breaking the larger story down into smaller pieces, and breaking those pieces into even smaller pieces, it's possible for him to move ahead with a really huge narrative without getting lost or discouraged.

Now, for those of us who aren't planning to write a narrative that runs for 10,000 pages, there are other ways you can run interesting variations on the Freytag pyramid that don't involve keeping track of hundreds of characters. For example, you can create something I'll call a leapfrogging or contrapuntal narrative.

There's a lot of variations to this, but I'll limit it to four. The first is a narrative that tells a single story, but tells it from the points of view of multiple characters, each one taking a turn before handing the story off to another character. Perhaps the most famous example of this is William Faulkner's novel *As I Lay Dying*. This book tells the story of the Bundrens, a family of Mississippi farmers, and how they cope with the death of the family's mother, Addie. Before she died, Addie made her husband Anse promise that he'd bury her in the town of Jefferson, which is an inconvenient distance away. The novel is a blackly comic account of how the family carries her coffin all the way to town.

He could have told the story in a straightforward fashion with a third-person narration, but instead Faulkner decided to narrate the entire novel from the points of view of 15 different characters. Each character speaks in the first person, trading off with the other members of the family as well as with people they meet along the way. It's a technically adventurous book, but it tells an old-fashioned story, one that includes all the elements of the Freytag Pyramid. The difference is that each piece of the story is told by a different character.

Another type of leapfrogging or contrapuntal narrative you could try is one that tells several equally important stories that remain separate for much of the book, but which come together at the end for a single climax. In fact, *A Song of Ice and Fire* is a crazily complex version of this type of narrative, but let's look at a slightly simpler version.

There's no more old-fashioned a storyteller than J. R. R. Tolkien, and his masterpiece *The Lord of the Rings* builds to one of the biggest climaxes in in the history of literature, namely the eruption of Mount Doom in the third volume of the trilogy, *The Return of the King*.

But if you look at how he gets there, Tolkien is a surprisingly adventurous plotter. By the end of the first volume, *The Fellowship of the Ring*, the story essentially splits into three, equally important strands. You have the story of

Frodo, Sam, and Gollum making their way to Mordor; you have the story of Merry and Pippin's kidnapping by the orcs; and you have the story of Aragorn, Legolas, and Gimli as they search for Merry and Pippin.

Again, there's an overarching story here—namely, the quest to destroy the One Ring. You also have a single, overarching chronology. But while you're reading *The Lord of the Rings*, you're shifting back and forth among the three stories, which take place at vast distances from each other, even if they take place at the same time. If you outline the whole story, taking into account all of its various branches, you'll see a lot of smaller Freytag pyramids, the way you would with *A Song of Ice and Fire*.

Let me recommend two more styles of contrapuntal narrative. One is commonly used by modern historical novelists. The old-fashioned historical novel focuses exclusively on a period or an episode in the past, but a number of contemporary historical novels weave two main stories together, usually a story from the past and a story from the present, which are linked somehow.

A great example is A. S. Byatt's novel *Possession*. The historical half of the novel is about a passionate love affair between two Victorian poets, and the contemporary half is about a group of modern academics who are competing with each other to find out the truth about this long-rumored affair. It's a fundamentally an old-fashioned plot, and it builds to a very spooky climax in a graveyard at night. It's made up of two equal plotlines which feature characters who can never meet with each other, because they live in different centuries. And yet the outcome of one plot determines the outcome of the other. There are other parallelisms as well: The pair of lovers in the 19th century are matched by a pair of lovers among the competing academics in the 20th century, for example.

And here's one more type of leapfrogging narrative. As I've said before, the basic murder mystery is usually a contrapuntal story. It's the most basic kind of binary plot there is—who killed the victim?—but answer is often arrived at in a complicated way. There's the present-day story, which usually starts with the discovery of the body and follows the progress of the investigation, and then there's the story of the recent past, which ends with the murder.

Looked at chronologically, one story—that of the murder—ends just as the other story—that of the investigation—begins. But the way most murder mysteries are structured, you start with the investigation and work backwards into the story of the murder, learning it in bits and pieces, and often out of chronological order. Nobody would call most murder mysteries avant-garde, but even the most run-of-the-mill of them does interesting things with plot and chronology.

In the next lecture, I'm going to talk some more about the traditional plot, taking a look at ways you can rearrange or adapt the individual pieces of it, plus some other common techniques you can use to make the plot more complex and intriguing. We'll be looking at examples from Shirley Jackson, James Baldwin, Toni Morrison, and Flannery O'Connor. And in the lecture after that, I'll talk about the plotless or nontraditional narrative. These narratives work outside the lines of the Freytag Pyramid, but each one nevertheless has a structure. Every work of fiction has a structure even if it doesn't have a plot.

In the meantime, I'll leave you with a very simple, but very fruitful exercise: Take some of your favorite books or movies or television shows and see if you can graph them on Freytag's Pyramid. I think you'll find a couple of interesting things: One is how common a structure it is, but you'll also find how often the structure of a narrative is not a single pyramid, but a more complicated tangle of many pyramids, like the structures of *As I Lay Dying*, or *Middlemarch*, or *A Song of Ice and Fire*.

If you don't want a traditionally structured plot to become a straightjacket, you need to walk a fine line between being too predictable on the one hand, and disappointing the reader on the other. You want the reader to be satisfied and not feel betrayed by your climax, but on the other hand, you don't want them to see it coming. This particular structure has survived for a couple thousand years partly because it can be reassuring. But it has also survived because it has turned out to be remarkably adaptable, and capable of being bent into all sorts of interesting shapes without breaking.

Adding Complexity to Plots
Lecture 11

In the last two lectures, we saw that many narratives have the same basic structure, and we saw that varying this structure, such as rearranging the chronology or braiding several plotlines together, can make plotting both interesting and challenging. The fairly large-scale approaches that we've looked at affect the structure of the narrative as a whole, but in this lecture, we'll look at several more focused techniques that can be used on a smaller scale to make a plot more subtle and satisfying. These include suspense, flash-forwards, flashbacks, and foreshadowing. We'll also explore the important topic of withholding information in structuring plots.

Withholding Information and Suspense

- Because plotting seems daunting to many writers, it's important to keep in mind that one of the fundamental principles of plotting is the withholding of information. At the beginning of a plot, you want readers to know very little—just enough to intrigue them—but at the end, you want them to know everything. We might even say that plotting is the mechanism by which the writer decides what information to withhold early on, what information to reveal, and in what order to reveal it.

- Because all books and stories are read over time and can't be imbibed all at once, the most fundamental thing a writer withholds from the reader is how the story ends. In the simplest kind of stories, this is the main reason to keep reading: to find out how it all turns out. But there are other kinds of withholding that result in more subtle plots.

- Consider, for example, Shirley Jackson's well-known story "The Lottery." It's about a small New England village that holds a lottery once a year among all the adult villagers; the person who "wins" the lottery is then stoned to death by the others. The main reason this story works is that Jackson introduces the concept of the lottery in the first paragraph but withholds its purpose from the reader until the end.

- The surprise ending is a fairly simple kind of withholding; yet another kind is the creation of suspense. In a story that involves a surprise, the writer withholds information from the reader and sometimes from the characters, but when a writer creates suspense, he or she generally withholds information from the characters while letting the reader in on the secret.

- Other kinds of withholding have to do with rearranging the elements of the traditional plot; these techniques are perhaps not so much about withholding information as they are about simply presenting it to the reader in an unusual order.

  o As John Gardner points out in *The Art of Fiction*, exposition can take place at any point in the narrative, but in most cases, you want to save a good deal of your exposition for later. At the beginning, you want to say enough about the situation and the major characters to intrigue the reader, but you don't want to explain too much. Parceling out exposition only as needed is an approach that often feels more natural than dropping all the information on the reader's doorstep at once; in many cases, you are providing the information to the reader at the same time that the characters are learning it.

  o In popular fiction, the inciting action—the moment conflict is introduced into the story and gets the plot going—often comes at the very beginning, before the exposition. A good example is the opening of the movie *Jaws*, when a young woman goes for a midnight swim and is eaten by the shark. Only after that do we meet Chief Brody, the first of the three main characters, and learn about the island community of Amity. The traditional elements of the Freytag pyramid are present but in a different order.

  o In fact, you can even structure a story so that you give away the climax in the first few moments, as in James Baldwin's novel *Giovanni's Room*. If we lay out the events of this story in chronological order, the results look like the Freytag pyramid. But Baldwin shrewdly gives us the most dramatic element right at the start, which has the effect of intriguing us, making us want to know exactly how things turned out so badly for the characters who have just been introduced.

Flash-Forwards and Flashbacks

- Both flash-forwards and flashbacks are scenes that take place out of the main chronological order of the story. A flash-forward is a glimpse of something that will happen to the characters in the future, at the end of or perhaps even after the main narrative, and a flashback is a scene that takes place before the main plotline started.

- Flash-forwards are often used in first-person narratives, with the narrator giving the reader a glimpse of an intriguing outcome before returning to the beginning and showing how the story worked its way up to that point. One famous first-person flash-forward is the beginning of Billy Wilder's great film about Hollywood, *Sunset Boulevard*, which opens with the narrator essentially starting his story from beyond the grave.

© Rasmus Rasmussen/iStock/Thinkstock.

Many detective stories consist largely of flashbacks as the detective or investigator hears from witnesses about the situation that led up to the murder.

- But using a flash-forward as a teaser to hook the reader at the beginning of a plot can occasionally come across as mechanical. You can use flash-forward elsewhere in a narrative, even at the end, skipping a period of time to show how the characters turn out years after the main chronology of the story. An effective example of this approach is Alice Munro's short story "The Beggar Maid."

- Flashbacks, of course, are much more common. Many detective stories employ flashbacks, but they can also be used to great effect in other genres or in more mainstream fiction. Indeed, flashbacks can often be used as replacements for, or in combination with, exposition, especially when you're trying to present the reader with important or dramatic information about the previous history of a character. Toni Morrison uses this technique to show the dramatic birth of a character in her novel *Beloved*.

Foreshadowing
- A flash-forward is usually a fully evoked and dramatized scene set in the future, but foreshadowing is a hint or a series of hints that a writer plants in the narrative early on to prepare the way for what comes later. In many cases, the success of the narrative's resolution depends on how carefully the writer has prepared the way for it. You want the resolution to be unpredictable but satisfying, and pulling that off requires a balance between withholding information and revealing just enough so that the reader doesn't feel cheated at the end.

- Some foreshadowing is fairly mechanical, such as making sure you introduce all the characters, context, and props you need for a story to pay off. The Russian playwright Anton Chekhov famously said that if you show the audience a pistol on the wall in the first act, then that pistol must go off in the third act. This is a fundamental insight about creating plot.
    - Part of what Chekhov means is simply that you have to play fair with the audience: You can't have a character suddenly waving a pistol around without giving some hint early on that waving a pistol was at least a possibility.

    - But Chekhov is also saying that you need to pay attention to what details you include and when you include them. If you show a pistol on the wall, and nobody uses it, you've set up an expectation in the reader, then thwarted it.

- Chekhov's rule about the pistol is also an implicit reminder that a plot is not like real life. In our ordinary lives, we see countless details every day, and we decide in the moment, usually subconsciously, what's important and what's not. But a narrative is not like real life: Every detail has a meaning and is included for a specific purpose; you must think about what details are important, what details you can ignore or leave out, and in what order you introduce them.

- One example of foreshadowing is found in Flannery O'Connor's short story "A Good Man Is Hard to Find," about a southern family that encounters a criminal on a road trip to Florida. At the beginning of the story, the family's grandmother tries to talk her son out of going by pointing out a story she's read in the newspaper about a criminal on the loose and headed toward Florida.

  - The first time you read the story, this episode comes across as nothing more than gentle family comedy, evoking an old woman's groundless paranoia and her son's taciturn refusal to be manipulated.

  - Indeed, most of the story is a comic account of the family's road trip, complete with bickering children and a colorful episode at a barbecue shack. It isn't until the final few pages, when the family encounters the criminal, that you realize how efficiently detailed and tightly constructed it is. Without that bit of foreshadowing in the first paragraph, the story simply wouldn't have the same effect.

- Another example is found in Joseph Conrad's *Nostromo*, a novel about a revolution in a fictional South American country. An Englishman named Charles Gould owns a silver mine in this country, and in the days before the revolution, he decides to hide his stockpile of silver so that the revolutionaries can't get it. To do this, he puts the silver on a barge, which he entrusts to an Italian sailor named Nostromo and a young journalist named Martin Decoud. They take the silver to an island off the coast to keep it safe from the rebels. In the end, the effect the silver has on Nostromo becomes the central moral dilemma of the book.

o The opening chapter of *Nostromo* is a masterpiece of exposition, consisting mainly of a long, evocative description of this fictional country's geography. In the third paragraph, Conrad relates a local legend about two foreigners who, years ago, ventured onto a remote peninsula in search of some legendary buried gold and were never heard from again. According to the legend, the ghosts of the two foreigners are still guarding the treasure they discovered: "Their souls cannot tear themselves away from their bodies."

Suggested Reading

Baldwin, *Giovanni's Room.*

Conrad, *Nostromo.*

Gardner, *The Art of Fiction.*

Jackson, "The Lottery."

Morrison, *Beloved.*

Munro, "The Beggar Maid."

O'Connor, "A Good Man Is Hard to Find."

Writing Exercise

1. Choose a particular situation and tell it first as a surprise, then as a passage of suspense. If you want to use a ticking bomb, you can, but the scene doesn't have to be violent—in fact, it can be a ticking bomb equivalent. Consider our story from the first lecture about Sarah and Brad. In the surprise version, you might tell it from Brad's point of view, in which case Sarah's announcement that she wants a divorce is as much as a surprise to the reader as it is to Brad. But you might also tell it from Sarah's point of view, in which case the reader would know from the start that she wants a divorce, and the scene becomes one of suspense as we wait anxiously for Brad to learn the truth.

Adding Complexity to Plots
Lecture 11—Transcript

In my first lecture on plot, I talked about the difference between story and plot. In the second lecture, I explained that many narratives have the same basic Aristotelian structure of situation, conflict, and resolution. This structure is also known as Freytag's Pyramid, with its separate stages of exposition, inciting incident, rising action, climax, falling action, resolution, and denouement.

I also said that you can play interesting variations on this basic plot structure that makes plotting both interesting and challenging. The underlying story in Joseph Conrad's *Lord Jim* fits Freytag's Pyramid fairly well if you lay it out chronologically, but the way Conrad rearranges that chronology helps make *Lord Jim* one of the greatest novels ever written.

And even if a narrative moves forward more or less chronologically, the way *Middlemarch* and *A Song of Ice and Fire* do, you can still complicate and enrich the plot by braiding together several stories or plotlines, or by leapfrogging separate narratives so that they come together in the end.

So far, I've been talking about the structure of a narrative as a whole, but in this lecture, I want to talk about techniques that you can use on a smaller scale to make a plot more subtle and satisfying. These include suspense, flash-forwards, flashbacks, and foreshadowing.

But before I get started, I want to introduce a sweeping generalization that may make plotting seem less daunting to you. As I've said earlier, John Gardner wrote that plotting is one of the hardest things a writer does. I know from my own experience that many talented writers are often more intimidated by the idea of constructing a plot than they are by any other facet of fiction writing. And what often intimidates them is not that they don't know how to get started or what they want to say, but that they have so much they want to get across that they're worried about bogging the narrative down.

So, here's my sweeping pronouncement: One of the fundamental principles of plotting is the withholding of information. At the beginning of a plot, you want to the reader to know very little, but at the end, you want the reader to know everything. You might even say this is the essence of every plot that ever existed: A plot is the mechanism by which the writer decides what information to withhold, what information to reveal, and in what order.

In many instances the writer himself doesn't know as he starts how a story is going to turn out, but he certainly knows by time he's finished writing it. A couple of lectures ago, I said that my high school English teacher, Mrs. Giltner, defined literature as the creation of order out of chaos. And way back in my lecture about evocation, I said that fiction suggests reality by choosing the most evocative details, rather than trying to include every single detail about a character, a setting, or a situation. If writing fiction was just a matter of recording all the facts as they happen, then trial transcripts and surveillance videos would be the greatest works of art ever made.

But in fiction we're trying to create meaning out of this relentless stream of events, so you have to choose what to keep, what to leave out, and what order you put them in. Since all books and stories are read over time and can't be imbibed all at once, the most fundamental thing a writer withholds from the reader is how the story ends. In the simplest kind of stories, the ones that E. M. Forster said only answer the question, "And then?" this is the main reason to keep reading, to find out how it all turns out.

But there are other kinds of withholding that result in more subtle plots. Take, for example, Shirley Jackson's famous story, "The Lottery." Most American high school students have read this story at least once. It's about a small New England village which, once a year, for reasons that are never explained in the story, holds a lottery for all the adults in the village. The person who "wins" the lottery, so to speak, is stoned to death by all the others. Assuming you've read it before and I haven't just ruined the ending for you, you will remember what a shock it is to read this story for the first time. I was introduced to it in a high school English class where the teacher had us all read it silently to ourselves, and you could tell when each reader "got" what was happening in the story by the separate little gasps all around the room.

It's a beautifully crafted story on a lot of levels, but the main reason it works is that the author introduces the concept of the lottery in the very first paragraph, but she withholds from the reader what the lottery is actually for.

What makes reading "The Lottery" especially gut-wrenching on a first reading is that the reader is the only person who doesn't know what's going on. The author certainly does, as do all the characters in the story. The story lulls you with its measured, uninflected evocation of the life of a seemingly normal country town, and then it springs the horror on you at the end. This kind of withholding puts the reader in a very lonely place. It's as if you're standing in a group of people you've known all your life, and you suddenly wake up to the fact that they're capable of killing you in cold blood.

There's one other thing I want to point out about Jackson's withholding of information in "The Lottery": this technique is not the same thing as an unreliable narrator, which we'll talk about in a later lecture. The narration of "The Lottery" is reliable: Everything the story tells us is true; it never misrepresents anything. It's just that the story withholds the single most important fact.

That's a pretty simple kind of withholding, the surprise ending. Yet another kind of withholding is the creation of suspense. In a story that involves a surprise, the writer withholds information from the reader, and sometimes from the characters. In a story that creates suspense, the writer withholds information from the characters, but lets the reader in on the secret.

Probably the most famous explanation of the difference between surprise and suspense comes from the great English film director, Alfred Hitchcock. In the mid-1960s, he gave a famous series of interviews to the French director Francois Truffaut. Hitchcock used the example of placing a ticking bomb under a table while two characters are talking. If you don't show the audience the bomb, then they will be as surprised as the characters are when it goes off. This, Hitchcock said, can be a very satisfying effect. In fact, one of Hitchcock's most famous sequences, the shower scene in *Psycho*, is exactly that sort of surprise.

But Hitchcock also says in the interview that he prefers suspense to surprise. In order to make that same situation suspenseful—two people talking while a bomb ticks down under the table—all you have to do is show the audience the bomb at the start of the scene without showing it to the characters. The result is that the audience feels anxious on behalf of the characters, who continue their conversation with no inkling of the danger they're in.

As Hitchcock himself put it, "In the first case we have given the public fifteen seconds of surprise at the moment of the explosion. In the second case we have provided them with fifteen minutes of suspense."

There are other kinds of withholding that have to do with rearranging of the elements of the traditional plot. These techniques are perhaps not so much about withholding information as they are simply about presenting it to the reader in an unusual order. Let's take exposition as an example.

As John Gardner points out in *The Art of Fiction*, exposition can take place at any point in the narrative. In fact, in most cases, you want to save a good deal of your exposition for later. At the beginning of a narrative, you want to explain enough to intrigue the reader and keep her reading, but you don't want to explain too much.

There are some exceptions to this practice: Writers of science fiction or historical fiction sometimes include a passage or a chapter at the beginning of a narrative in which they tell the reader everything she needs to know about the world of the story. This sort of exposition has an unlovely name, the *info dump*. These chapters can occasionally be tedious to read, even if they are the most efficient way of explaining a complicated world so that the writer can get the story going.

On the other hand, most mainstream writers, and a lot of science fiction authors and historical novelists, prefer to provide exposition as needed, and only then. If you manage to sneak the exposition in without the reader noticing that it's exposition, it can feel more natural than dropping it all on the reader's doorstep all at once. In many cases you can introduce exposition seamlessly by providing the information to the reader at the same time as the characters are learning it.

Much of the traditional mystery novel, for example, consists of backstory and exposition which gets parceled out in small doses. It would spoil the mystery to provide all the exposition at the start, because that would require saying who the murderer is. Instead, the reader helps to solve the mystery alongside the detective. Indeed, it's the withholding of backstory and exposition that makes a mystery novel a mystery novel.

Or consider the inciting action, which you may recall is the moment that conflict is introduced into a story and gets the plot going. In popular fiction, the inciting action often comes at the very beginning, even before the exposition. A good example is the opening of the movie *Jaws*. The first thing that happens in the movie is that a young woman at a party goes for a midnight swim on the beach and gets eaten by a shark. Only then are we introduced to Chief Brody, the first of three main characters, and only after we meet Chief Brody are we introduced to the island community of Amity. And later on, when the rising action of the story is well underway, we are introduced to the other two main characters: Hooper, the young marine biologist, and Quint, the grizzled old fisherman. In other words, we get the inciting incident in the first five minutes, then we get the exposition, and we don't even meet the third major character until halfway through the film. All the traditional elements of Freytag's Pyramid are there, but in a different order.

In fact, you can even structure a story so that you give away the climax in the first few moments—in other words, you put the climax ahead of everything else. The novel *Giovanni's Room* by James Baldwin is structured this way. *Giovanni's Room* is the story of a young American named David, who is living in Paris in the early 1950s and wrestling with his own sexuality. As a teenager, he had a sexual relationship with another boy, but he resists thinking of himself as gay. In fact, in the years since, he has gotten involved with a young woman. Meanwhile, living in Paris, he falls in love with another man, an Italian named Giovanni, who works as a bartender in a place owned by a Frenchman named Guillaume. Without going into all the details, suffice it to say that Giovanni ends up murdering Guillaume, that he is sentenced to death by guillotine, and that David feels responsible for Giovanni's fate. The novel is told in the first person by David.

Recalling Forster's distinction between story and plot, please note that the story of *Giovanni's Room* starts chronologically years before, with David recalling his childhood and teenage years in flashback. The plot, however, starts on the evening before Giovanni's execution, which is nearly the end of the story. By page two, we know that David and Giovanni had been lovers, and by page three we know that Giovanni is going to be executed the following morning. So, after only three pages, we know that David and Giovanni had an affair, that it led to disaster, and that David is wracked with guilt over it.

If you lay out the events of this story in chronological order—as opposed to its structure as a plot—it looks like a Freytag Pyramid. But instead of following that structure, Baldwin very shrewdly gives us the most dramatic element right from the start, namely the upcoming execution. This has the effect of intriguing the reader, making him want to know exactly how things turned out so badly.

In fact, Baldwin does an even more interesting thing later on: Even though he opens the novel by telling us that Giovanni is going to be executed, he never actually shows us the climax. The night before the execution, David is miles away from the prison in a house in the French countryside. Having promised that he would be present for the execution, David loses his nerve and refuses to go to the prison. In the last few pages of the book, he imagines what Giovanni's execution is like, but he doesn't actually witness it. The resolution of the plot, on the very last page, is David's descent into guilt, self-doubt, and self-recrimination.

It might seem that Baldwin isn't actually withholding anything in *Giovanni's Room*. After all, he's giving away the ending in the first three pages. But I think he's actually engaging in a more subtle kind of withholding—that is, he's withholding the full effect and meaning of Giovanni's impending death on David, which we don't really understand until the book's final pages. If you look at it as a conventional binary plot—will David and Giovanni find happiness together?—the book blows it in the first chapter. But if you look at it as a more subtle kind of binary narrative—will David accept his share of responsibility for Giovanni's predicament?—the novel works wonderfully well.

As much as I love "The Lottery" and the films of Alfred Hitchcock, their kind of withholding is more mechanical than what Baldwin is doing in *Giovanni's Room*. In "The Lottery," Shirley Jackson withholds what happens at the climax, while in *Giovanni's Room*, Baldwin withholds why the climax happens. In each case, the reader is compelled by the writer to read the whole narrative to get to the truth. In fact, what Baldwin is doing in the opening of *Giovanni's Room* is an especially extreme example of a flash-forward. As the name implies, a flash-forward is the opposite of a flashback. Both flash-forwards and flashbacks are scenes that take place out of the main chronological order of the story. A flash-forward is a glimpse of something that will happen to the characters in the future, at the end of and perhaps even after the main narrative, while a flashback is a scene that usually takes place before the main plotline started.

Flash-forwards are often used in first-person narratives. The narrator gives the reader a glimpse of an intriguing or dire outcome, as in *Giovanni's Room*, and then returns to the beginning and shows how the story worked its way up to that point.

Another famous first-person flash-forward is the beginning of Billy Wilder's great film about Hollywood, *Sunset Boulevard*. This film opens with the narrator, a screenwriter named Joe Gillis, starting to tell his story from beyond the grave, as we see his dead body floating in a swimming pool. The rest of the film then backs up and shows us how he ended up in the drink.

But flash-forwards don't necessarily have to appear only at the beginning of a plot. In fact, using a flash-forward as a kind of teaser to hook the reader can occasionally come across as a rather mechanical effect. Remember that you can use a flash-forward anywhere in a narrative. You can even do it at the end, when it's rather like fast-forwarding a video, skipping the intervening time to show how the characters turn out years after the main chronology of the story.

A very effective example is Alice Munro's long short story, "The Beggar Maid." This story is about Rose, a young working-class woman from a small Ontario town, who goes away to college, where she is courted by Patrick, an awkward young man from Vancouver who happens to be the heir to a fortune. It's a 33-page story, and the first 30 pages take place more or less chronologically, showing the awkward courtship of Rose and Patrick over the course of a year or two. The last four pages of the story fast-forward through their disastrous marriage and acrimonious divorce. The story ends in a final scene years later, when they simply glance at each other in passing in the Toronto airport, and Rose realizes for the first time just how much Patrick despises her.

The power of that devastating final scene comes, in part, from everything we know of their cumulative history. But the scene's power is also partly a product of that giant leap in chronology, showing us how two characters who have not met in years can still feel instantaneous rage at the sight of each other.

Flashbacks, of course, are much more common. As I said a few minutes ago, detective stories tend to be made up mostly of flashbacks, as the detective or investigator hears from witnesses about the situation that led up to the murder. But flashbacks can also be used to great effect in other genres, or in mainstream fiction. For one thing, flashbacks can often be used as replacements for, or in combination with, exposition. They are especially useful when you're trying to present the reader with necessary information about the previous history of a character. Flashbacks are often used in preference to a simple piece of exposition if the information about the character is particularly important or dramatic.

For example, early in Toni Morrison's novel *Beloved*, a young girl named Denver recalls what her mother told her about the circumstances of Denver's birth. To put it simply, Denver's mother, Sethe, was an escaped slave on the run when she gave birth to Denver in a patch of wild onions on the Kentucky side of the Ohio River, just across the river from freedom.

It's an important piece of information about Denver's past, and about Sethe's struggle to be free. Morrison could easily have taken care of it in a brief, expository summary, but instead, she has Denver remember her mother telling her the story of her own birth. This then segues effortlessly into a third-person account of the birth itself, showing it in graphic and powerful detail.

By using a dramatic flashback instead of a simple expository description, Morrison is emphasizing how important this episode is in the lives of Sethe and her daughter and how important it is to the rest of the plot. The main narrative of *Beloved* takes place in the years after the Civil War, but many of the scenes are flashbacks to the lives of its main characters before the war, when they were still slaves. Much of the power of the book comes from showing us how the past haunts the present, and that effect comes in large part from Morrison's frequent and skillful use of flashbacks.

This brings me now to foreshadowing, which is not the same thing as a flash-forward. A flash-forward is a fully-evoked and dramatized scene set in the future, but foreshadowing is a hint or a series of hints that a writer plants early in the narrative in order to prepare the way for what comes later. In many instances, the success of a narrative's resolution depends on how carefully the writer has prepared the way. Simply put, you want the resolution to be unpredictable but satisfying. And pulling that off requires a balance between withholding information, so that the reader can't predict what's going to happen, and revealing just enough information so that the reader doesn't feel cheated when the ending is revealed.

In other words, you want the end of the story to feel both surprising but inevitable. The response you want from the reader is, at the same moment, "Oh my God!" and "Of course!" You want the reader to think, "I should have seen that coming," but without actually allowing her to actually see it coming.

This is where foreshadowing comes in. Some of it is fairly mechanical. You want to make sure that you introduce all the characters, the context, and even the props that you need for a story to pay off. We've all felt cheated by stories or movies where the writer or filmmaker pulls something out of his hat at the last moment to make the ending work. But we've all also experienced narratives where everything suddenly and very satisfyingly makes sense and all the pieces of the narrative click into place.

On a number of occasions and in a number of different ways, the Russian playwright and short story writer Anton Chekhov famously said that if you show the audience a pistol on the wall in the first act, then that pistol has to go off in the third act. This has been quoted so often that it has become a cliché. But, like many clichés about writing, it's fundamentally true, and it is, indeed, a fundamental insight about creating a plot.

Part of what Chekhov means is simply that you have to play fair with the audience or the reader. You can't have a character suddenly waving a pistol around without giving us some hint early on that waving a pistol around was at least a possibility.

But he's also saying that you need to pay attention to what details you include, and when you include them. If you show a pistol on the wall, and nobody uses it, you've set up an expectation in the reader and then thwarted it—unless, of course, you intended it as a red herring, which is basically an act of false foreshadowing. But if that's not the case, then showing us the pistol and then never having it turn up again is just as bad as producing a pistol out of thin air.

Chekhov's rule about the pistol has an even deeper meaning, though, which lies its implicit reminder that a plot is not like real life. In our ordinary lives we see countless details pass before us every day—people, things, the weather, the news, all of it. In real life, we have to decide on the fly, usually subconsciously, what's important and what's not. But a narrative, as I keep reminding you, is not like real life. Every detail has a meaning; every detail has been placed there by the writer for a specific purpose. And as the writer, you have to think about what details are important, what details you can ignore or leave out, and in what order you introduce them. That is what foreshadowing is all about.

Let's look at two examples. The first comes from Flannery O'Connor's famous short story, "A Good Man Is Hard to Find," which is one of the most unsettling stories in American fiction. It's about a Southern family who take off on a fateful road trip to Florida. The story is told mostly, though not entirely, from the point of view of the family's unnamed grandmother.

The very first line is, "The grandmother didn't want to go to Florida." In the same paragraph, she tries to talk her son, Bailey, out of going, by pointing out a story she's just read in the newspaper:

"Now look here, Bailey," she said, "see here, read this," and she stood with one hand on her thin hip and the other rattling the newspaper at his bald head. "Here this fellow that calls himself The Misfit is aloose from the Federal Pen and headed toward Florida and you read here what it says he did to those people. Just you read it. I wouldn't take my children in any direction with a criminal like that aloose in it. I couldn't answer to my conscience if I did."

Now, spoiler alert, the grandmother and her family take off for Florida anyway, and along the way they do indeed run into The Misfit. Things do not go well.

But the first time you read this story, if nobody has given away the ending the way I just did, this little episode in the very first paragraph comes across as nothing more than gentle family comedy. All O'Connor seems to be doing is evoking an old woman's groundless paranoia, her clumsy attempt to manipulate her son, and her son's taciturn refusal to be manipulated. Indeed, until The Misfit himself turns up about two thirds of the way into the story, "A Good Man Is Hard to Find" is basically a comic account of the family's road trip, complete with bickering children and a colorful episode at a barbecue shack.

It isn't until the final few pages, when the story closes around your heart like a steel trap, that you realize how efficiently detailed and tightly constructed it is. Without that bit of foreshadowing in the first paragraph, the story simply wouldn't have the same effect. At the beginning of "A Good Man Is Hard to Find," O'Connor hides a hint of menace that we don't even realize is menace until it's too late to avoid it.

Let's take another, less spoilerish example. Joseph Conrad's *Nostromo* is an epic novel about a revolution in a fictional South American country called Costaguana. The main economic asset of Costaguana is a silver mine owned by an Englishman named Charles Gould. In the days before the revolution, Gould decides to hide his entire stockpile of silver so that the revolutionaries can't get their hands on it. To do this, he puts the silver put on a barge, which he entrusts to an Italian sailor named Nostromo and a young journalist named Martin Decoud. These two men take the silver to an island off the coast of Costaguana to keep it safe from the rebels.

Nostromo is a big, complicated novel with many characters, and like *Lord Jim*, it has a fractured chronology, but that's the central episode in the book. The silver is a metaphor not only for Gould's power as a colonialist, it's a symbol for the corruptibility of human beings. The title character, Nostromo, is admired above all for his reliability and trustworthiness, and in the end, the effect that the silver has on him becomes the central moral dilemma of the book.

Now, the opening chapter of *Nostromo* is a masterpiece of exposition, consisting mainly of a long, evocative description of this fictional country's geography. But starting in the third paragraph, Conrad tells us a local legend about two foreigners, whom he identifies as "Americanos, perhaps, but gringos of some sort for certain." Many years ago, they ventured onto a remote peninsula in search of some legendary buried gold and were never heard from again.

Their story goes on for two more paragraphs, ending with this:

> The two gringos, spectral and alive, are believed to be dwelling to this day among the rocks, under the fatal spell of their success. Their souls cannot tear themselves away from their bodies mounting guard over the discovered treasure. They are now rich and hungry and thirsty—a strange theory of tenacious gringo ghosts suffering in their starved and parched flesh of defiant heretics, where a Christian would have renounced and been released.

Now, the first time you read *Nostromo*, this reads as if it's just a bit of folklore, thrown in by Conrad for local color and nothing more. It isn't until you read the novel a second or third time that you realize that this episode, which is only a couple hundred words or so, is a foreshadowing of the entire story.

Specifically, it foreshadows the fates of Nostromo and Decoud. After depositing the silver on an island off the coast of Costaguana, Nostromo swims back to shore, leaving Decoud behind with the silver. While Nostromo becomes a hero by helping to defeat the revolution, Decoud, all alone on the lonely island, succumbs to despair. Finally he rows out to sea, weighs his body down with two ingots of silver, and shoots himself. Nostromo returns too late, and finds that Decoud is gone, and probably dead.

Because he believes he isn't getting as much credit for his heroism as he deserves, Nostromo tells everyone that the silver was lost at sea. Then, for the rest of his life, he slowly gets rich off the treasure, by retrieving it one ingot at a time. At the end of the book, in a rather melodramatic turn of events, he loses his life because of the silver.

So you can see that, by the end of the novel, the brief story of the Americans who haunt a missing treasure in the first chapter has happened again, in much more detail, with Decoud and Nostromo. Just like the two gringos, they experience both a spiritual and physical death because of treasure. This is an expert bit of foreshadowing, giving us not only the plot in a nutshell, but the novel's central theme. Even if you never read the novel more than once, this story registers in your subconscious and helps to prepare the way for the more complicated version that comes later on.

In this lecture, we've only scratched the surface of the variations you can play on the traditional plot. There are many, many more ways to vary a traditional plot than I've got time to explore here. But, as I've said, while the traditional plot is very sturdy and adaptable, it's not the only way to structure a narrative. In the next lecture, I'm going to do a brisk trot through the epiphany short story and the modernist and postmodernist novel, to show you some other ways that writers have structured fiction. We'll be looking specifically at Anton Chekhov's short story "The Kiss," James Joyce's story "The Dead," and Virginia Woolf's novel, *Mrs. Dalloway*.

In the meantime, here's a simple exercise to explore one of the techniques I talked about in this lecture. Take a particular situation and tell it first as a surprise. Then take the same situation and retell it as a passage of suspense. If you want to use a ticking bomb, have at it, but it doesn't have to be violent— in fact, it can be a ticking bomb equivalent. Take the story I concocted for the first lecture, about Sarah and Brad. In the surprise version, you might tell it from Brad's point of view, in which case Sarah's announcement that she wants a divorce is as much as a surprise to the reader as it is to Brad. But you might also tell it from Sarah's point of view, in which case the reader would know from the start that she wants a divorce. Then the scene becomes one of suspense, as we wait anxiously for Brad to learn the truth. Give it a try; you might have some fun with it.

Structuring a Narrative without a Plot
Lecture 12

E very work of fiction has a structure, but not every work of fiction has a plot, at least not a traditional plot. Even if it doesn't have a plot, however, every work of fiction has, or ought to have, something the writer John Gardner called "profluence," which he defined as the feeling that you're getting somewhere when you're reading a work of fiction. Whether or not a story has a plot, something should change over the course of reading it, if not in the story itself, at least in the heart or mind of the reader. In this lecture, we'll explore a few ways to structure fiction that don't involve using the Freytag pyramid or the traditional plot.

Chekhov's "The Kiss"

- The birth of the modern short story took place in the late 19th century with the Russian writer Anton Chekhov. In his story "The Kiss," the officers of an artillery regiment training in the Russian countryside are invited by a local landowner to spend the evening at his country house. During the evening, the main character, a shy officer named Ryabovitch, wanders into a dark room and receives a kiss from a woman who has mistaken him for someone else.

  o The woman flees the room, and Ryabovitch is unable to discover who kissed him. For days afterward, Ryabovitch fantasizes about the encounter, inventing a whole future life with this woman, even though he doesn't know who she is.

  o At the end of the story, when his regiment returns to the same town and the landowner invites the officers back to his house, Ryabovitch loses his nerve and stays behind in the barracks.

- "The Kiss" reads like a conventional story; the scenes are laid out in chronological order, with no flashbacks or flash-forwards. Yet the story doesn't come to a climax or resolve in the same way as a traditional story. Ryabovitch does not develop as a character. He has a brief glimpse of a more exciting life, but his only response is in his lonely imagination, and he does nothing about it.

- The genius of the story is not so much that it's plotless as that it suggests a potential conflict, then refuses to resolve it. Chekhov sets up a binary question—who kissed Ryabovitch, and will he ever find her again?—and technically, he answers the question—no, Ryabovitch won't find the girl. That disappointment is the point of the story: The real question is not whether Ryabovitch gets the girl, but whether he can rise above his own timid nature; that is a much more profound and unsettling question.

- Even though nothing "happens" in "The Kiss" in the traditional sense, something profound changes over the course of the story—not in the character or the situation but in the reader.

Joyce's "The Dead"
- "The Dead" is the final story in James Joyce's only volume of short fiction, *Dubliners*. Instead of a conventional climax or resolution, the stories in this book rely on what Joyce called an *epiphany*. In religious terms, the word *epiphany* means a deep spiritual insight or realization brought about by divine intervention; Joyce used it to refer to an individual experiencing a moment of profound, sometimes life-changing, self-understanding.

- "The Dead" is the longest story in *Dubliners*, and like "The Kiss," it reads conventionally; it's a chronological account of a party in Dublin in January 1904. Most of the story is told from the point of view of a successful middle-aged man named Gabriel Conroy. Near the end of the party, Gabriel witnesses his wife, Gretta, listening raptly to a singer performing an old Irish folksong.
    - In the cab on the way to the hotel room they've booked for the night, Gabriel experiences a powerful lust for his wife, but when they're alone in the room, he realizes that Gretta is upset. She tells him that hearing the folksong at the party has reminded her of a boy named Michael Furey who loved her when she was a young woman. Furey used to sing the same

song to her, and he probably died because he stood in the rain, waiting outside her window.

- o Gabriel realizes that to make love to his wife at this moment would be akin to an assault; thus, after she falls asleep, he simply lies awake in the dark next to her. Gabriel's epiphany is his realization that Gretta has never loved him as much she loved Furey, and he further realizes that he has never loved her, or anyone else, the way Furey loved Gretta. But instead of feeling rage or disappointment, Gabriel experiences a moment of expansive generosity for his wife, for himself, for Furey, and in Joyce's famous phrase, for all the living and the dead.

- You might think that Joyce could have evoked Gabriel's epiphany in a shorter story, one that focused only on the aftermath of the party, but that simply wouldn't have worked.
  - o The first 40 pages of the story, a chronological account of the party, are structurally essential to Joyce's purpose. Not only does he include details about Gabriel that pay off only at the end, but he shows us how a long-married couple present themselves to their friends and acquaintances in a public setting. This makes their moment of unexpected intimacy at the end even more poignant and piercing.

  - o We need to see, at length and in detail, the life that Gabriel thought he was living in order to understand his shock when he realizes that nothing he thought about his life was true.

- At first glance, the structure of "The Dead" is similar to that of "The Kiss." Both are chronological, both are centered on a party, and both are essentially a series of evocative scenes that do not make up a conventional plot. The final effect of "The Dead," however, is different from that of the "The Kiss" because Gabriel comes to a new understanding of himself and Ryabovitch does not.

- Think back to the distinction E. M. Forster made between a story and plot: that a story tells us what happened, but a plot tells us why. Then think back to how a conventional plot does this: by posing a question in the form of a conflict, then answering the question by resolving the conflict.
    - The structural brilliance of "The Dead" is that it does not set up a conflict at the start of the story; instead, it holds your interest by giving you a plotless but entertaining account of its main character and his social situation; it then blindsides you at the end with a conflict that neither you nor the main character even knew existed.

    - The conclusion of "The Dead" is powerful partly because of what it says—that happiness is rare and precarious and sometimes founded on a lie—but it's also powerful because of the way Joyce plays with our expectations. He gives us what looks like an ordinary day for its main character, then surprises both Gabriel and the reader with something extraordinary.

Woolf's *Mrs. Dalloway*

- The use of everyday moments to build a picture of a world at a particular moment in order to reveal something profound also lies behind Virginia Woolf's novel *Mrs. Dalloway*. The novel is set over a single day in London in the early 1920s and focuses on a 52-year-old woman named Clarissa Dalloway as she prepares for a party at her home that evening. Other major characters include

Virginia Woolf's stream-of-consciousness technique in *Mrs. Dalloway* requires more concentration than following a conventional plot, but it provides a more vivid evocation of a particular moment in time in the lives of the characters.

Peter Walsh, a former suitor of Clarissa's who has just returned from five years' service in India, and Septimus Warren Smith, a veteran of World War I who is suffering from shell-shock.

- There are only a few conventionally dramatic moments in *Mrs. Dalloway*, including the suicide of Septimus Smith and the meeting of Clarissa and Peter Walsh after many years, as well as a few flashbacks. Except for the death of Septimus, it's a fairly unremarkable day.

- Given that there's no conflict, no climax, and nothing to resolve at the end, what gives the book its structure? Instead of using a plot to structure the novel, Woolf uses two techniques, one of which governs the overall shape of the novel, and the other, its movement within and between scenes.

  o The overall shape comes from the fact that the novel is set over the course of one day, which allows Woolf to limit the number of incidents in the book and the scope of the characters.

  o The technique Woolf uses to make the novel flow from moment to moment is stream of consciousness. As you recall, when we read the passage in which Clarissa looks in a shop window, her thoughts shifted quickly and subtly from the world around her to her memories of girlhood, the last days of her uncle, and her relationship with her daughter. Each brief moment in that passage tells us something about Clarissa that we didn't know before. In other words, it is profluent enough without Clarissa having to confront or resolve a conflict.

- Perhaps the most remarkable feature of *Mrs. Dalloway* is the way Woolf effortlessly, often suddenly, shifts the narrative's point of view among a number of characters. These shifts also provide the sort of narrative momentum that other, more conventional books rely on plot to provide. They enable Woolf to evoke a particular moment in time and in the lives of her characters far more vividly than in a conventionally plotted narrative.

Postmodernist Techniques

- In this lecture, we've seen several ways to structure a piece of fiction that don't rely on a plot with a conflict and a resolution. Obviously, the techniques we've explored are not for everyone; most writers fall back on plot because it's easy and it's what most readers expect and enjoy. But trying to write a story or a book with an unconventional technique can make you a more observant, subtle, and engaged writer, even if you then go back and apply what you've learned to a more conventional narrative.

- The type of fiction known as *postmodernism* is even more adventurous than the modernist works we've explored in this lecture. In general, a postmodern novel is one that calls attention to itself as a novel, plays games with language and with narrative conventions of plot and character, and constantly calls attention to the fact that it is a work of fiction.

- Even if you have no interest in writing this kind of fiction yourself, it's worth looking into some of the stories and books of postmodernism, including David Foster Wallace's *Infinite Jest*, Roger Boylan's *Killoyle*, Jennifer Egan's *A Visit from the Goon Squad*, and Kate Atkinson's *Life after Life*.

Suggested Reading

Chekhov, "The Kiss."

Joyce, "The Dead."

Woolf, *Mrs. Dalloway*.

Writing Exercise

1. Choose a single character and write about an hour in that person's life, limiting yourself to five pages. Don't pick the hour when something significant happened to the character—when he or she committed a murder or fell in love, for example. Instead, pick one of the countless hours in a person's life where nothing particularly important is going on. But try to put in as much detail about that person as you can, including memories or flashbacks that might be provoked by something as simple as a smell or an overheard comment. By limiting the time period and the number of pages, you provide yourself with a structure that doesn't rely on plot, but if you include significant detail, you may be pleasantly surprised at how much you can get across about the character.

Structuring a Narrative without a Plot
Lecture 12—Transcript

Every work of fiction has a structure, but not every work of fiction has a plot, at least not a traditional plot like the ones I've been talking about in the last two lectures. But even if it doesn't have a plot, every work of fiction has to have something the writer John Gardner called "profluence." Gardner defined profluence as the feeling that you're getting somewhere when you're reading a work of fiction.

Let me suggest another way to think about it. Whether or not a story or a novel has a plot, something should change over the course of reading it, if not in the story itself, at least in the heart or mind of the reader. In this lecture, I want to suggest a few ways to structure fiction that don't involve using Freytag's Pyramid or the traditional plot. I'll use some examples that don't raise the usual expectations, or that raise the reader's expectations and then confound them in a profound and subtle way.

Let's start with short fiction. The short stories of the 19th century were generally plot-driven. Even though many of them were not quite long enough to accommodate all the features of Freytag's Pyramid, they usually set up a situation, invoked a conflict, and resolved it pretty quickly, often with a twist at the end.

Think of all the stories that you might have read in high school: Nathaniel Hawthorne's "Young Goodman Brown," Edgar Allan Poe's "The Tell-Tale Heart," Herman Melville's "Benito Cereno," Guy de Maupassant's "The Necklace," O. Henry's "The Gift of the Magi," and nearly all of Conan Doyle's Sherlock Holmes stories.

Each one of these stories has a sting in its tale, as a secret is revealed or a twist is administered. Some of them, such as "Young Goodman Brown" and "Benito Cereno," are quite profound, but compared to the modern short story, their effect is still pretty mechanical. This kind of story can be very satisfying, but it often doesn't quite feel like real life.

The modern short story begins in the late 19th century with the Russian writer Anton Chekhov. He is perhaps better known as the author of such plays as *The Cherry Orchard*, *Three Sisters*, and *Uncle Vanya*, but among fiction writers, he is one of the most influential short story writers of all time. One of the most vivid reading experiences of my life, in fact, was reading his story "The Kiss" as a sophomore in college. It was a revelation to me at the time, because not only did it show me something profound about life, it showed me a whole new way of storytelling.

What happens in "The Kiss" is very simple. The officers of an artillery regiment training in the Russian countryside are invited by a local landowner to spend the evening at his country house. During the course of the festivities, the main character, a very shy and buttoned-up officer named Ryabovitch, wanders off by himself through the house. At one point he walks into a completely darkened room. As he hesitates just inside the door, a woman rushes out of the dark, murmurs "At last!" and kisses him. An instant later, this woman realizes he isn't the man she was waiting for and she flees the room, leaving the stunned Ryabovitch in the dark. He steps into the lighted room where the party is going on and searches the faces of the women, but he never does discover who kissed him.

Ryabovitch and his regiment ride away the next morning. Up until now his life has been utterly without passion, and for days afterwards, Ryabovitch constantly fantasizes about this encounter. He even invents a whole future life, including marriage and children, with a woman whose name and face he doesn't even know. This is the most remarkable thing that has ever happened to him, and he spends the next few pages ringing like a bell that has been struck for the very first time. But at the end of the story, when his regiment returns to the same town, he loses his nerve as they pass the landowner's mansion. And when the landowner invites the officers back to his house that evening, Ryabovitch stays behind in the barracks.

And that's it. That's all that happens in the story. Scene by scene and sentence by sentence, it reads like a conventional story, full of vivid exposition, some sharply etched characters, and a fair amount of dry humor. The scenes are steadily laid out in chronological order, with no flashbacks or flash-forwards.

And yet, the story does not come to a climax or resolve like a traditional story. Ryabovitch does not develop as a character. He does not win or lose at the end. He's the same person all the way through the story. He has a brief glimpse of a more exciting life, but his only response is in his lonely imagination, and he does nothing about it. He was a grey little man at the beginning of the story; he's a grey little man at the end; and he will, Chekhov implies, be a grey little man for the rest of his life. And even though the story does not resolve in the traditional way, this realization about Ryabovitch has a very powerful effect on the reader.

If you really wanted to, I suppose you could plot "The Kiss" on a Freytag Pyramid: It opens with exposition—the description of Ryabovitch and his regiment. It has an inciting action—the kiss in the dark. It has a rising action—Ryabovitch brooding about the mystery woman for the next few weeks. And it even has a climax of a sort, when Ryabovitch decides not to go back to the country house at the end.

But the genius of the story is that it suggests a potential conflict and then refuses to resolve it, at least in the way the reader was expecting. Chekhov sets up a couple of binary questions—who kissed Ryabovitch and will he ever find her again? And then, technically, Chekhov answers at least half of the question—no, Ryabovitch won't find the girl. In fact, he won't even really look for her. That disappointment the reader feels at this turn of events is the point of the story. The real question is not whether Ryabovitch gets the girl, but whether he can rise above his own timid nature. And that is a much more profound and unsettling question.

To put it another way, Chekhov has performed a bait-and-switch on the unsuspecting reader. He starts with what looks like a sweet little love story and gives us instead a shattering and heartbreaking judgment of the main character. So, even though nothing "happens" in the traditional sense, something profound does change over the course of the story—not in the character or the situation, but in the reader.

The first time I read "The Kiss," at the age of 19 or 20, I approached the end of it with the expectation that it was going to resolve one way or the other. I expected that Ryabovitch was going to be either happy or heartbroken at the end. But what I didn't see coming was that he was going to be just the same as he was in the beginning.

I felt as if an abyss had opened at my feet as I realized that, yes, you can ruin your own life without even knowing that you're doing it. But I also felt exhilaration at the audacity and the tenderness of the story. Chekhov gives us an intimate and tragic portrait of a man who is presented with a vision of passion and does nothing about it. He does not find love, and he does not understand himself any better. And yet, even if nothing changed in Ryabovitch, the story changed me profoundly, and that's what makes it a great story.

I had a very similar feeling later that same semester, in the same class, when I read James Joyce's story "The Dead" for the first time. "The Dead" is the final story in Joyce's only volume of short fiction. Titled *Dubliners*, this volume of stories has been as influential for modern short story writers as Chekhov's short fiction, if not more so.

Instead of a conventional climax or resolution, the stories in *Dubliners* rely upon what Joyce called an "epiphany." This word comes from the ancient Greek word *epiphaneia*, which means an appearance or manifestation. In religious terms, the word "epiphany" means a deep spiritual insight or realization which has been brought about by divine intervention. Joyce used it to refer to an individual experiencing a moment of profound, and sometimes life-changing, self-understanding.

"The Dead" is the longest story in *Dubliners*, about 60 pages long. And like "The Kiss," it reads very conventionally, a steadily chronological account of a party in Dublin in the first week of January, 1904. It is full of evocative details, sharply observed characters, and gentle humor.

Most of the story is told from the point of view of a middle-aged man named Gabriel Conroy. Gabriel is the sort of successful and reliable fellow who is relied upon to carve the goose at the party and deliver a slightly pompous after-dinner speech. Near the end of the party, Gabriel witnesses his wife, Gretta, listening raptly to a singer performing an old Irish folksong. Then, in the cab to the hotel room that they've booked for the night, Gabriel is possessed of a powerful lust for his wife. His emotions have been stirred up by the happiness of the party and by the fact that they have a night to themselves without their children.

But when they're alone in the room, Gabriel realizes that Gretta is upset. She tells him that hearing the folksong at the party has reminded her of a boy named Michael Furey, who had loved her when she was a young woman. Furey used to sing that same song to her, years ago, and he probably died because he stood in the rain, waiting outside her window. Gabriel realizes that to make love to his wife at this moment would be akin to an assault, so after she falls asleep, he simply lies awake in the dark next to her.

Gabriel's epiphany is his realization that Gretta has never loved him as much she loved the boy who died for her years ago. He further realizes that he has never loved her, or anyone else for that matter, the way that Michael Furey did. But instead of feeling rage or disappointment, Gabriel experiences a moment of expansive generosity for his wife, for himself, for Michael Furey, and in Joyce's famous phrase, for all the living and the dead.

This is one of most glorious moments in all of literature. It knocked me flat when I first read it back in college, and it has knocked me flat every time I've read the story since, even though I know it's coming.

Looking at the story as a whole, you might think that Joyce could have evoked Gabriel's epiphany in a shorter story, one that focused only on the aftermath of the party, but that simply wouldn't have worked. The first 40 pages of the story are a chronological and very entertaining account of the events at the party, and those scenes are structurally essential to what Joyce is trying to do. In those first 40 pages, Joyce shows us how a long-married couple present themselves to their friends and acquaintances in a public setting, and he includes details about Gabriel that only pay off at the end. This makes their moment of unexpected intimacy at the end even more poignant and piercing. In other words, you need to see as vividly as possible, and at considerable length, the life that Gabriel thought he was living in order to understand his shock when he realizes that nothing he ever thought about his life was true.

At first glance, the structure of "The Dead" is similar to that of "The Kiss." Both are chronological, both are centered around a party, both are essentially a series of evocative scenes that do not really make up a conventional plot. The final effect of "The Dead," however, is different from that of the "The Kiss," because Gabriel comes to a new understanding of himself and Ryabovitch does not.

Think back to the distinction E. M. Forster made between a story and plot—that the story tells us what happened, but a plot tells us why. Now think back to how a conventional plot does this, by posing a question in the form of a conflict and then answering the question by resolving the conflict.

The structural brilliance of "The Dead" is that it does not set up a conflict at the start of the story. Instead, it holds your interest by giving you a plotless but an entertaining and exquisitely detailed account of its main character and his social situation. Then it blindsides you at the end with a conflict that neither you nor the main character even knew existed.

The conclusion of "The Dead" is powerful partly because of what it says—that happiness is precarious, and sometimes it's founded on a lie. But it's also powerful because of the way that Joyce plays with your expectations. If he had set up a conventional plot—opening the story with Gabriel wondering if Gretta was happy in their marriage, for example—the ending simply wouldn't have worked. The power of the story comes from the way it gives us what looks like an ordinary situation for its main character, and then surprises both Gabriel and the reader with something extraordinary. Pardon my bad pun, but a conventional plot would have killed "The Dead."

The use of everyday moments to build a picture of a world at a particular moment in order to reveal something profound also lies behind Virginia Woolf's great novel, *Mrs. Dalloway*. This book is set over a single day in London in the early 1920s, and it focuses on a well-to-do, 52-year-old woman named Clarissa Dalloway as she prepares for a party at her home that evening.

There are a couple of other major characters as well: Peter Walsh, a former suitor of Clarissa's who has just returned from five years' service in India, and Septimus Warren Smith, a veteran of World War I who is suffering from what used to be called shell-shock and what we now call post-traumatic stress disorder. Other characters include Septimus Smith's Italian wife, Rezia, Mrs. Dalloway's husband, Richard, and her daughter, Elizabeth, as well as a woman named Sally Seton, with whom Mrs. Dalloway was in love when they were both young women.

There are only a few conventionally dramatic moments in *Mrs. Dalloway*. These include the suicide of Septimus Smith and the meeting of Clarissa and Peter Walsh after many years. They also include Clarissa's flashback of the moment when Sally Seton kissed her, and Peter's flashback to the moment when Clarissa rejected his proposal of marriage, both of which happened 30 years before. Otherwise, most of the incidents in the book are pretty ordinary. Except for the death of Septimus, of course, it's a pretty unremarkable day.

So given that there's no conflict as such, no climax, and nothing to resolve at the end, what gives the book its structure? What gives it profluence? What changes over the course of *Mrs. Dalloway*?

Instead of using a plot to structure the novel, Woolf uses two techniques. One of them governs the overall shape of the novel. The other governs its movement from scene to scene, and from moment to moment within each scene. The overall shape is determined by the fact that the novel is set over the course of one day. This allows Woolf to limit the number of incidents in the book, and to limit the scope of the characters. There's only so much the characters can do and only so far they can go in a single day. And, taking into account Clarissa and Peter's flashbacks to their youth, there's only so much of their past they can remember in a day.

One way to structure the formless chaos of an entire life in a narrative would be to select the most important or dramatic events and string them together in a plot, the way Hollywood biopics often do. Instead, Virginia Woolf picks one day and writes about the most important events, actions, meetings, and memories of that day. The intention is that these events are representative enough to give us a vivid impression of the character's whole life.

The technique of setting a novel or story in a single day is fairly common. A few years earlier, James Joyce had used the same technique on a much larger scale, in his novel *Ulysses*. Over the years, the technique has also been used by such writers as Eva Figes in her short but very beautiful novel, *Light*, which is about a day in the life of the family of the painter Claude Monet; by Malcolm Lowry in *Under the Volcano*, which is about a day in the life of an alcoholic Englishman living in Mexico; and by yours truly in my novel, *Next*.

And there are also more conventionally plotted novels take place in one day. There are lots of thrillers in which the hero is working against the clock, and it's easy to imagine an historical novel about the day Lincoln was assassinated, for example.

What's important to note about *Mrs. Dalloway*, however, is that it's not a particularly significant day in the life of any of the characters (except for Septimus, of course). Instead, the idea behind it is that by very closely observing the thoughts of a few characters over a limited period of time, you can evoke a particular period and a way of life, the way you might infer the ocean from a drop of water.

In my first lecture about plot, I talked about the lesson I learned from my high school English teacher, when she said that fiction imposes order on the chaos of reality. What we learn from the example of *Mrs. Dalloway* and other novels that take place in one day, is that the order you impose doesn't necessarily need to be a conventional plot. You don't have to arrange the story's events in the usual way to have them mean something. The order you impose on reality can as simple as focusing on the important details of a particular time period. The illumination of character or the evocation of a particular way of life in this way can be as satisfying as an old-fashioned plot.

But even if you limit the events of your narrative to a single day, how do you make the narrative move forward if there's no conflict to be resolved? This brings us to the second method that Virginia Woolf uses in *Mrs. Dalloway*, the one that makes the novel flow from scene to scene, and moment to moment. This is accomplished by Woolf's use of the stream-of-consciousness technique.

In one of my lectures about character, I quoted a scene from the book that let us hear what Clarissa Dalloway was thinking as she looked in a shop window. As you may recall, the passage shifted very quickly from the sights and sounds of the world around Clarissa, to memories of her girlhood, to the last days of her uncle, to her relationship with her daughter.

Each brief moment in that passage tells us something about Clarissa Dalloway and her world that we didn't know before: what sort of girl she was, what sort of person her uncle was, what sort of relationship she has with her daughter. Using Gardner's term, this passage is profluent even without Clarissa having to confront or resolve a conflict.

The book devotes this kind of attention not just to Clarissa, but also to Peter Walsh; to her husband, Richard; to Septimus Smith; and to Smith's wife, Rezia. Not all of these scenes are written in the same dense style Woolf uses to evoke Clarissa Dalloway's consciousness. A long central passage from the point of view of Peter Walsh is written in a more conventional, expository style, while the passages from the point of view of Septimus Smith are feverish and full of violent imagery that evokes his spiritual agony.

In fact, perhaps the most remarkable and influential feature of *Mrs. Dalloway* is the way Woolf effortlessly shifts the narrative's point of view from one character to another. These narrative shifts are what provide the momentum that other, more conventional books rely on plot to provide.

There are long passages of Mrs. Dalloway where the point of view is limited to one character or bounces back and forth between two characters. But there are also several bravura sequences where the point of view shifts from one character to someone he or she has just passed in the street, then on to another person, and so on. For example, only a few pages into the book, Clarissa hears an automobile backfire in the street while she's in a shop, and at that moment, the point of view quickly shifts from Clarissa to Septimus, who sees the same car. Then it shifts to Rezia, then back to Clarissa, then to a woman selling flowers on the street, then to a couple of women and an old man outside the gates of Buckingham Palace, then back to Septimus and Rezia, then to a girl named Maisie Johnson who asks Rezia for directions, then to an old woman feeding the pigeons, and finally to a man standing on the steps of St. Paul's cathedral. Over the course of 15 pages, some of these characters get a couple of pages each, while others are inhabited by Woolf for only a few sentences.

It's a breathtaking piece of prose that requires more concentration from the reader than just following a plot. But if you stick with it, you end up with a more vivid evocation of a particular moment in the lives of these particular characters, than you would have gotten from a more conventional narrative.

So far, we've seen several different ways to structure a piece of fiction that don't rely on a plot. In Chekhov's "The Kiss" and Joyce's "The Dead," the narrative uses a single moment to illuminate the rest of a character's life, while in *Mrs. Dalloway*, a chronology limited to a single, ordinary day and a close attention to each character's most intimate thoughts evoke each character's entire life and a particular moment in history.

Obviously, this sort of technique is not for everybody, and maybe not even for most writers. For all the difficulties we writers have with plot, and particularly with making a plot seem lifelike and not really like a plot, most of us fall back on it because, frankly, it's easier to do, and it's what most readers expect. An epiphany narrative like "The Dead" or a plotless evocation of a single day like *Mrs. Dalloway* require more effort and concentration from a reader than, say, the relentless, addictive, one-damn-thing-after-another forward momentum of a popular novel like *Game of Thrones*.

Lots of readers don't see the point to a story like "The Kiss." Or they try to read *Ulysses* or *Mrs. Dalloway* only because guys like me tell them they ought to, and then they give up after 25 pages. There's nothing wrong with that. I know lots of intelligent, sophisticated readers who have no patience for *Mrs. Dalloway*. But I will say this: If you're willing to make the extra effort, *Mrs. Dalloway* reaches places in a reader that a conventionally plotted novel, even a great one, simply cannot.

And, more to the point, trying a write a story or a book with an unconventional technique can make you a better writer. It can make you more observant, more subtle, and more engaged, even if all you plan to do is apply what you've learned to a more conventional narrative. Four of the five books I've written so far are conventionally plotted. But my fifth book, *Next*, was my attempt to apply the technique of *Mrs. Dalloway* to a different sort of life, only with more jokes. I'd like to think it's my best book, but even if it isn't, it made me dig deeper as a writer than I ever have before.

As a matter of fact, the type of fiction I've been talking about in this lecture isn't even considered all that radical anymore. You'll notice that the three examples I've cited so far—"The Kiss," "The Dead," and *Mrs. Dalloway*—all date from the late 19th or early 20th century. Since then, another, even more adventurous literary technique has grown up, known as postmodernism.

This is a huge topic which takes us beyond the scope of these lectures, and indeed, beyond my own area of expertise. So without getting into the whole history of prose fiction since World War II, suffice it to say that a postmodern novel is one that plays games with language and with the usual narrative conventions of plot and character, and which consistently calls the reader's attention to the fact that he or she is reading a work of fiction.

One of the hallmarks of postmodern writers is that they love jokes and puns, and they often like to play with structure. For example, David Foster Wallace's *Infinite Jest* includes 388 footnotes that appear at the end of the book. Roger Boylan's novel *Killoyle* includes footnotes on the same page as the text. These notes are often directly addressed to the reader and provide a sort of cranky, and very funny, commentary on the rest of the book.

Even if you have no interest in creating this kind of fiction yourself, these books and stories are worth looking at because, over the past 40 or 50 years, many of the techniques of postmodernism have made their way into the mainstream.

Take, for example, Jennifer Egan's Pulitzer Prize-winning novel *A Visit from the Goon Squad*. This is a novel-in-stories about a group of people who revolve around a rock-and-roll producer named Bennie Salazar.

Written in very accessible literary prose, the individual stories and the novel as a whole are humane and moving in a conventionally satisfactory way, but at the same time, Egan very cleverly uses a lot of techniques from the postmodernist toolbox. She arranges the stories out of chronological order, she tells one story in the second person, and, most famously, she tells one of the stories in the form of a PowerPoint presentation. It's the best of both worlds, incorporating postmodern techniques in a very entertaining way, but delivering all the emotional satisfaction of a mainstream novel.

An even more adventurous combination of experimental literary technique and old-fashioned storytelling is the British writer Kate Atkinson's *Life After Life*. In this remarkable novel, the main character, Ursula Todd, lives her life over and over again, with each parallel life playing out differently than all the others. Ursula dies at the end of each chapter, and then her life begins again in the next chapter with her birth in England in 1910.

Several of the early chapters are very short, as Ursula dies in childbirth, or as an infant, or as a young girl. She goes on to die several times during the influenza epidemic of 1918. She is also killed by an abusive husband, and in one chapter, she dies during the Blitz in World War II.

As the novel goes on, however, each of her lives is longer and more satisfying, almost as if Ursula is learning from each iteration of her existence. Like *A Visit from the Goon Squad*, *Life After Life* is written in an accessible literary style. The characters that recur throughout the novel—Ursula's parents, siblings, friends, and lovers—remain more or the less the same in each life, even as Ursula's relationship with them changes from version to version. But the overall structure not only suggests that each of our lives is a series of accidents or coincidences over which we have little control, it also raises interesting questions about the nature of literary character: namely, how many changes can Atkinson make in Ursula and still have her be the same person?

More importantly, the novel tests the very foundations of storytelling, which is what makes it postmodern. In most narratives, when the writer makes a choice about a moment in the plot, she closes off all the other possible plotlines. But in *Life After Life*, Atkinson deliberately works against that idea of closure. She can't show us all of Ursula's possible lives—that would take an infinitely long book—but she can suggest infinity by showing us a wide variety of them. Like *A Visit from the Goon Squad*, it's a remarkable and very satisfying combination of vivid storytelling and postmodern playfulness.

If you think you might like to try some of the techniques I've talked about in this lecture, here is an exercise: Take a single character and write about an hour in that person's life, limiting yourself to five pages. Do not pick the hour when something significant happened to the character—when he killed somebody or fell in love, for example. Instead, pick one of countless hours in a person's life where nothing particularly important is going on.

But do try to put in as much detail about that person as you can, including memories or flashbacks, which might be provoked by something as simple as a smell or an overheard comment. By limiting the time period and the number of pages, you provide yourself with a structure that doesn't rely on plot. But if you put a lot of detail in, I think you'll be pleasantly surprised at how much you can get across about the character. You may even get more than five pages out of it.

Whether you want to tell a good, old-fashioned story with a beginning, middle, and an end, or a crazy ambitious postmodernist epic, the point is to engage the heart and mind of the reader and keep her turning the pages. And perhaps the most daunting part of creating a plot or a structure is knowing how and where to begin. In my next lecture, I'll talk about some strategies for getting started, using examples from William Faulkner, Mark Twain, and Marilynne Robinson.

In the Beginning—How to Start a Plot
Lecture 13

Getting a plot started is a daunting prospect for most writers, but the reason it's daunting varies from writer to writer. Some writers know so much about the story even before they start that they don't quite know where to begin. Others have only a single episode or character in mind, and they're not sure how to spin that situation into a complete narrative. In this lecture, we'll explore three ways to work a writer works out plot, outlined by John Gardner: "by borrowing some traditional plot or an action from real life … by working his way back from the story's climax; or by groping his way forward from an initial situation."

Working out Plots

- Gardner's first method of approaching plot is borrowing, but it's important to note that this is not the same as plagiarism, which generally involves passing off someone else's work as your own. Borrowing, in contrast, usually involves changing an earlier plot in significant ways or using it for a purpose that the original author may not have intended or even foreseen. Many writers, for example, have retold Homer's *Odyssey*, setting it in completely different contexts. Others have retold well-known stories from a different point of view.

  o Of course, historical novels take their stories from famous people or events in history. As with novels that adapt earlier works of literature, the best historical novels reimagine history in interesting ways. For example, Robert Graves's novel *I, Claudius* and Marguerite Yourcenar's *The Memoirs of Hadrian* each tell the story of a Roman emperor from the emperor's point of view.

  o Sometimes, writers borrow types of plots rather than specific stories. Beginning writers of mysteries or romance novels, for example, probably have templates for those sorts of stories in their minds. Although such a template can be a straightjacket, it can also be a convenient way to at least get a plot started, even if you plan to change it later on.

- o And sometimes writers borrow a plot when they need to provide a structure for the material that truly interests them. The science fiction writer William Gibson structured his first novel, *Neuromancer*, as an old-fashioned noir thriller in the style of Dashiell Hammett or Raymond Chandler. He was interested in evoking a rich, complex, and colorful future and in playing with the cultural, social, and political implications of the computer revolution; thus, he used a thriller plot to provide a framework for this material.

- Another approach to plotting is to start with the end of a story and structure the rest of the work so that it leads to a particular climax. Obviously, this method requires that you know how the story ends before you start writing. It also probably works best if you're writing a binary narrative, that is, one with an either/or conclusion.
    - o With this type of narrative, figuring out how to start by working backward should be relatively easy: If there's a crime to be solved, you start with the crime or its immediate aftermath; if the two lovers finally get together, you need to start with their meeting or the situation that leads to their meeting.

    - o This is the method where you're most likely to find that an outline is useful. If you already know what happens at the end, that means you know, or at least can infer, what the plot needs to do to reach that point: what characters you'll need, what the setting will be, and roughly what steps the characters need to take to get there.

- Finally, many writers start with an image, a character, or a situation and, as Gardner put it, "grope" their way forward. William Faulkner famously said that he created his great novel *The Sound and the Fury* by starting with a single image of a little girl with muddy underpants sitting in a tree, peering through a window at a funeral. This method is probably more time-consuming and frustrating than sticking to an outline, but it may result in a more complex narrative structure.

- The methods of structuring a plot are not limited to these three, of course, and the methods can be combined in interesting ways. Even if you're borrowing a plot, you may find yourself monkeying with it, and even if you're trying to stick to the facts of a famous life—such as the life of Hadrian or Copernicus—it's what you discover in the process of writing, as you imagine yourself into their minds, that makes the narrative come alive.

Starting *in Medias Res*

- As mentioned in an earlier lecture, many stories begin *in medias res*, "in the middle of things." In fact, it's tempting to say that all stories begin *in medias res* because there's really no such thing as a story that begins *ex nihilo*, "from nothing." Even if you start a novel with the birth of the main character, that character already has parents and relations, a family history, and a social and historical context.

- What *in medias res* usually means is starting the plot at a point where the story is already underway. Homer's *Iliad* is not really about the Trojan War in its entirety; by the time the *Iliad* opens, the war has already been going on for 10 years, and the present-time narrative depicts only a few weeks near the end of the siege of Troy. Even though it makes reference to how the war began and how it ends, the *Iliad* does not dramatize the kidnapping of Helen, which started the war, or the fall of Troy, which ended it.

- Starting *in medias res* shows us that choosing where to begin is not so much a matter of figuring out the chronological beginning of a story as it is choosing the most dramatically productive moment. Shakespeare could have started *Hamlet* with the funeral of Hamlet's father or the subsequent marriage of Hamlet's mother to his uncle Polonius, but he chose to open it with the moment that was most likely to make Hamlet reconsider recent events, namely, the appearance of his father's ghost, demanding vengeance.

Limiting Choices

- Another way to approach the start of a plot is to limit your choices. As we've mentioned, real life flows ceaselessly and infinitely in all directions; it's knowing what to leave out that turns life into fiction. Thus, you could limit your time frame, having the story or novel take place in a single day, week, or month, or you could limit the point of view, telling the story from the point of view of only one character.

  o Neither of these limits necessarily means that you have to leave out other settings or other times in the characters' lives.

  o You can start the narrative at a particular moment and limit it to particular time, the way Virginia Woolf limits *Mrs. Dalloway* to the events of one day, yet still range backward and forward in time and place, incorporating flashback scenes that take place at other times and in different settings.

- You also have a number of choices with the first line of a narrative, which will both dictate and be dictated by what comes later.

  o If you're telling a story from the point of view of a character who dies at the end, for example, you will be limited to third-person narration—unless you want the character to narrate the story from beyond the grave. If you're writing a story that features a surprise later on, you might want to start in the first person present tense or in the close third person, so that the reader lives in the moment right alongside the main character and is just as stunned as the character when the surprise finally comes.

  o Look at the openings of books and stories you admire, paying attention to not just the immediate effect of the opening moment but also how the opening prepares the reader for what comes later.

Opening Examples

- One category of story opening is simply beginning at the beginning, the way Tolkien does in *The Hobbit*: "In a hole in the ground there lived a hobbit." This opening sounds like the beginning of a fairy tale, with an unspoken "once upon a time" at the start of the sentence. As brief and to the point as it is, that simple 10-word sentence tells us right away that we're in a fantasy world, inhabited by creatures called hobbits, and it tells us something important about hobbits, that they live underground.

- Another way to begin at the beginning is simply to state the premise of the story as bluntly as possible, the way Franz Kafka does in the first line of his story "The Metamorphosis": "One morning, upon awakening from agitated dreams, Gregor Samsa found himself, in his bed, transformed into a monstrous vermin." This sentence is only 19 words, but at the end of it, we know the name of the main character, that he is a man ridden with anxieties, and that he has undergone a horrific transformation. The rest of the story works out all the implications of a man being transformed overnight into a giant cockroach.

- Both of those openings are in the third person, but many of the most famous American novels begin with a first-person narrator speaking directly to the reader. Herman Melville's *Moby-Dick* begins with "Call me Ishmael," and Mark Twain's *The Adventures of Huckleberry Finn* begins with "You don't know about me, without you have read a book by the name of *The Adventures of Tom Sawyer*, but that ain't no matter."

- As we've said, writing is about imposing order on chaos, about making decisions—often arbitrary ones—out of what seems to be an infinity of choices. It's also as much about what you leave out as what you leave in. Your decision about when, where, and with whom to begin a narrative opens one path for you even as it closes off many others.
  - Just like making decisions in real life, you sometimes don't realize what the consequences of your choices are until much later. But unlike life, if you find you've made a wrong decision about the opening of your novel or short story, you can always go back and change it or even start over.

  - Writing, especially plotting, is not a science; it's an organic and wildly inefficient process of trial and error. But it's the stuff you don't plan for, the stuff that surprises you, that makes fiction worth reading and makes the writing of it simultaneously frustrating and rewarding.

Suggested Reading

Faulkner, *The Sound and the Fury.*

Gardner, *The Art of Fiction.*

Hynes, *Next.*

Kafka, "The Metamorphosis."

Robinson, *Housekeeping.*

Tolkien, *The Hobbit.*

Writing Exercise

1. Without thinking about it too much, imagine some sort of striking or intriguing situation. For example, imagine a man and woman who are eating at a candlelit table in a romantic restaurant, but they aren't speaking to each other; in fact, they don't even look at each other. Or imagine a woman standing in an alley in the rain at night, holding a knife. Then, again without thinking about it too much, try imagining the very next thing that happens, then the next, and the next. If you find yourself running out of steam or boxing yourself into a corner, go back to the original situation and try something completely different.

In the Beginning—How to Start a Plot
Lecture 13—Transcript

Getting a plot started is a scary prospect for many writers, but the reason it's scary varies from writer to writer. Some of us know so much about the story and characters even before we start that we can't decide where to begin. On the other hand, some of us only have a single episode or a single character, and we're not sure how to spin them into a complete narrative.

In the first case, it can be hard to pick the right moment out of all the stuff in the story, and in the second case, it's hard to begin if you have no idea where the story's going to end up. Let's see if we can make this less scary.

In *The Art of Fiction*, John Gardner says that

> [A] writer works out plot in one of three ways: by borrowing some traditional plot or an action from real life (the method of the Greek tragedians, Shakespeare, Dostoevsky, and many other writers, ancient and modern); by working his way back from the story's climax; or by groping his way forward from an initial situation.

Let's take these one at a time.

First, I want to make clear that borrowing a plot is not the same thing as plagiarism, though there have been instances when writers, even very famous ones, have copied ideas so slavishly that they come right up to the edge of, and sometimes over, what we call plagiarism today.

Plagiarism generally involves passing off someone else's work as your own. Usually the plagiarist copies the original word for word, or very close to word for word. The kind of borrowing that Gardner is talking about is different. For one thing, it isn't disguised. If a writer bases a story or a novel on a Greek legend, for example, he or she is usually up front about it. The proof is in the story itself, for all to see. For another, most writers who borrow a plot usually change it significant ways, or use it for a purpose that the original author may not have intended or even foreseen.

For example, many writers have retold Homer's *Odyssey*. The most famous retelling is James Joyce's *Ulysses*, which uses the *Odyssey* as a roadmap for the comings and goings of two men in Dublin on one day in 1904. More recently, the Coen Brothers used the story of the *Odyssey* to tell the comic story of three men who escape from a Southern chain gang during the Great Depression, in their film *O Brother, Where Art Thou?* In each case, the writers took Homer's story and did something new with it, or at least set it in a completely different context. But the debt that these two works owe to the original is clear. Nobody accuses Joyce or the Coen Brothers of ripping off Homer.

Many writers have done something similar with other great works of literature, telling a well-known or beloved story from a different point of view. Many of these works show us the original in a new light. John Gardner himself retold the story of *Beowulf* from the point of view of the monster in his novel *Grendel*.

And a number of writers in recent years have reimagined famous stories through the lens of feminism. The American novelist Jane Smiley set Shakespeare's *King Lear* on an Iowa farm in her novel *A Thousand Acres*, suggesting that the reason that two of Lear's three daughters reject him so badly is that he had sexually abused them when they were girls.

In *Wide Sargasso Sea*, Jean Rhys imagines the backstory of *Jane Eyre* from the point of view of the first Mrs. Rochester, the famous "madwoman in the attic." And Valerie Martin's novel *Mary Reilly* retells Robert Louis Stevenson's *Dr. Jekyll and Mr. Hyde* from the point of view of a poor Irish servant who works in Dr. Jekyll's household.

Other writers have had fun by putting a famous story in a new context. In his very clever novel *Fangland*, the novelist John Marks, who used to work as a producer at *60 Minutes*, moves the story of *Dracula* from the late 19th century and sets it backstage at a TV newsmagazine in the present day.

In each of these examples, the starting point for the writer is determined by the source material. John Marks begins *Fangland*, for example, with a young American journalist, recently engaged to be married, who is on her way to interview a mysterious Romanian businessman. This reproduces the opening of *Dracula*, in which a recently engaged English lawyer travels to visit a mysterious Transylvanian nobleman.

Then, of course, there are historical novels that are based on the lives of famous people or on events in history. In these narratives, the story (if not the plot) is already laid out for the writer. And, as with novels that adapt earlier works of literature, the most interesting historical novels reimagine the history in interesting ways.

Robert Graves's novel *I, Claudius* and Marguerite Yourcenar's *The Memoirs of Hadrian* each tell the story of a famous Roman emperor from the emperor's point of view, giving us access to the private lives behind public events. John Banville's *Doctor Copernicus* is a fictionalized biography of the famous Polish astronomer. It tells the story of Copernicus in chronological order from his early childhood to his death, while giving us something only a novel can provide, namely access to Copernicus's most intimate thoughts. Other novelists have shown us famous people from the point of view of the less famous people around them. In his novel *Quarantine*, the British novelist Jim Crace reimagines Christ's 40 days in the wilderness from the points of view of several other people who were living in the Judean desert at the time.

Sometimes, writers borrow types of plots rather than specific stories. Any beginning writer of mysteries or romance novels probably has a template for that sort of story in her head, whether she likes it or not. And while such a template can be a straightjacket, it can also be convenient way to at least get a plot started, even if you plan to change it up later on.

And sometimes writers borrow a plot not because they're particularly interested in the plot per se, but because they need to provide a structure for what they are interested in. The science fiction writer William Gibson decided to structure his famous first novel, *Neuromancer*, as an old-fashioned noir thriller in the style of Dashiell Hammett or Raymond Chandler. What he really wanted to do, however, was evoke a complex and colorful future, and play with the cultural, social, and political implications of the computer revolution. So he used a thriller plot to provide a framework, then he attached to it the stuff that really interested him.

I did a similar thing with my first published novel, *The Wild Colonial Boy*. I wanted to write about political violence in Northern Ireland, so I modeled the book after the literary thrillers of writers I'd admired, including Joseph Conrad, Robert Stone, and John le Carré.

And the last of the three novellas in my second book, *Publish and Perish*, is based explicitly on a famous (and public domain) horror story by the English writer M. R. James, *Casting the Runes*. James's story is one of the best horror stories ever written, and my version follows his plot pretty closely. But my version also plays what I hope are some interesting variations on the original, by changing the gender of the protagonist, setting it in Texas in the present day, and telling a lot more jokes than the original did.

Gardner's next suggestion for getting a plot going is to start with the ending and then structure the rest of the story so that it leads to that particular climax. Obviously, this method requires that you know how the story ends before you start writing. It probably works best if you're writing what I called a binary plot a couple of lectures ago. I'll be talking in much more detail about binary endings in the next lecture, but for now, suffice it to say a binary narrative is one that has a yes/no or an either/or conclusion. The detective catches the murderer or he doesn't; the two lovers get together or they don't; or the main character experiences some sort of clear-cut victory or defeat.

With a binary narrative, figuring out how to start by working backwards from the ending should be relatively easy. If there's a crime to be solved, you want to start with the crime or its immediate aftermath. If the climax requires two lovers getting together, you need to start with their meeting, or the situation that leads to their meeting. The rest of it is just working out the details. This is the method where you're most likely to find that an outline is useful.

If you already know what happens at the end, that means you know what the plot needs to do to reach that point. You'll know which characters you'll need, what the setting will be, and roughly what steps the characters have to take to get there. I'm not much of a cook, but I imagine that working backwards from the ending is sort of like a chef tasting a dish and then reverse engineering the recipe to get that taste again.

Of course, there are outlines and there are *outlines*. In my very first lecture, I suggested that a writer might sketch out a story by using the five Ws of journalism and making a list of the various story elements: Who's in it, when it's set, where it's set, what happens, and why things happen. Making such a list in itself doesn't necessarily constitute an outline. It doesn't really tell you how to structure all these elements, but it certainly helps by cutting through the clutter and helping you focus on what's important.

But sometimes a more formal outline can be very helpful. I've only used an outline myself once, for my novel *The Lecturer's Tale*. This was the longest and most ambitious book I'd ever attempted up to that point in my career. It is a big, sprawling satire about an English department, with lots of characters who interact with each other in complicated ways. I didn't start with an outline, but about halfway through, I began to feel overwhelmed by everything I had to keep straight. So I took a few days off from actually writing the book and made a giant wall-chart. This chart had all the major characters down one axis and all the chapters in the book along the other, and I graphed the movement of each character through the narrative.

At first, making the chart was mostly an excuse not to work. I spent way too much time driving all over Austin, Texas, looking for just the right sketch pad and just the right set of colored markers. And then, after putting the chart up on the wall of my office, I quickly found it even more oppressive than trying to keep all the characters straight in my head, so I took it down. But in retrospect, the actual creation of the thing was enormously useful to me, and I'm not sure I ever would have made it to the end of the novel without it.

On the other hand, I have more often written things using Gardner's third method of plotting, that is, starting with an image or a character or a situation and groping my way forward. You often hear writers talking about making a start without knowing where they're going. William Faulkner famously talked about how he started his great novel *The Sound and the Fury* with only a single image of a little girl with muddy underpants sitting in a tree, peering through a window at a funeral.

259

If he was telling the truth, and nobody ever mythologized the life and career of William Faulkner the way William Faulkner did, then the fact that he started this way is especially impressive. From that simple beginning, *The Sound and the Fury* ended up as one of the most structurally complex novels in American literature.

In fact, the novel may be complex because of this method, not in spite of it. The book has four major sections, told from various points of view. Each section is focused on a single day, with flashbacks and flash-forwards. According to Faulkner, this structure was the direct result of trial and error. Here's what he had to say about it:

> I tried first to tell [the story] with one brother, and that wasn't enough. That was Section One. I tried it with another brother, and that wasn't enough. That was Section Two. I tried the third brother, because Caddy was still to me too beautiful and too moving to reduce her to telling what was going on, that it would be more passionate to see her through somebody else's eyes, I thought. And that failed and I tried myself—the fourth section—to tell what happened, and I still failed.

Of course, Faulkner's claim that he failed is more than a little disingenuous. What he calls failure turns out to be an incredibly productive way of constructing a complex novel.

But it's important to point out that this method is certainly more time-consuming and, along the way, probably more frustrating than constructing an outline and sticking to it. One thing you learn pretty quickly as a writer is that writing fiction is not an efficient process. And that's as it should be. As the example of *The Sound and the Fury* shows us, most of the time you discover the good stuff by accident along the way.

The methods of structuring a plot are not limited to simply three, of course, as I'm sure even John Gardner would have admitted. You can certainly combine the three methods in interesting ways. Even if you're borrowing a plot, you may find yourself monkeying with it. And even if you're trying to stick to the facts of a famous life—such as the life of Hadrian or Copernicus—it's what you discover as you imagine yourself into that person's head that makes the narrative come alive.

And it's certainly possible to know how a story ends, and still grope your way forward from the beginning, which is how I wrote my novel *Next*. I knew four things about the story when I started: how it ended, where it was set, the fact that it took place in one day, and roughly who my main character was. Apart from that, I knew nothing about what happened between the opening scene and the climax of the book. And yet, even though I knew what the ending was, I still wrote the book as if I didn't. This effort was helped by the fact that the entire narrative is told from the point of view of Kevin, my main character, who, of course, has no idea either what's going to happen to him on that particular day.

Much of the book is just Kevin walking around Austin, Texas, in the heat of a summer's morning as he kills time before a job interview. As he walks, he takes stock of his life and remembers scenes from his past in flashback. I honestly had no idea what Kevin's history would turn out to be before I started, and I had only a rough idea of where he was going to walk. But I did have two advantages: I had a basic chronological structure to work with—a single day in Kevin's life—and I had the advantage that I was writing a book set in the town where I live. Each day, I simply rolled out of bed and walked the bit of Austin where Kevin was going to walk. I took note of everything and everyone I saw, and much of what I saw ended up in the novel.

What surprised me as I wrote the book, however, was how much those sights and sounds in Kevin's present-day experience provoked ideas for Kevin's previous history. I never would have gotten these ideas if I'd just sat at my desk and tried to outline his backstory.

For example, one of the biggest and most complex scenes in the book takes place in a chain supermarket called Gaia Market, which is my off-kilter version of Whole Foods. In this scene, Kevin stands in Gaia and witnesses a lover's argument. And as he listens to the young couple arguing, he remembers the time that he and his new girlfriend ran into his ex-girlfriend in the Gaia Market in Ann Arbor, Michigan, where he lives. The juxtaposition of a present-day scene with a flashback in a similar setting ended up working really well. In fact, it became one of the key scenes in the book. And it didn't come from an outline. Instead, it was the direct result of me wandering into Whole Foods one morning. The main lesson here is that no matter how you decide to structure your plot—whether you outline it in every detail ahead of time, or you just wing it, or you split the difference and do a little of both— you should be prepared to take advantage of happy accidents.

Now, if you're still daunted by taking that first step, here are some ideas that may make it easier. First, remember that many stories begin *in medias res*, which is Latin for "in the middle of things." In fact, it's tempting to say that all stories begin *in medias res*, because there's really no such thing as a story that begins *ex nihilo*, or from nothing. Even if you start a novel with the birth of the main character, the way Dickens starts *David Copperfield*, that character already has parents and relations, a family history, and a social and historical context. Or consider the opening line of Genesis, which is probably the least *in medias res* opening in history—"In the beginning, God created the heavens and the earth." Even here, there is already a character in place, namely, God.

What *in medias res* usually refers to, however, is starting the plot at a point where the story is already underway. Homer's *Iliad* starts *in medias res*. By time the *Iliad* opens, the siege of Troy has already been going on for 10 years, and the present-time narrative of the *Iliad* only depicts a few weeks near the end of the siege. Even though the story makes reference to how the war began and how it ends, the *Iliad* does not dramatize the kidnapping of Helen, which started the war, nor does it dramatize the fall of Troy, which ended it.

In Shakespeare's *Hamlet*, the ghost of Hamlet's father appears in the first scene, and he tells Hamlet that he was murdered. This mean the play has the same structure as a classic murder mystery, where half the story has already taken place by time the body is found.

More recent examples of *in medias res* include nearly every James Bond film, the opening scene of which usually shows 007 already fighting for his life. Another striking example is opening scene of the television series *Breaking Bad*, which shows high-school-teacher-turned-meth-cook Walter

White, wearing only his underpants and a gas mask, driving an RV frantically through the desert. This scene happens to be a flash-forward. The rest of the episode backs up to show how his recent diagnosis of lung cancer has led him to cooking meth.

When we consider the technique of *in medias res*, we see that choosing where to start a narrative is not necessarily about finding the chronological beginning of the story. Instead, it's about deciding what the most dramatically productive moment is. In other words, what's the beginning moment out of which you can get the most mileage as a storyteller. Shakespeare could have started *Hamlet* with the funeral of Hamlet's father, or with the marriage of Hamlet's mother to his uncle Polonius. Instead, he chose to open it with the moment that was most likely to make Hamlet reconsider recent events, namely the appearance of his father's vengeful ghost.

And the opening of *Breaking Bad* hooks viewers immediately, making us want to know why this pudgy, middle-aged guy is running around in the desert in his tighty-whities, waving a gun. The opening of *Breaking Bad* does what an opening is supposed to do. It strongly suggests what the story is about—in this case, middle-class, middle-aged desperation—but it does not explain everything.

Yet another way to approach the start of a plot is to limit your choices. As I've said before, real life flows ceaselessly and infinitely in all directions. It's knowing what to leave out that turns life into fiction. You could limit your time frame, for example: Have the story or novel take place in a single day, or a single week, or a single month. You could also limit the point of view: Tell the story from the point of view of only one character. And if that doesn't work (the way it didn't work for Faulkner when he was writing *The Sound and the Fury*), you could introduce other points of view. You could use leapfrogging narrators, the way Faulkner does in one of his other novels, *As I Lay Dying*, or the way George R. R. Martin does in his *Song of Ice and Fire* series.

But limiting the time frame doesn't necessarily mean you have to completely leave out other times in the characters' lives. This brings us back to *in medias res*. You can start the narrative at a particular moment and limit it to a particular time, the way Virginia Woolf limits *Mrs. Dalloway* to the events of one day. And yet, you could still range backwards and forwards in time and place, the way *Mrs. Dalloway* incorporates flashback scenes that take place years earlier, in completely different settings.

But what about that first line, that very first step? Here you have a lot of choices, too, each one of which will both dictate and be dictated by what comes later. If you are telling a story from the point of view of a character who dies at the end, for example, you're going to be limited to a third-person narration—unless you want the character to narrate the story from beyond the grave, the way William Holden's character narrates the film *Sunset Boulevard*, or the way the murdered girl in Alice Sebold's *The Lovely Bones* narrates the story of her own death.

If you're writing a story that features a surprise later on, one that the main character never sees coming, you might want to start in the first person, present tense, or in the close third person. Using these points of view means that the reader lives in the moment right alongside the main character, seeing no more than she sees and knowing no more than she knows. The result is that the reader is just as surprised as the character is when the moment of surprise finally comes.

Perhaps the best thing to do is to take a look at the openings of books and stories you admire. Take into account not just the immediate effect of that moment, but also how the opening prepares the reader for what comes later on. There are as many ways of doing this as there are writers, of course, but we can still group them into some useful categories. There are too many different ways to open a story for me to talk about them all, but here are some examples.

One category, of course, is simply beginning at the beginning, the way Tolkien does in *The Hobbit*: "In a hole in the ground there lived a hobbit." This is a very fairy-tale way to begin, of course. Even if Tolkien doesn't actually say it, there's an unspoken "once upon a time" at the beginning of that sentence. But as brief and to the point as it is, that simple, 10-word sentence tells us right away that we're in a fantasy world, inhabited by creatures called hobbits. It also tells us something important about hobbits, namely that they live underground (which, if you know Tolkien, you'll have to admit turns out to be surprisingly important: Large sections of *The Hobbit* and *The Lord of the Rings* take place underground).

Another way to begin at the beginning is simply to state the premise of the story as bluntly as possible. Consider the first line of Franz Kafka's story "The Metamorphosis": "One morning, upon awakening from agitated dreams, Gregor Samsa found himself, in his bed, transformed into a monstrous vermin," and by vermin, Kafka means a cockroach. In this particular translation, the opening sentence is only 19 words. But at the end of it, we know the name of the main character, we know that he is a man riddled with anxiety, and we know that he has undergone a horrific transformation. The rest of the story is essentially just working out all the implications of what it means for a man to be transformed overnight into a giant cockroach.

Both of these openings are in the third person, but what if we begin at the beginning in the first person, with the narrator directly addressing the reader? I don't want to say that this is a uniquely American way of opening a novel—this is how *David Copperfield* begins, after all, as well as Salman Rushdie's *Midnight's Children*—but certainly many of the most famous American novels begin with the narrator speaking directly to the reader.

Herman Melville's *Moby-Dick* begins with, "Call me Ishmael." And Mark Twain's *Adventures of Huckleberry Finn* begins with these famous sentences: "You don't know about me without you have read a book by the name of *The Adventures of Tom Sawyer*, but that ain't no matter. That book was made Mr. Mark Twain, and he told the truth, mainly. There was things which he stretched, but mainly he told the truth." In this case, the opening is not particularly dramatic, but it draws us in with one of the most distinctive voices in American literature—direct, humorous, and folksy.

The opening of *Huckleberry Finn* also sets the tone of the novel. Whatever happens later, whether it's funny or desperate and profound, we know that we will hear about it from a character who is simultaneously lively and humane.

The opening of another great American novel, Marilynne Robinson's *Housekeeping*, combines the directness of Melville with a straightforward summary of the important characters and the premise of the plot: "My name is Ruth. I grew up with my younger sister, Lucille, under the care of my grandmother, Mrs. Sylvia Foster, and when she died, of her sisters-in-law, Misses Lily and Nona Foster, and when they fled, of her daughter, Mrs. Sylvia Fisher."

The deceptive simplicity of this draws the reader in, but there is a lot packed in this sentence: orphaned sisters, the death of a grandparent, abandonment. It also sets up the reader for the slow-motion surprise of the rest of the novel, as Ruth and Lucile's final guardian, Sylvia, turns out to be one of the most eccentric characters in modern American fiction.

Everything in that first sentence is true, but the working out of that situation—two little girls being cared for by a series of older relatives who either die, flee, or turn out to be strange—leads the reader into one of the most mysterious and complex experiences I've ever had as a reader. And it's the straightforward directness of Ruth's voice, her willingness to tell us everything, that keeps us engaged with the novel, no matter how weird and unsettling things get.

As I keep saying in these lectures, writing is about imposing order on chaos, about making decisions. These decisions are often arbitrary ones, out of what seems to be an infinity of choices. Writing fiction is also as much about what you leave out as what you leave in. Your decision about when, where, and with whom to begin a narrative opens one path for you even as it closes off a lot of others. And just like making decisions in real life, sometimes you don't realize what the consequences of your choices are until much, much later.

But unlike life, you can always go back and fix a bad decision, or even start over from scratch. Writing, and especially plotting, is not a science. It's an organic and wildly inefficient process of trial and error. But it's the stuff you don't plan for, the stuff that you don't see coming, the stuff that just presents itself—surprise!—as you go along—that's the stuff that makes fiction worth reading, and makes the writing of it simultaneously frustrating and rewarding.

In the next and final lecture about plot, I'll talk about bringing a narrative to a conclusion, and I'll be focusing on three examples: Henry James's novella *The Aspern Papers*, Flannery O'Connor's short story "A Good Man Is Hard to Find," and Katherine Mansfield's story "Miss Brill."

In the meantime, here's an exercise to help you jump-start the opening of a story. Imagine, at random and without thinking about it too much, some sort of striking or intriguing situation. For example, imagine a man and woman who are eating at a candlelit table in a romantic restaurant, but they aren't speaking to each other—in fact, they don't even look at each other. Or imagine a woman standing in an alley in the rain at night, holding a knife.

Then, again without thinking about it too much, try imagining the very next thing that happens, and then the next, and then the next. If you find yourself running out of steam or boxing yourself into a corner, then go back to the original situation and try something completely different. I think you'll be surprised at how productive this can be.

Happily Ever After—How to End a Plot
Lecture 14

If starting a narrative is daunting, bringing one to an end can be tricky. What readers think of the end of a plot often colors their opinions of the entire narrative. A plot that has a successful or, at least, a vivid ending can make a mediocre narrative seem better than it is, while a weak ending can make an otherwise superb narrative lose its luster. Endings are also difficult because what people consider a good ending depends on individual taste and because what writers and readers consider a good ending has changed over time. In this lecture, however, we'll look at two fundamental qualities that nearly everyone agrees an ending should have: believability and satisfaction.

Believability and Satisfaction

- In part, believability depends on what we as readers bring to a story, specifically our own individual understanding of how the real world works and what real people are like.

  - This doesn't mean that the rules of the real world can't be bent: Your readers are willing to accept that the laws of nature can be altered, broken, or ignored in fantasy, horror, and science fiction, as long as you provide an alternative set of rules for your fictional world and stick to them.

  - Readers of any genre, however, are less likely to buy into a character whose final actions violate their beliefs about human psychology. Different readers have different ideas and expectations about how human beings think and behave or how they ought to think or behave. An ending that strikes one reader as completely plausible and even admirable may strike another as preposterous and even offensive.

- Consider the ending of *Jane Eyre*. The brooding, sexually magnetic Mr. Rochester persuades Jane to fall in love with him without bothering to tell her that he's already married and that he keeps his first wife locked in the attic. At the end of the novel, after a series of plot twists, Jane happily marries Mr. Rochester.

- o Most readers accept this ending, given the narrative conventions of the time and because Jane is such an admirable character that we want her to be happy. Still, it's possible to imagine a reader who just can't believe that someone as smart and independent as Jane would give someone as manipulative and self-serving as Mr. Rochester a second chance.

- o If you believe that character is more fundamental to fiction than plot, then the key to crafting a believable ending is staying true to the nature of your characters. You can make an ending believable if you can get the reader to play along with the premise and if you play fair with the reader by obeying the rules of your own world but especially by respecting your own characters.

- Just because an ending is believable doesn't mean it's satisfying. In the terminology of philosophy, believability is a necessary condition of a satisfying ending, but it is not a sufficient one.

- o As we've seen, believability isn't an absolute quality, but satisfaction is even more dependent on taste and personal experience.

- o We can conceivably make a case for the believability of an ending, but we can no more convince a skeptic to be satisfied by an ending than we can make people change their minds about foods they don't like.

Resolution

- In *The Art of Fiction*, John Gardner says that there are two ways a narrative can end: "in resolution, when no further event can take place … or in logical exhaustion." Of course, there are other types of endings, but these two definitions probably cover most possibilities. Let's start with resolution, which is what we've termed a binary ending—one that resolves an either/or situation or answers a simple question posed at the beginning of the narrative.

- Plots with binary endings are often dismissed as mechanical and contrived, and many of them are. We could even argue that the ending of some simple binary narratives is the least important thing about them; the real reason we enjoy them is that we enjoy the setting or characters. This is often the case with well-written genre narratives: The journey is interesting, even if the destination turns out to be unmemorable.

Binary endings are the kind we find in most bestselling novels and popular movies and television shows: Who committed the crime? Will the star-crossed lovers get together?

- But it's also true that many binary endings are both immensely satisfying and unforgettable, perhaps even the high point of the story.

  o John le Carré's novel *Tinker, Tailor, Soldier, Spy* is the story of a veteran British spy named George Smiley who is asked by the British intelligence service to find a Soviet mole in its midst.

  o Le Carré complicates the ending of the novel by making the mole an upper-class Englishman and a former lover of Smiley's wife. It's a binary ending with layers, because the mole's betrayal is at once political, social, and personal.

- Many literary novels also have binary endings. Perhaps the most satisfying binary ending of a literary story can be found in Henry James's *The Aspern Papers*. Here, James not only imagines a binary situation that generates suspense, but he peoples the plot with three vivid and sharply defined characters and stays true to them throughout.

Logical Exhaustion
- Gardner's "logical exhaustion" is the point at which a narrative has reached its deepest understanding of a character or a situation, beyond which it would just be repeating itself. This sort of ending does not rely

on raising a binary expectation in the reader, but it does require the early pages to draw the reader into the narrative, setting up an expectation that some sort of revelation will occur.

- One variety of this kind of ending is the epiphany, exemplified in Katherine Mansfield's short story "Miss Brill." Like many epiphany stories, this one doesn't have a plot, but like the best of them, it is carefully constructed to deliver a devastating emotional blow at the end.
  - Every sharply observed detail and every slight shift of emotion in this story builds toward a single piercing epiphany. Mansfield starts by introducing a late-middle-aged woman who lives alone and whose most elegant possession is an old fox stole, which reminds her of her youth.

  - In the middle section, Mansfield shows us the park Miss Brill visits every Sunday and allows us to participate in what she sees there. We see how she prides herself on her gift of quiet observation, and we share the slight superiority she feels toward the people she observes so sharply.

  - We share Miss Brill's moment of communion with the people in the park: She's one of the players in a kind of play they all put on each Sunday. She even takes a brief respite from her loneliness by indulging in the fantasy of them all singing together. But then, her illusions are shattered by two thoughtless lovers who sit on the end of her park bench, and in the end, she sees herself as the world sees her—old, unfashionable, and alone.

  - There's no binary plot here, no situation to resolve, but the story moves with ruthless efficiency to an ending that's every bit as precision engineered—and every bit as powerful—as the ending of *The Aspern Papers*.

Hybrid Ending
- The hybrid ending exists halfway between the binary ending and the epiphany. We see an example in Flannery O'Connor's story "A Good

Man Is Hard to Find," about a southern family that takes a drive to Florida and ends up murdered on a lonely country road by a serial killer.

- The killer, who is called The Misfit, is mentioned in the first paragraph of the story, when the grandmother of the family reads aloud from the newspaper about his recent escape from prison. Then, The Misfit is mentioned only once more, briefly, in the middle of the narrative, before he and his henchmen turn up later.

- The reappearance of The Misfit might have been a Dickensian coincidence in the hands of a lesser writer, but his appearance in the newspaper in the first paragraph is played for laughs so that when he reappears at the end full of genuine menace, the reader's experience mirrors that of the family members as they slowly realize that they're about to die.

- The ending of "A Good Man Is Hard to Find" falls halfway between a binary ending and an epiphany. On the one hand, it ends definitively, with the murder of several of its characters, but like an epiphany story, it changes everything the reader thought about what came before. It doesn't answer a question that was openly posed at the beginning of the story but instead answers a question that the reader didn't even realize was being posed until the story is finished: Is the world a safe place? O'Connor answers with a definitive no.

Thoughts on Endings

- The endings of "A Good Man Is Hard to Find," *The Aspern Papers*, and "Miss Brill" are all satisfying in part because they are all prepared for early in the narrative. All three of these endings also essentially leave the reader with nothing left to know. The major questions are answered, and we have gained our deepest understanding of the situation or the characters.

- The fact that all three of these endings are more or less airtight and perfectly prepared for doesn't necessarily mean that James, Mansfield, and O'Connor knew the ending of each story before he or she started.
  - o It might seem that knowing the ending in advance is the easiest way to write, because you can craft the story to head in that

direction. But you may also find yourself forcing the characters in a particular direction whether they want to go there or not, with the result that your plot can seem contrived and your characters can seem more like puppets than real people.

o Not knowing where you're going may sometimes be easier than planning ahead and may even lead to a more satisfying ending. You may find that your ending arises effortlessly and organically from the situation and the characters—an inevitable result of your choices along the way. Of course, with this method, you may also find that you have painted yourself into a corner or drafted a narrative that just peters out.

- We've noted repeatedly that literature is the creation of meaning out of an otherwise meaningless existence. The ending of a narrative is where that meaning is most sharply defined. It's where the hidden patterns are finally revealed, and we at last have a moment, however fleeting, where we understand everything that came before. In other words, the secret of a satisfying ending is not that it's definitive or revelatory, happy or unhappy, but that there's nothing left to say.

Suggested Reading

Forster, *Aspects of the Novel*.

James, *The Aspern Papers*.

Mansfield, "Miss Brill."

O'Connor, "A Good Man Is Hard to Find."

1. Choose a story or a novel that you love, imagine a different ending for it, and then work backward to see what you'd have to change to make the new ending believable and satisfying. Consider *Jane Eyre* as an example. Jot down a rough outline of everything in the book that leads to Jane's marriage to Mr. Rochester, then imagine a different ending: She marries someone else in the novel, or she decides to live by herself on her inheritance money. Go back through your outline to see what you'd have to change in the story to make the new ending work.

Happily Ever After—How to End a Plot
Lecture 14—Transcript

Starting a narrative is daunting. Bringing one to an end can be tricky. You just can't win.

The end of a plot is the last thing a reader sees, and what she thinks of the ending often irreversibly colors her opinion of the entire narrative. A plot that has a successful or at least a vivid and memorable ending can make a mediocre narrative seem better than it is, while a weak or unconvincing ending can make an otherwise superb narrative lose its luster.

Our old friend E. M. Forster thought that wobbly endings were a common problem for novels in particular. He had this to say about it in *Aspects of the Novel*:

> Nearly all novels are feeble at the end. This is because the plot requires to be wound up. Why is this necessary? Why is there not a convention which allows a novelist to stop as soon as he feels muddled or bored? Alas, he has to round things off, and usually the characters go dead while he is at work, and our final impression of them is through deadness. … Incidents and people that occurred at first for their own sake now have to contribute to the denouement. In the end even the author feels he is being a little foolish. … [M]ost novels do fail here—there is this disastrous standstill while logic takes over the command from flesh and blood.

I suspect that this is a bit tongue-in-cheek. Given that *Aspects of the Novel* is essentially a celebration of careful craftsmanship, I doubt that Forster is entirely serious when he wishes that novelists could just stop as soon as they get "muddled or bored." And remember that Forster was notoriously ambivalent about plot; remember how he said in a "droopy, regretful voice" that "Yes—oh dear yes—the novel tells a story."

But even so, Forster is expressing a peevishness that all writers feel at one time or another. He's also right that it's not uncommon for novels, even great ones, to fall apart at the end. The last quarter of Mark Twain's *Adventures of*

Huckleberry Finn is notoriously weak, especially after Tom Sawyer turns up in the story. The comedy turns labored, the narrative loses momentum, and the plot is resolved in a series of unconvincing contrivances. You can tell that Twain got, well, muddled and bored, and just wanted to wrap things up.

One of my favorite books, Joseph Conrad's *Nostromo*, has the most brilliant opening third of any novel I've ever read, but the last third of it is much more melodramatic and conventional than the rest of the book. It's almost as if Conrad got tired or lost his nerve toward the end.

There are some other factors at play that make endings difficult to talk about. For one thing, what people consider a good ending is dependent on individual taste. For example, many readers are disappointed if a romance doesn't end with the couple getting together, while others think a conventional happy ending is sentimental and unrealistic.

For another thing, what writers and readers consider a good ending has changed over time. The endings of many great 19th century novels now strike many modern readers as contrived and unconvincing. Charles Dickens is an indisputably great writer, but some of his novels have endings that seem ludicrously sentimental to a modern reader. The good characters find love, security, and happiness, while the bad characters are either humiliated or killed off. Or, in the case of Fagin in *Oliver Twist*, they are humiliated *and* killed off.

Some classic novels seem unconvincing to a modern reader because our cultural, social, and moral assumptions have changed. Women who have sex outside of marriage are no longer expected to kill themselves, the way they do in several famous 19th century novels. And some famous 19th century endings have been so widely imitated that they have become hackneyed. At the end of *Jane Eyre*, a poor but intelligent and virtuous woman wins the love of a brooding, sexually magnetic rich guy. However original this may have been when Charlotte Brontë was alive, now it's a trope in modern romance novels and a cliché of Hollywood romantic comedies.But even if they disagree about the particulars, nearly everyone agrees on the two fundamental qualities that a good ending should have. Namely, it should be both believable and satisfying.

Believability and satisfaction are not the same, however, and they are not interchangeable. It's possible for an ending to be believable without being satisfying. In real life, for example, killers often get away with murder, or two lovers who seem perfect for each other never actually get together. Neither of these outcomes would be very satisfying in a conventional narrative.

However, on the other hand, it's not possible for an ending to be both satisfying but not believable. If the killer is caught or the lovers are brought together as a result of a blatant contrivance on the part of the author, the ending is unsatisfying because we don't believe it.

And it should go without saying that a satisfying ending is not necessarily a happy one. Some of the greatest literary novels ever written have unhappy endings. And in recent decades, a lot of first-rate genre fiction has come to rely on unhappy but dramatically satisfying endings. George R. R. Martin's *A Game of Thrones*, the first novel in his *Song of Ice and Fire* series, ends with the death of the novel's noblest character.

So what do we mean when we say that an ending is believable? In part, believability depends on what we as readers bring to a story. Our own, individual understanding of how the world works and what real people are like helps determine what we will believe in a work of fiction. This doesn't mean the rules of the real world can't be bent. Readers are willing to accept that the laws of nature can be altered, broken, or ignored in fantasy, horror, and science fiction, as long as you provide an alternate set of rules for your fictional world and stick to them.

Readers of any genre, however, are less likely to believe a character whose final actions violate their understanding of human psychology. Different readers have different expectations of how human beings think and behave, or how human beings ought to think or behave. An ending that strikes one reader as completely plausible and even admirable will strike another reader as preposterous and even offensive.

Take the ending of *Jane Eyre* again. Mr. Rochester may be brooding and sexually magnetic, but he persuades Jane to fall in love with him without bothering to tell her that he's already married and that he's keeping his crazy first wife locked in his attic. And yet at the end of the novel, after a series of twists that include a surprise inheritance for Jane and a house fire that conveniently kills the first Mrs. Rochester, Jane Eyre happily marries Mr. Rochester.

Most readers accept this ending. For one thing, we take into account the narrative conventions of the time the novel was written. For another, we want Jane to be happy because she is such an admirable character. Still, it's possible to imagine a reader who just can't believe that someone as smart and independent as Jane would give someone as manipulative and self-serving as Mr. Rochester a second chance. Our willingness to believe the ending of *Jane Eyre* depends partly on our general understanding of human nature, but it also depends on our understanding of Jane Eyre herself as an individual character.

If character is more fundamental to fiction than plot, as I argued in Lecture 3, then the key to crafting a believable ending is staying true to the nature of your characters. You can make an ending believable if you can get the reader to play along with the premise of your narrative and if you play fair with the reader by obeying your own rules. But respecting your own characters is especially important.

But, as I said a moment ago, just because an ending is believable doesn't make it satisfying. In the terminology of my long dormant bachelor's degree in philosophy, believability is a necessary condition of a satisfying ending, but it is not a sufficient one. And as we've just seen, believability isn't an absolute quality. Reasonable people can disagree over whether an ending is credible or not.

But satisfaction is an even more ineffable and unquantifiable quality, one that is even more dependent on taste and personal experience. You can at least make a case that a particular ending is believable. You can argue that it's prepared for, that the writer played by the rules, and so on. But you cannot convince a skeptic that an ending is satisfying, any more than you can to make someone change his mind about a food he doesn't like. If you don't like onions, no amount of argument is going to make you like onions.

Consider the passionate arguments that erupt online or around water coolers after the final episodes of such popular television series as *The Sopranos* or *Breaking Bad*. If you were annoyed and unsatisfied at the abrupt disappearance of Tony Soprano in the very last moments of his final episode, no amount of passionate exegesis from me is going to change your mind. Just as it is with onions, satisfaction is a wholly subjective judgment. Endings are a matter of taste, and as the Latin maxim has it, *de gustibus non est disputandum*: "In matters of taste, there can be no dispute."

At this point, perhaps we should throw up our hands like E. M. Forster, but as even he would admit, yes—oh dear yes—a work of fiction must have an ending. So, let's just accept the fact that an ending cannot be all things to all people, and let's take a look at three endings that are considered satisfying by most readers.

In *The Art of Fiction*, our other old friend, John Gardner, says that there are two ways a narrative can end:

> In resolution, when no further event can take place (the murderer has been caught and hanged, the diamond has been found and restored to its owner, the elusive lady has been captured and married), or in logical exhaustion, our recognition that we've reached the stage of infinite repetition; more events might follow, perhaps from now till Kingdom Come, but they will all express the same thing.

Now, this is an oversimplification, because there are other types of endings, not to mention hybrid varieties, but these two definitions probably cover most possibilities.

Let's start with the sort of ending Gardner calls resolution, but which I have called a binary ending. As you may recall, this is the kind of ending that resolves an either/or situation or answers a simple question that was posed in the opening pages of the narrative. This is the sort of ending you find in most bestselling novels, popular movies, and television shows. Who committed the crime? Will the two star-crossed lovers get together? Will the intelligence agent foil the supervillain's plot? Will the hero of the epic fantasy complete his quest?

Plots with binary endings are often dismissed as mechanical and contrived, and, to be honest, many of them are. You could even argue that the endings of some of these simple binary narratives is the least important thing about them, and the real reason we enjoy them is that we enjoy the setting or the characters.

For example, I used to watch reruns of the television drama *Law and Order* obsessively. Even when I knew I'd seen an episode once or twice already, I'd watch it again anyway, because I could never remember how it turned out. I came to realize that my pleasure in watching the show didn't come from the ending, but from the time I spent in the company of characters like Sam McCoy or Lenny Briscoe. This is often the case with well-written genre narratives: The journey is interesting, even if the destination turns out to be unmemorable.

But let's not dismiss binary endings out of hand. There are a lot of great narratives where the ending is both immensely satisfying and unforgettable, and maybe even the high point of the story. John le Carré's great spy novel *Tinker, Tailor, Soldier, Spy* is the story of a veteran British spy named George Smiley who is asked by the British intelligence service to find a Soviet mole in their midst. This is a binary ending with a vengeance, along the lines of a classic country-house murder mystery: Smiley assembles a list of suspects and investigates each one. Then, in a sweaty-palmed climactic scene, he discovers which one of his colleagues actually is a Soviet spy.

Much of the fun of the book lies in the twists and turns of the investigation, and in le Carré's sharp delineation of his large cast of characters. But the ending is tremendously satisfying, and not mechanical or contrived at all. This is because le Carré complicates the ending by making the mole an upper class Englishman and a former lover of Smiley's wife. This means that the mole is not just a traitor to his country, but a traitor to his class and to his professional colleagues. It's a binary ending with layers, because the mole's betrayal is at once political, social, and personal.

Many literary novels also have binary endings. Will Elizabeth Bennett marry Mr. Darcy in *Pride and Prejudice*? Will Ahab catch and kill Moby-Dick?

Will Jay Gatsby win Daisy Buchanan back from her brutish husband in *The Great Gatsby*?

One literary story in particular has perhaps the most satisfying binary ending I've ever read. Henry James's novella *The Aspern Papers* is narrated by an unnamed literary critic whose passion is a long-dead American poet named Jeffrey Aspern. The critic has learned that some letters from Aspern may still be in the possession of the poet's former lover, who is now a very old woman living in Venice. The critic then goes to Venice, where he learns that the old woman, Juliana Bordereau, is living in a decaying old palazzo in the company of her plain, middle-aged niece, Miss Tina. Because Juliana and Miss Tina are living in poverty, the critic insinuates himself into their house by renting a room from them. And because he suspects that Juliana has no intention of letting anyone see the letters, he tries to allay her suspicions by pretending to be romantically interested in Miss Tina.

This is a tight little triangle of characters—the unscrupulous narrator, the suspicious old woman in possession of a priceless literary treasure, and the lonely middle-aged woman—and it sets up not one, not two, but three binary questions: Will the critic get the letters? Will Juliana discover his true intentions? Will the critic callously break Miss Tina's heart?

James shows us the wary dance of these three characters through a series of impeccably crafted scenes, each one of which ratchets the tension up a little higher. The novella culminates in an almost gothic climax in the middle of the night, when the narrator tries to break into the desk where he thinks the letters might be hidden and is caught in the act by Juliana. She curses him, and he flees the house. Juliana dies soon thereafter, and the narrator returns to the house to ask Miss Tina if she might let him have the papers. Miss Tina hints that she might—if he agrees to marry her. The narrator flees again, because he can't imagine marrying someone he thinks of as "a ridiculous pathetic provincial old woman." (It goes without saying that the narrator of *The Aspern Papers* is no prince.)

But he's desperate for the papers, so in the final pages of the novella, when the narrator returns once more to the palazzo, where Miss Tina has changed somehow. As he puts it:

Her look of forgiveness, of absolution, made her angelic. It beautified her; she was younger; she was not a ridiculous old woman. This trick of her expression, this magic of her spirit, transfigured her, and while I still noted it I heard a whisper somewhere in the depths of my conscience: "Why not, after all—why not?" It seemed to me I could pay the price.

In other words, at the end of the story, the critic is tempted to marry Miss Tina in order to get the letters. Then, on the very last page of the novella, Henry James springs the trap he has expertly laid for both the narrator and the reader, when Miss Tina reveals that she burned the letters one by one, the night before.

And so *The Aspern Papers* fulfills the reader's expectations by answering all three of the binary questions it posed at the start: No, the critic does not get the papers. Yes, Juliana discovers his true intentions. As for the third question—will Miss Tina's heart be broken?—the answer turns out to be the most satisfying twist in the story, because Miss Tina turns out to be as skillful and ruthless a player as the narrator. If the narrator did break her heart, Miss Tina earns her revenge by breaking his, by denying him the one thing he ever really wanted.

This is storytelling of the highest order. Henry James not only imagines a binary situation that generates suspense, he peoples the plot with three vivid and sharply defined characters and stays true to them. There is the conniving narrator who isn't nearly as clever as he thinks he is. There is the mistrustful old woman who has spent a lifetime living in the shadow of a famous poet. And there is the watchful spinster who shines with beauty in her one moment of bitter triumph. The reversal at the end is the best kind of surprise, where the reader is thinking simultaneously, "I did not see that coming," and, "Of course!"

Now let's talk about the sort of ending that Gardner calls a case of "logical exhaustion." This is the point at which a narrative has reached its deepest understanding of a character or a situation, and beyond which it would just be repeating itself. This sort of ending does not rely on raising a binary expectation in the reader, but it does require the early pages to draw the reader into the narrative by setting up an expectation in the reader that some sort of revelation is going to occur.

A variety of this kind of ending is the epiphany, which I explained a couple of lectures ago. The example I used then was James Joyce's long story "The Dead," but this time I want to talk about the short story "Miss Brill" by Katherine Mansfield, one of Joyce's contemporaries. It's only five pages long, and, like many epiphany stories, it doesn't really have a plot. But like the best of the epiphany stories, it is carefully constructed to deliver a devastating emotional blow at the end.

Miss Brill is a late-middle-aged Englishwoman who lives alone in a rented room in a seaside town in France, where she makes her living teaching English. Every Sunday, she sits on a bench in the public gardens, listening to a brass band and watching the crowd pass by. She especially enjoys eavesdropping on the conversations of the other people who sometimes share her bench.

In the opening paragraph, Miss Brill is seated on the bench on a bright but slightly chilly Sunday afternoon. She is wearing a fox stole, the sort of fur wrap that still has the head, feet, and tail of the fox at either end, and she recalls the pleasure she took in lifting it out of its box and brushing it before she put it on and left her room.

The middle section of the story is like George Seurat's brilliantly detailed pointillist painting, *A Sunday on La Grand Jatte*, as Miss Brill observes the old married couple on the bench next to her, watches children play, and witnesses an old woman trying unsuccessfully to flirt with an elderly man.

She takes delight in thinking of the scene as a kind of a play in which she's one of the actors. She even enters into a lovely fantasy in which everyone in the park starts to sing along with the band:

> The young ones, the laughing ones who were moving together, they would begin, and the men's voices, very resolute and brave, would join them. And then she too, she too, and the others on the benches— they would come in with a kind of accompaniment—something

low, that scarcely rose or fell, something so beautiful—moving. … And Miss Brill's eyes filled with tears and she looked smiling at all the other members of the company. Yes, we understand, we understand, she thought—though what they understood she didn't know.

This moment when Miss Brill feels a communion with all the other people in the park is immediately ruined, however. An amorous young couple sit on the bench next to her, and the girl refuses to kiss the boy because of "that stupid old thing" at the end of the bench. It takes a moment for reader and Miss Brill to realize that the "stupid old thing" she's referring to is Miss Brill herself. The girl goes on to make fun of Miss Brill's beloved fox stole, by comparing it to a dead fish. The story then jumps abruptly to its last two paragraphs, where Miss Brill returns to her tiny, shabby room and sits on the bed for a long time.

The story ends like this: "The box that the fur came out of was on the bed. She unclasped the necklet quickly; quickly, without looking, laid it inside. But when she put the lid on she thought she heard something crying."

I'm not sure my summary can evoke the story's power, but I hope it gives you at least an idea of the elements that make it work. Every sharply observed detail and every slight shift of emotion builds toward a single piercing epiphany.

Mansfield starts by introducing a woman whose most elegant possession is an old fox stole, which she treats with loving care because it reminds her of her youth. Then, in the middle section, in the manner of *Mrs. Dalloway*, Mansfield shows us the park through Miss Brill's eyes and allows us to participate in Miss Brill's reactions.

We see how she prides herself on her gift of quiet observation, and we share the slight superiority she feels towards the people she observes so sharply. Then we share her moment of communion: She is one of people in the park, after all, one of the players in this play they all put on each Sunday. She takes brief respite from her loneliness by indulging in the fantasy of everyone singing together—only to have her illusions shattered by two thoughtless young lovers. And just as the end of *The Aspern Papers* clicks shut like a trap on the last page, so does the last paragraph of "Miss Brill." The title character suddenly and unexpectedly sees herself as the world sees her. And, from that slight observational remove that she was so proud of in the park, she can hear herself weeping.

There is no binary plot here, no situation to resolve. But we have reached the point that Gardner called "logical exhaustion": Miss Brill has had a devastating insight into her own life, and the reader has shared that devastating insight. This insight changes everything that Miss Brill and the reader had thought up to this point, and it cannot be taken back. Her life will go on, but there is nothing new left to learn. The story moves sentence by sentence with ruthless efficiency to an ending that's every bit as precision-engineered, and every bit as powerful, as the end of *The Aspern Papers*.

Let's look now at a sort of hybrid ending, existing halfway between the binary ending and the epiphany. Flannery O'Connor's story "A Good Man Is Hard to Find" is about a southern family who take a drive to Florida and end up being murdered on a lonely country road by a serial killer. The killer, who is called The Misfit, is mentioned in the story's very first paragraph. The grandmother of the family, who is the story's main point-of-view character, reads aloud from the newspaper about his recent escape from prison. After that, The Misfit is mentioned only once more, briefly, before he and his henchmen turn up later in the story, after the family has driven its car into a ditch. Meanwhile, the central portion of the story is a comic portrayal of the family bickering with each other in the car and stopping for barbecue.

The reappearance of The Misfit might have been a Dickensian coincidence in the hands of a lesser writer. But his appearance in the newspaper in the first paragraph is played for laughs. As a result, when he reappears at the end full of genuine menace, the reader's experience mirrors that of the family as they slowly realize that they're about to die. "This can't be happening," you think the first time you read the story, which is exactly what the family must be thinking. But because it is so skillfully prepared for, the ending leads you to a radical change of perspective. Instead of finding the coincidence unbelievable, you find instead that the ending alters your understanding of everything that came before.

The grandmother's foolishness, for example, which was funny and kind of sweet for most of the story, ends up becoming tragic and pitiable. The offhand references to The Misfit in the first paragraph and briefly again in the middle of the story turn out to be foreshadowing. They are hints, if only we'd picked up on them, of a version of the world that is both profound and terrifying.

The story closes with the same finality as *The Aspern Papers*. O'Connor prepares for her ending with as much skill as Henry James does. But where Henry James lays his plot points out where the reader can see them, O'Connor hides hers behind a scrim of irony. The Misfit is foreshadowed in the first paragraph, but in such a way that a first time reader doesn't suspect he's important; he's just the groundless fear of an old woman.

And O'Connor also skillfully underplays the plot twists that lead to the family's death. It is the grandmother's insistence that they take a side trip to visit a house she used to know that leads to their accident. And what seals the family's doom is the fact that she calls The Misfit by his nickname as soon as she sees him. These two mistakes by the grandmother are simultaneously shrewdly observed bits of her character and tripwires that lead inevitably to her death and to the deaths of her loved ones.

The ending of "A Good Man Is Hard to Find" falls halfway between a binary ending and an epiphany. On the one hand it ends definitively, with the murder of several of its characters, but like an epiphany story, it radically changes everything the reader thought about what came before. It doesn't answer a question that was openly posed at the beginning of the story, but instead it answers a question that the reader didn't even realize was being posed until after he finishes the story. The question is, "Is the world a safe place?" and the story answers with a definitive "No."

What makes these three endings satisfying? I can't say for certain, because not every reader will necessarily find them as satisfying as I do. But I can tell you what they have in common. Each one is prepared for, starting with the first page or even the first paragraph of the narrative. The opening of *The Aspern Papers* sets up all three binary questions that the ending answers. The Misfit is mentioned in the very first paragraph of "A Good Man Is Hard to

Find." And Miss Brill's faded fox stole, the symbol of her own faded appeal, is mentioned in the very first paragraph.

Think back to John Gardner's definitions of how a narrative can end: that a story either resolves, or it logically exhausts itself. All three of these endings essentially leave the reader with nothing left to know. Each writer has taken us as far as we can go. All the major questions are answered, and we have gained our deepest understanding of the situation or the characters.

In the last lecture, I talked about two ways of starting a plot. One is to work toward an ending you already know. The other is to let the plot tell you what the ending should be. All three of these endings are more or less airtight, and perfectly prepared for. But that doesn't necessarily mean that Henry James, Katherine Mansfield, and Flannery O'Connor knew the ending of each story before they started. They may very well have—I don't actually know—but it seems to me that either method may generate a satisfying ending.

At first glance, it might seem that knowing the ending in advance is the easiest way to write, because you can direct the story at every point to head in that direction. But you also run the risk of forcing the characters in a particular direction whether they want to go there or not. In that case, your plot can seem contrived and unlifelike, and your characters seem more like puppets than living, breathing people.

It may be that not knowing where you're going is easier than planning ahead. Not knowing where you're going may even lead to a more satisfying ending. You may also find that your ending arises effortlessly and organically from the situation and the characters, as a natural and inevitable result of your choices along the way. Of course, with this method you may also find that you have painted yourself into a corner, or have drafted a narrative that just peters out. Either way, you're running the risk of having to go back and start again, but hey, that's showbiz.

Way back in the second lecture, I talked about how literature is the creation of order out of chaos, the creation of meaning out of an otherwise meaningless existence. The ending of a narrative is where that meaning is most sharply defined. The ending is where the hidden patterns are finally revealed. The ending is where, at least for a fleeting moment, we understand everything that came before.

In other words, perhaps the secret of a satisfying ending, of any variety, is not that it's definitive or revelatory, or happy or unhappy. Perhaps the secret of a satisfying ending is that there's nothing left to say.

With the next lecture, I'll be starting a block of three lectures about point of view. In the first lecture, I'll be talking in general about the wide range of points of view, touching briefly on a variety of works, including George Eliot's *Middlemarch*, Marilynne Robinson's *Housekeeping*, and Nabokov's *Lolita*.

In the meantime, here's an exercise to help you think about crafting an ending. Take a story or a novel that you really love and imagine a different ending for it. Then work back to see what you'd have to change to make the new ending believable and satisfying. Take *Jane Eyre* as example. Jot down a rough outline of everything in the book that leads to Jane's marriage to Mr. Rochester, then imagine a different ending. Perhaps she marries someone else in the novel, or she decides to go live by herself on her inheritance money. Then go back through the outline and see what you'd have to change in the story to make the new ending work.

And how can you tell I have reached the end of this lecture? Because I have nothing left to say!

Seeing through Other Eyes—Point of View
Lecture 15

A s we've seen throughout these lectures, writing fiction is all about making choices, and deciding what point of view and voice to adopt in a narrative is one of the most important choices you have to make. This choice not only determines the perspective from which the story and plot are viewed, but it can determine what actually happens, and it has a powerful effect on what characters you include and how you depict them. In this lecture, we'll take a quick tour of the most important types of point of view; then, in the next two lectures, we'll look at the first person point of view and the third person point of view in more detail.

Point-of-View Tour
- If you imagine your story as a landscape, you can think of point of view as the dome of the sky arching over the story. The different possible points of view are points on that curve: from the highest point, overlooking the entire landscape, to the lowest point, where a character or a narrator can see only what's directly in front of him or her.

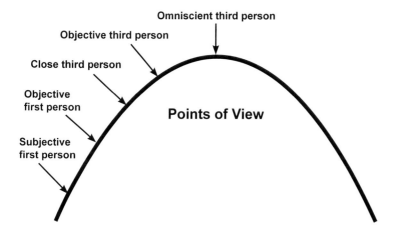

- The most all-inclusive point of view is the omniscient third person. This is the point of view in which the author and the narrator seem to be more or less the same person, though that's not necessarily the case. This sort of narration sees, knows, and usually reveals everything about the characters in the story. This point of view is often called godlike because, like an all-powerful, all-knowing deity, the narration can see into the hearts and minds of its characters, revealing their most intimate secrets.

- A little closer to the ground but still fairly high up on the curve is the objective third-person point of view. One of the best examples of this point of view is Dashiell Hammett's *The Maltese Falcon*. In this novel, although we see and hear everything every character does, we never get inside their minds.
  - Unlike an omniscient point of view, which generally shows us what characters are thinking and feeling, the objective third person is more like a video camera, recording and reporting everything it sees but allowing readers to make up their own minds about the characters' feelings, thought, and motivations.

  - This may be the most lifelike point of view because it reproduces what it feels like for each of us to move through the real world, trying to infer what other people around us are thinking from their speech or actions but never really knowing for sure. Although it's perhaps more lifelike, it's also colder than third-person omniscient, which engages more deeply and intimately in the lives of its characters.

- About halfway down the dome of our imaginary sky is the close or limited third-person point of view. More recently, this has come to be known as *free indirect discourse*. In this point of view, the narration uses third-person pronouns, and like the omniscient third person, it gets inside the minds of its characters. But in many narratives of this sort, the whole story or novel is generally told from the point of view of only one character.
  - Because this close third-person point of view can often shift among several characters in the same narrative, it can easily turn into the omniscient third person. George Eliot's *Middlemarch* is written in this way, as is Faulkner's *Light in August*.

- The traditional omniscient third person is often more remote from its characters and capable of making sweeping judgments about society, whereas modern novels written in the more intimate close third person generally shy away from that.

- Still, the close third person allows the author occasionally to pull back the camera and either comment directly on the action as the author or show us something the point-of-view character can't or doesn't know. Free indirect discourse is the default mode of much contemporary fiction.

- In the objective first person, the narration uses first-person pronouns, but it maintains a certain distance from the action of the narrative. In other words, the story or novel is narrated by a fictional character who plays only a minor part in the story or isn't present in the story at all. Two good examples are Ishmael in *Moby-Dick* and Nick Carraway in *The Great Gatsby*.

- At ground level in our landscape is the subjective first person, in which the first-person narrator is the main character or one of the main characters in the story. For example, Huck Finn is both the narrator and the main character of Mark Twain's *The Adventures of Huckleberry Finn*. We see and hear everything in the book through Huck's eyes, and we know only what Huck witnesses or hears about. In more recent times, the subjective first person has become more prevalent.

- This curve of sky representing different points of view is a continuum, of course, and narratives can and do find points between the ones we've just described. In addition, many books mix and match points of view.

The Narrator's Audience

- One question related to point of view is this: Is the narration addressed to an unknown reader in the real world, or is it addressed to some person or group of people who exist in the world of the story?

- Consider, for example, three of the most famous first-person narratives in literature: Brontë's *Jane Eyre*, Twain's *The Adventures of Huckleberry*

Finn, and Nabokov's *Lolita*. In all three, there are at least hints of the narrator's awareness that he or she is addressing the reader of the book.

- o Jane Eyre narrates her story as if she were writing her memoir for posterity. In the most famous line from the book, she makes it clear that she knows she's writing a book when she says about Mr. Rochester, "Reader, I married him." This is a memorable example of a fictional character speaking directly to the real readers of her book.

- o Huck Finn bridges the gap between fiction and reality in his first sentence: "You don't know about me without you have read a book by the name of *The Adventures of Tom Sawyer* … by Mr. Mark Twain." Here, we have a fictional character speaking directly to the reader and referencing a real book by a real author, in which he, Huck, first appears as a fictional character.

- o *Lolita* opens with an introduction by a fictional psychiatrist, and the rest of the book is pitched as a confession written by Humbert Humbert in prison. Unlike Jane Eyre and Huck Finn, who cross the divide between the fictional world and the real world, Humbert Humbert remains more constrained within the pages of his book because he knows he's writing something that may only ever be read by the authorities who locked him away.

- This question becomes even more complicated when we consider first-person narrators who speak in the present tense. Such a narration contributes to the pace and immediacy of an exciting story, but there's something fundamentally improbable about it: Are we to understand that the character is silently narrating his or her own actions in the moment?

- The uses of the third person can be just as diverse. The 19th-century third-person omniscient voice of George Eliot and Leo Tolstoy is very much a public, authoritative voice. The more feverish voice of Dickens, however, sounds more like a particular person, even though he often writes in the third person.

- There are also third-person narrations that presume the reader's intimacy with the social setting and the worldview of the author, such as Jane Austen in *Pride and Prejudice*.

- In the 20th century, the stream-of-consciousness third person of such books as *Mrs. Dalloway* doesn't seem as though it's speaking to anyone outside of the character, let alone outside of the novel. Even though the novel is technically in the third person, the effect of reading *Mrs. Dalloway*'s narrative voice is like eavesdropping on each character's thoughts as they happen.

Temporal Distance

- The other element of point of view and voice that we need to consider is the distance in time from which the story is told. Partly, this is simply a matter of verb tense, but it's also about a larger issue, namely, the distance of the first-person narrator or the third-person narrative voice from the events being depicted.

- With a first-person narrator, you have to decide just how close the narrator is to the events he or she is describing. Huck Finn is told mainly in the past tense, but the implication of Huck's voice throughout the book is that he is still a boy, telling us about a series of events that have happened in the recent past. In other words, it's a story about a child told by the child.

- We get a slightly different effect from Harper Lee's *To Kill a Mockingbird*, where the distance of Scout, the first-person narrator of the novel, is deliberately ambiguous. At times, her narration is immediate and limited to what she knew as a young girl, but the novel also steps back and narrates the events from the point of view of Scout as a grown woman, looking back on her childhood. We get a child's-eye view of childhood leavened with an adult's retrospective explanation of events that Scout as a child wouldn't have fully understood.

- This element of temporal distance from the events in the narrative is just as important with third-person narratives. Being the default tense of so many narratives, the past tense doesn't necessarily mean the distant past:

Tolstoy's *Anna Karenina* is told in the past tense, for example, but it was both written and set during the 1870s. George Eliot's *Middlemarch*, on the other hand, was published in the early 1870s but set 40 years earlier, in the 1830s. Tolstoy uses the past tense to tell a contemporary story, while Eliot uses the past tense to tell a story of the recent past, giving the reader some distance from the events.

o   The 40-year timespan may not seem like much, but if we transfer the difference to the present day, we can see that Eliot's use of the past tense is significantly different from Tolstoy's.

o   Consider the difference between watching the two television shows *Breaking Bad* and *Mad Men*: *Breaking Bad* was set more or less in the present moment, allowing no temporal distance between the story and the viewers. But with *Mad Men*, set in the early 1960s, we can at least cling to the illusion that we are better behaved than the people who worked on Madison Avenue were at that time.

Suggested Reading

Brontë, *Jane Eyre*.

Eliot, *Middlemarch*.

Fitzgerald, *The Great Gatsby*.

Lee, *To Kill a Mockingbird*.

Melville, *Moby-Dick*.

Nabokov, *Lolita*.

Robinson, *Housekeeping*.

Tolstoy, *Anna Karenina*.

Twain, *The Adventures of Huckleberry Finn*.

1. Choose an opening from one of the books discussed in this lecture, another book you've read, or something you've written and try rewriting it from a different point of view, in a different verb tense, or in a different voice. Would *The Adventures of Huckleberry Finn* work if it were narrated in the third person or in the first person by an elderly Huck looking back on his childhood? Would George Eliot be able to create as broad a portrait of the community in *Middlemarch* if it were narrated by only one character? What would *I, Claudius* feel like if it was written in the present tense? Would it make the Roman emperor's court feel more immediate, or would it just feel bizarre?

Seeing through Other Eyes—Point of View
Lecture 15—Transcript

As I said in my earlier lectures about character, fiction gives us access to the consciousness of other people. This is just another way of saying that fiction allows us to see the world from someone else's point of view.

Point of view is just as fundamental to fiction as character and plot. It's hard, if not impossible, to imagine a work of fiction without any characters in it, and by the same token, it's pretty much impossible to imagine a work of fiction that has no point of view. Even the most remote third-person narrative, which watches human behavior without judgment as if through a security camera, is a particular point of view.

Just as there are different ways to create character or structure a plot, there are a wide variety of points of view. There's the imperial, godlike, third person of the great 19th century authors such as George Eliot or Leo Tolstoy. There's the intimate, limited third person of a high modernist novel like *Mrs. Dalloway*, shifting from one character to the next. Or there's the distinctive first person of books as different from each other as *Jane Eyre*, *The Adventures of Huckleberry Finn*, *Heart of Darkness*, *Lolita*, or *Housekeeping*.

Choosing a point of view is not just about deciding whether to use the third person or the first person. Choosing a point of view also determines the style and tone of the narration, specifically the quality that writers call *voice*. Think about a favorite novel or short story, especially one that is narrated in the first person, and I'll bet that what you remember mainly is the narrator's voice. Long after most of us have forgotten the plot details of *The Adventures of Huckleberry Finn*, we remember the sly, slangy voice of Huck himself. We remember Jane Eyre's grit and restrained passion. We remember Humbert Humbert's creepy erudition in *Lolita*.

Each one of these individual voices not only evokes the character who is telling the story, it also determines the tone, sensibility, and moral stance of the narrative. Jane Eyre's decency and stubborn determination aren't just a reflection of her own personality, they represent Charlotte Brontë's view of what people are like and how the world works.

It's important to remember that Mark Twain is not Huck Finn, Charlotte Brontë is not Jane Eyre, and that Nabokov is not Humbert Humbert. In the next lecture, I'll talk more about the double consciousness of the first-person narrator. It's even possible for a writer to create a first-person narrator who may not be telling the truth, the way Eudora Welty does in her short story "Why I Live at the P.O." I'll also talk about that technique, known as an unreliable narrator, in the next lecture.

But as distinctive as a first-person narration can be, it's not as if first-person narrators have all the fun. A third-person narration can have as distinctive a voice as a first-person narrator. One of the hallmarks of a great author, in fact, is the way his or her distinctive voice can become another character in the narrative, even if that voice isn't actually participating in the story.

You can't read Dickens, for example, without coming away with a vivid impression of the author himself, even when he's writing in the third person, maybe even especially when he's writing in the third person. His great novel *Bleak House* is written in both the first and the third person, and you can't read it without getting a vivid idea of which characters Dickens approves of and which ones he doesn't. It's clear what makes Dickens angry, what makes him laugh, and what he thinks is the moral thing to do. His unique view of humanity, expressed with his boundless energy, is present on every page.

George Eliot's great novel *Middlemarch* is written in the third person, but it also features frequent comments directly from the author. As a result, when you read *Middlemarch*, you're not only following the characters and the story, you're engaging with one of the sharpest and least sentimental intellects in English literature. And if you read *Bleak House* and *Middlemarch* one right after the other—and that's a lot of reading, because they are both great, big books—you can see right away that you could never mistake Eliot's voice for Dickens', or vice versa.

As I keep reminding you throughout these lectures, writing fiction is all about making choices. When it comes to point of view, you have to decide whether your story will be told by someone in the story or by an outside narrator. You also have to decide what voice that character or that narrator is going to use. Choosing a point of view and a voice not only determines the perspective from which the story and the plot are viewed, it also determines which characters you include and how you depict them, as well as what actually happens in the narrative. Choosing a point of view is one of the most important decisions you will make.

In this lecture, I want to take a quick tour of the most important types of point of view. Then, in the next two lectures, we'll look at the first-person point of view and then the third-person point of view in more detail.

I have found that it sometimes helps to think of point of view as something literal, as a way of looking at a landscape, for example. Imagine your setting as an actual landscape, with plains, mountains, valleys, forests, and deserts. Your story is what happens to your characters as they move across this landscape. Let's think of the different types of point of view as actual points along the curve of the sky arching over the story, from the highest point, overlooking the entire landscape, to the lowest point, right at ground level, where a character or a narrator can only see what's directly in front of him or her.

Let's start with the third-person point of view. As we'll discover in more detail in a subsequent lecture, there are different types of third person. The most all-inclusive variety is the third-person omniscient point of view, right at the zenith of our metaphorical sky. This is the point of view in which the author and the narrator seem to be more or less the same person, though that's not necessarily the case. As John Gardner puts it, the omniscient narrator is a persona of the author. Whether or not this narrator is the same person as the author, this sort of narration sees all and is capable of revealing everything there is to know about the characters.

This point of view is often called godlike, because the narration is like an all-powerful, all-knowing deity who can not only see the entire landscape beneath, but into the hearts and minds of its characters. This type of narration can place a character in her historical, political, and social context at the same time as it can reveal her most intimate secrets. This variety of the third-person point of view is often associated with the 19th century, when it was used without irony by such great writers as George Eliot and Leo Tolstoy.

With the rise of modernism and postmodernism, the omniscient point of view came to be used more ironically. Even so, it was the point of view that dominated fiction right through the middle of the 20th century, often in large-scale novels that have a lot of characters and often evoke whole communities. A good example is Paule Marshall's *The Chosen Place, the Timeless People*, an epic novel about life on a Caribbean island which was published in 1969. More recently, Jonathan Franzen, in his novels *The Corrections* and *Freedom*, has adopted a godlike point of view. So has the British novelist Nicola Barker in her novel *Darkmans*, which depicts the members of a community even as it enters into the consciousness of each of its characters as intimately as *Mrs. Dalloway* does.

A little closer to the ground along our curve of sky, but still pretty high up, is the third person objective point of view. We've already encountered a good example of this point of view in Dashiell Hammett's detective novel *The Maltese Falcon*. As I said when we were discussing this novel earlier, the interesting thing about the point of view of *The Maltese Falcon* is that we see and hear everything each character does, but we never get inside their heads.

The omniscient third person of Tolstoy or Eliot can dip into the heads of an individual character like Anna Karenina or Dorothea Brooke and inhabit her consciousness for a time, showing us what she is thinking and feeling. But the objective third person is more like a video camera. It records and reports everything it sees, but it doesn't tell us anything about the characters' private feelings, thoughts, or motivations.

This point of view may even be the most lifelike one. After all, we can't read the minds of other people in real life, and the objective point of view reproduces what it feels like as we try to guess, from their speech, actions, and gestures, what other people around us are thinking. But even though it's more lifelike than the third-person omniscient, it's also a colder point of view, because it cannot engage intimately with the minds of its characters.

Moving down along the dome of our imaginary sky, we find a spot about halfway down, midway between the omniscient third person and the most intimate first-person narration. This point of view is known as the close third person or the limited third person. More recently it has also come to be known as "free indirect discourse."

In the close third person, the narration uses third person pronouns such "he," "she," and "they" instead of first-person pronouns such as "I" or "we." And, like the omniscient third person, it gets inside the heads of its characters. But in the limited third person, the whole story or novel is generally told from the point of view of only one character. John Updike, for example, used the close third person in his series of four novels about the life of Harry "Rabbit" Angstrom. These novels are written in the third person, but they are mainly told from the point of view of Rabbit himself. The close third person, in fact, is the default mode of much contemporary fiction.

But the close third person doesn't have to be limited to one character. Often, writers will alternate the point of view between several characters within the same narrative, the way Toni Morrison does in *Beloved*. William Faulkner's *Light in August* also shifts between several different point-of-view characters, all of them expressed in the third person. In fact, the close third-person point of view can easily turn into the omniscient third person. Much of George Eliot's *Middlemarch*, for example, is written from the point of view of one character or another, but Eliot often shifts into the omniscient point of view, often within a chapter, or even within a paragraph.

However, the traditional omniscient third person is usually more remote from its characters, and capable of making sweeping judgments about society or whole classes of people. For whatever reason, modern novels written in the more intimate close third person tend to shy away from those kinds of judgments. Still, the close third person allows the author to pull back the camera, if he wants to. It allows him to comment directly on the action or to show us something the point-of-view character can't or doesn't know.

Moving further down the curve of the sky, the close third person shades into what you might call the objective first person. Like the close third person, which uses third-person pronouns to limit itself to the perspective of one character, the objective first person is a hybrid point of view. It uses the first-person pronoun, "I," but still maintains a certain distance from the action of the narrative.

In other words, in the objective first person, the story or novel is being narrated by a fictional character, but one who either plays only a minor part in the story or isn't actually present in the story at all. Two good examples are Ishmael in *Moby-Dick* and Nick Carraway in *The Great Gatsby*.

In much of *Moby-Dick*, Ishmael acts mainly as a recording eye, telling what he sees and hears, even though he's technically a crew member of the *Pequod* and a character in the story. He involves himself in the work of the crew, but his story is not the main story of the book, and he is not the main character. Captain Ahab is. Instead of taking center stage, Ishmael does two things. One is to tell us the story of Captain Ahab's obsession with the great white whale. The other is to evoke, almost like a documentary filmmaker, the way of life aboard a whaling vessel. In the second half of the novel, in fact, much of Ishmael's narration is in effect in the third person. There are even scenes that take place when Ishmael isn't even present.

In *The Great Gatsby*, Nick Carraway is slightly more important to the story. The character of Daisy is his cousin, and he plays a role in bringing Gatsby and Daisy together over the course of the book. Furthermore, it's Nick's voice that passes judgment on the events of the story, and it's his voice that sums up the meaning of the book in those famous final lines. But the main story is not about Nick. It's about Gatsby and Daisy. You could easily imagine a version of *The Great Gatsby* written in the third person, where Nick is just a minor character, and F. Scott Fitzgerald himself takes on the responsibility of passing judgment at the end.

A variant of this type of first person is the first person plural narration, in which the author uses the pronoun "we" and adopts the collective point of view of a community of people.

One of the best known examples is William Faulkner's famous gothic short story, "A Rose for Emily," which is narrated from the point of view of the town itself. In this classic story, the first person plural has the effect of

301

drawing the reader in and making her a de facto member of the community. In fact, the complicity implied in the use of the pronoun "we" has the further effect of making the story's chilling ending even more shocking. The first person plural isn't used very often, but it's still a technique that can generate interesting results. In recent years, the American writer Joshua Ferris wrote his first novel, *Then We Came to the End*, from the point of view of a group of office workers at a Chicago advertising agency.

Now let's move along the curve of the sky as far down as we can go. Here, right down at ground level, is the subjective first person. In this point of view, the first-person narrator is one of the main characters in the story, and often the main character. Unlike Ishmael in *Moby-Dick*, who is the narrator but not the main character, Huck Finn is both the narrator and the main character of *The Adventures of Huckleberry Finn*. We see and hear everything in the book through Huck's eyes, and we can only know what Huck witnesses or hears about. Not only that, but Huck's moral journey is the heart of the novel, as he befriends the escaped slave Jim and decides not to turn him in to the authorities.

In more recent times, as the subjective first person has become much more prevalent, we have narrators like Ruth in Marilynne Robinson's *Housekeeping*. Ruth is one of three main characters in the book, and her decision about how she wants to live her life represents the book's climax. And there's the chilling Humbert Humbert in Nabokov's *Lolita*, who tells us of his illicit passion for the 12-year-old Dolores Haze. This is one of the most disturbing uses of the subjective first person in all of literature.

The curve of sky representing the different points of view is a continuum, of course, and these are just the principal compass points on it. Narratives can and do find points in between the ones I've just described. For example, a first-person narrator can be an unreliable narrator, who lies or withholds certain crucial information, or misunderstands what's actually going on.

And many books mix and match points of view. In *Anna Karenina* and *Middlemarch*, both Tolstoy and George Eliot vary the scope of their third person. Sometimes they give us a wide-angle, omniscient view, encompassing whole groups or communities of people. But sometimes they use the limited third person to get deep inside the head of a single character. Tolstoy, for example, goes so deep inside Anna's head near the climax of *Anna Karenina* that he approaches the extremely intimate third person you find in high modernist novels like *Mrs. Dalloway*.

Some books jump back and forth between the third and first person. Dickens's great novel *Bleak House* is told from both the third person and the first-person point of view. Even more recently, John Burnham Schwartz's novel *Reservation Road* has three main characters, two of whom we hear from in the first person, while the third character we see only in the close third person.

When you're deciding on the point of view of your story, however, you're not just deciding who tells it. There's also the question of to whom the writer is telling the story, as well as the question of the time and distance from which a story is told. Let's take these one at a time.

When I say that you have to consider to whom the story is told, I'm not talking the trying to decide who your audience is. That's a different question, and not necessarily an artistic one. Rather, I'm talking about a different question: Is your narration addressed to an unknown reader in the real world, or is it addressed to some one person or some group of people who exist in the world of the story?

Take, for example, three of the most famous first-person narratives in literary history, Charlotte Brontë's *Jane Eyre*, Mark Twain's *The Adventures of Huckleberry Finn*, and Nabokov's *Lolita*. In the first two examples, the narrator is the title character. In *Lolita*, the narrator is the poet Humbert Humbert, and the title character is the 12-year-old girl who is the object of his sexual obsession. In all three examples, there are at least hints that the character is aware that he or she is addressing the actual reader of the book. Jane Eyre narrates her own story with great force and intimacy as if she were writing her memoir for posterity. In the novel's single most famous line, she makes it clear that she knows she's writing a book, when she says about Mr. Rochester, "Reader, I married him."

Here you have one of the most memorable examples of a fictional character speaking directly to the real readers of her book. Or seeming to—what's really happening, of course, is that Charlotte Brontë, a real person, is causing Jane Eyre, a fictional person, to speak directly to the reader. Or if you prefer a more mystical interpretation, Jane Eyre is speaking through Charlotte Brontë.

Huck Finn bridges the gap between fiction and reality in his very first sentence: "You don't know about me without you have read a book by the name of *The Adventures of Tom Sawyer*." In this case a fictional character not only speaks directly to the reader, he refers to a real book by the real author, in which he, Huck, first appears as a fictional character. Again, of course, it's not really Huck, but Mark Twain, using Huck to refer to himself and his own earlier book.

In *Lolita*, Humbert Humbert's first-person narrative is a little less philosophically complex. The book opens with an introduction by a fictional psychiatrist, and the rest of the novel is written as a confession of his crimes that Humbert Humbert wrote in prison. Unlike Jane Eyre and Huck Finn, who cross the divide between the fictional world and the real world, Humbert Humbert remains constrained within the pages of his book. He knows he's writing something that may only ever be read by the authorities who locked him away.

The question of a book's intended reader gets even more complicated when you consider first-person narrators who speak in the present tense. We often find this kind of narration in thrillers—"I walk into the room and pull my gun," that sort of thing. Such a narration contributes to the pace and immediacy of an exciting story, but there's something fundamentally improbable about it: Are we to understand that the character is silently narrating what he's doing as he does it?

And then there are the first-person narrators of historical novels. Robert Graves's *I, Claudius* and Marguerite Yourcenar's *Memoirs of Hadrian* are fictional memoirs by real Roman emperors. We are meant to believe that Claudius and Hadrian are speaking explicitly to posterity, to readers who may live centuries after the author himself has died.

The uses of the third person can be just as diverse. The 19th century, third-person omniscient voice of George Eliot and Leo Tolstoy is very much a public, authoritative voice. While you wouldn't mistake Eliot or Tolstoy for each other, they share a certain godlike distance from the story and their characters. The voice of Dickens, however, is more feverish and engaged in the lives of his characters, even though he also often writes in the third person.

There are also third-person narrations that presume the reader's intimacy with the social setting and the worldview of the author. Take, for example, the famous first line of Jane Austen's *Pride and Prejudice*: "It is a truth universally acknowledged, that a single man in possession of a good fortune must be in want of a wife." Now, Austen was an ironic writer, so presumably even she understood the hyperbole of this statement. Outside of early 19th century Britain, and a very narrow slice of British society at that, this is patently not a universal truth. But even if you don't believe it, the first sentence implicates the reader in Austen's world right from the very first words.

Moving into the 20th century, you have the stream-of-consciousness third person of such books as *Mrs. Dalloway*. Much of that book doesn't feel as though it's speaking to anyone outside of Mrs. Dalloway's head, let alone outside of the novel. Even though the novel is technically in the third person, the effect of reading *Mrs. Dalloway*'s narrative voice is like eavesdropping on a character's thoughts in real time.

With a first-person narrator, you have to decide just how close the narrator is to the events he or she is describing. *The Adventures of Huckleberry Finn* is told mainly in the past tense, but that famous opening sentence is told in the present tense—"You don't know about me without you have read a book [called] *The Adventures of Tom Sawyer* … by Mr. Mark Twain." The clear implication of Huck's particular voice throughout the book is that he, the narrator, is still a boy, and he is telling us about a series of events that happened very recently. In other words, it's a story about a child told by the child. He's telling us about more or less contemporary events. It is a past-tense story told by a present-tense narrator, or a narrator who is speaking to us as we're reading.

You get a slightly different effect from Harper Lee's *To Kill a Mockingbird*. The narrator of that novel is Scout, who was a child during the events of the novel, but who is remembering them from the perspective of an adult. At times her narration is immediate and limited to what she knew when the events were actually happening. At other times, the novel steps back and narrates the events from the point of view of a grown woman, looking back on her childhood. In this respect, you might say we get the best of both worlds: a child's eye view of childhood, leavened with an adult's perspective on events that the young Scout would not have fully understood. It's a very subtle and sophisticated use of voice, and one of the elements of the book that accounts for its continuing popularity.

In Marilynne Robinson's *Housekeeping*, the narrator announces herself in the first person, present-tense in the book's first line—"My name is Ruth." But the rest of the book is told in a retrospective past tense. Even more so than Scout in *To Kill a Mockingbird*, Ruth is clearly telling the story from the point of view of a grown woman, at a distance of many years.

And in Thomas Berger's epic Western *Little Big Man*, the narrator, Jack Crabb, speaks about events that happened a lifetime ago, including his friendship with Wild Bill Hickok, his days as a gunfighter, and his life among the Sioux. This gives his narration the quality of a tall tale—among other things, Jack Crabb claims to be the only white survivor of the Battle of the Little Big Horn—and it helps define Jack himself as a talkative old man who loves spinning yarns.

The idea of a narration's temporal distance from the events in the narrative is just as important with third-person narratives. The past tense is the default tense of many novels and stories, but the use of the past tense doesn't necessarily mean the events of the story took place in the distant past. For example, Tolstoy's *Anna Karenina* is told in the past tense, but it was both written and set during the 1870s. George Eliot's *Middlemarch*, on the other hand, was published in the early 1870s, but it was set 40 years earlier, in the 1830s. Tolstoy is using the past tense to tell a contemporary story, while Eliot is using a similar past tense to tell a story of the recent past, giving the reader some distance from the events.

If you transfer this difference to the present day, you can see that one use of the past tense is significantly different from the other. Consider the difference between watching the two television shows *Breaking Bad* and *Mad Men*. *Breaking Bad* is set more or less in the present moment, forcing the viewer to confront the fact that Walter White's desperation and increasingly bad behavior are a result of a way of life in which we all participate. *Mad Men*, on the other hand, is set half a century in the past. This distance allows the viewer to look back on Don Draper's lies and infidelities with the smugness of hindsight. *Breaking Bad* jangles our nerves because there's no temporal distance between the story and us: This is how we live now. But with *Mad Men*, we can at least cling to the illusion that we are better behaved than the people who worked on Madison Avenue in the early 1960s.

So, as if choosing among all the myriad possibilities for creating character and sketching out a plot weren't complicated enough, you have to contend with all the complicated choices that come with deciding what point of view to use and which voice to use.

Do you want to survey the landscape from a great height? Do you want to try and encompass as wide a view as possible, showing the whole scope of society while diving at will into the heads of a variety of characters? Or do you want to look only at that little patch of territory you can see at ground level, from the point of view of a single character? Do you want to adopt the godlike authority of a third-person, past-tense narration that sees and understands all? Or do you want a first-person, past-tense narrator, who can look back with more experience on her younger self? Or do you want a third-person, present-tense narration that relates events as they happen, with no hint of what's coming?

It's a lot to think about, so here's an exercise that might help you sort things out. Take the opening of any of the books I talked about in this lecture, or the opening of a book of your own choosing, or the opening of something you've written yourself, and try it in a different point of view, a different verb tense, a different voice.

Would Huck Finn work if it were narrated in the third person? What if it were narrated by an elderly Huck looking back on his childhood? Would George

Eliot be able to create as broad a portrait of the community in *Middlemarch* if it were narrated by only one character within the story? What would *I, Claudius* feel like if it was written in the present tense? Would it make the Roman emperor's court feel more immediate, or would it just feel bizarre? I don't know if these alternate versions would be better or worse, but they would certainly be different than the ones we know.

In the next lecture, I'll take a more detailed look at the first person, and I'll be talking again about Ishmael in *Moby-Dick* and Nick Carraway in *The Great Gatsby*. But I'll also be talking about unreliable narrators in the works of Henry James, Eudora Welty, and Mohsin Hamid. Then, in the following lecture, we'll look at the varieties of the third person.

Each of these points of view has its advantages and disadvantages, and by exploring their use in the work of other authors, you'll be able to think about how to use different types of point of view and voice in your own work.

I, Me, Mine—First-Person Point of View
Lecture 16

T he inherent improbability of first-person narration was summed up by Henry James in the preface to one of his novels, when he remarked how strange it was to make a first-person narrator both "hero and historian" of his own story. In other words, first-person narration can be peculiar because it often (though not always) must accomplish two goals at once: tell the story and evoke one of the story's characters, often the most important character. But it's also true that first-person narration can be one of the most intimate, seductive, and natural-seeming ways to tell a story. In this lecture, we'll look at several varieties of the first-person narrator and how you can use each of them.

Objective First Person
- The objective first-person narrator is present in the story but is not the most important character. This kind of narration is halfway between the close third person and a more intimate first person.

- One of the most obvious examples of objective first-person narration is Ishmael in *Moby-Dick*. Ishmael, of course, introduces himself in the first line of the novel, and for much of the book, we hear a great deal about his experiences. But the book is more about Captain Ahab than it is about anyone else, and indeed, Ahab and many of the other characters are more interesting than Ishmael. Further, Ismael doesn't develop in the way that characters in modern novels often do.

- In *The Great Gatsby*, Nick Carraway takes much more of a role in the story than Ishmael does, but on the whole, he serves mainly as a recording eye. He is also an outsider to the world he depicts; thus, he's able to record the story of the wealthy characters around him with more objectivity and distance than Gatsby or Daisy could.

- The slightly remote first-person narration allows readers to feel that they are witnessing the events of the novel firsthand but with no pressure to endorse a particular opinion of any of the characters or actions in the story.
  - A version of *Moby-Dick* narrated by Ahab or a version of *The Great Gatsby* narrated by Gatsby would require us to take sides for or against the narrator, while an objective third-person version of these two novels would not be nearly as engaging.

  - Objective first-person narration is especially effective when the central character—as opposed to the narrator—is both charismatic and slippery, as Ahab and Gatsby are. Ishmael and Nick Carraway allow us to get close but not too close.

The Heroic Narrator
- The heroic narrator is usually the main character or one of the main characters and takes an active role in the events of the story. In this case, the narration's evocation of character is equally important to telling the story.

- Both objective first-person and heroic narration invite readers to take the narrator at face value and assume that he or she is telling the truth. But heroic narration also invites readers to actively endorse the narrator's judgments of the other characters and situations in the story.

- We don't root for Nick Carraway in *The Great Gatsby* because he's not the main character, and Nick's slight remove from the action enables us to make up our own minds about Gatsby. But in *Jane Eyre*, we are not only asked to assume that Jane is telling the truth throughout, but we are also actively encouraged to endorse Jane's judgments of the other characters and to root for things to turn out well for her.

- With a heroic narrator, there is not much difference between the narrator's opinion of the other characters and the author's. Consider Philip Marlowe, the hard-boiled private investigator who is the main character and narrator of the detective stories of Raymond Chandler.

At first glance, it might seem as if Marlowe is just a recording-eye narrator, but if we listen to his voice carefully, we realize that he is passing judgment on a world that doesn't share his strict sense of morality.

The distance between the author's view of the world and that of the heroic narrator, such as Raymond Chandler's Philip Marlowe, is not very great, allowing both the author and the reader to live through the narrator.

- A more complex version of the heroic narrator is Huck Finn, a classic example of the *double consciousness* of a first-person narrator. With this technique, a skilled writer can simultaneously evoke the beliefs and prejudices of his narrator while letting the reader see through the narration to what's really going on.

  o This double consciousness manifests itself at the moral climax of Huck's book, when he must decide whether to allow Jim to be sold back into slavery or to help Jim gain his freedom. Everything about the moral code of Huck's world tells him that letting a slave run away is a kind of theft, and Huck truly believes that sanctioning this theft will send him to hell. But then, he recalls the way he and Jim looked after each other as they floated down the river, and he says, "All right, then, I'll *go* to hell."

  o In this episode, Twain allows us to revel in hearing Huck's reasoning in his unique voice—staying true to the character—but Twain himself also peeks through the character, letting readers know that Huck is doing the right thing, even if Huck doesn't know it for himself.

The Retrospective Narrator

- With retrospective narration, the narrator recalls events from a distance of many years, looking back on a time when he or she was younger. In this type of narration, there is also an emotional and intellectual distance between the character as a younger person and the character at the time of the narration. Many stories and books fulfill the first requirement here but not the second.

- Jane Eyre, for example, looks back on her struggles as a young woman from the perspective of an older woman, fulfilling the first requirement. But Jane doesn't write very critically or objectively about herself as a younger woman—we're encouraged to root for her throughout the book; thus, her narration doesn't fulfill the second requirement.

- One of the best examples of the sort of narrator who fulfills both requirements is Ruth in Marilynne Robinson's novel *Housekeeping*. Much of this book is about how Ruth and her sister, Lucille, two young girls who have either been abandoned or orphaned by all the other adults in their family, end up being looked after by their unconventional aunt, Sylvia.

  o Sylvia makes an attempt to create some stability for her nieces in the family home in Idaho, but she can't resist the pull of a restless life, and in the end, the young Ruth chooses to run off with her aunt while Lucille chooses to stay behind and live a more conventional life. The story is told many years later by the grown-up Ruth, who is now a vastly different person from the young girl she had been.

  o Ruth looks back on her childhood without regret or nostalgia but, instead, with a kind of bemused, mysterious calm that passes no judgment and does not require the reader to make a judgment either.

  o Written in limpid, poetic prose, Ruth's narration takes readers on a spiritual journey that requires us to reconsider everything we may have thought was true about family life, motherhood, and the relations between sisters. Ruth's voice puts us in the mind of an unusual character and shows us the world in a whole new light.

- There are also retrospective first-person narrators who look back on their former selves with disappointment or even contempt, as we saw with David in James Baldwin's novel *Giovanni's Room*. Indeed, we might say that David is an antiheroic narrator: We are expected to take David's story at face value and to endorse his judgment of himself—though in this case, we are meant to share his contempt for himself, rather than endorse his heroism.

The Unreliable Narrator

- The unreliable narrator is one who cannot be trusted by the reader. The simplest version of this narrator simply lies to the reader, revealing his or her deceit at the end of the story. In John Banville's novel *Doctor Copernicus*, there's a section written in the first person by a scholar named Rheticus, who was Copernicus's student but is angry with his teacher. His chapter is full of gossip and criticisms of Copernicus, and only at the end does he confess that a crucial element in his story was invented, casting doubt on nearly everything he has said.

- There are also unreliable narrators who lie to the other characters in the story and often end up deluding themselves. As we saw earlier, the unnamed first-person narrator of Henry James's novella *The Aspern Papers* is a literary critic who is desperate to acquire some old love letters by a long-dead American poet. Throughout the novella, the narrator wrestles with his conscience over what he has done to get the letters, but in the end, he stifles his guilt.

- Another sort of unreliable narrator deludes both himself or herself and the reader. The experience of reading Eudora Welty's story "Why I Live at the P.O." is like being cornered by a talkative and slightly unhinged woman who believes she has been wronged by her family. Because of the narrator's self-pity and her unconscious comic exaggeration, it's clear that her version of events is extremely biased, if not untrue. But unlike Rheticus, who ultimately admits that he has lied to the reader, Welty's narrator sticks to her guns.

- Finally, another variation on the unreliable narrator is the narrator who may or may not be unreliable, but whose truthfulness is never revealed to the reader.
  - One of the most interesting recent examples of such a narrator is in Mohsin Hamid's *The Reluctant Fundamentalist*. The novel is narrated in the first person by a Pakistani man who has attended Princeton and worked on Wall Street, but who, after the events of 9/11, has found himself in reluctant sympathy with the goals of the terrorists.

  - The novel is framed as a long monologue, in which the unnamed narrator tells his life story to an American listener. What makes this narration so unusual is that there are increasing hints that the narrator may be a terrorist and that his listener may be an American intelligence agent sent to kill him. The potential unreliability of the narrator is essential to the final impact of this unsettling and thought-provoking book.

Suggested Reading

Baldwin, *Giovanni's Room*.

Chandler, *The Long Goodbye*.

Fitzgerald, *The Great Gatsby*.

Hamid, *The Reluctant Fundamentalist*.

Melville, *Moby-Dick*.

Robinson, *Housekeeping*.

Twain, *The Adventures of Huckleberry Finn*.

Welty, "Why I Live at the P.O."

1. Try your hand at either the double consciousness that Twain uses in *The Adventures of Huckleberry Finn* or the unreliable narrator technique used by Eurdora Welty or Mohsin Hamid. In the first instance, pick a character whose worldview you disagree with and write in his or her voice, trying to let your own worldview peek through. In the second instance, write from the point of view of a character who is clearly lying about something; try to stay true to the voice while letting the reader know that everything the narrator says is not necessarily true.

I, Me, Mine—First-Person Point of View
Lecture 16—Transcript

There is something inherently improbable about a first-person narrator. How often in real life have you ever listened to someone tell you a story about themselves that included not only their thoughts and actions, but elaborate evocations of the setting, not to mention verbatim dialogue from other people? Not very often, I'm guessing. As I said in my lecture about evocation, most people in real life tell stories the way they tell jokes, with just enough detail to get the point across. But in fiction, first-person narrators often pay attention to the purely literary requirements of setting a scene. They evoke sights and sounds and feelings, and they vividly render other characters.

And if that narrator is in a novel, the first person becomes even more improbable, because the narrator is likely to go on, without interruption, for a hundred thousand words. In case you're wondering, that would take about 12 hours to speak aloud.

In the preface to one of his novels, the American writer Henry James summed up the inherent improbability of the first-person narration when he said how strange it was to make a narrator both "hero and historian" of his own story. In other words, a first-person narration is peculiar because it has to do two things at once: It has to tell the story, but it also has to evoke one of the story's characters. And in many cases, the narrator is the story's most important character. What can make it even more peculiar is the fact that the narrator and the author don't always see eye to eye. As we'll see, this can lead to some interesting results.

But it spite of its fundamental weirdness, or maybe even because of it, a first-person narration can be one of the most intimate, seductive, and natural-seeming ways to tell a story, if it's done well. Certain varieties of third-person narration have an authoritative, public voice—think of George Eliot or Tolstoy—which can make you feel as if you're being lectured to as part of a large audience. But a first-person narrator can feel as if he or she is speaking to you alone, confiding his or her story to you, and to no one else.

"This is what happened to me," the narrator is telling you. "I saw this with my own eyes."

A first-person narration can offer the reader the same feeling of immediacy and truthfulness we get when we hear testimony in a court case, read an intimate memoir, or, God forbid, sneak a peek at someone else's diary. And because a fictional character has the potential to reveal more of him or herself than any real person possibly could, a first-person narration can offer you an experience that you usually can't get in real life.

This intimacy accounts for the deep affection we feel for certain famous fictional narrators. Consider how badly we want Jane Eyre to come up trumps and marry Mr. Rochester. Consider how much we want Huckleberry Finn to do the right thing and help the slave Jim gain his freedom. And consider how many people love J. D. Salinger's Holden Caulfield for his bluntness and his smart-alecky wit.

But even so, this intimacy is still not real. A first-person narrator is an arbitrary literary conceit that is mutually agreed upon by the writer and the reader. It creates an *illusion* of intimacy that requires, on the part of the writer, fidelity to the voice of the narrator, not only as the source of the story, but as a character within the story. On the part of the reader, this illusion of intimacy requires a willingness to go along with the fantasy that this fictional person is real and is telling you the truth.

On the one hand, you have the inherent improbability of hearing a complex story told to you by one of its participants, and, on the other, you have the illicit thrill of hearing something that no one else knows. The tension between these two factors accounts for much of the power and the mystery of the first person.

In this lecture, I want to look at several different varieties of first-person narrator and talk about how you can use each of them. Let's start with the least intimate variety. In the previous lecture, I called this the objective first person, or the first-person narrator as recording eye. This is a narrator who is present in the story, but who is not the most important character.

In the continuum of points of view, an objective first-person narrator is about halfway between the close third person and a more intimate first person. The narrator's role in telling the story is more important than his or her role in creating character. The most obvious examples from American literature are Ishmael in *Moby-Dick* and Nick Carraway in *The Great Gatsby*.

Ishmael, of course, introduces himself to the reader in the very first line of the novel—"Call me Ishmael"—and early in the book, we hear a great deal about his experiences. But it becomes obvious pretty quickly that the book is more about Captain Ahab than it is about anyone else. As it turns out, not only is Ahab more interesting than Ishmael, most of the characters in the book are more interesting than Ishmael.

In fact, one of the curious things about *Moby-Dick* is that its first-person narrator simply disappears for pages at a time. There are scenes in the novel where Ishmael isn't even present. For example, there's a scene between Ahab and his first mate, Starbuck, which takes place when they are alone in Ahab's cabin, and which is therefore written in a de facto third person. What's more, Ishmael doesn't develop in the way that characters in modern novels often do. He goes through some tremendous experiences, including the sinking of his ship and the death of everyone else in the story. But in the end, he's essentially the same person as he was at the beginning. There are no epiphanies for Ishmael.

In *The Great Gatsby*, Nick Carraway takes much more of a role in the story than Ishmael does in *Moby-Dick*. Nick is Daisy's cousin, his house is the site of Gatsby and Daisy's reunion, and he's present for many of the big scenes. But on the whole, he serves mainly as the recording eye for the story. Unlike the other major characters—Gatsby, Daisy, and Daisy's husband, Tom—Nick has to work for a living, which makes him an outsider to the world he's depicting. He is able to record the story of the stinking rich characters around him with more objectivity and distance than Gatsby or Daisy could.

Nick is certainly more engaged in the story than Ishmael is in *Moby-Dick*. So the novel's famous last line—"So we beat on, boats against the current, borne back ceaselessly into the past"—represents Nick's epiphany and no one else's. But even so, he's still not essential to the playing out of the plot. He gives an intimate portrait of a man he knew personally, but from a slight remove.

This, I think, is the hallmark of the slightly remote first-person narrator. He is not quite as remote as the third person and not quite as intimate as a more active first-person narrator. This kind of narrator allows you to feel you are witnessing the events of the novel firsthand, but with no pressure from the narrator to endorse a particular opinion of any of the characters or any of the actions in the story. A version of *Moby-Dick* narrated by Ahab or a version of *The Great Gatsby* narrated by Jay Gatsby would require us to take sides for or against our narrator, which I personally think would have diminished the power of these two novels. So perhaps the objective and remote first-person narrator is especially effective when your central character is both charismatic and slippery, the way Ahab and Gatsby are. Ishmael and Nick Carraway allow us to get close, but not too close.

Now let's talk about what I called, in my previous lecture, the subjective first person, and let's break it down into several different varieties. The first variety is what I'm going to call the heroic narrator. This sort of narrator is usually the main character, or at least one of the main characters, and she takes an active role in the events of the story. In this case, the narration's evocation of her own character is equally important to telling the story.

This sort of narrator has something in common with the objective first-person narrator. In both cases, the reader is invited to take the narrator at face value and assume that what she is telling you is the truth.

But heroic narration takes this assumption a bit further and invites the reader to actively endorse the narrator's judgments of the other characters and situations in the story. We don't root for Nick Carraway in *The Great Gatsby*, because he's not the main character. Nick's slight remove from the action enables us to make up our own mind about Gatsby himself. But in Charlotte Brontë's *Jane Eyre*, we are not only asked to assume that Jane is telling the truth throughout, but we are also actively encouraged to endorse Jane's judgments of the other characters, and to root for her.

In the book's wonderful first paragraph, which I quoted in an earlier lecture, we are encouraged to feel Jane's righteous anger at her mistreatment by her foster family. Later on, we are encouraged to sympathize with her feeling of betrayal when she discovers that Mr. Rochester is already married. And at the end, we are encouraged to feel her joy and triumph when she is finally able to marry him.

Let me put this another way: In a story with a heroic narrator, there is not much difference between the narrator's opinion of the other characters and the author's. In some cases, and in some very good books, this can become a kind of wish fulfillment.

For example, consider Philip Marlowe, the hard-boiled private investigator who is the main character and the narrator of the great detective stories of Raymond Chandler. At first glance, it might seem as if Marlowe is an objective first-person narrator, simply recording what he sees and hears.

Listen to the first paragraph of Chandler's novel *The Long Goodbye*:

> The first time I laid eyes on Terry Lennox he was drunk in a Rolls-Royce Silver Wraith outside the terrace of The Dancers. The parking lot attendant had brought the car out and he was still holding the door open because Terry Lennox's left foot was still dangling outside, as if he had forgotten he had one. He had a young-looking face but his hair was bone white. You could tell by his eyes that he was plastered to the hairline, but otherwise he looked like any other nice young guy who had been spending too much money in a joint that exists for that purpose and for no other.

At first this seems to be an objective bit of description that happens to be written in the first person, but if you listen carefully to Marlowe's voice, you realize that the narrator is passing judgment. Marlowe's voice is that of a cool, slightly weary man of the world. You can tell by listening to him that he has a lot of experience with people of all sorts, and that he can recognize when a man is drunk just by looking at his eyes.

The kicker is the last part of the last sentence. Marlowe refers to the nightclub The Dancers not just as a "joint," but as the sort of joint that exists for no other reason than to take money off nice young guys like Terry Lennox. This is a judgment. It tells us that Marlowe (and by proxy, Chandler himself) accepts that he has to live in this crummy world, but he doesn't have to approve of it.

As Marlowe moves through the rest of the novel, most of the story is about other people. But on every page, Marlowe continues to crack wise and make sharp judgments of everything and everybody around him. He makes mistakes, of course, but he usually recovers from them later on. And in nearly every scene, Marlowe is the one in control, the one who understands what's really going on, and the one who gets off the best jokes. The distance between the Philip Marlowe's view of the world and Raymond Chandler's is not very great. This kind of wish-fulfilling narration allows both the reader and the author to live through the narrator without any guilt or second thoughts. It allows us to move through an exciting story full of danger and intrigue as the coolest, smartest, and most righteous person in the room.

Now let's take a look at a more complex version of the heroic first person. Let's return to one of the most famous narrators in literary history, namely Huck Finn in Mark Twain's *Adventures of Huckleberry Finn*. Huck is not only a superbly entertaining narrator, he's one of the great characters in American fiction. He is a plainspoken, semi-literate, but verbally inventive boy who is by turns gullible and devious, resourceful and accident-prone, and who gets by on what today we would call street-smarts. In fact, Huck implicitly warns the reader in the very first paragraph that not all of what follows may be true—what he says is, "I never seen anybody but lied, one time or another." And indeed, throughout the book, Huck repeatedly uses lies to get himself out of trouble.

Let's look at the ways in which Huck is a more complex narrator than Philip Marlowe. While Marlowe's narration certainly uses the slang and idioms of mid-20th-century urban America, Huck's dialect is even more specific, representing rural Missouri in the years before the Civil War. Indeed, one of the greatest pleasures of reading the book is just being able to listen to the cadences, rhythms, and rich idioms of Huck's speech.

But the more important reason that Huck is a more interesting narrator is that his boyish, semi-educated view of the world does not necessarily represent the views of his author. Huck is shrewd, wily, and fundamentally decent, but he's also young and immature and badly educated. His creator, however, is much more mature and better educated. The result is that Huck Finn represents a classic example of what you might call the *double consciousness* of a first-person narrator. This is when a skilled writer evokes the beliefs and prejudices of his narrator, while at the same time letting the reader see through the narration to what's really going on.

This double consciousness accounts for much of the humor in *Huckleberry Finn*. Some of the best passages are Huck's guileless descriptions of adult behavior that he doesn't understand. One such moment comes in Chapter 1 when the Widow Douglas, one of the prim and proper adults in Huck's life, tries to read to him from the Bible:

> After supper she got out her book and learned me about Moses and the Bulrushers, and I was in a sweat to find out all about him; but by and by she let it out that Moses had been dead a considerable long time; so then I didn't care no more about him, because I don't take no stock in dead people.

The humor in this passage comes from the double-consciousness of the narration. On the one hand, we understand and maybe even sympathize with the boredom of a child who is being told a long, involved story about some old dead guy. On the other hand, Mark Twain is winking at us over Huck's shoulder, letting us know that he knows as well as we do that Huck is missing the point.

More importantly, though, the double consciousness of *Huckleberry Finn* explicitly manifests itself at the moral climax of the book in Chapter 31. This is the moment when Huck has to decide whether to allow his friend, the slave Jim, to be sold back into slavery, or whether he should help Jim go free. Everything about the moral code of Huck's world, everything ever told to him by white teachers, ministers, and other authority figures tells him that letting a slave run away is a kind of theft. Huck truly believes that sanctioning this theft will send him to hell.

But then, in a heartfelt paragraph, he recalls fondly the way he and Jim looked after each other as they floated down the river. Finally he says, in one of the most famous sentences in American literature, "All right, then, I'll *go* to hell." Then he says:

> It was awful thoughts and awful words, but they was said. And I let them stay said; and never thought no more about reforming. I shoved the whole thing out of my head, and said I would take up wickedness again, which was in my line, being brung up to it, and the other warn't. And for a starter, I would go to work and steal Jim out of slavery again; and if I could think up anything worse, I would do that, too; because as long as I was in, and in for good, I might as well go the whole hog.

There are three things, at least, going on in this thrilling paragraph. One is that Huck is simply telling us the story of his decision. Another is that Twain is allowing us to revel in the sheer pleasure of hearing Huck reason this out for himself, in his own unique voice.

But the most important thing is that Twain is peeking through his own character at this point. Twain is letting the reader know that Huck is doing the right thing even if Huck himself doesn't know it. Remember, at this point Huck really thinks he's consigning himself to eternal damnation. On the one hand, Twain stays absolutely true to his character. Huck sounds like Huck all the way through this passage, with his rough grammar, his folksy idioms, and his phonetic spellings. But on the other hand, Twain allows the reader to see through Huck and to understand the larger issue, which is the immorality of slavery. Huck comes down on the side of love versus the letter of the law. And even though we, as readers, may fault his reasoning, we can't fault his conclusion. Using Huck's own voice, Mark Twain allows us to see Huck and the world he lives in even more clearly than Huck himself could.

Now, the very last paragraph of *The Adventures of Huckleberry Finn* makes it clear that Huck is still a boy when he narrates his own story, and that his adventures have happened only in the recent past. This brings me to the next variety of the heroic first-person narration, which I'm going to call the retrospective narrator.

One of the hallmarks of the retrospective narrator is that she is recalling events in her own life from a distance of many years. Unlike Huck Finn, she is looking back at herself when she was younger. But there's more to it than simply the distance in time. In this type of narration, the narrator is also expressing the emotional and intellectual distance between her younger self and the person she is now at the time she's narrating the story.

There are many stories and books that fulfill the first requirement of this type of narration, but not the second. For example, Jane Eyre is looking back on her struggles as a young woman from the perspective of an older woman, happily married to Mr. Rochester, so her story fulfills the first requirement. But she doesn't really write very critically or objectively about herself as a younger woman—remember, we're encouraged to root for Jane throughout the book—so her narration does not fulfill the second requirement.

One of the best examples of the sort of narrator who does fulfill both requirements is the character Ruth in Marilynne Robinson's novel *Housekeeping*. Following in the footsteps of other classic American narrators such as Ishmael, Huck, and Nick Carraway, Ruth introduces herself directly to the reader in the first sentence: "My name is Ruth." Then, with characteristically American directness, she goes on to summarize her backstory in a few words: "I grew up with my younger sister, Lucille, under the care of my grandmother, Mrs. Sylvia Foster, and when she died, of her sisters-in-law, Misses Lily and Nona Foster, and when they fled, of her daughter, Mrs. Sylvia Fisher."

The majority of the book is about how Ruth and Lucille, two young girls who have been either abandoned or orphaned by all the other adults in their family, end up being looked after by Sylvia, their very unconventional aunt. Sylvia has lived her adult life drifting from town to town, but for the sake of her nieces, she makes an attempt to create some stability for them in the family home in a small town in Idaho. But try as she might, Sylvia finally can't resist the pull of a restless life. In the end, the young Ruth chooses to run off with her aunt, while Lucille chooses to stay behind and live a more conventional life.

The simplicity of this belies the dreamlike strangeness of this novel. It is told many years later by the grown-up Ruth, who is a now vastly different person from the young girl she had been. Unlike Jane Eyre, who starts as an outsider and achieves the conventional goals of marriage, security, and children, Ruth chooses (as Huck Finn puts it at the end of his book) to "light out for the Territory," and live an unsettled life in the company of her strange aunt.

In other words, Ruth is the opposite of Jane Eyre. She leaves a conventional life to become an outsider, and writes her narrative from that perspective. She looks back on her childhood without regret or nostalgia, but instead with a kind of bemused, mysterious calm that passes no judgment.

Written in limpid, poetic prose, Ruth's narration takes the reader on a spiritual journey that requires to the reader to question the conventional wisdom about family life, about motherhood, and about the relations between sisters. Ruth's voice truly puts us in the head of someone very, very unusual. Her narration allows us to see a way of living we may not want to inhabit in real life, but which has the profound effect of showing us the world in a whole new light.

There is also another kind of retrospective first-person narrator, namely one who looks back on his former self with disappointment or even contempt. In an earlier lecture, I talked about James Baldwin's novel *Giovanni's Room*, which is narrated by an American expatriate in Paris named David. As you may recall, David struggles with his sexuality throughout this brief novel. He is powerfully attracted to men, but he loves and hopes to marry a young American woman named Hella.

The bulk of the story is about David's intense affair with a bartender named Giovanni. David lives with the man for a time, but he eventually leaves Giovanni in favor of Hella. David's rejection of Giovanni leads indirectly to Giovanni's murder of a bar owner and his execution. At the end of the book, Hella leaves David as well. Finally David, in a last moment of cowardice, decides not to attend Giovanni's execution.

David's narration is not told at a great distance in time from the events of the story. It is suffused throughout with David's mixed emotions about being gay, but most of all, his narration is dominated by his self-contempt for the way he treated Giovanni. As early as the end of the second chapter, David considers the fact that Giovanni will be "rotting soon in unhallowed ground," and then he says "Until I die there will be those moments, moments seeming to rise up out of the ground like Macbeth's witches, when his face will come before me, that face in all its changes, when the exact timbre of his voice and the tricks of his speech will nearly scorch my ears, when his smell will overpower my nostrils."

In fact, you might say that David is an anti-heroic narrator, but he still has something in common with a heroic narrator. In *Jane Eyre*, we are expected to take Jane's judgments of herself and the other characters at face value. By the same token, we are meant to take David's story at face value and to endorse his judgment of himself. It's just that in his case, we are meant to share his contempt for himself, rather than endorse his heroism.

This brings us to the unreliable narrator, or the sort of narrator who cannot be trusted by the reader. Unreliable first-person narrators come in several varieties. The simplest version is the narrator who is simply lying to the reader, and who reveals his lies at the end.

John Banville's novel *Doctor Copernicus* is a fictional account of the life of the famous astronomer. Most of the book is told in the close third person, from Copernicus's point of view, but there is a fascinating section written in the first person by a scholar named Rheticus. This young scholar was a student of Copernicus, who, in the manner of ambitious students of famous teachers, is full of rage at Copernicus for all sorts of reasons. His chapter is full of pernicious gossip and severe criticisms of the older man. Only at the end of his section does Rheticus confess that a crucial element in his story was invented, which casts into doubt nearly everything else he said for the previous 60 pages.

There is another kind of unreliable narrator, namely the one who lies to other characters in the story and often ends up deluding himself. The unnamed first-person narrator of Henry James's novella *The Aspern Papers* is a literary critic who is desperate to acquire some old love letters by a long-dead American poet named Jeffrey Aspern. These letters are in the possession of

Aspern's former lover, now a very old woman. The narrator attempts to get the papers away from her by pretending to be romantically interested in the old woman's unattractive niece.

It all goes wrong, of course. The critic's scam is discovered, and on the final page, the niece, who at last understands the game he was playing, tells the narrator that she has burned the letters. Throughout the novella, the narrator has wrestled with his conscience, but in the end he stifles it. In the very last line of the story, as he looks at a picture of the poet that hangs in his study, he says, "When I look at it I can scarcely bear my loss—I mean of the precious papers." Notice he says the loss of the papers—not the loss of his honor, his dignity, or any compassion for a lonely woman whose heart he broke.

There is yet another sort of unreliable narrator, one who manages to delude both herself and the reader. The experience of reading Eudora Welty's hilarious story, "Why I Live at the P.O.," is like being cornered by a talkative and slightly unhinged woman. This narrator believes she has been wronged by her family and is determined to tell you her side of the story, whether you want to hear it or not.

Here's the first paragraph:

> I was getting along fine with Mama, Papa-Daddy and Uncle Rondo until my sister Stella-Rondo just separated from her husband and came back home again. Mr. Whitaker! Of course I went with Mr. Whitaker first, when he first appeared in China Grove, taking "Pose Yourself" photos, and Stella-Rondo broke us up. Told him I was one-sided. Bigger on one side than the other, which is a deliberate, calculated falsehood: I'm the same. Stella-Rondo is exactly twelve months to the day younger than I am and for that reason she's spoiled.

And it just gets weirder and funnier from there, and it ends with the narrator explaining why she moved out of the family home and started living at the local Post Office.

Much of the effect of the story comes from the way it mimics the cadences of someone who is telling you a story in person. Much of it in the present tense, with dialogue in the manner of, "So I says to her," and then, "So she says to me," and so on. Because of the narrator's self-evident self-pity and her unconscious comic exaggeration, it's clear by the end of the story that her version of events is extremely biased, if not flat out untrue. Unlike Rheticus, however, who admits at the end of his story that he has lied to the reader, Welty's narrator sticks to her guns, right to the end: "And if Stella-Rondo should come to me this minute, on bended knees, and attempt to explain the incidents of her life with Mr. Whitaker, I'd simply put my fingers in both my ears and refuse to listen."

Once again, as with Mark Twain and Huck Finn, we have a narration with a double consciousness. On the one hand there's the narrator, pleading her case with the reader unconvincingly, and on the other there's Eudora Welty, winking at us over her narrator's shoulder.

Yet another version of the unreliable narrator is the narrator who may or may not be unreliable, but whose truthfulness is never finally revealed to the reader. One of the most interesting recent examples is the Pakistani writer Mohsin Hamid's *The Reluctant Fundamentalist*. This novel is told in the first person by a Pakistani man who attended Princeton and worked on Wall Street, but who, after the events of 9/11, has found himself in reluctant sympathy with the goals of the terrorists. The novel is framed as a long monologue delivered in a café in the city of Lahore, as the unnamed narrator tells his life story to an American listener who never speaks.

There are increasing hints throughout the book that the narrator may possibly be a terrorist himself. There are also hints that his listener may possibly be an American intelligence agent sent to kill him. The potential unreliability of the narrator is essential to the final impact of this very unsettling and thought-provoking book, and it could only have been done in the first person.

In the next lecture, we'll look at a variety of things you can do with the third person voice, and we'll be talking about how it's used in George Eliot's *Middlemarch*, George R. R. Martin's *A Song of Ice and Fire* series, and George Pelecanos's detective novel *The Cut*.

In the meantime, you might want to experiment with the first person voice by attempting either the double consciousness that Twain uses in *Huckleberry Finn* or the unreliable narrator technique used by Eudora Welty or Mohsin Hamid.

In the first instance, pick a character whose worldview you disagree with and write in their voice, while trying to let your own worldview peek through. In the second instance, write from the point of view of a character who is clearly lying about something. Try to stay faithful to the character's voice while also letting the reader know that what the narrator is saying is not necessarily true.

Writing in the first person can be a tricky thing to pull off, but when it's done well, and the reader finds herself caught up in the story as well as the voice, it can be one of the satisfying experiences a writer and reader can share.

He, She, It—Third-Person Point of View
Lecture 17

As mentioned in the last lecture, a first-person narration can be intimate and immediate, but first-person narrators can usually convey only those events that they have witnessed or heard about from another source. The third person, in contrast, has much more range and flexibility. A third-person narration can encompass all sorts of things that a first-person narrator wouldn't know or be able to express. Paradoxically, the third person can also go deeper into an individual character's consciousness than the first person. Perhaps most importantly, the third person is often a more instinctive and natural way to tell a story. In this lecture, we'll look at several varieties of third-person narration and see how they are combined by modern writers.

Close Third Person

- The close third person seems to be the default mode of most contemporary fiction. Here, the writer adopts the point of view of only one character at a time. This narration is similar to the first person because, on the whole, it stays close to what one character knows, thinks, and feels.

- Still, the close third person contains at least the possibility of going deeper into the character's head than a first-person narration does because the third person allows the writer to reveal things about the character's thoughts, feelings, intentions, and prejudices that the character may not know or understand or may not want anybody else to know. In this respect, the close third person can be more comprehensive than the first person, because it allows the writer to show everything about a character, not just what that character chooses to reveal.

- As with other choices in creative writing, using this point of view means that you gain some things and you lose others. With the first person, for example, you can create a unique voice for the character, as Twain does for Huck Finn, and by choosing to tell a story in the close third person, you lose that distinctive voice. In contrast, in the close third person, you can dive as deeply into your characters' minds as Virginia Woolf does in *Mrs. Dalloway*.

- o The moment in *Huckleberry Finn* where Huck decides to help Jim win his freedom—"All right then, I'll *go* to hell"—would not be nearly as thrilling in the close third person because much of the scene's power comes from watching Huck work out the problem for himself.

- o By the same token, the scene in *Mrs. Dalloway* where Clarissa looks into a shop window and her mind skips around with lightning speed would be clumsy in the first person. The intimate but slightly remote view afforded by the close third person allows us to understand Clarissa even better than she understands herself.

- With the close third person, you also can switch from one character to another with relative ease, avoiding the need to reinvent the voice of the narration each time. In other words, you can use the same authorial voice to evoke different characters.
  - o The most bravura example of this, of course, is *Mrs. Dalloway*, which often switches point of view within a scene. In most instances, however, writers shift point of view from chapter to chapter. This technique broadens the scope of the story beyond what only one character can know.

  - o Alternating points of view in the close third person is a powerful way to tell a long story because it gives you the best of both worlds: Each chapter allows you to inhabit the mind of a single character, but by changing the point of view, you can broaden the scope of the narrative and present different perspectives on the same events. At the most mechanical level, this technique ensures that the reader is present for all the important scenes.

- You can add another dimension to the close third person by including the point-of-view character's first-person thoughts within the third-person narration. A character's thoughts may be indicated by italics or quotation marks, although those treatments may not be appropriate in all cases.

Objective Third Person

- In the objective or remote third person, the narration simply describes what the characters do and say without giving the reader access to their thoughts. At first glance, this narration might seem the same as the recording-eye first person, in which a character who is tangential to the main story relates the events. But there's a crucial difference: With the recording-eye first person, the events are still filtered through a fictional consciousness, who often passes judgment or makes educated guesses as to what the other characters are thinking.

  o Nick Carraway is not central to *The Great Gatsby*, but he views the story of Gatsby and Daisy from a particular point of view—as Daisy's cousin and Gatsby's friend—and his take on the events of the novel colors the reader's understanding.

  o We can compare this with the remote third-person narration in Dashiell Hammett's *The Maltese Falcon*, which watches everything the characters do but doesn't give us direct access to their thoughts and feelings. This kind of third person keeps us at arm's length from its characters, which helps to build suspense but at the cost of a certain iciness.

- The opposite of this remote and noncommittal third person is what we might call the engaged or judgmental third person, in which the narration has a strong opinion about the events it relates, even though that opinion doesn't come from an actual character in the story. This type of third-person narration is commonly found in the novels of the 18th and 19th centuries, when authors often passed judgment on the follies of their characters.

  o This kind of voice works especially well with comic or picaresque novels, such as *Tom Jones*, by the 18th-century English writer Henry Fielding.

- A generation later, we hear a similar voice in Jane Austen, who seems to stand halfway between the warm-blooded, judgmental third person of the 18th century and the cooler but still sympathetic close third person of the 20th century. Much of *Pride and Prejudice* is told in the close third person from Elizabeth Bennet's point of view, but there are also memorable passages in which the author herself passes direct and unmediated judgment.

- Perhaps the most enthusiastically judgmental narrator of all time is Charles Dickens, whose third-person narration often has great fun at the expense of his characters and doesn't shy away from stern moral outrage, especially at the injustices of society.

- Modern writers are no less opinionated than their predecessors, but rather than telling the reader what to think, most contemporary novelists prefer to stand back and let the events of the novel and the actions and ideas of the characters speak for them.

Omniscient Third Person

- The omniscient third person is often described as godlike, but not just because it allows the writer complete access to the created world and the inner lives of the characters. It also allows the writer to give readers the same range of perspectives—from the most all-encompassing views of a community, to the most intimate exchange between two individuals, to a character's most private thoughts.

- There's an overlap here with plotting. As mentioned in an earlier lecture, constructing a plot requires you to choose what to reveal to the reader and when, and when you're writing in this kind of third person, those choices usually depend on which perspective you use.

- The hallmark of the omniscient third person is that you can often swoop in a single chapter—and sometimes in a single passage—from the widest view of the story to the most intimate. A good example of this kind of narrative dexterity is found in chapter 11 of George Eliot's *Middlemarch*.

- o   In the first part of the chapter, Eliot tells us, in a straightforward fashion, about a doctor named Lydgate, who is new to the town of Middlemarch, and his interest in marrying a pretty young woman named Rosamond Vincy. Eliot bluntly states that Lydgate is "young, poor, and ambitious" and that the chief quality he wants in a wife is beauty and charm. Eliot also lets us know that Rosamond is interested in Lydgate, too, because she considers herself too good for the boring young men she grew up with.

- o   Along the way in this passage of pure exposition, Eliot masterfully fits Lydgate and Rosamond within the social hierarchy of the town, while also discussing the fact that love and marriage can disarrange that social hierarchy. It is, in other words, as godlike a perspective as possible, mostly cool, even-handed, and remote, with a few flashes of authorial judgment.

- o   Then, Eliot narrows her focus to the breakfast table of the Vincy household, where Rosamond, her brother Fred, and their mother discuss a wide variety of topics. Here, Eliot vividly evokes the individual characters and their relationships, while taking care of an important moment in the plot and giving the reader information that will be important later on. And it's all done in a third-person point of view that is halfway between a recording eye and a judgmental authorial voice.

- •   It's important to note that an omniscient third-person narration can also incorporate the close third person. In *Anna Karenina*, Tolstoy writes much of the novel in the same omniscient third person that Eliot uses, keeping us at a slight remove from the characters. But he also delves into a modern-seeming close third person, especially with Anna herself.

Combining Points of View

- Although it may be true that the close third person remains the default mode for many writers, you'll also find that most writers feel free to mix and match the varieties of the third person in surprising and innovative ways.

- Much of the narration of the American detective novelist George Pelecanos, for instance, is of the recording-eye variety, with detailed descriptions in spare language of what his characters look like, what they wear, and what they say and do. But occasionally, his narration varies from the remote third person to the close third person. Interestingly, Pelecanos also occasionally allows himself to step in and pass judgment on his characters.

- Such judgments help make it clear that an author doesn't necessarily endorse everything his or her protagonist does. You can do this in the first person only by implication, but in the third person, you can come right out and say what you think.

Suggested Reading

Austen, *Pride and Prejudice*.

Dickens, *Bleak House*.

Eliot, *Middlemarch*.

Hammett, *The Maltese Falcon*.

Hynes, *The Wild Colonial Boy*.

Martin, *A Song of Ice and Fire*.

Pelecanos, *The Cut*.

1. Pick a stressful or contentious situation between two characters—an argument between a husband and wife, for example, or an interrogation scene in which a detective is trying to get a confession out of a suspect. Then, tell the scene three ways: once in the close third person from the point of view of one character, such as the detective; once in the close third person from the point of view of the other character; and once in the omniscient third person, showing the same situation from a godlike perspective.

He, She, It—Third-Person Point of View
Lecture 17—Transcript

It's not like I've done a survey or anything, but I think it's safe to say that some version of the third person is the default narrative voice of most contemporary fiction. With the rise of the memoir in recent years, the first person has given the third person a run for its money. But on the whole, most writers probably feel most comfortable writing in the third person.

Why should this be, I wonder? As I said at the beginning of the previous lecture, a first-person narration can seem more natural. And it can certainly be appealing, intimate, and immediate, providing the illusion that we are hearing the events of the story from one of its participants, or at least from a witness. But as I also pointed out, first-person narrators can be deluded, or they can be liars.

There is also another drawback which is common to nearly all first-person narrators, whether they're telling the truth or not. A first-person narrator can usually talk only about the events that he or she has witnessed or has heard about from another source. In addition, the first-person narration can be tricky for a writer, because of that double consciousness that I explained in the last lecture. You have a slightly more complicated job when you're writing in the first person. You are not only telling the story, you are also creating an important character at the same time and telling the story through that character's voice.

The third person, on the other hand, has a good deal more range and flexibility than the first person. A third-person narration can encompass all sorts of things that a first-person narrator wouldn't know or be able to express. The third person can also, paradoxically, go deeper into an individual character's consciousness than the first person can. If you adopt the godlike perspective of the omniscient third person, for example, every facet of a character's personality and history is made available to the reader.

But perhaps most importantly, the third person is probably a more instinctive and natural way to tell a fictional story, especially if you're telling a story about someone who isn't yourself, as most fiction writers are.

Most of us tell jokes in the third person. Nearly all fairy tales and folk tales are told in the third person. No one says, "Once upon a time, I went into the woods to my grandmother's house." And many of the great early texts of western literature are told in the third person, from the *Iliad* and the *Odyssey* to *Beowulf* and *Don Quixote*. In its most straightforward form, the third person adopts the easy cadence and authority of the traditional oral storyteller.

But of course, there are different varieties and flavors of the third person. Think back to my metaphor of the sky from my first lecture about point of view. I started at the zenith with the most omniscient variety of the third person and worked my way down the curve of the sky to the interior version of the first person on ground level. In this lecture, we're going to look at the varieties of the third person in more detail. I will start with the type of third-person narration that is most like the first person, and work my way back up to the godlike third person of the great 19th-century novelists. What we'll find by the end (spoiler alert!) is that most writers usually adopt more than one variety of the third person in same story or novel. This is different from the way writers tend to use the first person, where you are often locked into one version of the narration throughout the entire story.

So let's start with the close third person, or what is sometimes called "free indirect discourse." At the start of this lecture I said that the third person is the default mode of most contemporary fiction, and the close third person is the type that is most commonly used. In the close third person, you adopt the point of view of only one character at a time, while continuing to use the third person pronouns "he" or "she." It's very similar to the first person on the whole because the close third person sticks to what the character knows. It shows us only what that character has seen or heard about, and it shows us only that character's thoughts and feelings.

In fact, the close third person traffics in that same double consciousness that the first person does, only with more weight being given to the exterior point of view of the author. In some instances, this kind of third person is so close to the character that it ends up being a de facto first person. In fact, in some uses of the close third person, you could probably switch the narrative into the first person without having to change too much apart from the pronouns.

But that's rare. In most cases, the close third person at least contains the possibility of going deeper into the character's head than a simple first-person narration does. This is because the third person allows you to reveal things about the character's thoughts, feelings, intentions, and prejudices that the character himself may not know or understand. A close third person can also reveal a character's secrets. In this respect, the close third person can be more comprehensive than the first person. It allows you to show everything about a character, and not just what that character chooses to reveal.

As with any other choice in creative writing, choosing to use this particular point of view means you gain some things and you lose some things. In the first person, you can create a unique voice for the character, the way Twain does for Huck Finn. By choosing to tell a story in the close third person, you lose that distinctive voice. On the other hand, in the close third person you can dive as deeply into your character's head as Virginia Woolf does in *Mrs. Dalloway*.

Let's take a look at the difference. That moment in *Huckleberry Finn* where Huck decides to help Jim win his freedom would not be nearly as thrilling in the close third person. The power of that scene comes from watching Huck work it out for himself. If you were to change that passage into the third person, you'd have to pepper it with a lot phrases like "Huck thought that," or "It seemed to Huck that." And right there, you lose the immediacy of it. You lose the feeling that you're watching Huck Finn himself wrestling with his own conscience. "At last Huck decided, all right then, he'd *go* to hell" is not nearly as powerful a sentence as Huck himself saying, "All right, then, I'll *go* to hell."

Now think back to that moment in *Mrs. Dalloway* that I mentioned in an earlier lecture, when Clarissa Dalloway is looking at a shop window. In just a few words, her mind skips with lightning speed from a memory of her father buying suits, to a shop where you could buy perfect gloves, to her uncle saying that you could know a lady by her gloves, to the death of her uncle during the war, to her own passion for gloves, and finally to her remote relationship with her daughter. It's possible to imagine recasting that scene in the first person, but think how clumsy it would be: "As I stared in the window of a shop where you used to be able to buy almost perfect gloves,

I was reminded of my Uncle William saying that you could know a lady by her shoes and gloves, which reminded me of how he turned over in his bed one morning and died," and so on.

Not only is this horribly awkward, it actually changes Mrs. Dalloway as a character. It makes her a much more introspective and self-aware woman than she is in Woolf's version. It presumes that she understands her own thoughts as well as her author does. Instead, by using a very close, very intimate third person in that scene, we're getting an unself-conscious view of Clarissa Dalloway. We're seeing her intimately but remotely at the same time. We understand her even better than she could understand herself. Let me put it this way: The close third person is like eavesdropping. We're more likely to believe what a politician says when he doesn't know the microphone is on than when he's wearing his public face and repeating his talking points. The close third person is like an open mic: It lays bare the private Mrs. Dalloway, not just the version of herself that she wants the world to see.

Another reason the close third person is more flexible and comprehensive that the first person is that it's easier to shift point of view from one character to another. It's certainly possible to switch from one first-person narrator to another within the same story or book. William Faulkner does it brilliantly in *As I Lay Dying*, which is narrated by 15 different characters. It's a remarkable achievement, but before you rush off to imitate it, consider this: When you're writing in the first person, you're not only telling the story, you're creating an individual voice for that character. In Faulkner's case, that's 15 different narrators. And even though they all come from the same family or at least from the same community, they all have to sound at least a little bit different from each other. It's a lot of work, both for the writer and the reader, which is perhaps why this technique isn't used very often.

On the other hand, in the close third person, you can switch from one character to another with relative ease, because you don't have to reinvent the voice of the narration itself each time you switch point of view. You can use the same authorial voice to evoke different characters.

Mrs. Dalloway is a bravura example of this, of course, often switching point of view within a scene. However, in most instances, writers shift point of view from chapter to chapter. This technique broadens the scope of the story beyond what only one character can know. I learned this the hard way when I was writing my first published novel, *The Wild Colonial Boy*.

That novel was a thriller about a young Irish American named Brian who agrees to carry some explosives into Britain for an Irish terrorist. My first three drafts were in the close third person from Brian's point of view. The problem was that in each successive draft, the plot became more complicated. It reached a point where many of the most dramatic moments—a gunfight, a brutal interrogation, a terrorist bombing—happened when Brian wasn't present. This was supposed to be a thriller, and yet the most thrilling scenes entered the novel only as secondhand accounts or news reports.

Finally, a friendly agent who agreed to read the third draft suggested that I tell the novel from the alternating points of view of Brian and several other characters in the novel. That way, I could show the reader each dramatic moments from the point of view of one of the characters who was actually present, instead of just feebly telling the reader about them later on, from Brian's secondhand perspective. This suggestion opened up the book, gave it a much wider scope, and made it much more thrilling. It also forced me to get inside the heads of three more characters, two of whom were women, which was something I might never have attempted on my own.

And so I learned that alternating points of view in the close third person is a really powerful way to tell a long story or a novel. It gives you the best of both worlds. Each individual chapter allows you to inhabit the mind of a single character, but by changing the point of view with each subsequent chapter, you can broaden the scope of your narrative. In fact, by using several different point-of-view characters, you can show different perspectives on the same event. And, at the most mechanical level, you can make sure the reader is present at all the most important scenes.

Switching between several point-of-view characters with the close third person is an especially useful technique for very long, epic narratives. It can balance intimacy with a sort of widescreen, cinematic expansiveness. George R. R. Martin uses this technique very effectively in his *Song of Ice and Fire* novels. Each book is told from the points of view of many different characters, and the point of view switches with each chapter. Not only does this allow the reader to see the complex events of the story from multiple points of view, it allows Martin to evoke a vast imaginary world in vivid and evocative detail. And by showing different and often competing perspectives on the same series of events, the series reads less like a simplistic fable of good versus evil and more like a gritty contemporary account of conflicting interests.

Martin also does something else that many writers do when using the close third person. He includes the point-of-view character's thoughts in the first person, but within the third-person narration. Usually these thoughts are set off from the rest of the narration by using italics. Here's the character Jaime Lannister as he being ferried down a river in a rowboat as a captive in chains, and he's trying to catch a little sleep on the fly:

> He must have drifted off then. The wine had made him sleepy, and it felt good to stretch, a luxury his chains had not permitted him in his cell. Jaime had long ago learned to snatch sleep in the saddle during a march. This was no harder. [Then, in italics:] *Tyrion is going to laugh himself sick when he hears how I slept through my own escape.* [Then, back to roman type:] He was awake now, though, and the fetters were irksome.

When it's done seamlessly, as it is here, this can add yet another dimension to the close third person.

And some writers, such as Leo Tolstoy in *Anna Karenina*, set aside their characters' thoughts with quotation marks rather than italics, using "she thought" or "she said to herself" rather than the usual dialogue tag "she said."

Other writers incorporate the first-person thoughts of a character without using italics or quotation marks. The entirety of my novel, *Next*, is told from the close third-person point of view of a single character, named Kevin. Before publication, I had a friendly disagreement with the copyeditor, who wanted to put Kevin's first-person thoughts in italics. Because the whole book was essentially in Kevin's head, I was afraid that all those italics would simply be distracting, so I insisted on leaving his thoughts in roman type.

Now let's take a quick look at another variety of the third person, namely the objective or remote third person. This is the sort of third-person narration that simply describes what the characters do and say without giving the reader access to their thoughts.

At first glance, this kind of narration might seem the same as the recording eye first person I talked about in the last lecture, in which a character who is tangential to the main story tells the events of the narrative, the way Ishmael and Nick Carraway do. But there's a crucial difference. With the recording eye first person, the events are still being filtered through a fictional consciousness. And this fictional consciousness often passes judgment or makes educated guesses as to what the other characters are thinking. Nick Carraway may not be central to *The Great Gatsby*, but he does narrate the story of Gatsby and Daisy from a particular point of view. Nick's take on the events of the novel still colors the reader's understanding.

Compare this with the remote third-person narration in Dashiell Hammet's *The Maltese Falcon*. This narrative perspective watches everything the characters do like a camera, but without giving us direct access to their thoughts and feelings.

Here's a moment when Sam Spade is embracing his partner's wife. He's been carrying on an affair with her, and this excerpt comes from the moment when they have found out that his partner, and her husband, is dead:

> He grimaced again and bent his head for a surreptitious look at the watch on his wrist. His left arm was around her, the hand on her left shoulder. His cuff was pulled back far enough to leave the watch uncovered. It showed ten-ten.
>
> The woman stirred in his arms and raised her face again. Her blue eyes were wet, round, and white-ringed. Her mouth was moist.
>
> "Oh, Sam," she moaned. "Did you kill him?"

Spade stared at her with bulging eyes. His bony jaw fell down. He took his arms from her and stepped back out of her arms. He scowled at her and cleared his throat.

It's pretty clear from this that Spade may be heartless cad, but he's probably not a murderer. But since we don't know what he's actually thinking, we can't be absolutely certain. This kind of third person keeps us at arm's length from its characters. This builds suspense and keeps the reader on his toes, but at the cost of a certain coldness.

The opposite of this remote and noncommittal third person is what you might call the engaged or judgmental third person. Even though this variety of third person is not tied to a character in the story, the voice still has a strong opinion about the events it is relating. You find this type of third person much more commonly in the novels of the 18th and 19th centuries, when authors had no problem passing judgment on the follies of their characters. There is no pretense of objectivity in the narrative voice, which passes judgment right and left without filtering it through a character.

This kind of voice works especially well with comic or picaresque novels, like those of the 18th-century English writer Henry Fielding. His big comic novel *Tom Jones* regularly passes judgment on the follies of its characters. A generation later, you still hear something of the same voice in Jane Austen, who was a much more subtle writer than Henry Fielding, but also a very sharp judge of flawed characters. Much of *Pride and Prejudice* is told in the close third person from Elizabeth Bennett's point of view, but there are also memorable passages in which the author herself passes a direct and unmediated judgment. Here is a paragraph from the first chapter, which sums up the badly mismatched marriage of Elizabeth's parents, even before we have met any of their daughters:

Mr. Bennett was so odd a mixture of quick parts, sarcastic humour, reserve, and caprice, that the experience of three and twenty years had been insufficient to make his wife understand his character. Her mind was less difficult to develop. She was a woman of mean understanding, little information, and uncertain temper. When she was discontented she fancied herself nervous. The business of her life was to get her daughters married; its solace was visiting and news.

If this is a bit too 19th century for you, let me translate it: Mr. Bennett is a quick-witted, intelligent man who keeps his opinions to himself and hides behind his sarcasm. Mrs. Bennett is uneducated and not very intelligent, and she loves gossip and is terrified that her daughters will not marry well. Jane Austen is telling us rather bluntly that this is not a match made in heaven.

Perhaps the most enthusiastically judgmental narrator of all time is Charles Dickens. His third-person narration often has great fun at the expense of his characters, and it also doesn't shy away from stern moral outrage.

In the opening pages of one of his greatest novels, *Bleak House*, Dickens is already passing judgment before he has introduced any characters at all, when he describes at length the baleful effect of a complicated Chancery court lawsuit:

> Jarndyce and Jarndyce drones on. This scarecrow of a suit has, in the course of time, become so complicated that no man alive knows what it means. The parties to it understand it least; but it has been observed that no two Chancery lawyers can talk about it for five minutes without coming to a total disagreement as to all the premises. Innumerable children have been born into the cause; innumerable young people have married into it; innumerable old people have died out of it. Scores of persons have deliriously found themselves made parties in Jarndyce and Jarndyce, without knowing how or why; whole families have inherited legendary hatreds with the suit.

And so on. Dickens being Dickens, this goes on for several pages.

Modern writers are no less opinionated than Dickens, of course, but they usually don't tell the reader what to think. Instead, most contemporary novelists prefer to stand back and let the events of the novel and the actions of the characters speak for themselves (often while discreetly stacking the deck). Still, there are some modern novelists, such as John Irving and Tom

Wolfe, who sometimes use their third-person narrative voice to pass an overt judgment.

Let's move now up to the zenith of my imaginary dome, to the omniscient third person. This is the magisterial point of view of the great 19th century novelists such as George Eliot and Leo Tolstoy.

This version of the third person is often described as godlike, but not just because it allows the writer complete access to the world she has created and the inner lives of her characters. Every writer already has that power, of course, no matter what point of view she's using. The omniscient third person is called godlike, rather, because it presents the reader the full range of perspectives, from the most all-encompassing view of a community, to the most intimate exchange between two individuals, to a character's most private thoughts.

The hallmark of this kind of third-person narration, especially in hands of a great writer like George Eliot, is that it can swoop in a single chapter, and sometimes in a single passage, from the widest view of the story to the most intimate. A good example of this kind of narrative dexterity is Chapter 11 of Eliot's *Middlemarch*.

This is a huge Victorian novel with a lot of characters and a lot of story to tell, and it is set in a small fictional English community called Middlemarch in the 1830s. The whole of Chapter 11 is about 3,500 words, and in the first 1,300 words, Eliot directly tells us about a doctor named Lydgate. Dr. Lydgate is new to the town, and he is interested in marrying a very pretty young woman named Rosamond Vincy. Over the course of the passage, Eliot tells us bluntly that Lydgate is "young, poor, and ambitious." She also tells us that the chief quality he wants in a wife is beauty and charm, which is why he has already ruled out the novel's main character, Dorothea Brooke, because Dorothea is too brainy and serious.

Eliot also simply tells us that Rosamund Vincy is likewise interested in Lydgate, because he is a handsome and accomplished outsider, and because she considers herself too good for the boring young men of Middlemarch. In this long passage of pure exposition, Eliot masterfully fits Lydgate and

Rosamund within the social hierarchy of the town, and she also takes time to show how love and marriage can disarrange that social hierarchy. Her perspective in the first section of Chapter 11 is as godlike as possible. It is cool and even-handed and remote, with a few flashes of authorial judgment in the manner of Jane Austen or Henry Fielding.

Then, in the second part of the chapter, Eliot deftly narrows her focus from the general to the particular. She focuses on the breakfast table conversation of Rosamund's family on a particular morning. We get to watch Rosamund, her brother Fred, and their mother bantering about Rosamund's marriage prospects, the rules of social class in their community, and Fred's opinion of Lydgate, among other things.

It's one of my favorite scenes in all of literature, because Eliot does so many things at once, and does them so well. At the same time as she vividly evokes each individual character and shows their complicated relationships with each other, she also takes care of an important moment in the plot and gives the reader information that will be important later on. And it's all done in a third person that is halfway between a recording eye and the more judgmental third person Eliot was using in the first half of the chapter. The only variety of the third person she doesn't use is the close third person, allowing us to see the scene strictly from the inside the mind of Fred, Rosamund, or their mother.

Eliot very effectively places us in the room with these characters. She allows us to witness each twist and turn of their conversation and to watch their body language. But, with the reserve of the 19th century novelist, she does not encourage us to see through the eyes of any of the characters in the scene, or even to identify with any one of them.

Which is not to say that an omniscient third-person narration can't incorporate the close third person as well. In *Anna Karenina*, which was published only a few years after *Middlemarch*, Tolstoy writes much of the novel in the same magisterial omniscient third person that Eliot uses, and he keeps us at a slight remove from the characters. But at certain points in the novel, especially with Anna herself and another character named Levin, he also delves into a close third person that seems very contemporary to a modern reader.

In the famous climax of the book, when Anna rushes about Moscow in a panic before her fateful encounter with a locomotive, the novel delves deep into her mind, mixing her first-person thoughts with an extremely intimate close third person. The omniscient third person of the rest of the novel keeps us at arm's length from these Russian aristocrats, but in this passage, the distance between the reader and the character is almost completely erased. Anna's pain and desperation are visceral, and whether you approve of her choices or not, you can't read about her fate without a racing pulse.

Modern writers, of course, have all of these techniques at their disposal. While it may be true that the close third person remains the default mode for many writers, you'll also find that most writers feel free to mix and match the varieties of the third person in surprising and innovative ways.

The contemporary American crime novelist George Pelecanos stands in direct line of descent from Dashiell Hammett and Elmore Leonard. And, like Hammett and Leonard, much of his narration is of the recording eye variety. In very spare language, Pelecanos gives us detailed descriptions of what his characters look like, what they wear, and what they say and do. His novel *The Cut*, for example, is told mostly from the point of view of a young private investigator in Washington, DC, named Spero Lucas. Much of the story follows Spero closely as he gets involved in a complicated case involving drug dealers.

But occasionally the narration varies from the remote third person into the close third person. In this passage, for example, Spero, in the manner of all warm-blooded private detectives, is leaving the home of a woman named Lisa Weitzman, with whom he's just had a one-night stand:

> His father had once told him, "Don't let anything walk past you," and Lucas knew well what that meant. There are opportunities that are there for only a short period of time, and only available to people of a certain age. He and Lisa Weitzman understood. They'd had fun. He didn't want to be one of those sad middle-aged

guys who think about the women they should have bedded in their youth, if only they'd been less sensible. He planned to age with good memories.

This is one of the rare moments in the book when we get direct access to Spero's thoughts and feelings, but in the context of a detective thriller, it's enough.

What's even more interesting, however, is that Pelecanos himself very occasionally steps in to pass judgment on his character, in the 19th century manner. Here's Spero not long after his one-night stand, delivering a bunch of roses to Lisa's door:

> He went up the steps of Lisa Weitzman's home and laid the roses, heavily wetted, on her doorstep, along with a note he had written in a childish scrawl before getting out of his vehicle. The note was corny and obvious, something about how nice it was to hang out with her. He had no plans to try and see her again, but he wanted to do something respectful for her, at least. Flowers had come to mind. He was a resourceful but not particularly original young man.

Much of the judgment in this paragraph is implicit—the childish scrawl of the note, its corny and obvious wording—but then there's a stinger in the tail of the paragraph. Like George Eliot passing bemused judgment on Dr. Lydgate's distaste for brainy women, Pelecanos himself briefly steps in to let us know that Spero still has some growing up to do. Little moments like this help to make it clear that the author doesn't necessarily endorse everything his protagonist does. You can do this in the first person only by implication, but in the third person, you can come right out and say what you think.

In the next lecture, I'll be talking about the various ways setting can be used in fiction, and we'll be looking at some famous bits of scene setting from Dickens's *Bleak House* and *The Lord of the Rings*, as well as some different uses of setting from Mr. Pelecanos and the British writer Rosemary Sutcliff.

In the meantime, here's an exercise that explores some of the power and flexibility of the third person. Pick a stressful or contentious situation between two characters, such as an argument between a husband and wife, or an interrogation scene where a cop is trying to get a confession out of a suspect. Then tell the scene three different ways, each in the third person: once in the close third person from the point of view of one character—the cop, for example—and then tell the same situation again in the close third person from the point of view of the suspect. Then, in the third paragraph, try to go all George Eliot and look on the scene from the omniscient third person, showing the same situation from a godlike perspective.

Evoking Setting and Place in Fiction
Lecture 18

E very story has a setting, but setting is not equally important to all stories. For some narratives, setting is a sort of painted theatrical backdrop against which the story plays out, and that backdrop can be changed for another one without fundamentally changing the story itself. In most contemporary fiction, however, setting is important, and much of what makes a novel or story memorable is the author's careful evocation of a particular place and time. In this lecture, we'll talk about some of the purposes to which setting can be put in a narrative and some of the ways in which setting can be evoked.

Setting as a Metaphor
- In many narratives, setting can be a metaphor for the narrative as a whole. One of the most famous examples here is the opening paragraph of *Bleak House*, Charles Dickens's novel about a complicated and never-ending lawsuit in mid-19th-century England.
  - Before we meet a single character in *Bleak House* and before the plot even starts, Dickens indelibly evokes a vision of dark, dirty London, full of filthy animals, ill-tempered pedestrians, and people wheezing and shivering in the all-encompassing fog.

  - This exceptionally vivid evocation of setting serves two purposes: It vividly evokes the sensory details of London in the mind of the reader—the darkness, the cold, the dirt—and it makes the setting serve as a metaphor for the misty, insinuating, impenetrably foggy coils of the lawsuit itself.

- In J. G. Farrell's historical novel *Troubles*, which is about the Irish rebellion against British rule in the years after World War I, the main setting is a giant resort hotel on the Irish coast called the Majestic, and it serves throughout the novel as a metaphor for the grand, ornate, and crumbling edifice of the British Empire.

- o At the end of the novel, the Irish Republican Army burns the hotel to the ground, not only destroying the hotel but metaphorically destroying the dominance of the Protestants and British in Ireland. On the last page, a gentle and befuddled retired British army major surveys the ruins, including the skeletons of the hundreds of cats that lived in the hotel.

  - o Even readers who don't know anything about the history of the Irish Revolution understand that the major is surveying the ruins of an empire, not just a burned-down hotel.

- Note that the descriptions of foggy, dirty London in *Bleak House* and the Majestic Hotel in *Troubles* are also full of vivid sensory details that draw readers into the scene, putting them in the moment even if they don't consciously pick up on the metaphor. Even when a setting is used for a metaphorical purpose, it should be visceral and vivid, allowing us to experience that imaginary world as if we were characters in the story.

Setting to Evoke Mood

- Setting can also be used to evoke mood, especially when the point is to evoke a strong vicarious emotion, such as the feeling of fear readers get from a horror story or the feeling of suspense they get from a thriller.

- Consider part of the description of a haunted house from the early pages of Judith Hawkes's marvelously creepy novel *Julian's House*:

  Inside the gate a silence falls. Leaves stir and are still. At the foot of the porch steps the silence deepens, wrapped around with the fragrance of the shallow pink roses that twine the uprights and shadow the wide boards with their leaves. And yet it is more than a silence, as the leaves stir and again are still: it is a silence of breath held, of a sob stifled in a pillow, the silence that follows the blow of a fist upon a table. In the moving leaves this silence seems to murmur in its sleep—of too many closed doors, keys turning smoothly in well-oiled locks, glances exchanged without words. (p. 12)

- Even if we hadn't already been told that this is a haunted house, it would be impossible for anybody to read this description and not understand immediately that there is something wrong with this house—that there is something bad waiting inside.

- Notice that Hawkes uses the word *silence* six times in this description. Although normally the repetition of a word that many times in so short a passage would be anathema to writers, here, it has the effect of making the silence ominous. Note, too, that *silence* is paired with active verbs— *falls*, *deepens*, *murmur*[*s*]—changing it from an absence of sound to an active presence in the house.

Setting to Evoke Character

- In addition, setting can be used to tell readers about the characters in a story. For example, a description of a room or a house is often used to tell us something about the person who lives there.

- One of the major plotlines in George Eliot's *Middlemarch* is the ill-advised marriage between Dorothea Brooke, an intense young woman in her early 20s, and Edward Casaubon, a dry and humorless scholar who is 30 years her senior. Early in the book, after their surprise engagement, Dorothea goes to visit Mr. Casaubon's home:

  > The building, of greenish stone, was in the old English style, not ugly, but small-windowed and melancholy-looking …. In this latter end of autumn … the house too had an air of autumnal decline, and Mr. Casaubon, when he presented himself, had no bloom that could be thrown into relief by that background. (pp. 73–74)

- Nearly everything that Eliot says about the house—that it is "not ugly, but small-windowed and melancholy" and that it has an air of "autumnal decline"—could also be said about Casaubon himself. The last clause of the passage is one of the great backhanded insults in English literature: the fact that there is nothing about Casaubon himself that could be "thrown into relief" by his joyless home.

Setting to Evoke Time and Movement

• Setting can also be used to evoke the passage of time and the movement of characters through a landscape. Tolkien is especially skillful at evoking the geography of Middle Earth—in part, simply because he delights in evoking the natural world but also because these passages literally slow the narrative down, which has the effect of evoking the slow passage of the characters, moving on foot through a vast and often spectacular landscape.

In a chase scene, Rosemary Sutcliff skillfully evokes both motion and the landscape of the Scottish highlands with such phrases as "skirting a reed-fringed upland pool" and "swerving from a patch of bog."

© Lesley Jacques/iStock/Thinkstock.

    o A passage in *The Two Towers* in which Frodo and Sam pass through the land of Ithilien evokes both the vastness of the landscape through which they are moving and their own sense of wonder at it. The fact that the reader is required to slow down during this passage and to literally stop and smell the flowers also evokes the slowness of their journey.

    o Among other techniques, the passage effectively shifts focus from the long distance to the close-up: We first see the mountains as "a long curve that was lost in the distance," but in the next sentence, we get particular types of trees—"fir and cedar and cypress." Finally, we see individual harbingers of spring: fronds piercing moss, green-fingered larches, and flowers opening in the turf.

- Of course, setting doesn't have to slow down the narrative; it can also evoke speed and danger. In a chase scene from Rosemary Sutcliff's *The Eagle of the Ninth*, we delight in the vivid evocation of the landscape in its own right—luminous green bogs, bronze tides of dying heather—but we also note that Sutcliff skillfully interweaves flashes of landscape description with breathless action.

A Continuum of Setting

- The many ways in which setting can be evoked fall between two ends of a continuum: At one end, setting is evoked by stopping the narrative in its tracks and describing a place or a time period. At the other end, setting is evoked only minimally.

  - In general—though not always—the first method is used in narratives similar to *Bleak House* or *Troubles*, where the setting is important to the story, while at the other extreme, when the setting isn't that important, writers don't bother with it as much.

  - In between, there are many variations, including evoking setting as you go, inserting a few telling details along the way without stopping the action. As always, most novels and short stories fall somewhere in between, combining the various methods.

- In narratives that include standalone descriptions of setting, how the writer uses them depends on the point of view of the novel, whether it's the omniscient third person, limited third person, or first person.
  - The omniscient third person is almost cinematic. The opening of *Bleak House*, for example, is like a crane shot in a movie, starting high up—"smoke lowering down from chimney-pots, making a soft black drizzle"—and slowly descending to street level—"dogs, undistinguishable in mire." This passage gives the mind's eye something to look at, and it introduces a central metaphor for the plot.

o When a standalone description of setting is told from the limited third-person or first-person point of view, it also evokes character. How the character sees the setting—what details he or she picks out as important—tells us something about the person through whose eyes we, the readers, are seeing them.

o When setting is described from the first-person point of view, it can become even more multilayered. For example, setting is important to the novels of Raymond Chandler, but it's also important that the setting is seen through the eyes and mind of Chandler's protagonist, the private detective Philip Marlowe. Marlowe's descriptions tell us a great deal about himself.

• Writers who only scarcely evoke setting often use a kind of shorthand, relying on the fact that certain places, street names, or even brand names are familiar to the reader and will be evocative of time and place. The crime thrillers of George Pelecanos, for example, are specifically set in Washington, DC, and Pelecanos skillfully mixes real street and place names in Washington with brief bits of description.

• Whether you choose to lavish your reader with a richly detailed description or simply say that your detective walked into a Starbucks, remember that in most cases, how you use setting depends on the overall purpose of your narrative. Scene by scene, you want to lavish detailed descriptions on settings that recur or are especially important, but you need only a line or two to evoke settings that don't matter quite as much or that appear only once.

Suggested Reading

Austen, *Pride and Prejudice*.

Chandler, *The Big Sleep*.

Dickens, *Bleak House*.

Eliot, *Middlemarch*.

Farrell, *Troubles*.

Hawkes, *Julian's House*.

Pelecanos, *The Cut*.

Sutcliff, *The Eagle of the Ninth*.

Tolkien, *The Two Towers*.

Writing Exercises

1. Try describing the same setting from the point of view of two different characters who want different things. For example, consider Sarah and Brad, the unhappily married couple in our narrative from the first lecture. As you may recall, they're at a baseball game; try to describe the ballpark from Sarah's point of view, bearing in mind that she's about to ask for a divorce, and then from Brad's, bearing in mind that he has no idea what she's about to ask him.

2. You might also explore the importance of a particular setting to a narrative by setting a scene from a famous novel or story in a radically different place or time from the original version. Can you rewrite a scene from, say, *The Adventures of Huckleberry Finn* that is set someplace other than the Mississippi? Could one of the scenes from *The Great Gatsby* take place at any other place or time than Long Island in the Jazz Age?

Evoking Setting and Place in Fiction
Lecture 18—Transcript

Every story has a setting, but setting is not equally important to all stories. For some narratives, setting is just a painted theatrical backdrop against which the story plays out, and that backdrop can be changed for another one without fundamentally changing the story itself. Think of those modern-dress Shakespeare productions where Richard III is played as a fascist from the 1930s, or Macbeth is played as an ambitious investment banker, or the Montagues and the Capulets in *Romeo and Juliet* are portrayed as rival street gangs in Miami.

And it's not just Shakespeare: One of the best films ever made from a Jane Austen novel is the 1990s teen comedy *Clueless*. This film very successfully, and surprisingly faithfully, sets Austen's novel *Emma* in a contemporary Los Angeles high school.

Here's another example: Christina Stead's brilliant novel about a dysfunctional family, *The Man Who Loved Children*, was originally set in Stead's native Australia. But in order to make it more appealing to American readers, she was persuaded by her publisher to move the setting to Washington, DC.

In most contemporary fiction, however, setting is important. Much of what can make a novel or story memorable is the author's careful evocation of a particular place and time. To pick two obvious examples, Raymond Chandler's Philip Marlowe novels are inextricably linked with Los Angeles in the middle part of the 20th century, and Flannery O'Connor's stories will be forever associated with the rural American South.

An evocative and memorable setting doesn't even have to be real. Much of the appeal of Tolkien's Lord of the Rings comes from the way its characters and the reader move through the lovingly detailed landscape of Middle Earth. Tolkien's settings are so detailed and evocative that, if you've read Lord of the Rings more than once, as I have, chances are you could be dropped anywhere in Middle Earth and find your way around.

Setting can also mean a particular time period, as well. The British novelist Hilary Mantel is famous for her attention to historical accuracy in her novels set in the court of Henry VIII, *Wolf Hall* and *Bring up the Bodies*. And the thrillers of Alan Furst owe much of their excitement to his detailed evocation of Europe during the rise of the Nazis.

Another writer who is known for her evocative settings is Rosemary Sutcliff, who is best known for her series of young adult novels about Roman Britain, *The Eagle of the Ninth*, *The Silver Branch*, and *The Lantern Bearers*. Each of these books skillfully evokes both the time period and the landscape of ancient Britain and Scotland. Sutcliff had a keen appreciation of the natural world and a sharp eye for the telling detail.

Of course, all fictional narratives are set somewhere, whether the particular setting is essential or not. At the very least, setting establishes a context for the characters and the plot, since not even fictional characters come out of nowhere. Sometimes it's just a backdrop—"Two households, both alike in dignity, / In fair Verona, where we lay our scene"—but more often than not, setting does more in the narrative than just situating us in time and place. In this lecture, I want to talk first about some of the purposes to which setting can be put in a narrative. After that, I'll talk about how you can evoke setting in a story, which depends on the purpose of the setting.

Let's start by looking at some of the ways that you can use setting in a story or novel.

In many narratives, setting can be a metaphor for the narrative as a whole. One of the most famous examples is the opening paragraph of *Bleak House*, Charles Dickens's great novel about a complicated and never-ending lawsuit in mid-19th-century England. Here are the opening words:

> London. Michaelmas term lately over, and the Lord Chancellor sitting in Lincoln's Inn Hall. Implacable November weather. As much mud in the streets as if the waters had but newly retired from the face of the earth, and it would not be wonderful to meet a Megalosaurus, forty feet long or so, waddling like an elephantine lizard up Holborn Hill. Smoke lowering down from chimney-pots,

making a soft black drizzle, with flakes of soot in it as big as full-grown snowflakes—gone into mourning, one might imagine, for the death of the sun. Dogs, undistinguishable in mire. Horses, scarcely better; splashed to their very blinkers. Foot passengers, jostling one another's umbrellas in a general infection of ill temper, and losing their foot-hold at street-corners, where tens of thousands of other foot passengers have been slipping and sliding since the day broke (if this day ever broke), adding new deposits to the crust upon crust of mud, sticking at those points tenaciously to the pavement, and accumulating at compound interest.

The next paragraph is an equally detailed and equally unsettling account of the London fog. Dickens describes how it creeps everywhere and obscures everything, how it gets into the eyes and throats of ancient pensioners by their firesides and pinches the toes and fingers of a ship's apprentice boy. And so before we ever meet a character and before the plot even starts, Dickens has indelibly evoked a vision of dark, dirty London, full of filthy animals, ill-tempered pedestrians, and poor people wheezing and shivering in the all-encompassing fog.

This exceptionally vivid setting sets up two purposes. On the one hand, it vividly evokes the sensory details of London in the mind of the reader—the darkness, the cold, the dirt. On the other hand, the setting serves as a metaphor for the misty, insinuating, impenetrably foggy coils of the lawsuit itself.

Here's another example. J. G. Farrell's historical novel *Troubles* is about the Irish rebellion against British rule in the years after World War I. The main setting is a giant resort hotel on the Irish coast called the Majestic. This baroque old building serves all the way through the novel as a metaphor for the grand, ornate, crumbling edifice of the British Empire.

At the end of the novel, the Irish Republican Army burns the hotel to the ground. The actual destruction of the hotel represents the metaphorical destruction of the dominance of Protestants and the British in Ireland. On the last page, the novel's main character, a gentle and befuddled retired British army major, surveys the ruins, which includes the skeletons of the hundreds of cats that lived in the hotel:

> There was very little to see except that great collection of wash-basins and lavatory bowls which had crashed from one burning floor to another until they reached the ground. He inspected the drips of molten glass which had collected like candle-grease beneath the windows. He noted the large number of delicate little skeletons (the charred and roasted demons had been picked clean by the rats). He stepped from one blackened compartment to another trying to orientate himself and saying, 'I'm standing in the residents' lounge, in the corridor, in the writing-room.' Now that these rooms were open to the mild Irish sky they all seemed much smaller—in fact, quite insignificant.

This evocative but brief excerpt can't convey the full effect of this final scene, but take my word for it. The vast, crumbling, mostly empty Majestic is an oppressive presence all the way through the whole book, with its clueless Anglo-Irish owners, its sullen Irish servants, and a surrounding countryside seething with resentment. Even if he or she doesn't know anything about the history of the Irish Revolution, every reader will understand that in that final scene, the Major is surveying the ruins of an empire, and not just a burnt-out old hotel.

I want to emphasize that each of these two settings, foggy, dirty London in Bleak House and the Majestic Hotel in Troubles, are also full of vivid sensory details that draw you into the scene and into the book. They put you in the moment even if you aren't consciously picking up on the metaphor. A setting should be visceral and vivid even when you are using it for a metaphorical purpose. Whatever its symbolic intent, a carefully evoked setting should allow us to experience that imaginary world as if we were characters in the story.

You can also use setting to evoke mood, especially when the point of the book is to evoke a strong, vicarious emotion. This is especially true in genre fiction such as horror, where you want to evoke fear in a reader. Here's part of a description of a haunted house from the early pages of Judith Hawkes's marvelously creepy novel, Julian's House:

> Inside the gate, so overgrown with honeysuckle that it no longer swings freely but seems to protest against being opened, the yard slopes ever so slightly down to the house and you may find your pace quickening in spite of yourself as you approach. The broad flagstones leading the way are cracked now and worn with the pressure of feet going back and forth across them; grass springs up in the cracks and the once-sharp edges are soft with moss. Inside the gate a silence falls. Leaves stir and are still. At the foot of the porch steps the silence deepens, wrapped around with the fragrance of the shallow pink roses that twine the uprights and shadow the wide boards with their leaves. And yet it is more than a silence, as the leaves stir and again are still: it is a silence of breath held, of a sob stifled in a pillow, the silence that follows the blow of a fist upon a table. In the moving leaves this silence seems to murmur in its sleep—of too many closed doors, keys turning smoothly in well-oiled locks, glances exchanged without words.

Even if we hadn't already been told that this is a haunted house, it would be hard to read this description and not sense immediately that there is something wrong with this house, that there is something bad waiting inside.

There are a lot of nifty little details in this passage, but I'll just point out one. You might not notice it on a first reading, but Hawkes uses the word *silence* six times in the paragraph. Normally the repetition of a word that many times in so short a passage is anathema to writers (or at least to copyeditors), but here the repetition has the effect of making the silence ominous, like a thundercloud building on the horizon.

More importantly, the word *silence* is paired with such active verbs as *falls*, *deepens*, and *murmur[s]*. The use of these verbs change the silence from an absence of sound to an active presence in the house. This is a very skillful bit of scene-setting.

You can also use setting to tell us about the characters in a story. A description of a room or a house is often used to tell us something about the person who lives there. One of the major plotlines in George Eliot's *Middlemarch* is the ill-advised marriage of Dorothea Brooke, an intense young woman in her early 20s, to Edward Casaubon, a dry and humorless scholar who is 30 years her senior.

Early in the book, after their surprise engagement, Dorothea goes to visit Mr. Casaubon's home:

> The building, of greenish stone, was in the old English style, not ugly, but small-windowed and melancholy-looking: the sort of house that must have children, many flowers, open windows, and little vistas of bright things, to make it seem a joyous home. In this latter end of autumn, with a sparse remnant of yellow leaves falling slowly athwart the dark evergreens in a stillness without sunshine, the house too had an air of autumnal decline, and Mr. Casaubon, when he presented himself, had no bloom that could be thrown into relief by that background.

Even if the reader hadn't already begun to suspect that Dorothea's marriage to Casaubon was a bad idea, this description should make up his mind. Nearly everything Eliot says about the house, that it's "small-windowed and melancholy," that the grounds around it are dark, still, and without sunshine, and that it has an air of "autumnal decline," could also be said about Casaubon himself. The last clause of the passage is one of the great backhanded insults in English literature, when Eliot says that there is nothing about Casaubon himself that could be "thrown into relief" by his joyless home.

Setting can also be used to evoke the passage of time and the movement of characters through a landscape. Tolkien is especially skillful at describing the geography of Middle Earth. In part this is simply because he delights in evoking the natural world. But these passages also literally slow the narrative down, and this has the effect of evoking the slow passage of characters who are moving on foot through a vast and often spectacular landscape.

363

Here are the hobbits Frodo and Sam passing through the land of Ithilien, in *The Two Towers*:

> Day was opening in the sky, and they saw that the mountains were now much further off, receding eastward in a long curve that was lost in the distance. Before them, as they turned west, gentle slopes ran down into dim hazes far below. All about them were small woods of resinous trees, fir and cedar and cypress, and other kinds unknown in the Shire, with wide glades among them; and everywhere there was a wealth of sweet-smelling herbs and shrubs. The long journey from Rivendell had brought them far south of their own land, but not until now in this more sheltered region had the hobbits felt the change of clime. Here Spring was already busy about them: fronds pierced moss and mould, larches were green-fingered, small flowers were opening in the turf, birds were singing. Ithilien, the garden of Gondor now desolate, kept still a dishevelled dryad loveliness.

This lovely passage evokes both the vastness of the landscape through which Frodo and Sam are moving, as well as their own sense of wonder at it. Notice how the passage effectively shifts our focus from the long-distance to the close-up. We see the mountains as "a long curve that was lost in the distance," but in the next sentence we get particular types of trees—"fir and cedar and cypress." And finally we get the individual harbingers of spring: fronds piercing moss, green-fingered larches, flowers opening in the turf. And the fact that the reader is required to slow down during this passage and to stop and smell the flowers also evokes the slowness of Frodo and Sam's journey.

But setting doesn't have to slow down the narrative. You can also use setting to evoke speed and danger. Here's part of a chase scene from Rosemary Sutcliff's *The Eagle of the Ninth*. Her two main characters, the Roman soldier Marcus and his slave Esca, are fleeing on horseback across the Scottish highlands from a band of Pictish tribesmen:

> He was riding for his life with the dark hunt in full cry behind him, putting out all his skill to keep clear of hidden pitfalls, the

hummocks and snags and snarls among the heather that might bring disaster, grimly aware that he could not grip strongly enough with his right knee, and if the pony stumbled at this flying gallop, he would go clean over its head. On and on they hurtled, now skirting a reed-fringed upland pool, now swerving from a patch of bog luminously green in the fading light; uphill and down, through bronze tides of dying heather, startling here a flock of plover, there a stray curlew from the bents, and always, behind them, the hunt drawing nearer. Marcus could hear the hounds giving tongue above the soft thunder of the ponies' hooves, nearer, steadily nearer; but there was no time for looking back.

Here, as in Tolkien, we can delight in the vivid evocation of the landscape in its own right—the luminous green bogs, the bronze tides of dying heather. But we should also note how Sutcliff skillfully interweaves the flashes of landscape description with breathless action.

It should be obvious from the examples we've already looked at that there are many different ways to evoke setting in fiction. As always, the various methods for evoking setting fall between two ends of a continuum. At one end, you evoke setting by stopping the narrative dead in its tracks and describing a place or a time period in detail. At the other end, you barely evoke setting at all. In general, the method of stopping the narrative in its tracks is used in narratives such as *Bleak House* or *Troubles*, where the setting is important to the story. At the other extreme, when the setting isn't that important to the story, you simply don't bother with it. Most novels and short stories fall somewhere in between, combining the various methods.

Let's take a look at some examples. We'll start with the two opposite poles, and then examine some examples that fall somewhere in between.

In narratives that rely upon stand-alone descriptions of setting, the point of view the writer is using determines how she evokes the setting. The omniscient third person is going to be more cinematic, like an objective camera eye. Take the opening of *Bleak House* that we looked at earlier. It's like a crane shot in a movie, one that starts high up—"smoke lowering down from chimney-pots, making a soft black drizzle"—and then slowly descends to street level—"dogs, undistinguishable in mire." There it becomes a tracking shot, showing us the masses of Londoners struggling through the mud and the fog, but not from any individual person's point of view—"foot passengers, jostling one another's umbrellas in a general infection of ill temper." And remember, this passage does two things simultaneously: It gives our mind's eye something to look at, and it introduces a central metaphor for the plot.

Now, when a stand-alone, set-piece description of setting is told from the limited third-person or the first-person point of view, it also does one more thing: namely, it evokes character. How the character sees the setting, what details he or she picks out as important, tell us something about the person through whose eyes we, the readers, are seeing them.

J. G. Farrell's *Troubles* is told in the close third person from the point of view of Major Archer, a shell-shocked veteran of World War I. A diffident and sometimes befuddled man, Archer walks through the burnt-out ruins of the Majestic at the end of the book and merely takes note of the melted glass and the skeletons of dead cats. The metaphorical intent of the scene is lost on the Major. He does not draw any of the connections between the Majestic Hotel and the British Empire. Instead, it's the author who makes that connection, by using that narrative double consciousness that I talked about in a previous lecture. In the last sentence of the paragraph I quoted earlier, Farrell writes: "Now that these rooms were open to the mild Irish sky they all seemed much smaller—in fact, quite insignificant." This is an oblique, sly, but sharp comment about the end of empire. And it doesn't come from Major Archer, but from the author.

A setting can become even more multilayered when it is described from the first-person point of view. A few minutes ago, I said that setting is part of the appeal of the novels of Raymond Chandler because of the way he records the city of Los Angeles during a particular time in its history. But what makes the setting especially distinctive in Chandler is the fact that it is seen through the eyes and mind of Chandler's main character and protagonist, the private detective Philip Marlowe.

Here's the second paragraph of Chandler's first novel, *The Big Sleep*, in which Marlowe is entering the Los Angeles mansion of a rich client named General Sternwood:

> The main hallway of the Sternwood place was two stories high. Over the entrance doors, which would have let in a troop of Indian elephants, there was a broad stained-glass panel showing a knight in dark armor rescuing a lady who was tied to a tree and didn't have any clothes on but some very long and convenient hair. The knight had pushed the vizor of his helmet back to be sociable, and he was fiddling with the knots on the ropes that tied the lady to the tree and not getting anywhere. I stood there and thought that if I lived in the house, I would sooner or later have to climb up there and help him. He didn't seem to be really trying.

This goes on for another couple of paragraphs, but this is enough to make my point. This paragraph does several things all at once. First, it sets the scene visually, so we know where we are. Second, it tells us right from the start that General Sternwood is very rich, an impression that is immediately reinforced by the next two paragraphs and several other passages of description later in the chapter. Third, it tells us a good deal about Marlowe himself. We learn that he is an alert, sharp-eyed, and witty observer of his surroundings. We learn that he quickly takes the measure of his environment and the people he meets. Fourth, the stained-glass window with the knight and the naked lady foreshadows the plot: General Sternwood is being blackmailed by a photographer who has taken nude pictures of his youngest daughter. Marlowe is being hired to become, in effect, the knight in dark armor whose job it is to free her from the pornographer's clutches.

Let's take a look now at a writer who scarcely evokes setting at all, at least not in the modern sense: Jane Austen. Compared to a modern writer, Austen hardly ever describes anything, either settings or characters. Mr. Darcy is the leading man of *Pride and Prejudice*, and here is only the physical description he gets in the entire book: "Mr. Darcy soon drew the attention of the room by his fine, tall person, handsome features, noble mien." That's it, that's all we get of him, a description that could fit any number of men. Well, the same goes for Austen's evocations of setting. Her description of Mr. Darcy's mansion, Pemberley, is slightly more extensive than her description of Darcy himself, but not by much:

> The eye was instantly caught by Pemberley House, situated on the opposite side of the valley, into which the road with some abruptness wound. It was a large, handsome stone building, standing well on rising ground, and backed by a ridge of high woody hills;—and in front, a stream of some natural importance was swelled into greater, but without any artificial appearance.

That's all there is, and none of it is particularly evocative. Note in particular the abstract adjectives she uses to describe the house itself, as opposed the landscape in which it sits. All she tells us about the house is that it is large, handsome, and made of stone. Just as Darcy's description could describe half the titled landowners in England, the description of his home could fit nearly every other English country house at the time.

And yet, it's not fair to say that Austen was completely uninterested in evoking setting. Jane Austen could rely upon the fact that she and her readers shared a social and geographical context, and so she could use a kind of shorthand. Reading novels was still mostly an elite practice in Austen's day. She knew that her educated readers would recognize the real places she cited in the text, and then be able to interpolate the nature and approximate location of the fictional places.

The village of Longbourn in *Pride and Prejudice*, for example, is fictional, but it is situated is in the real English county of Hertfordshire, and Austen could count on her readers knowing what Hertfordshire looks like. In the same novel, another family, the Gardiners, live on Gracechurch Street, a real street in London, and Austen knew that her readers would know where Gracechurch Street is and what sort of people lived there. To put it in modern terms, you might say that Jane Austen was relying on the brand names of her day to evoke setting, which is a technique many of our contemporary writers rely upon.

The crime thrillers of George Pelecanos, for example, are very specifically set in Washington, DC, and they are often set in a specific year. He evokes the time period by telling you what pop songs a character hears on the radio, and he often describes characters by telling us the brand names of their clothes. On the very first page of his novel *The Cut*, for example, we're told that the main character, Spero Lucas, is wearing Carhartt jeans and that he's taking notes in a black Moleskine notebook. And throughout the novel, Pelecanos skillfully combines real street and place names with brief bits of description.

Here's a passage in which Spero Lucas drives out of the city and then rides his bicycle to reconnoiter a suspicious location:

> He drove out to Hyattsville, Maryland, via Queens Chapel Road and Hamilton Street, and stopped in the lot of the 38th Street Park, through which ran the paved Northwest Branch trail. He got onto his bike and pedaled southeast, staying in the middle gears, through open fields, past woods, across Rhode Island Avenue, and finally across Alternate Route 1, navigating through fast vehicular traffic. He dipped down into Tanglewood Drive, entered the industrial district of Edmonston, and cruised at a steady pace.

All these places are real: You can get on Google Streetview like I did when I read *The Cut* and follow this route in every detail.

The downside to a description like this is that if you don't know Hyattsville, Maryland as well as Spero Lucas or George Pelecanos do, your eye is likely to glide over these names. On the other hand, the author's use of these real place names bespeaks an authority and an intimacy with the setting that can be just as compelling to a reader as a more detailed description. In the context of a fast-paced thriller, this sort of description may be even more compelling. Even if you have never crossed Rhode Island Avenue through traffic, the passage evokes the confidence and expertise of Spero Lucas.

And, of course, there's that vast middle ground of narratives between those that use stand-alone, set-piece descriptions and those that rely simply on place names. Let's go back to that breathless chase scene from Rosemary Sutcliff's *The Eagle of the Ninth* and look at one particular sentence:

On and on they hurtled, now skirting a reed-fringed upland pool, now swerving from a patch of bog luminously green in the fading light; uphill and down, through bronze tides of dying heather, startling here a flock of plover, there a stray curlew from the bents, and always, behind them, the hunt drawing nearer.

Note how this long sentence starts with action—"On and on they hurtled"—and then launches into a series of adjective phrases with a participle at the start of each phrase—skirting, swerving, startling. Each one of these adjective phrases modifies the pronoun "they" at the beginning of the sentence. Now note how within each phrase, the participle is linked with a vivid feature of the landscape—"skirting a reed-fringed upland pool," "swerving [round] a patch of bog," "startling … a flock of plover." In this way, Sutcliff skillfully evokes both motion and landscape, not only in the same paragraph, not only in the same sentence, but in the same phrase.

Now, whether you choose to lavish your reader with a richly detailed Technicolor description or just say that your detective walked into a Starbuck's, remember that in most cases, how you use setting depends on the overall purpose of your narrative. Scene by scene, you want to lavish detailed descriptions on settings that recur or are especially important. But you only need a line or two to evoke settings that don't matter as much, or that only turn up once.

If a particular setting looms over the whole narrative, the way the Majestic Hotel looms over J. G. Farrell's novel *Troubles*, then you will constantly return to the setting as the story goes on, the way Farrell does. If you want to evoke the slow passage of travelers on foot across a landscape, then you will slow the narrative down for long descriptions of that landscape, the way Tolkien does in *Lord of the Rings*. But if you want to evoke an intense, energetic young private investigator speeding on his bicycle through a modern-day industrial park, you'll want to pick up the pace and just use place names, the way George Pelecanos does in *The Cut*.

Now here are a couple of different exercises you could try, in order to explore the use of setting in a narrative. As I said earlier, one of the things you can do with setting is evoke character, so try describing the same setting from the point of view of two different characters, who want different things.

Take Sarah and Brad, for example, the unhappily married couple in my narrative from the first lecture. As you may recall, they're at a baseball game, so try describing the ballpark two different ways. Show it first from Sarah's point of view, bearing in mind that she's about to ask for a divorce, and then show it from Brad's, bearing in mind that he has no idea what she's about to ask him.

You could also explore just how important a particular setting is to a narrative by taking a famous novel or story and setting it in a radically different place or time from the original. As I said at the start of the lecture, people do this with Shakespeare all the time, and even with Jane Austen upon occasion. But you could rewrite a scene from, say, *Huckleberry Finn* that was set someplace other than the Mississippi. Or could one of the scenes from *The Great Gatsby* take place at any other place or time other than Long Island in the Jazz Age?

Meanwhile, in the next lecture, I'll be talking about pacing in fiction, and we'll be looking at a variety of works, including Leo Tolstoy's novella *The Death of Ivan Ilyich*, Alice Munro's great short story "The Beggar Maid," Eleanor Catton's Booker Prize-winning novel *The Luminaries*, and John le Carré's classic spy thriller, *Tinker, Tailor, Soldier, Spy*.

Pacing in Scenes and Narratives
Lecture 19

E very narrative has a tempo. Some stories are fast-paced and breathless, some are slow and meditative, and as always, there's a vast middle ground of narratives where the tempo varies throughout the work, depending on what the writer is trying to evoke at a particular moment. In fiction, this tempo is called *pacing*—a rather slippery concept because it's so subjective. Some readers crave constant action and clever plot twists, while others want a story that lingers over the intimate details of a character's sensibility and relationships. Given that no book can be all things to all readers, the trick for the writer becomes finding the right tempo, or variety of tempos, for his or her particular story.

Introduction to Pacing

- Pacing in fiction encompasses two levels: the pace of the narrative as a whole and the pace of individual chapters and scenes. Both of these ways of looking at pacing are based on a sort of proportion or balance. Indeed, the essence of pacing is a kind of juggling act, by which writers gauge how much information they want to get across, how many words or pages they have to do it in, and how much patience they hope the reader has.

- One feature of pacing a writer must address is the length of time a story or scene takes in the world of the narrative versus the time it takes for someone to read it. On the whole, a long book that depicts a short period of time will probably be slower paced than a short book or a short story that depicts a long period of time.

- But length itself is not a reliable measure of the pace of a narrative. You also have to consider the balance between the length of the story and the number of incidents and characters within it. We might call this the *density* of the narrative.

- A third kind of balance to consider is that between action and exposition or between scene and summary.
  - In most narratives, the writer shifts back and forth between modes of storytelling. On the one hand, writers usually dramatize the most important and interesting events as separate scenes, with the full complement of action, dialogue, and setting. On the other hand, writers often need to get across a good deal of important background or expository information that isn't necessarily very dramatic.

  - Expository passages often stand outside the time sequence of the narrative—such as when you pause the action to describe a setting or to tell a character's backstory—or you might simply summarize a long period of time in a few paragraphs in order to get the characters quickly from one place to another or from one dramatic moment in the story to the next.

Pacing a Whole Narrative

- Leo Tolstoy's *The Death of Ivan Ilyich* opens with a short chapter in which a group of Ivan Ilyich's fellow lawyers talk about his recent death. After that, Tolstoy spends the next 11 pages or so of this 50-page narrative summarizing the events of the first 44 years of Ivan's life. The son of a civil servant, he becomes a civil servant himself, and his professional life is devoted to rising through the bureaucracy, while his personal life is devoted to social climbing, marriage, and fatherhood.
  - The overall effect of the story depends on Tolstoy convincing us of Ivan's ordinariness, but because the first 44 years of his life are the least dramatic part of the story, Tolstoy summarizes them at a rapid clip. He tells us what we need to know—and no more—as quickly and efficiently as possible.

  - About halfway through the novella, Ivan falls off a ladder, and his injury leads to a mysterious illness that ends up killing him only three months later. Suddenly, this Everyman's life has become dramatic, and having raced through the first 44 years of his life in 11 pages, Tolstoy spreads his last three months out over 35 pages. The pace slows, and there's a greater amount of detail and a sharper focus on his day-to-day moments as Ivan weakens. As the story reaches Ivan's last day, it slows down even more, devoting the last page and a half to the final hour of his life.

o Except for the opening chapter, *The Death of Ivan Ilyich* starts out as fast-paced exposition and becomes slower and more dramatic as it goes on, until the end, where it lingers over the very last moment in Ivan Ilyich's life.

• Let's compare this story with Alice Munro's "The Beggar Maid." This story goes for 33 pages, the first 30 of which depict the first year of the relationship between its two main characters, Patrick and Rose.

o Instead of segregating the exposition and putting it all at once at the beginning, the way Tolstoy does, Munro shifts effortlessly back and forth between vividly dramatized moments and sharp passages of exposition.

o At the center of the story is a fully dramatized scene in which Rose breaks up with Patrick, which is then followed by a more expository scene in which she changes her mind. Then, in the last three pages of the story, Munro

The nature of Alice Munro's "The Beggar Maid" dictates the story's pacing, starting slow and speeding up to lead us to the devastating scene at the airport in the end.

© vadimguzhva/iStock/Thinkstock.

summarizes Rose and Patrick's unhappy 10-year marriage in five paragraphs before giving us a final scene 9 years after their divorce: They see each other in the airport in Toronto, and Rose is shocked when Patrick makes a hateful face at her, a "timed explosion of disgust and loathing."

- The pacing and the balance between action and exposition of each of these stories reflect the different intents of their authors.
  - Tolstoy wants to show us that most of Ivan Ilyich's life has been shallow and selfish; thus, he races through the first 44 years in order to linger on the last three months, when Ivan's suffering allows him to feel compassion for his wife and son in his last moments. In order to do this, the novella needs to start at a rapid pace and slow down as it goes, reflecting Ivan's own moral and spiritual journey.

  - In "The Beggar Maid," however, Munro is more like a lawyer building a case. To prepare for that focused moment of loathing on the last page, she needs to show in slow, patient, dramatic detail why Patrick and Rose should never have married in the first place and why they did anyway. Having done that, she can then fast-forward through the marriage itself and through the 9 years after it before dramatizing the final encounter.

- Eleanor Catton's *The Luminaries* is set during a gold rush on the west coast of New Zealand during the 1860s, and it has a complicated plot involving secrets, conspiracies, and betrayals. Interestingly, Catton chooses not to dramatize many of the most striking scenes—including a shipwreck and a possible murder—and, instead, structures the novel as a series of long conversations between various combinations of her large and diverse cast of characters.
  - During these conversations, the buried plot of the novel is slowly revealed. There are a few passages of scene setting and action, and in nearly every chapter, Catton pauses the conversation to tell us something about the history or

psychology of one or more of the characters in it. But on the whole, the novel moves at a steady and unvarying pace, as the reader eavesdrops on these conversations in real time.

    o   In the end, the novel is more about the nature of storytelling itself—about how people construct reality out of the stories they tell each other—than it is about the working out of the actual mystery.

- Written by a veteran of World War I under the shadow of World War II, *The Lord of the Rings* is a narrative about the end of one world and the dawn of a new one and the effect of the cataclysm on both individuals and whole races of people.

    o   Because he wishes to immerse us in this epic tale, Tolkien varies the pace throughout the book, letting us know what's important and what's mere background or scene setting by slowing down and dramatizing the most important moments and summarizing the less important ones.

    o   Unlike Catton, whose intent is more postmodern and cerebral, Tolkien's intent is to allow the reader to visit Middle Earth and participate in its history. Thus, he skillfully varies the pace, alternating thrilling or dramatic scenes with passages of exposition or backstory, partly to give the reader a breather and partly to prepare us for what comes next.

Pacing Individual Scenes

- How a scene is paced depends partly on its function in the narrative as a whole and partly on the author's intent: Is it important or not? Is it inherently dramatic or not?

- Scenes that introduce new characters to a narrative tend to be played out at a slow pace, in real time. This is also true of scenes of domestic life that are intended to show the characters at home, in a setting that is familiar to them.

- In contrast, intensely dramatic or violent scenes can be played out either fast or slow, depending on your intent. At the end of Melville's *Moby-Dick*, for example, Captain Ahab and the crew of the whaling ship *Pequod* chase the great white whale for three days, and the suspense is stretched out for 40 pages. But then, Ahab's death happens in a flash. The effect is shocking and ruthless—a dazzling example of how a sudden shift in pacing can open the abyss at the reader's feet.

- Slowing the pace of a scene can allow you to wring the last bit of suspense or mystery out of it. In John le Carré's *Tinker, Tailor, Soldier, Spy*, the aging spy George Smiley has been assigned to discover the identity of a Soviet double-agent, who has been working at the highest level of British intelligence for 30 years.
    - The book's pace varies throughout, but in its climactic scene, Smiley is hiding with a gun in the kitchen of a safe house, where he has lured the double-agent. He knows that the next voice he hears will tell him which of his trusted friends and colleagues is a traitor. At this point, le Carré slows the narrative down, telling us every detail, making us sweat alongside Smiley.

    - The events in this passage—an unseen man coming to the door and Smiley's racing thoughts—would take only a few seconds in real life, but le Carré almost cruelly slows them down, making us wait for the big reveal.

Suggested Reading

Burroway, *Writing Fiction*.

Catton, *The Luminaries*.

Eliot, *Middlemarch*.

Le Carré, *Tinker, Tailor, Soldier, Spy*.

Melville, *Moby-Dick*.

Munro, "The Beggar Maid."

Pelecanos, *The Cut*.

Tolkien, *The Lord of the Rings.*

Tolstoy, *The Death of Ivan Ilyich.*

Writing Exercise

1. Select one incident from something you've written and try writing it
    several different ways—as a summary, as a close third-person narrative,
    or as a long dialogue scene; take note of how the difference in pace and
    approach changes the effect. Then compare the results and see which
    one best serves the intent of the narrative you've written.

Pacing in Scenes and Narratives
Lecture 19—Transcript

Just as every piece of music has a beat, every narrative has a tempo. Some stories are fast-paced and breathless; some are slow and meditative. And there's that vast middle ground of narratives that are like symphonies, where the tempo varies throughout the work, depending on what the writer is trying to evoke at a particular moment.

In fiction, we call this tempo *pacing*, and pacing is a rather slippery concept, because it is so subjective. There are all sorts of different stories, and all sorts of different readers. Readers who crave action and clever plot twists in every chapter are going to find George Eliot's *Middlemarch* glacially slow, while readers who want a story that lingers over the intimate details of a character's sensibility and her intricate relations with her family and her community are going to find Dashiell Hammett's *The Maltese Falcon* rather abrasively frenetic. Of course, there are many, many readers who, depending on their mood, enjoy both *Middlemarch* and *The Maltese Falcon*. However, since no one book can be all things to all readers, the trick for the writer is to find the right tempo, or variety of tempos, for her particular story.

Pacing is also slippery because you have to account for it on at least two different levels. There is the tempo of the narrative considered as a whole, and then there's the tempo of individual chapters and scenes, which may vary enormously. But both of these types of pacing are based on a sort of proportion or balance. Whether you're considering the overall pace of a 33-page short story like Alice Munro's "The Beggar Maid," or the pace of a short, individual scene in an enormous novel like Tolkien's *The Lord of the Rings*, you have to balance the amount of information you want to get across with the number words or pages you have to do it in. You also have to factor in how much patience the reader is likely to have.

In fact, there are three kinds of balance that you have to keep in mind, so let's take them one at a time. The first kind is the balance between the length of time a story or scene takes in the world of the narrative versus the amount of time it takes the reader to read it. On the whole, a long book that depicts a short period of time is probably going to be slower paced than a short book or a short story that depicts a long period of time. For example, James Joyce's *Ulysses* takes 265,000 words to depict about 20 hours in the life of its two main characters, Stephen Daedelus and Leopold Bloom. On the other hand, Alice Munro's short story "The Beggar Maid" takes only 13,000 words to depict approximately 20 years in the life of Rose and Patrick, a couple who meet, marry, and then divorce. Both narratives provide intimate portraits of their two main characters, but I think it's safe to say that Munro's short story does it at a faster pace than Joyce's epic novel.

But length all by itself is not a reliable measure of the pace of a narrative. You also have to consider the balance between the length of the story—its number of words or pages—and the number of incidents and the number of characters within it. You might even call this the *density* of the narrative.

"The Beggar Maid" considers the rise and fall of a romantic relationship over 30 pages, and apart from a few minor characters along the way, it focuses almost entirely on Rose and Patrick. At the other extreme is Tolkien's *The Lord of the Rings*, which totals more than 480,000 words. This is nearly twice as long as *Ulysses*. But instead of taking place over the course of a single day and telling the story of only two major characters, *The Lord of the Rings* takes place over 18 months and contains dozens of important characters and multiple interlinked plotlines. Most of these separate plotlines take place at the same time. This means that on any given day in the world of the book, several things might be happening at once, hundreds of miles apart. So even though it's much longer than *Ulysses*, *The Lord of the Rings* tells a more complicated, lengthy, and action-packed story. Therefore, it moves at a faster pace than *Ulysses*.

And even though it's much, much longer than "The Beggar Maid," *The Lord of the Rings* has many, many more characters and much more story to tell, not to mention many more scenes of adventure and violent action. As a result, even though "The Beggar Maid" is shorter and it takes place over a longer period of time, many of the scenes and chapters in *The Lord of the Rings* move at faster pace than some of the scenes in "The Beggar Maid."

Which brings me to the third kind of balance, between action and exposition, or what the writer and teacher Janet Burroway calls the balance between scene and summary. In most narratives, you shift back and forth between modes of storytelling. On the one hand, you usually dramatize the most important and interesting events as separate, individual scenes. You give them the full complement of action, dialogue, and setting. You dramatize these scenes because you want the reader to remember these moments in particular. The fact that you lavish your full attention on these scenes reinforces the reader's impression that they are important.

On the other hand, you often need to get across a good deal of important background or expository information which, in itself, isn't necessarily very dramatic. Expository passages often stand outside the time sequence of the narrative. For example, you might pause the action to describe a setting or tell a character's backstory. Or you might simply summarize a long period of time in a few paragraphs, in order to get the characters more quickly from one place to another, or from one important moment in the story to the next one.

For the rest of this lecture, I want to talk about how you can achieve these three kinds of balance: the balance between the passage of time in the story and the time it takes to read it, the balance between the length of the work and the number of incidents that occur in it, and the balance between action and exposition. To begin with, we'll look at how some writers have paced a whole narrative, and then we'll look at the pacing of an individual chapter or scene.

Let's start with two relatively short narratives. One of them is Leo Tolstoy's novella *The Death of Ivan Ilyich*, and the other is the story I've already mentioned, Alice Munro's "The Beggar Maid." Each of these stories encompasses quite a bit of time within the relatively small number of pages. Tolstoy's novella tells the story of a Russian lawyer from his birth to his death at the age of 45 in 22,000 words, or about 50 pages. Alice Munro's story depicts about 20 years in the life of Rose and Patrick in 13,000 words, or about 30 pages. Each takes a different approach, for reasons that will become apparent.

The Death of Ivan Ilyich opens with a short chapter in which a group of Ivan Ilyich's fellow lawyers talk about his recent death, and then we never hear from these characters again. After that opening chapter, Tolstoy spends the next 11 pages summarizing the events of the first 44 years of Ivan Ilyich's life. This life is ordinary, uneventful, and even boring. The son of a civil servant, Ivan Ilyich becomes a civil servant himself, and his professional life is devoted to rising through the bureaucracy while his personal life is devoted to social climbing, marriage, and fatherhood.

Here's a typical passage that describes his marriage:

> Ivan Ilyich worked out an approach to married life. He asked no more of it than the conveniences which it was able to provide— dinner at home, a housewife, and a bed, and, above all, that propriety of external forms required by public opinion. For the rest, he looked for pleasure and good cheer, and when he found them, was very grateful. If, on the contrary, he met with antagonism and querulousness, he immediately retreated into his palisaded world of work and found his pleasure there.

As I say, Ivan is not a very interesting guy. The overall effect of the story depends on Tolstoy convincing us of his Ivan's ordinariness, and because the first 44 years of his life are the least dramatic part of the story, Tolstoy summarized them at a rapid clip. He tells us what we need to know and no more, as quickly and efficiently as possible.

Then about halfway through the novella, Ivan Ilyich falls off a ladder while he is hanging some curtains, and his injury leads to a mysterious illness that ends up killing him only three months later. Suddenly, this boring Everyman's life has become dramatic. Having raced through the first 44 years of his life in 11 pages, Tolstoy slows the pace and spreads Ivan's last three months over 35 pages. There is a greater amount of detail and a sharper focus on his day-to-day moments as he weakens. Here's a scene from a month before his death, when he is being waited on by his wife and by his butler, whose name is Gerasim:

> His wife returned late that night. She came in on tiptoe, but he heard her, opened his eyes, and hastily shut them again. She wanted

to send Gerasim out and sit with him herself. He opened his eyes and said, "No. Go."

"Are you suffering a lot?"

"It doesn't matter."

"Take some opium."

He consented and drank it. She went away.

This is slower than anything in the first 11 pages, where nothing at all was dramatized in detail, but it's still pretty brisk and efficient. It's the bare bones of a scene, enough to plant a rudimentary image in the reader's mind, but not enough to linger over. But as the story reaches Ivan Ilyich's last day, the pace slows down even more. The last page and a half of the story is devoted to the final hour of Ivan's life.

And so the balance between action and exposition in *The Death of Ivan Ilyich* is pretty easy to diagram: Except for that opening chapter, it starts out as fast-paced exposition and then becomes slower and more dramatic as it goes on, until the end, where it lingers over the very last moment in Ivan Ilyich's life.

Let's compare this with what happens in "The Beggar Maid." This story goes for 33 pages, and the first 30 pages depict only the first year of the relationship between its two main characters. In these pages, we watch Patrick, a graduate student, fall in love with Rose, who is an undergraduate at the same Canadian university. They have a complicated and rather prickly courtship. Patrick is embarrassed by his rich family in Vancouver, while Rose is embarrassed by her working class mother in a small town in Ontario. Each one grapples with his or her own emotions, and together they fumble at sex.

You can already see how the pacing of this story is different from that of *The Death of Ivan Ilyich*. The majority of the story takes place over eight months or so. Whereas Tolstoy puts all the exposition in at once at the beginning,

Munro shifts effortlessly back and forth between vividly dramatized moments and sharp passages of exposition. And she does this paragraph by paragraph and sometimes sentence by sentence, all the way through the story.

Here's an example. The Dr. Henshawe in this excerpt is a professor who is also Rose's landlady:

> There was something edgy, jumpy, disconcerting, about [Patrick]. His voice would break under stress—with her, it seemed he was always under stress—he knocked dishes and cups off tables, spilled drinks and bowls of peanuts, like a comedian. He was not a comedian; nothing could be further from his intentions. He came from British Columbia. His family was rich.
>
> He arrived early to pick Rose up, when they were going to the movies. He wouldn't knock, he knew he was early. He sat on the top step outside of Dr. Henshawe's door. This was in the winter, it was dark out, but there was a little coach lamp beside the door.
>
> "Oh, Rose! Come and look!" called Dr. Henshawe, in her soft, amused voice, and they looked down together from the dark window of the study. "The poor young man," said Dr. Henshawe tenderly.

Note how quickly and seamlessly this passage moves from an abstract, expository description of Patrick—that he is edgy, jumpy, disconcerting, and that his family in British Columbia is rich—to a specific, dramatized moment that evokes just how jumpy and edgy he is, by showing us that he's too nervous to knock on Rose's door. These two modes of narrative sit adjacent to each other on the page. The story doesn't segregate the exposition from the action, but weaves them together throughout.

At the center of "The Beggar Maid" is a long, fully dramatized scene in which Rose breaks up with Patrick. This is then followed by a brief, more expository scene in which she changes her mind, and they end up getting married. Then, in the last three pages of the story, Munro summarizes Rose and Patrick's unhappy 10-year marriage in five paragraphs before giving us a final scene nine years after their divorce. In this brief, wordless, devastating encounter, they see each other in the airport in Toronto, and Rose is shocked when Patrick makes a hateful face at her, a "timed explosion of disgust and loathing."

Both the pacing and the balance between action and exposition in each of these stories reflect the different intents of their authors. Tolstoy wants to show us that most of Ivan Ilyich's life has been shallow and selfish, so he races through the first 44 years in order to linger on his last moments, when Ivan Ilyich's suffering allows him to feel compassion for his wife and son. In order to evoke this emotional journey, the novella needs to start at a rapid pace, with very little detail, and then slow down as it goes. This pace reflects Ivan Ilyich's own moral and spiritual education.

In "The Beggar Maid," however, Munro is more like a lawyer building a case. In order to prepare for that focused moment of loathing on the last page, she needs to show us in slow, patient, dramatic detail why Patrick and Rose should never have married in the first place, and why they did anyway. Having done that, she can then fast forward through the marriage itself and through the nine years after it in order to dramatize their final encounter. The nature of each story dictates the pace at which it is told.

Now let's take a look at two much longer narratives, Eleanor Catton's Booker Prize-winning novel, *The Luminaries*, and Tolkien's *The Lord of the Rings*. Both of these novels are long, with complicated plots and a large cast of characters. *The Luminaries* clocks in at over 800 pages, while *The Lord of the Rings* is over a thousand pages. But because they are different types of stories, and because the intents of their authors are different, they are paced very differently.

The Luminaries is a pastiche of such 19th-century potboilers as Wilkie Collins's *The Moonstone*. It is set during a gold rush on the west coast of New Zealand during the 1860s, and it has a complicated plot involving secrets, conspiracies, and betrayals. What's interesting about the telling of this long and complex story, however, is that Catton chooses not to dramatize many of the most striking scenes—including a shipwreck and a possible murder.

Instead, she structures the novel as a series of long conversations between various combinations of her large and diverse cast of characters.

During these conversations, the buried plot of the novel is slowly revealed as the characters confide in, threaten, and negotiate with each other. There are a few passages of action and scene setting, and in nearly every chapter Catton pauses the conversation to tell us something about the history or psychology of one or more of her characters. But on the whole, the novel moves at a steady and unvarying pace throughout, as the reader eavesdrops on these conversations in more or less real time.

In the end, the novel is more about the nature of storytelling itself than it is about the actual working out of the mystery. In other words, it's about how people construct reality out of the stories they tell each other.

On the other hand, *The Lord of the Rings* is also full of scenes in which the characters tell each other stories, not to mention many scenes of negotiation, debate, and outright aggression, but the intent of *The Lord of the Rings* is different. Tolkien was a veteran of World War I and he wrote much of *The Lord of the Rings* during World War II. Partly because of these experiences, the novel is a narrative about the end of one world and the dawn of a new one. It is also about the effect of a catastrophic war on both individuals and whole races of people.

Because he wishes to immerse us in this epic tale, Tolkien varies the pace throughout the book. In order to let us know which scenes are important and which passages are mere background or scene-setting, he slows down and dramatizes the most important moments and merely summarizes the less important ones. There are long passages of exposition; in some cases, whole chapters do nothing but tell backstory. But for the most part, Tolkien's story regularly shifts between action and exposition as his characters move across the vast landscape of Middle Earth.

For example, early in the novel, as Frodo and his companions are leaving the village of Bree on their way to Rivendell (not to get too geeky on you), Tolkien devotes only about a page to the first five days of their trip. However, later, when Frodo and his companions enter the Mines of Moria to pass under the Misty Mountains, Tolkien devotes two entire chapters to the two and a half days they spend underground.

It's easy to see why he devotes more time to the second sequence than he does to the first. In the first instance, nothing terribly important happens during those five days, but Tolkien has to get his characters from one place to another. So, he tells us just enough to let us know that time has passed and what sort of landscape they moved through.

In the second instance, a great deal happens in the Mines of Moria that is essential to the plot, not the least of which are a couple of exciting fight scenes and the apparent death of a major character. So Tolkien slows down and dramatizes much more of it. He gives us action and dialogue, as well as a vivid and detailed evocation of the setting.

Tolkien also slows down the pace for his great, set-piece action scenes such as the Battle of Helm's Deep and the Battle of Pelennor Fields. He does this because they are important to the story, but he also slows down these scenes because they are inherently thrilling. Unlike Catton, whose intent is more postmodern and cerebral, Tolkien's intent is to allow the reader to visit Middle Earth and participate in its history. And so he skillfully varies the pace, alternating thrilling or dramatic scenes with passages of exposition or backstory. The purpose of the expository scenes is partly to give the reader a breather, and partly to prepare us for what comes next.

Our discussion of how Tolkien paces *The Lord of the Rings* points the way to our next discussion, about how to pace individual scenes. As my remarks about Tolkien suggest, how a scene is paced depends partly on its function in the narrative as a whole and on the author's intent. When you're thinking about the pacing of a scene, you need to ask yourself, is the scene important or not? Is it inherently dramatic or not?

Let's look at several different types of scene and talk about the tempo their authors choose for them. And bear in mind that different writers, with different intents, may treat the same sort of scene completely differently.

Scenes which introduce new characters to a narrative tend to be played out at a slow pace, in real time. This is also true of scenes of domestic life that are intended to show the characters at home, in a setting that is familiar to them.

A couple of lectures ago, when I was talking about point of view, I talked about a scene that does both, namely, Chapter 11 of George Eliot's *Middlemarch*. The first half of the chapter is pure exposition, introducing us to Lydgate, a handsome doctor who is new to the community. The second half of the chapter is fully dramatized, introducing us to two major characters, Fred and Rosamond Vincy, who are brother and sister, and a minor character, their mother.

This second scene is about 2,200 words long. Late one morning, Mrs. Vincy and Rosamond are working at embroidery in the dining room, and Fred comes down late for breakfast. The scene is 90 percent dialogue, and in the bantering exchanges between Fred and Rosamond, the irritability and competitiveness of young adult siblings is vividly evoked, as is their mother's patient attempt to mediate.

In this excerpt, Fred, an arrogant young college student, bickers with his sister over their mother's use of lower-class slang:

> "Are you beginning to dislike slang, then?" said Rosamond, with mild gravity.
>
> "Only the wrong sort. All choice of words is slang. It marks a class."
>
> "There is correct English: that is not slang."
>
> "I beg your pardon: correct English is the slang of prigs who write history and essays. And the strongest slang of all is the slang of poets."
>
> "You will say anything, Fred, to gain your point."
>
> "Well, tell me whether it is slang or poetry to call an ox a leg-plaiter."

"Of course you can call it poetry if you like."

"Aha, Miss Rosy, you don't know Homer from slang. I shall invent a new game; I shall write bits of slang and poetry on slips, and give them to you to separate."

"Dear me, how amusing it is to hear young people talk!" said Mrs. Vincy, with cheerful admiration.

Notice how their mother chimes in at the end to smooth things over. In its perceptiveness and subtle shifts of mood, not to mention the immediate familiarity we feel with Fred and Rosamond, it's a nearly perfect scene, and it would have played out in real time at the same pace it takes to read it out loud.

On the other hand, you can play intensely dramatic or violent scenes either fast or slow, depending on your intent. For example, at the end of Herman Melville's *Moby-Dick*, Captain Ahab and the crew of his ship chase the great white whale Moby-Dick for three days. The chase takes place over the course of three thrilling chapters, stretching out the suspense for 40 pages. Much of the previous 800 pages, of course, have been dedicated to Ahab's obsession with killing Moby-Dick, who severed Ahab's leg in an earlier encounter.

When Ahab's whaling boat is at last within harpooning distance of the whale, Melville slows the narrative down to let Ahab make one last, crazy speech—"to the last I grapple with thee; from hell's heart I stab at thee; for hate's sake I spit my last breath at thee." But then, in the very final moment of the last encounter between Ahab and Moby-Dick, Ahab's death happens in an instant:

The harpoon was darted; the stricken whale flew forward; with igniting velocity the line ran through the groove;—ran foul. Ahab stooped to clear it; he did clear it; but the flying turn caught him round the neck, and voicelessly as Turkish mutes bowstring their victim, he was shot out of the boat, ere the crew knew he was gone. Next instant, the heavy eye-splice in the rope's final end flew out of the stark-empty tub, knocked down an oarsman, and smiting the sea, disappeared in its depths.

After 800 pages of listening to Ahab rant about Moby-Dick, readers are usually shocked when Moby-Dick kills him in a heartbeat, jerking him by the neck out of the boat. There's no 19th century melodrama about Ahab's death. It's shocking and pointless, and after the last three chapters of pursuit and one last, flowery rant, it's told in only 88 words. It's a dazzling example of how a sudden shift in pacing can open the abyss at the reader's feet.

Alternately, you may want to show the skill of your hero at physical combat, and so you might slow down the action, the same way an Asian martial arts picture shows certain spectacular moves in slow motion to emphasize the skill of the performers. Here's Spero Lucas, the detective in George Pelecanos's detective novel *The Cut*, being attacked at night in a parking lot by an assassin:

> They moved at the same time. The man swung the knife, and Lucas stepped out of its arc and back. The man swung again. His reach was not sufficient, and Lucas knew he would have to come in. The man flipped the knife, switching it to a down-grip, and brought it across from his right shoulder as if he were swinging a bat. He caught only air. He brought blade back from the other direction and swung with a grunt, and it took him too far. Lucas stepped to the side, and then came in quickly, grabbed the man's wrist, and struck a hammer blow to the knife arm's elbow. The man's hand opened like a stunned flower, sending the knife skittering across the asphalt. Lucas pushed him away.

This is thrilling stuff, and it goes on for another four paragraphs before Spero finally kills the guy with his bare hands. On the one hand, this certainly looks fast-paced, because a lot happens in this paragraph, in only 129 words. But in real time the fight would probably take less than a minute, and if you put that time against the time and concentration it takes for the reader to slow down and follow every blow and knife thrust, you discover that Pelecanos actually slows the pace of his narrative here. And by doing so, he shows us just how skillful Spero Lucas can be in hand-to-hand combat.

You can also slow the pace of a scene in order to wring the last bit of suspense or mystery out of it. Let's take John le Carré's classic spy novel, *Tinker, Tailor, Soldier, Spy*, as an example. In *Tinker, Tailor*, the aging spy George Smiley has been assigned to discover the identity of a Soviet mole, or double-agent, who has been working at the highest level of British intelligence for 30 years. The book's pace varies throughout, shifting between long dialogue scenes, extended flashbacks, and long, detailed expository passages. In the book's climactic scene, Smiley is hiding with a gun in the kitchen of a safe house. He has lured the double-agent, whom he has nicknamed "Gerald," and Gerald's Soviet handler to the safe house in order to catch them red-handed.

As he waits, Smiley knows that the next voice he hears will tell him which of his trusted friends and colleagues is a traitor. This is the climax of the novel, the secret both Smiley and the reader have been working to learn. In order to heighten the drama and the suspense, le Carré slows the narrative down. He tells us every detail, he makes us sweat alongside Smiley in the kitchen:

> He heard the tread of a pair of feet on the gravel, brisk and vigorous. They stopped. It's the wrong door, Smiley thought absurdly; go away. He had the gun in his hand, he had dropped the catch. Still he listened, heard nothing. You're suspicious, Gerald, he thought. You're an old mole, you can sniff there's something wrong. Millie, he thought; Millie has taken away the milk bottles, put up a warning, headed him off. Millie's spoilt the kill. Then he heard the latch turn, one turn, two; it's a Banham lock, he remembered—my God, we must keep Banham in business. Of course: the mole had been patting his pockets, looking for his key. A nervous man would have it in his hand already, would have been clutching it, cossetting it in his pocket all the way in the taxi; but not the mole. The mole might be worried but he was not nervous.

Now, *Tinker, Tailor, Soldier, Spy* is of one of the best popular novels ever written, but in this passage, le Carré is writing stream-of-consciousness with nearly the intensity and density of the detail of Virginia Woolf. Not only are we in the kitchen with Smiley, clutching a pistol, we are inside his head, following his every anxious thought. Again, as with the fight scene in the

Pelecanos novel, the events in this paragraph—an unseen man coming to the door and patting his pockets for the key, and Smiley's racing thoughts—would take only a few seconds in real time. But le Carré almost cruelly slows it down. He makes us wait for the big reveal.

These, of course, are only a few, rather obvious examples of how the pacing of a scene can heighten its emotional effect. There are many other fruitful examples I don't have time to get into: Scott Spencer's epic 40-page sex scene in his novel *Endless Love*; the ending of James Joyce's "The Dead," in which Gabriel Conroy's epiphany about his marriage and his life is evoked over several pages; and the first conversation between Elizabeth Bennett and Mr. Darcy in *Pride and Prejudice*, which Jane Austen paces so that it reads like gladiatorial combat. I urge you to check these out on your own.

In the meantime, you can experiment with pacing by trying this simple exercise: Take an incident from something you've written and try writing it several different ways—as a summary, as a close third-person narrative, or as a long dialogue scene—and take note of how the difference in pace changes the effect. Then compare the results and see which one best the serves the intent of the narrative you've written. The result may surprise you. This exercise will also serve as a good transition for my next lecture, when I'll be talking about constructing scenes, and we'll look at some examples from Alice Munro, Eleanor Catton, and yours truly.

Building Scenes
Lecture 20

W riters approach the day-to-day process of composition in many ways, and of course, what you do as a writer each day depends on the overall shape of your narrative and on the purpose of the particular passage you're working on. Writers also differ on what they consider the fundamentals of writing fiction: the plot, character development, ideas to be conveyed, the crafting of elegant sentences, and so on. In the end, no matter how you approach the day-to-day process, every writer is faced with the prospect of making the whole thing hang together. We'll talk about that in our next two lectures, but in this lecture, we'll discuss what a writer does each day, that is, creating individual scenes.

Defining *Scenes*

- In his book *The Art of Fiction*, John Gardner defines a scene as everything "that is included in an unbroken flow of action from one incident in time to another." For Gardner, this unbroken flow can include movement through space from one place to another, as long as there isn't a big jump in time. In other words, a scene shows more or less everything that happens to a character, or between two or more characters, during a particular, discrete span of time, without any interruptions in the flow of that time, except for flashbacks or brief passages of exposition.

- There are, of course, many types of scenes, ranging from brief scenes featuring only a few characters in a narrowly defined setting to epic scenes that show many characters in a vast setting. There are scenes that are merely transitional, scenes that are pivotal moments in the plot, scenes where we learn the thoughts of only a single character, scenes in which the only action is conversation among the characters, and scenes full of violent, thrilling action.

- Deciding what you make into a scene as opposed to what you choose to reveal through exposition—in other words, what you choose to dramatize rather than summarize—is generally fairly easy. You usually want to dramatize the most important or interesting parts of the story, while relying on exposition to get across essential but less interesting information.

Requirements of Scenes

- An individual scene must meet at least two requirements at the same time: It must advance the larger narrative, or at least fit into it, and it must be interesting in its own right. In other words, a writer needs to balance the scene's position in the whole story with its own inherent drama. The way to achieve this balance is to remember that a scene should be no longer than it needs to be for its purpose within the story as a whole.

- These two balanced requirements—the intent of the narrative and the inherent interest of the scene—can vary enormously from one narrative to another.
    o George Pelecanos's hard-boiled detective novel *The Cut* is a fast-paced narrative, written with efficiency and economy. Its young detective, Spero Lucas, occasionally takes time out from the case he's working on to have an erotic interlude with a young woman. Such scenes move at the same brisk pace as the rest of the book, and they serve to tell us something we wouldn't otherwise know about Spero, but because they aren't central to the story, they tend to be much shorter and more expository than the scenes that advance Spero's investigations.

    o In a more expansive narrative, such as *Ulysses* or *Moby-Dick*, a scene can go on for pages simply because the author thinks it is inherently interesting. Melville, for example, devotes long passages or even whole chapters to describing the work of a whaling vessel, the natural history of whales, and other topics. These scenes advance the overall purpose of the book, which is to evoke a way of life in as much detail as possible, but they aren't necessarily concerned with advancing the plot.

    o And with some books, the point of the novel isn't the plot at all but the individual scenes that make up the plot. Even though

The Lecturer's Tale has a plot, the true purpose of the book is to make fun of the excesses of modern literary theory. For this reason, the book is basically a series of satirical set pieces. These set pieces aren't entirely self-contained—each pushes the plot a little further along—but each chapter or scene is mainly intended to be amusing for its own sake.

- Again, how long a scene goes on and whether it should be included at all depends on the intent of the narrative as a whole.

  o A crime novel, such as *The Cut*, needs to move quickly; if it slows down, it dies. Trying to squeeze in a long chapter about the history of detective work would throw off the whole story.

© Comstock Images/Stockbyte/Thinkstock.

The Lecturer's Tale satirizes academics who put literary criticism above actual works of art; its scenes are more focused on amusing the reader than advancing the plot.

  o *The Lecturer's Tale*, however, has a different metabolism. The reader is not meant to race through it but to enjoy each scene as it comes. The scenes in each book have a different pace and structure because the intent of each book is different.

Scene Transitions

- Transitioning into and out of scenes can vex even experienced writers. Such transitions can vary enormously, depending on the intent of the scene, its length, its importance in the narrative, and so on.

- Scenes that take place early in the narrative need more setup, on the whole, than scenes that appear later. When you're introducing characters, situations, or settings for the first time, you need to spend more time describing them than you do later on, when the reader already knows who the character is or what the setting looks like. You can often take your time in these early scenes, describing the setting and characters in some detail and letting the characters talk a bit more digressively than they might in later scenes.

- Short scenes tend to need less introduction than longer, more dramatic scenes. You can signal the start of a new scene with something as simple as a space break in the text or, if time has passed since the last section, with a simple phrase, such as "The next day …" or "A few hours later …." Scenes that are longer, more important, or more dramatic require more buildup at the start.

  o For example, in "The Beggar Maid," Alice Munro begins the scene in which Rose breaks up with Patrick with a brief description of Rose's walk from her room to Patrick's apartment. This description slows down the narrative and lets us know that something important is about to happen, providing a bumper between the fast-paced mix of exposition and miniature scenes that came immediately before it and the slower and more dramatic scene that's about to start.

  o Munro then ends the scene abruptly and dramatically, befitting the emotionally turbulent nature of the encounter, as Rose storms out of Patrick's apartment: "'I don't want to see you, ever!' she said viciously. But at the door she turned and said in a normal and regretful voice, 'Good-bye.'" (p. 96)

- Another way to transition into a scene is to begin it *in medias res*. The chief advantage of this approach is that it adds energy and urgency to the narrative. It also engages readers on a deeper level, forcing them to pay attention to what's going on.

  o For example, the opening sequence of Eleanor Catton's epic historical mystery *The Luminaries* introduces a character named Walter Moody, who has just arrived at a remote gold rush community on the west coast of New Zealand in 1866. In the opening pages, he finds himself in a hotel lounge with 12 other men, who tell him a long, complicated story about a suspicious death, a suicide attempt, and a fortune in gold, all of which happened two weeks before Moody even arrived.

- o Catton runs the risk here that the reader might feel overwhelmed, rather like Moody himself does, walking into a group of people he's never met before who are talking about something complicated that happened before he arrived. But she constructs this opening scene so expertly, with such attention to the detail, that she hooks the reader into a mystery that isn't fully explained until 800 pages later.

- Transitioning out of a scene is perhaps a little less difficult than transitioning into one. Once the main purpose of the scene has played out—the new character has been sufficiently introduced or the plot point has been made—you generally want to wrap it up as quickly as possible. For some kinds of narrative, you might want to end with a sort of punchline—a witticism from a character or a sudden revelation—but even with narratives that aren't driven by plot, you don't want to linger over the scene after its purpose has been fulfilled.

- There can also be transitions within a scene, such as when a writer pauses to provide some exposition or segue into a flashback.
    - o Again, *The Luminaries* is made up mostly of long, dramatized scenes, but because the plot is so complicated, Catton often pauses the action to introduce an extended flashback or some exposition about a character's history or psychology.

    - o Because the novel is written in the style of a 19th-century novel, sometimes Catton directly addresses the reader in a manner that calls attention to the transition itself. At other times, she slips effortlessly from drama to exposition with hardly any transition at all.

- Transitioning into and out of flashbacks is generally fairly straightforward. If it's a short flashback, you might signal the shift by putting the whole episode in italics. If the flashback is from the point of view of a particular character, you can simply write something like, "Leo thought back to the conversation he'd had with Anna the day before." A more subtle way to signal a flashback is with a change in verb tense—from the present tense to the past or the simple past to the past perfect.

Stories within Stories

- Although some scenes are just small bursts of drama that can be truncated or incomplete, most of the weight in a narrative is carried by fully dramatized scenes with a beginning, middle, and end. These major scenes are basically small stories within the larger story.

- Even if a major scene couldn't stand alone outside the context of the whole narrative, it should have the structure of a simple story. Earlier, we discussed fractals, the mathematical concept of a pattern that repeats itself at every level of magnification. It's not true that each individual scene should reproduce the structure or plot of the larger narrative, but it helps to remember that any story made of scenes is basically made of smaller stories.

Suggested Reading

Catton, *The Luminaries*.

Gardner, *The Art of Fiction*.

Hynes, *The Lecturer's Tale*.

———, *Next*.

———, *The Wild Colonial Boy*.

Munro, "The Beggar Maid."

1. Choose an undramatized moment from a story of your own or from a story or novel you admire and turn it into a full-fledged dramatic scene. In other words, take a moment from a story that is only alluded to or is depicted only briefly in an expository passage and dramatize it fully. For example, you might dramatize the moment that Hamlet is told that his father has died, a scene that doesn't appear in Shakespeare's play. Use as many words or pages as you need and turn that scene into a little story, with a beginning, middle, and end, making sure that the scene you write contributes to the larger narrative. This exercise will give you practice in making a scene self-contained, as well as making it an integral part of the larger story.

Building Scenes
Lecture 20—Transcript

Writers approach the day-to-day process of composition in many different ways. They differ in their aesthetic approach, they differ in temperament, they differ in willpower and discipline. And of course what approach you take each day depends on the balance between the overall shape of your narrative and the needs of the particular passage you're working on.

Writers also differ on what each one considers to be the fundamental unit of writing fiction. Some writers conceptualize the whole narrative in terms of plot points. Some writers think in terms of character arcs. Some think in terms of the larger ideas they want to get across, and so on.

Some writers focus mainly on crafting elegant sentences. In a famous interview in the *Paris Review*, the Russian novelist Vladimir Nabokov claimed to write novels the way someone might fill in a crossword puzzle. He paid no particular attention to chronology, at least to begin with. Instead, he wrote a few sentences at a time on index cards and then assembled the cards later into a narrative.

But no matter how you approach the day-to-day process, every writer—even Nabokov—is eventually faced with the prospect of making the whole thing hang together. We'll talk about that in our next two lectures, when we look at how the processes of composition and revision go hand in hand. But right now, I want to talk about what a writer does each day. And for me, that means creating individual scenes.

What exactly do I mean by a "scene"? As I discussed at length in my previous lectures about evocation and pacing, most narratives are divided between passages of exposition, in which the author summarizes the information the reader needs to know, and fully dramatized passages, which include action, dialogue, and setting. It's these dramatized passages that I'll be talking about, even though some of what I'll say applies to expository passages as well.

In his book *The Art of Fiction*, John Gardner defines a scene as everything "that is included in an unbroken flow of action from one incident in time to another." According to Gardner, this unbroken flow of action can include movement through space from one place to another, as long as there isn't a big jump in time. In other words, a scene shows more or less everything that happens to a character, or between two or more characters, during a discrete span of time. In order to qualify as a scene in this definition, there can't be any interruptions in the flow of that time, except for flashbacks or brief passages of exposition.

Of course, there are many different types of scene. For example, there are brief scenes that last only a few sentences and feature only a few characters in a narrowly defined setting, such as the opening scene of Flannery O'Connor's short story "A Good Man Is Hard to Find." On a larger scale, there are epic scenes that go on for many pages and show many characters doing many things in a huge setting, such as the vast battle scenes in Tolkien's *Lord of the Rings.*

There are scenes that are merely transitional; there are scenes that are pivotal moments in the plot; there are scenes where nothing happens but the thoughts of a single character; there are scenes where all the characters do is talk to each other; and there are scenes which are full of violent, thrilling action.

There are also scenes within scenes, which I'll talk about later in this lecture. As I said in my lecture on pacing, it is usually pretty easy to decide what you should make into a scene as opposed to what you should reveal through exposition—in other words, what you choose to dramatize rather than summarize. As I also said last time, you usually want to dramatize the most important or interesting parts of the story and rely on exposition to get across necessary but less interesting information. If you simply want the reader to know a bit of backstory, that's exposition. But if you want to have the reader experience something along with the characters, that's a scene.

Way back in my lecture about evocation, I said that scenes in which the readers vicariously participate are much more vivid and memorable than passages in which they are simply told something. If you want the reader to remember something, have it happen right in front of her.

A good example of this distinction comes from Alice Munro's story "The Beggar Maid," which, as you may recall, is about the courtship, marriage, and eventual divorce of two young Canadians, Rose and Patrick. As you may also recall, the story takes 30 pages to cover the first eight months of their relationship, and then summarizes their subsequent marriage, divorce, and final meeting in the last three pages of the story. For most of the story's first 25 pages, Munro shifts effortlessly between exposition and little bits of drama, often within the same paragraph. In fact, most of the dramatized bits only go on for a paragraph or two.

At the end of those first 25 pages, however, Munro gives us a fully dramatized scene. It's the scene in which Rose shows up at Patrick's room early in the morning and tells him she doesn't want to marry him. This scene goes on for three and half pages, which is a lot of real estate in a 33-page story. Munro chooses to give this scene more time than any other scene in the story because it is the most dramatic moment in Rose and Patrick's relationship, showing them at their most raw and intimate. It also sets up the startling reversal in the next, much shorter scene, when Rose's resolve weakens and she decides to marry him after all, leading both herself and Patrick into years of misery.

In other words, the scene in which Rose breaks up with Patrick is the heart of the story. This is why Munro lets this moment play out in real time in front of the reader. Without it, the rest of the story simply wouldn't have the same impact.

This particular scene also illustrates another important point about scenes in general. An individual scene needs to do at least two things at the same time: It needs to advance the larger narrative, and it needs to be interesting in its own right. In other words, a writer needs to balance the scene's position in the whole story with its own inherent drama. And one way to achieve this balance is to remember that a scene should be no longer than it needs to be in order to serve its purpose within the story as a whole.

Please note that I'm not saying that a scene should necessarily be short, efficient, and economical, but rather that no individual scene should go on so long that a reader begins to wonder why she's still reading it. The length of a scene depends on the narrative as a whole as well as the inherent interest of the individual scene, but these two balanced intentions can vary enormously from one narrative to another.

Take George Pelecanos's hard-boiled detective novel *The Cut*, for example. This is a fast-paced narrative, written with efficiency and economy. Even so, its young detective, Spero Lucas, occasionally takes time out from the case he's working on to have an erotic interlude with a young woman—in fact, over the course of the book, he strings along two different women, because he's that kind of guy.

These brief scenes about his love life add complexity to the character, and they serve to tell us something we wouldn't otherwise know about Spero. But because they aren't central to the story, they tend to be much shorter and more expository than the scenes that actually advance the investigation. Pelecanos properly devotes more space and detail and dramatic energy to those scenes in which Spero is interviewing a witness or stalking a suspect.

On the other hand, in a more expansive, less plot-driven narrative such as *Ulysses* or *Moby-Dick*, a scene can go on for pages simply because it is inherently interesting. These novels are more interesting for the quality of the language, the richness of the world being evoked, or the inherent interest in the subject matter than they are for the story.

In *Moby-Dick*, Herman Melville devotes long passages and even whole chapters to describing the work of a whaling vessel, the natural history of whales, and other topics that don't advance the plot. However, these scenes still advance the overall purpose of the book. They evoke an entire way of life in as much detail as possible, but they aren't necessarily concerned with advancing a story.

And with some books, the point of the novel isn't the plot at all, but the individual scenes that make up the plot. With your indulgence, I'll offer up one of my own novels, *The Lecturer's Tale*, as an example.

Now this book does have a plot. It's about a failing academic named Nelson who uses a supernatural power to rise through the English department of a fictional Midwestern university. But the purpose of the book wasn't necessarily to tell a story, but to allow me to make fun of the worst excesses of modern literary theory.

As I was writing it, I realized that the book was basically a series of satirical set pieces, each one of which was more over-the-top than the one before. These set pieces weren't entirely self-contained, since each one did push my silly plot a little further along. But each chapter or scene was mainly intended to be amusing for its own sake. It became clear to me early on that the point of the plot was to set up the scenes, not the other way around.

One of the plot points in *The Lecturer's Tale* is the fact that Nelson's department has a job opening, and even though Nelson isn't qualified for the position, he decides to sabotage the three main candidates. So in a chapter entitled "The Three Stooges," Nelson uses his supernatural power to get each candidate to embarrass him or herself. The chapter is made up of three major scenes, and in each scene, one of the job candidates self-destructs in public. The second scene, for example, features a charismatic Englishman who studies popular culture, and I had him deliver a lecture in which he deconstructs an Elvis Presley movie called *Viva Vietnam!* When somebody in the audience of the lecture points out that such a movie never existed, I had the Englishman argue that it didn't matter whether the movie existed or not, what mattered was his analysis.

The satirical target of this scene was academics who put literary criticism above actual works of art, but part of my incentive for writing it was simply to amuse myself, and, I hope, the reader. And so it became an extended comic riff on a fake Elvis Presley movie set in Vietnam, complete with fake Elvis Presley song titles like "Dien-Bien-Phooey," "You Broke My Heart of Darkness," and "The Moonlight, the Minefield, and You." I easily could have shown the Englishman's self-destruction in a much shorter scene, but it wouldn't have been as much fun.

My point here is that how long a scene goes on, and whether it should be included at all, does not depend on the plot necessarily, but on the intent of the narrative as a whole. A plot-driven crime novel like *The Cut* needs to move through the water like a shark. If it slows down, it dies. Trying to squeeze in a long chapter about the history of detective work or Spero Lucas's history with women would throw the whole novel out of whack.

On the other hand, *The Lecturer's Tale* has a different metabolism than a thriller. You're not meant to race through it the way you read a novel like *The Cut*; you're meant to enjoy each scene as it comes. As a result, the scenes in that book are longer and slower than the scenes in *The Cut*. The scenes in each book have a different pace and structure, because the intent of each book is different.

Transitioning into and out of a scene is something that vexes some writers, even experienced ones. These transitions can vary enormously, depending on the intent of the scene, its length, its importance in the narrative, and so on. For example, scenes that take place early in the narrative are going to need more of a set-up, on the whole, than scenes that appear later. When you're introducing characters, situations, or settings for the first time, you need to spend more time describing them than you do later on, when the reader already knows who the character is or what the setting looks like. You can take your time in these scenes. You can describe the setting and the character in some detail, and let the characters talk a bit more digressively than they might in later scenes.

For example, in the very first paragraph of *The Maltese Falcon*, Dashiell Hammett gives us a detailed physical description of his detective, Sam Spade. You may recall that Spade is described as looking like "a blond satan." Hammett provides this detailed and evocative description first thing so that later on he can start a scene with Spade's name or some action or gesture, without having to tell us all over again what he looks like.

The same goes for Spade's office: Having described it once, Hammett doesn't need to do it again, unless some particular feature of the setting needs to be pointed out for a particular purpose in that particular scene. For example, if Hammett wants to make it clear that a scene is happening in Spade's office at sunset, he might start the scene by saying something like, "The last light of the sun slanted through the slats of the blinds." There's no need for him to describe everything in the office again.

Also, short scenes need less of an introduction than longer, more dramatic scenes. You can signal the start of a new scene with something as simple as a space break in the text, or, if time has passed since the last section, with a simple phrase like "The next day ..." or "A few hours later ...."

On the other hand, if the scene is going to be longer or more important or more dramatic, you might want to make more of a fuss at the start. Alice Munro begins that significant scene in "The Beggar Maid," the one in which Rose breaks up with Patrick, with a description of Rose's walk from her room to Patrick's apartment:

> She woke up early, got up and dressed and let herself out the side door of Dr. Henshawe's garage. It was too early for the buses to be running. She walked through the city to Patrick's apartment. She walked across the park. Around the South African War Memorial a pair of greyhounds were leaping and playing, an old woman standing by, holding their leashes. The sun was just up, shining on their pale hides. The grass was wet. Daffodils and narcissus were in bloom.

As I said earlier, most of the story before this point moves at a brisk pace. This paragraph immediately slows down the narrative and lets us know that something important is about to happen. It provides a bumper between the fast-paced mixture of exposition and miniature scenes that came immediately before it and the slower and more dramatic scene that's about to start.

After that little prologue, Munro lets the encounter between Rose and Patrick play out before the reader in more or less real time. But then she ends the scene abruptly and dramatically, befitting the emotionally turbulent nature of the encounter, as Rose storms out of Patrick's apartment: " 'I don't want to see you, ever!' she said viciously. But at the door she turned and said in a normal and regretful voice, 'Good-bye.' "

After easing us into the scene, and letting it play out in front of the reader, Munro then cuts the scene off as sharply as Rose cuts off her relationship with Patrick. It's a skillful mimetic effect, evoking the same shock in the reader that both Rose and Patrick must feel at that moment.

Another way to transition into a scene is to begin it *in medias res*, which, as I've mentioned in an earlier lecture, is a Latin expression that means "in the middle of things." This is one of the oldest and most reliable tricks in a fiction writer's repertoire—namely, starting a scene in the middle of the action, or at least after the action of the scene is already underway. The chief advantage of entering a scene already in progress is that it adds energy and urgency to the narrative. It also engages the reader on a deeper level, by forcing him to sit up and pay attention to what's going on. It's as if he's walked into a lively party full of interesting people that started an hour before he got there.

In fact, this is exactly what happens in the opening sequence of Eleanor Catton's epic historical mystery *The Luminaries*. In her bravura opening chapter, Catton introduces us to a character named Walter Moody, who has just arrived at a remote gold rush community on the west coast of New Zealand in 1866. In the opening pages of the book, he finds himself in a hotel lounge with 12 other men. He has never met any of these men before, but they proceed to tell him a long, complicated story about a suspicious death, a suicide attempt, and the discovery of a fortune in gold, all of which happened weeks before Moody even showed up. By throwing both Moody and the reader into the deep end of the pool, Catton risks making the reader feel overwhelmed, the way Moody does himself, at first. But she constructs that opening scene so energetically and with such attention to detail, that she hooks us into the mystery that isn't fully explained until 800 pages later.

Now, when it comes to making a transition from one scene to another, usually you can accomplish it without any fuss. Here's another example from "The Beggar Maid." This is a brief passage that starts as exposition and shifts suddenly into a little bit of drama. It comes during a sequence where Patrick has taken Rose back to British Columbia to meet his family:

> The sisters Joan and Marion were younger than Patrick, older than Rose. Unlike Patrick they showed no nervousness, no cracks in self-satisfaction. At an earlier meal they had questioned Rose.

"Do you ride?"

"No."

"Do you sail?"

"No."

"Play tennis? Play golf? Play badminton?"

No. No. No.

Here, two, simple expository sentences about Patrick's sisters lead immediately, with hardly any transition, into a brief scene in which we can hear, in only 17 words, Joan and Marion's snobbery and Rose's embarrassment.

Transitioning out of a scene is perhaps a little less vexing than transitioning into one. Again, it depends on the scene's purpose in the narrative as a whole, but in general, you can round off a scene more briskly than you can start one. Once the main purpose of the scene has played out—the new character has been sufficiently introduced, the plot point has been made—you usually want to wrap it up as quickly as possible, but without coming across like a host pushing his guests out the door.

For some kinds of narrative, you might end a scene with a sort of punchline—a witticism from a character, or even a sudden revelation—but even with narratives that aren't driven by plot, you don't want to linger over the scene after its purpose has been fulfilled.

As I said earlier, there can also be transitions within a scene, such as when a writer pauses to provide some exposition or segues into a flashback. Eleanor Catton's *The Luminaries* is made up mostly of long, dramatized scenes. But because the plot is so complicated, she often has to pause the action to introduce an extended flashback that lasts for many pages before returning to the original scene.

Because *The Luminaries* is written in the style of a 19th-century novel, sometimes Catton directly addresses the reader in a formal manner that calls attention to the transition itself: "We shall therefore intervene, and render

Sook Yongsheng's story in a way that is accurate to the events he wished to disclose, rather than to the style of his narration."

At other times, she slips effortlessly from drama to exposition with hardly any transition at all. The entire passage is too long to quote here, but here are the beginning and the end of an important piece of exposition about Walter Moody, which comes in the middle of a conversation Moody is having with a character named Gascoigne. The two men are discussing a prostitute named Anna, who has been wearing another woman's clothes for reasons that are too complicated for me to explain.

Here's how the scene transitions from drama to exposition:

> "Mr. Gascoigne," Moody said, holding up his hand, "despite my youth, I possess a certain store of wisdom about the fairer sex, and I can tell categorically that women do not like it when other women wear their clothes without their asking."
>
> Gascoigne laughed. Cheered by this joke, he applied himself to finishing his luncheon with a renewed energy, and a good humor.
>
> The truth of Moody's observation notwithstanding, it must be owned that his store of wisdom, as he had termed it, could be called empirical only in that it had been formed upon the close observation of his late mother, his stepmother, and his two maternal aunts: to put it plainly, Moody had never taken a lover, and did not know a great deal about women.

After this, there are nearly two pages of Moody's history with women, particularly his lack of experience with prostitutes. Then, two pages later, this exposition transitions back to the scene's present moment, with Moody addressing Gascoigne again:

> The truth was that he had never spoken two words together to a woman of Anna Wetherell's profession or experience, and would hardly know how to address her—or upon what subject—should the chance arise.

"And of course," he said now, "we ought to be cheered by the fact that Miss Wetherell's trunk did not follow her to the Wayfarer's Fortune."

"Did it not?" said Gascoigne in surprise.

The transition into the exposition is simple: It happens with a paragraph break, as the text jumps from Gascoigne's "good humor" to the beginning of the next sentence, "The truth of Moody's observation notwithstanding." Then, at the end of the expository section, the transition back into drama is signaled with another paragraph break, after the phrase "should the chance arise." Then comes a line of dialogue beginning "And of course," and the adverb "now" after "he said." These further signal the reader that the exposition is over and we're back at luncheon with Moody and Gascoigne.

The previous example was about pausing a scene to provide exposition, but there are also scenes within scenes, which are usually flashbacks. Getting in and out of flashbacks can be pretty straightforward as well.

If it's a short flashback, you might signal the shift in time by putting the whole flashback in italics, but that can be cumbersome. Too many words in italics can bristle at a reader. An easier way to transition into a flashback, especially if it's from the point of view of a particular character, is simply to say something like, "Leo thought back to the conversation he'd had with Anna the day before," or "Leo remembered what Anna had said to him," or something like that.

There's a more subtle way, though, which I have often used in my own work over the years. I've always thought that starting a flashback with "Kevin remembered …" or "Stella thought back to when …" was clunky and mechanical. It seems like the literary equivalent of the transition to a flashback in an old movie, the kind where the screen goes wavy or newspaper headlines come spinning toward the camera. So instead, I usually try to signal a flashback with a simple change in verb tense.

In my novel *Next*, my character Kevin spends much of the story thinking about his past. The present-day action of the novel is about Kevin's trip to

Austin, Texas, for a job interview, and those scenes are written in the present tense. His memories and flashbacks, on the other hand, are in the past tense.

Sometimes the text just switches straight from the present tense to the past, as in this excerpt. Kevin is standing on a pedestrian bridge in Austin and thinking about his father, who died when he was a teenager:

> Now Kevin knows why his father sang melancholy Sinatra songs in the shower, and the memory of his father's bass-baritone—too low for Sinatra, he strained for the high notes—unexpectedly tightens Kevin's throat. It kills him to think he never put it together, the difference between what his father sang when he was alone and thought no one could hear, and what he sang when he was harmonizing with his barbershop quartet buddies two Saturdays a month.

As you can see, Kevin's thoughts are in the present tense, but his father's actions are in the past tense. This passage leads to a two and half page flashback about the death of Kevin's father, all of which takes place in the past tense.

At the end of the flashback, a policeman speaks to the young Kevin, with his dialogue tag in the past tense. Then, in the next sentence, we return to Kevin in the present day, and he is thinking in the present tense:

> "Are you Kevin?" [the policeman] said with surprising tenderness.
>
> Wow, thinks Kevin on the bridge … [and he] palms the tears out of his eyes. I don't need this now, I really, really don't, but there's no stopping it: thirty-five years later, the night of his father's death can still sneak up on him.

Now, this technique won't work, of course, if the present day of your narrative is already in the past tense, which is the default verb tense of most fiction. In that case, you can signal a shift into a flashback by switching briefly into the past perfect tense. In that case, instead of saying "Kevin's father sang Sinatra songs in the shower," you'd say "Kevin's father *had sung*

Sinatra songs in the shower." And then, to get out of the flashback and back to the present, you'd use the past perfect again just for a moment at the end. Instead of saying " 'Are you Kevin?' the policeman said" you would write, " 'Are you Kevin?' the policeman *had said*" in order to signal the return to the main story.

Let me give you a longer example. Here's a brief flashback scene from my first novel, *The Wild Colonial Boy*, in which a character named Jimmy Coogan, who is a member of the Irish Republican Army, remembers the time he stole an expensive mackintosh raincoat from a shop in London:

> He started along the beach through a fine mist of sea spray, and he pulled the wide lapel of the mackintosh all the way across and buttoned it. The mac was an expensive one, a Burberry. He had tried it on in a posh men's store in Bond Street, turning this way and that in front of the tall mirrors like a woman while the clerk fussed around him and tugged at his cuffs. Coogan had no intention of taking it until he realized how his wife would scold him for it—and she did, telling him that it was his business to remain inconspicuous, that the mac made him look like a bloody television correspondent—and even then he had no intention of paying for it; he sent the man into the back for a box, and when man was gone he had slipped out door as someone else came in.

As this passage starts, Coogan "started along the beach" and "buttoned" his mackintosh in the past tense. But when he starts to remember how he stole it, the verb tense shifts into the past perfect: "He *had* tried it on in a posh men's store." Then the bulk of the flashback takes place in the simple past tense, because it's too awkward to write a long passage in the past perfect. Just like a long passage in italics, all those "had's" would bristle at the reader. Then, to signal the end of the flashback, I stick in one more instance of the past perfect—"when the man was gone he *had slipped* out the door" just before Jimmy returns to the present moment of the story. The effect is almost subliminal, and in principle, anyway, the reader follows the shift into the flashback and out of it again without really having to think about it.

So, to sum up, there some scenes are just little bursts of drama that can be truncated or incomplete, the way most of the early scenes in "The Beggar Maid" are, but most of the time, most of the weight in a narrative is carried by fully dramatized scenes. These major scenes are basically little stories within the story. Even if a major scene couldn't stand alone outside the context of the whole narrative, it should have the structure of a simple story, with a beginning, middle, and end.

In an earlier lecture, I talked about fractals, the mathematical concept of a pattern that repeats itself at every level of magnification. Now, I'm not saying that each individual scene should necessarily reproduce the structure or plot of the larger narrative, but it helps to remember that any story made of scenes is basically made of smaller stories. It's stories all the way down.

Here's an exercise to help you think about crafting scenes: Take an un-dramatized moment from a story of your own or from a story or novel you admire and turn it into a full-fledged dramatic scene. In other words, take a moment that is only alluded to or depicted only briefly in an expository passage, and dramatize it fully.

For example, the moment that Hamlet learns that his father has died is never shown in Shakespeare's play, so you might dramatize that. Take as many words or pages as you need and turn it into a little story, with a beginning, middle, and end. Don't worry about how long it is. But you also want to make sure that it contributes to the larger narrative. This will give you practice in making a scene self-contained as well as making it an integral part of the larger story.

In the meantime, in the next two lectures we're going to explore how the process of composition and the process of revision are linked, and we'll also talk about how to think about your completed narrative as a whole.

Should I Write in Drafts?
Lecture 21

From day to day, most writers focus on the individual elements that go into the writing of fiction: characters, dialogue, plot, setting, and so on. But sooner or later, you will have a completed draft, and you'll have to start worrying about whether or not the whole thing works. In this lecture and the next one, we'll talk about working with the narrative as a whole. The next lecture covers the process of revision, but as we'll discover, that process is closely linked with the process of composition. In this lecture, then, we'll talk about composing drafts. We'll begin with the pros and cons of writing the whole narrative out from beginning to end before you start changing it.

First Drafts

- Every completed writing project has at least a first draft. For some writers, that first draft is also the final draft, but most of the time, writers don't intend the first draft to be the finished work of art. In fact, it's not even supposed to be very good.

- The fact that first drafts are notoriously bad is not just an unfortunate byproduct of the creative process; it's a necessity. Think of writing a first draft as mining for gold the way it was done in such films as *The Treasure of the Sierra Madre*. Imagine yourself squatting awkwardly in a stream, sifting through dirt by hand to get a few flakes of gold. Expecting your first draft to be perfect is about as likely as the possibility that you will pick nuggets straight out of the dirt with your fingers.

- It's also true, however, that the experience of writing a first draft can be thrilling, and it's often more fun than the more grueling and painstaking work of revision. In many cases, writing a first draft is your only opportunity to experience the story in the way the reader will; that is, it's the only chance you'll have to find your way through the story scene by scene, without necessarily knowing what comes next or how it turns out.

It's the only time in the creative process when you can fully experience the thrill of discovery.

- Obviously, if you've created a detailed outline of your narrative or you know how it will end, you won't be experiencing it in complete ignorance of what comes next, the way a reader would.

- But even if you think you know where the story is going, you're likely to encounter any number of fruitful surprises while writing the first draft—surprises that will deepen or complicate the outline you worked out in advance. These surprises may lead you to change the outline or even throw it away. They may also lead you to change the ending.

- Even if you're working from an outline or think you know what your final destination is, during the early days of composition, you are an explorer moving through territory that no one else has ever crossed before.

- Writing a first draft can also be fun because a first draft is not supposed to be economical.

- You will probably find it fruitful to make your first draft the longest draft, putting in everything you can think of, then putting in some more. Especially at the beginning of a project, you're likely to be bursting with ideas and possibilities, and it's in your best interest to put as many of them down on paper as you can, without worrying too much about plausibility, consistency, or logic.

- You don't have to worry about whether your first draft will be interesting, because chances are that no one will ever see it except yourself and a few trusted readers.

- The reason for writing a long first draft is twofold: (1) The more material you put into it, the more material you have to work with later on, and (2) as we've said, writing a first draft is a process of exploration. You won't know for certain what the story is or who the characters are until you have the whole thing in front of you. The experience of writing everything down can change what you thought you were doing in profound ways.

- Another good practice is to write your first draft as quickly as possible. The time for the careful calibration of phrases, sentences, and paragraphs comes later. To begin with, you don't want to worry too much about pacing, about what works and what doesn't, or even about consistency. Keep in mind the motto of the songwriter and performer Nick Lowe: "Bash it out now and tart it up later."
  - o Not only will speed help you get as many ideas on the page as you can, some of that energy may well survive into the finished work.

  - o In an interview in *The New York Times*, the mystery writer Michael Connelly talked about his technique for writing fiction: "I have always felt that the books I have written fastest have been my best—because I caught an unstoppable momentum in the writing."

- The suggestion that you write a long first draft quickly can apply to any writer, at every level of experience, but it may be especially true for writers who are just starting out, especially for first novelists. Creative writing courses can be helpful, but in the end, you learn how to write a book by writing one. You learn by trial and error, and you give yourself the most scope for that process to be fruitful if you write an expansive, baggy, inconsistent, very likely unpublishable, and maybe even unreadable first draft.

Evolution of the Writing Process
- During the heyday of the novel in the 19th century, it was probably uncommon for a writer to compose several complete drafts of a novel before publishing it because many novels at the time were published as serials. These sections of novels appeared in weekly or monthly installments in newspapers or magazines over the course of a year or two.
  - o Charles Dickens is especially famous for having written his novels in installments, sometimes working only two weeks ahead of publication. He started writing *David Copperfield*,

for example, in February 1849, and the first installment was published only three months later. He didn't complete the book until November of 1850, so that the public had already started reading the novel long before he finished writing it.

- o This means that Dickens never did more than one complete draft of *David Copperfield*, and it means that he must have thought the novel through in great detail before he started writing.

- o Dickens may have done drafts of individual chapters or sections; he certainly rewrote things as he went along; and it's entirely possible that he may have changed his mind about the later chapters that he had outlined but hadn't written yet. But Dickens didn't have the option of making changes to the chapters that had already been published.

- o That may have handicapped him as far as plotting went, but even so, much of Dickens's work has an irresistible narrative momentum that is partly a reflection of his own boundless energy and partly a product of how he wrote the books—on deadline, a chapter at a time, just two weeks ahead of the printer.

- The commercial realities of publishing serial fiction in the 19th century affected the daily creative process of writers, dictating that books be written on the fly, without repeated drafts. In our own time, changes in technology have also caused changes in the way writers compose a whole narrative.

  - o Many writers who once wrote

Writing by hand is more time consuming than typing on a computer, but it can be a fruitful way to make yourself slow down and think about what you're trying to accomplish.

multiple drafts out in longhand now write only one complete draft of their work on the computer, making as many changes as they need to during the writing process.

- In other words, although each individual chapter may go through multiple drafts, many writers no longer compose one complete draft of a whole book; they don't advance to the next chapter until the current one is more or less finished.

One Draft versus Multiple Drafts
- If you've thought about a book for a long time, when you sit down to actually write it, you may find that you spend the most amount of time on the first three or four chapters. Once you have a firm foundation for the characters, the plot, and the setting, the later chapters may come easier.

- The creative process may also become easier for you as you gain experience as a writer. When you're writing your first story or novel, you're learning as you go, but as you become more experienced, you no longer have to teach yourself how to write dialogue, build suspense, and so on.

- Of course, there is always more than one way of doing things. No doubt, there are many experienced writers who continue to write in multiple complete drafts throughout their careers, and no doubt there are some rare novices who dash out a masterpiece in a first draft. As always, you should do what works best for you.

- In the end, whether you write multiple drafts or only one depends on the nature of the project. A plot-driven story that takes place in chronological order may be easier to write in one draft than a story that encompasses flashbacks or other nonchronological events.

- Note, too, that as you gain experience, you may no longer follow the advice to write long first drafts. You might find that your early drafts of individual scenes—not to mention the finished manuscript—are shorter than later drafts. In other words, you may become an "accretive" writer:

With each subsequent draft, you gather a little more material and go back to earlier scenes to fill in more details.

Suggested Reading

Ackroyd, *Dickens*.

Lamott, *Bird by Bird*.

Writing Exercise

1. Try some of the different writing techniques mentioned in this lecture with one of your own scenes or chapters. For those who are more accustomed to using a computer, try drafting a scene in longhand to make yourself slow down and think as you write. You might also think about how you usually compose a scene or chapter, then try the opposite technique. In other words, if you're the sort of writer who dashes through a scene without looking back, try slowing down and revising as you go, writing your first paragraph multiple times until you think it's perfect before proceeding to the next one. If you're already the sort of writer who revises as you go, try typing out a scene as fast and furiously as possible, without stopping and looking back. With either approach, you may hate the result—in which case, you can go back to your old way of doing things—or you might find that sometimes, for certain purposes, changing your process can lead to interesting results.

Should I Write in Drafts?

Lecture 21—Transcript

Up until this point in the lectures, we've mainly been talking about the individual elements that go into the writing of fiction. We've looked at creating characters, writing dialogue, constructing a plot, evoking setting, and choosing a point of view, among other things. And in the previous lecture, we talked about what I consider to be the fundamental building block of fiction writing, the creation of an individual scene.

Focusing on these things makes sense, because from day to day and from moment to moment, you will spend most of your time as a fiction writer thinking about the particular task at hand, whether it's creating a vivid scene, providing a little bit of exposition or backstory, or just crafting the next sentence. The final shape of the whole narrative may always be present in the back of your mind, but in the heat of composition, you are more likely to be focused on the particular scene in front of you.

But sooner or later, you will have to put the whole narrative down on paper—if you're old school—or you will have a complete computer file. Either way, whether it's a pile of pages or a pile of pixels, you'll have a completed draft. And at that point you have to start worrying about whether the whole thing works or not. In this lecture and the next one, we're going to talk about working with the narrative as a whole.

The process of composition and the process of revision are very closely linked, and you can't separate them completely. So I'll be talking a little bit about the process of revision in this lecture, but I'll talk about it in more detail in the next lecture. But to start with, let's talk about composing drafts.

Many writers tend to create their works in complete drafts, and by this I mean that they write the whole narrative down, from beginning to end, before they start to revise, often several times in a row. I say "many" and not "all," because some writers never write in complete drafts. Other writers take a different approach with each different project, sometimes writing in complete drafts, sometimes not. I'm one of the latter: I've done it both ways, and I'll talk later on about how my practice has changed over the years.

I'll also talk about some other ways of dealing with the whole narrative that other writers have used. But to begin with, I'm going to talk about the pros and cons of writing the whole narrative out, beginning to end, before you start changing it.

Every completed writing project has at least a first draft. For some projects, for some writers, that first draft is also the final draft. But for most writers, most of the time, the first draft is not intended to be the finished work of art. In fact, it's not even supposed to be very good.

In her excellent writing guide *Bird by Bird*, the writer Anne Lamott came up with a famously salty way to describe that first effort. Please pardon my French, or rather, please pardon Anne Lamott's French: It's what she calls "the idea of shitty first drafts." Here's what she says about them:

> All good writers write them. This is how they end up with good second drafts and terrific third drafts. People tend to look at successful writers, writers who are getting their books published and maybe even doing well financially, and think that they sit down at their desks every morning feeling like a million dollars, feeling great about who they are and how much talent they have and what a great story they have to tell; that they roll their necks a few times to get all the cricks out, and dive in, typing fully formed passages as fast as a court reporter. But this is just the fantasy of the uninitiated. I know some very great writers, writers you love who write beautifully and have made a great deal of money, and not one of them sits routinely down feeling wildly enthusiastic and confident. Not one of them writes elegant first drafts.

I think Lamott and I must know some of the same people, or at least the same sort of people. I've read the first drafts of many of my writer friends, and none of them were ever very good. As a matter of fact, some of them shook my confidence in just how good my friends were. And when the finished story or book turned out to be very good indeed, I was secretly amazed that such a bad beginning led to such a great finished product. And to be fair to my friends, I'm sure they've have the same experience reading my first drafts. But that, I think, is Ann Lamott's point: The fact that first drafts are notoriously crummy is not an unfortunate byproduct of the creative process, it's a necessity. I'm going to commit a rather clumsy metaphor here, but think of writing a first draft as mining for gold.

Bear in mind that everything I know about gold mining is from movies like *The Treasure of Sierra Madre* or Charlie Chaplin's *The Gold Rush*. It's my understanding that you have to spend days and weeks squatting awkwardly in a rushing stream, sifting by hand through tons of dirt to get a few flakes of gold. I'm not saying that the proportion of dirt to gold in a first draft is necessarily tons to ounces, but expecting that first draft to be perfect is about as likely as Charlie Chaplin picking nuggets straight out of the dirt with his fingers. It just doesn't happen.

Perhaps I'm laying it on a bit thick—I did warn you that it was a clumsy metaphor—because it's also true that the experience of writing a first draft can also be thrilling. It's often a lot more fun than the more grueling and painstaking work of revision, and probably a lot more fun than panning for gold.

In many cases, writing a first draft is your only opportunity to experience the story the way the reader will. In other words, it's the only chance you'll have to find your way through the story, scene by scene, without necessarily knowing what comes next or how it turns out. It's the only time in the creative process when you can fully experience the thrill of discovery.

This isn't always the case, obviously. If you've already created a detailed outline of your narrative, or you know how's it's going to end, you won't be reading it in complete ignorance of what comes next, the way a reader would. But, as I've said in earlier lectures, you're likely to encounter fruitful surprises while writing the first draft, even if you think you know where the story is going. These surprises will deepen or complicate the outline you worked out in advance. You may find yourself changing the outline, or even throwing it away. You may even change the ending.

I know that in my own work, most of the best bits, whether it's a plot twist or a sudden revelation about a character, came to me while I was actually writing a draft. I hardly ever get my best ideas by planning a story in advance. Even if you're working from an outline, and even if you think you know your final destination, during those early days of composition you are an explorer moving through territory nobody else has ever crossed before.

Writing a first draft can also be thrilling because it's not supposed to be very good. It's not supposed to be elegant or shapely, and it's especially not supposed to be economical. In fact, perhaps the most fruitful approach you can take is to make your first draft your longest draft.

In that first attempt, you should put in pretty much everything you can think of, and then put in some more. It's in your best interest to put as many of your ideas down on paper as you can, without worrying too much about plausibility, consistency, or logic. Especially at the beginning of a project, you're likely to be bursting with ideas and possibilities, and you want to run with that energy as long as you can. So, dare to be crazy. Dare to be over the top.

Also, dare to be boring. You don't have to worry about whether the first draft is ever going to be interesting to anybody else. Chances are nobody's ever going to read it anyway, except yourself and maybe a few of your trusted readers. To sum up, a first draft doesn't need to be elegant, but it does need to be as comprehensive and all-inclusive as possible.

There are two good reasons for writing a long first draft. One is pretty simple: The more stuff you put into it, the more stuff you have to work with later on. It's much easier to write more than you need in an early draft and then cut the superfluous stuff, than it is to take a structure which may already have become fixed in your mind and pry it apart to add new scenes or characters.

The other reason you want a long first draft is because, as I've already said, writing a first draft is a process of exploration. Until you have the whole thing down on paper, you won't even really know what the story is, or who the characters are. No matter how much you plan in advance, the experience of making the story flow through your pen or through your keyboard can change what you thought you were doing in profound ways.

My first novel, *The Wild Colonial Boy*, was about the Irish Republican Army. When I started it, I thought I was writing a politically radical defense of the IRA's guerilla war against the British Army in Northern Ireland in the 1970s and 1980s. I was young then, in my late 20s, and I still had romantic notions about revolution. But by time I had put the whole novel down on paper, my attitude toward my own narrative had changed completely. I realized I wasn't writing a pro-IRA novel anymore. Instead, I was writing a novel about the futility and cruelty of terrorism. It not only changed my view of the book, it changed my view of myself.

It turned out I wasn't nearly as radical as I thought I was, and it took the process of writing down the whole story from beginning to end for me to see that. As Anne Lamott puts it, "Very few writers really know what they are doing until they've done it."

I would also suggest that you write your first draft as quickly as possible. The time for the careful calibration of phrases, sentences, and paragraphs comes later. To begin with, you don't want to worry too much about pacing, and what works and what doesn't, or even about consistency.

As I said in my very first lecture, I've been fond of quoting a slogan from the English rock-and-roll musician Nick Lowe. Along with being a great songwriter and performer, Nick Lowe has also earned a reputation as producer for other artists such as Elvis Costello, and his nickname as a producer has always been "Basher." This comes from his motto in the recording studio, which is "Bash it out now and tart it up later."

I think this motto works just as well for fiction writing. Not only will writing quickly help you get as many ideas on the page as you can, something of that energy may very well survive into the finished work.

The mystery writer Michael Connelly has said something similar. In an interview in the *New York Times*, he talked about how his years as crime reporter informed his technique for writing fiction. Here's what he said:

> Momentum in writing means momentum in reading. There is a
> prevailing school of thought that something good must take time,

sometimes years to create and hone. I have always felt that the books I have written fastest have been my best—because I caught an unstoppable momentum in the writing.

I don't endorse Connelly's philosophy entirely. I don't believe that writing faster is always better. But there's a lot of truth to what he says. The headlong momentum of a first draft can often carry over even into the finished product.

Any writer, at every level of experience, can take advantage of this advice. But I think it's especially true that writers who are just starting out, and especially first novelists, should write their first drafts quickly. MFA programs, creative writing classes, and a course like this one can be very helpful, but in the end, you learn how to write a book by writing one. You learn by trial and error, and for that process to be fruitful, it may actually help you to write an expansive, baggy, inconsistent, very likely unpublishable, and maybe even unreadable first draft.

This is the way I learned how to write novels, at any rate. I never even finished my first attempt at a novel. Instead, I gave up after writing 200 truly bad and spectacularly dull pages, which will never again see the light of day. But I then went on to write four handwritten drafts of *The Wild Colonial Boy*. As soon as I finished the first draft of that book, I typed it up—on a typewriter, because that's how old I am. Then I showed it to a few people and got some advice. After that, I sat down and wrote the whole thing out again in longhand, and typed it up again.

Then, after a third handwritten draft, also painstakingly typed by me, I sent it to an agent. This guy very generously gave me some of the best advice I've ever gotten on a manuscript, and I wrote the final draft, again in longhand, while I was attending the Iowa Writers Workshop during the late 1980s. I typed this final draft on my first computer—a Leading Edge Model D, for those of you who remember the Paleolithic Era of personal computing. With some minor revision, that was the version that ended up as my first published novel. And I'm convinced that it wouldn't have been publishable at all, and I wouldn't be here, talking to you, if I hadn't slogged through those four handwritten drafts.

But not everyone writes books that way. In fact, during the heyday of the novel in the 19th century, it was probably uncommon for a writer to compose several complete drafts of a novel before publishing it. Back then many novels were published as serials, meaning that they were published in weekly or monthly installments in newspapers or magazines over the course of a year or two. Charles Dickens is especially famous for having written his novels in installments, sometimes working only two weeks ahead of publication.

For example, he started writing *David Copperfield* in February 1849, and the first installment was published only three months later, on the first of May. He didn't complete the book until November of 1850, which means that the public had already started reading *David Copperfield* long before Dickens finished writing it. This also means that Dickens never really did more than one complete draft of *David Copperfield*. Because he wasn't working with complete drafts, he needed to have thought the novel through in great detail before he even started writing. As the British writer Peter Ackroyd says in his biography of Dickens,

> Never was a writer so exact, so thorough, so careful in his plans.
> He told one contemporary that "… the plot, the motive of the book,
> is always perfected in my brain for a long time before I take up my
> pen." And he told another that "… he never began to write before
> having settled the work in its minutest detail, in his head."

Dickens may have done drafts of individual chapters or sections, and he certainly rewrote things as he went along. And the further he got into the story, it's entirely possible that he may have changed his mind about the later chapters, the ones that he had outlined but hadn't written yet. For example, his novel *Great Expectations* originally had a different ending than the one he ended up publishing.

But Dickens did not have the option of making any changes to the chapters that had already been published. He could not go back and change an early chapter to make it consistent with a new understanding of the story or a character. That may have handicapped him as far as plotting went, at least in comparison to a modern writer, who has the freedom to go back and fix a mistake.

And yet, much of Dickens's work has an irresistible narrative momentum. This momentum is partly the result of Dickens's own boundless energy, but it is also a product of how he wrote the books: on deadline, a chapter at a time, just two weeks ahead of the printer.

And so the commercial realities of publishing serial fiction in the 19th century affected the daily creative process of writers. The publishing business back then dictated that books be written on the fly, without repeated drafts. In our own time, changes in technology have also caused changes in the way that writers compose a whole narrative.

As I mentioned at the start of the lecture, my own process has changed over the years. I haven't written more than one complete draft of anything since my second book, a collection of three novellas called *Publish and Perish*. In that case, one of the novellas went through at least two complete drafts, and the second one was significantly different from the first. But at least one of the novellas, called "Queen of the Jungle," was written essentially as one draft, in a white heat. And the published versions of each of my three subsequent books, all of them novels, are essentially first drafts. I didn't do this because I wanted to emulate Dickens. Rather, the reason I changed my method is because I started to use a computer.

Even before PCs, I knew people who actually composed on a typewriter, but I could never work that way myself. When I'm writing, I make a lot of false starts, and I change a lot things as I go. I often go back to the very beginning of whatever section I'm working on and change it significantly. Sometimes I just scrap the beginning entirely and start over from scratch.

This means that when I was still writing fiction in longhand on yellow legal pads, my manuscript pages were full of sentences that I had drawn a line through, and even whole passages that I had crossed out. I also made a lot of changes by turning the page sideways and writing in the margins.

Back in the era of the typewriter, there was something final about actually typing up these handwritten drafts. Any change you made after you typed up your draft meant at the very least messing about with White Out or correction tape. Sometimes you'd have to retype an entire page or even several pages, and sometimes you had to repaginate the whole thing. Changing the typescript was so cumbersome and time consuming that it made sense to do all my actual composing in a handwritten draft, where I could be as messy and indecisive as I needed to be.

But when I started to use a personal computer, I discovered that the handicaps of typewriting disappeared. I could make changes in a computer file just as easily as I could write passages sideways in the margins of a page. Even more easily, in fact: I no longer had to transcribe changes from a manuscript by correcting or retyping a typescript. And I no longer had to decipher my own dodgy handwriting while I was typing.

I could make the change instantly in the file, at will, without having to print anything out. For example, if I wanted to move a whole passage from one chapter to another, I could simply copy and paste it, rather than having to retype the whole section. And if I wanted to save different versions, I could do that too, without wasting any paper. As a result, I composed nearly all of my second book, *Publish and Perish*, on a computer—though, as I say, I did at least two complete drafts of one of the novellas.

When I wrote *The Lecturer's Tale*, my third book and second novel, I never did more than one complete draft of the whole book, even though each of the individual chapters went through multiple drafts. As I explained in my last lecture, the plot of *The Lecturer's Tale* is basically an excuse to string together a series of satirical set pieces, and each one of those set pieces was rewritten several times. If you were to add up all the different versions of each chapter, it would probably amount to several complete drafts of the whole book.

But it was still different from the way I wrote *The Wild Colonial Boy*, where I wrote all the way to the end of the book without revising individual scenes before going back to the beginning and starting over. With *The Lecturer's Tale*, I didn't advance to the next chapter until the previous one was more or less finished, so that by time I finished the final draft of the last chapter, the book was essentially done.

With my next book, *Kings of Infinite Space*, I moved even further away from doing complete drafts. This novel is an office comedy about a failed academic who ends up working as a temp for a Texas state agency. I got the idea for it while I was still working on *The Lecturer's Tale*, so I couldn't get to it right away. As a result of this delay, the book marinated in my brain for a year before I ever started writing it. When I finally got around to it, I wrote it faster than I've ever written a novel before or since, in a rather feverish eight months.

Kings is a plot-driven book, and since I'd had a year to work the story out in my head, writing it down was actually pretty easy. As a result, I moved even further away from doing drafts than I had in writing *The Lecturer's Tale*.

I spent the most amount of time on the first three or four chapters. I wrote them over and over again, slowly perfecting them, so that each time I rewrote them, I made fewer changes. Then, when I had the opening section of the book more or less squared away, the later chapters came easier, because I already had a firm foundation for the characters, the plot, and the setting. In fact, the further I got into the book, the fewer drafts of each chapter I did. Many of the later chapters in the book are essentially first drafts, with only minor changes from the version I created on the day of their first composition.

This was a pretty radical shift in my creative process, and there are several reasons for it. One, as I've already said, is the change in technology. Making changes to a text on my laptop is easier than scribbling in the margins of a handwritten draft, and a lot faster. Though it may or may not be easier on my hands, since I've probably just exchanged writer's cramp for carpal tunnel syndrome. But perhaps just as significant is the fact that I'd become a more experienced writer. When I was writing *The Wild Colonial Boy*, I was essentially teaching myself how to write a novel. Plowing through all those handwritten drafts and hammering out all those typescripts on my Smith Corona was the best boot camp this young writer ever had. By the time I was writing *Kings of Infinite Space*, I was no longer teaching myself how to write dialogue or build suspense. I could just sit down and do it.

As always, I don't want to say that there's only one way of doing things. No doubt there are many experienced writers who continue to write in multiple complete drafts throughout their career, and no doubt there are some rare novices who dash out a masterpiece on the first go. The Beat writers, for example, believed in the motto "first thought, best thought," which was coined by the poet Allen Ginsberg. Not being a fan of the Beats myself, I'm not sure I'd endorse that sentiment, but you should do what works best for you and not necessarily listen to me. As I recall, Allen Ginsberg and Jack Kerouac didn't do too badly.

In the end, whether you write multiple drafts or only one depends on the nature of the project. Even though I haven't written in complete drafts since my first book, I also haven't used the same method twice. Each book has been written in a slightly different way.

My most recent novel, *Next*, was written in a similar fashion to *Kings of Infinite Space*, but with a crucial difference. As with *Kings*, I wrote the opening section of *Next* over and over again until I was more or less happy with it before proceeding to write the rest of the book. But *Kings* was a plot-driven story that happened in chronological order. Much of the story of *Next* takes place in flashbacks that do not occur in chronological order. In one chapter I might have my main character, Kevin, think about something that happened only a few months ago, but in the following chapter, he might recall something that happened 40 years ago, during his childhood. As a result, the further I got into the book, the more I learned about Kevin. And the more I learned about him, the more I had to go back and incorporate my new understanding into chapters that I had finished many months earlier. This happened all the way through the book. Even as I was writing the final chapter, I found myself having to reconfigure and revise earlier sections, and even the opening pages.

Writing *Next* was like the composition of *Kings of Infinite Space* in one respect: By time I had finished the first complete draft of each book, I was more or less done. But on a daily basis, writing *Next* was a much messier and more complicated process than writing *Kings*. It also took much longer: two-and-a-half years as opposed to eight months.

I also have to admit that, as I've gotten more experienced, I no longer follow one piece of advice I gave you earlier in the lecture. The first draft of my first novel, *The Wild Colonial Boy*, was indeed the longest and the most rambling and digressive of the four drafts. But now that I write in drafts of individual scenes rather than complete drafts of the whole manuscript, I find that my early drafts of each scene are usually shorter than the later drafts, not to mention the finished version.

In fact, at this point in my career I've turned into a different type of writer. One reader of mine called me an "accretive" writer, by which he meant that each new draft I write gathers a little more material, the way you might roll a snowball through the snow to turn it into the bottom half of a snowman. This may not work for you, obviously, but it's worth taking a look at, and I'll explain my current practice in more detail in the next lecture.

It's been difficult to think of an exercise for this lecture, because any exercise that involves the creation of a complete draft goes well beyond being an exercise, obviously. But I can suggest that you take some of the different techniques I'm mentioned in this lecture and try them out for yourself with a scene or a chapter.

For my younger viewers, who have spent their whole lives on a keyboard, you might try picking up a pen and a pad of paper and seeing if you can draft a whole scene in longhand, without typing a word. Even though I no longer write whole books or even whole chapters by hand anymore, I still sometimes sit down with one of my old yellow legal pads and write a few paragraphs in my indecipherable handwriting. Writing by hand is more time-consuming than typing. It can be a very fruitful way to make yourself slow down and think about what you're trying to accomplish.

But if that sounds too 19th century for you, try something like this: Think about how you normally compose a scene or chapter, and then try the opposite technique. In other words, if you're the sort of writer who dashes through a scene without looking back, try slowing down and revising as you go. Write your first paragraph over and over until you think it's perfect before proceeding to the next one.

Or, on the other hand, if you're already the sort of writer who revises as you go, throw caution to the winds and try typing out a scene as fast and furiously as possible. Don't stop and don't look back.

In either case, you may hate the result, in which case you can go back to your old way of doing things—no harm, no foul. Or you might find that sometimes, for certain purposes, changing your process can lead to interesting results. As I say, I've done it both ways, and both ways have worked for me.

In my next lecture, we'll look at the process of rewriting and revision, which most writers will tell you is about as much fun as doing your taxes—but most writers will also tell you that revision is where the real work of fiction writing gets done. So sharpen your red pencils!

Revision without Tears
Lecture 22

In the early stages of composing a work of fiction, you're often caught up in the thrill of discovery, creating unique situations and characters. Whatever frustrations you may experience in the act of creation are offset by the sheer pleasure of making something new. But then, having created a beautiful, imaginative draft, you have to sit down and look for everything you did wrong. Revision is about confronting your own mistakes and fixing them in such a way that the reader never knows there were any mistakes to begin with. It can be hard and unpleasant work, but in this lecture, we'll look at strategies for revision that can make it less intimidating.

The Daunting Task of Revision

- Much of what makes revision difficult is that you have to consider your draft on every level, more or less all at once. It's the one time in the whole process where you cannot avoid having to think about everything. You have to ask yourself not only if the entire narrative works as a whole, but if all its individual parts do what they're supposed to do and whether they all pull in the same direction. Is each character complete and believable? Are the point of view, verb tense, and setting appropriate? Does each chapter and scene round off and lead to the next? Are your sentences interesting, elegant, and memorable?

- One way to make this daunting task less intimidating is to prepare for revision from the very start. The motto "Bash it out now and tart it up later" is a reminder to forge ahead energetically, but it also serves to underscore the idea that getting the story down on paper is only the beginning of the process; you will have to "tart it up"—change things—later on.

- Composing and revising are inextricably linked, and how you revise depends in large part on how you composed the draft in the first place.

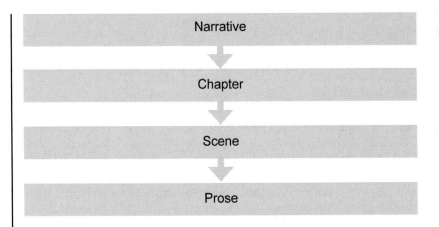

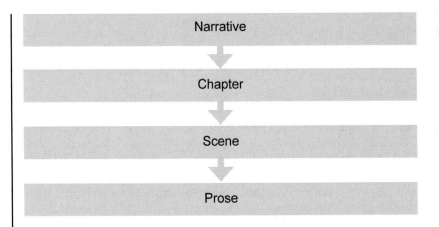

When revising, you need to think about every level of your work, from the narrative as a whole to individual chapters, scenes, and sentences.

- o If you write a whole draft without looking back and don't start revising until it's done, then you've got all the revision to do all at once. This may make facing the revision more daunting because you're looking at rewriting days or months of previous work. Still, forging ahead without having to worry every day about what you wrote the day before can make writing that first draft easier.

- o If you rewrite each individual section before you proceed to the next one, you'll be revising as you go. This approach may make the revision a little less daunting, but it's no guarantee that when you've reached the end, you still won't have to go back and fix mistakes or even make major changes. Even with this method, you still reach a point where you have to think about everything at once—whether the narrative works as a whole and whether all the individual parts work.

Case Study: Revision
- *The Lecturer's Tale* is the story of Nelson Humboldt, a failing academic who, in the first chapter of the book, loses his right index finger in a

freak accident on the quadrangle of the campus where he teaches. After Nelson's finger is reattached, he discovers that he can make anybody do anything he wants by touching them with that finger. He uses this power to save his own teaching job, and as he becomes more corrupt, to work his way to the top of his university's English department.

- The original opening of this novel reads, in part, as follows:

> Crossing the Quad at noon on a grey Halloween, Nelson Humboldt's finger was severed in a freak accident. Oddly enough, he hadn't been hurrying as he usually did at this time of day, and anyway, Nelson was a tall fellow, standing a full head taller than many of the young people around him. If anyone could see where he was going, it was Nelson Humboldt. …

> But today Nelson was unusually distracted, and this, he decided later, was the reason for the accident. He had just come from the cramped office of the undergraduate chair of the English department, where Nelson was a lecturer, and just ten minutes before she had told him compassionately but briskly that the department was being forced by budget necessities to terminate his appointment at the end of the semester. … Nelson had no savings to speak of and no prospects, the job market being what it was, and now he was about to have to no job, and he moved much more slowly than usual through the press on the Quad, still in shock, his mind elsewhere, letting himself be buffeted by the currents and eddies of passing students. The loss of his finger was just the last straw.

- This opening doesn't work on either the micro level of sentences and phrases or the macro level of the narrative as a whole. Many of the sentences are just plain clumsy, and the first paragraph doesn't intrigue the reader or suggest something about the narrative to come. The opening is nothing but exposition—an undramatic summary—and there is no evocative detail.

- In the second-draft version, the bare, unevocative summary of the first version is eliminated, and we begin to get the rudiments of an actual scene between Nelson and the chair of the English department, Victoria Victorinix:

> [Nelson] had just come from the spartan seventh-floor office of Victoria Victorinix, the undergraduate chair of the English department, where Nelson was a visiting adjunct lecturer. Just five minutes before the accident Professor Victorinix had told Nelson politely but coolly that the department was being forced by budget necessities to terminate his appointment at the end of the semester. Professor Victorinix was a small, slender, steely woman, with cropped, silvery hair, a penetrating gaze, and the trace of a bemused smile always about her mouth. Nelson appreciated her forthrightness, and the fact that she looked at him as she sacked him; indeed, it was Nelson's glance that roamed all over the white walls and spare, elegant shelves of her office, as he swallowed hard and tried not to cry. The emotion would have been an honest response on Nelson's part, but tears wouldn't have changed anything: Professor Victorinix had suffered twenty-five years of a being ignored, condescended to, and worse as a gay woman in academia, and she was unusually immune to the self-pity of wounded young men.

> "You have our gratitude, of course," she said, "for all your efforts on behalf of the department. Though I realize that under the circumstances, that may not mean much to you."

- The second version is better because it is dramatic and because it starts to show rather than tell. This opening puts the reader in the middle of a situation, providing just enough information to make it intriguing and to suggest what's coming without giving everything away. Not only does the new version work better on the macro level of the whole narrative, but it also works better on the micro level of sentences and evocative details.

- During the course of writing *The Lecturer's Tale*, the character of Professor Victorinix changed from a minor character to a major one. She also changed from merely chair of the English department to, possibly, a vampire. These changes forced additional revisions to the opening scene, the final version of which is more evocative, dramatic, and full of physical details:

  > Professor Victorinix was a small, slender, thin-lipped woman with cropped, silvery hair, and a bloodless manner barely masked by a disinterested politesse. Even during the day she kept the blinds of her office drawn, and today she sat in the shadows just beyond the direct glare of the lamp. The reflected glow off her desktop emphasized the sharpness of her cheekbones, the deep groove between her eyebrows, the smooth skullcap curve of her forehead. She regarded Nelson with a gaze that seemed to him aristocratic, ancient, bored.

  > "Under the circumstances," she said, "I realize that our gratitude may not mean much to you."

- The additional details here reinforce the fact that Victorinix is powerful and a bit menacing and that she will be important later on. And the use of Nelson's point of view in the opening reinforces the fact that he's the main character of the book.

- Notice that these revisions serve every level of the book. The larger narrative is served by introducing Nelson's point of view and by providing a more vivid and memorable introduction to Professor Victorinix. The chapter is served by starting with a brief description of the accident, then backtracking to show a bit of what happened just before it. The scene is served by providing more action and dialogue to evoke the situation rather than just describing it. And the prose is served by making the sentences clearer and more dynamic.

Lessons Learned

- As these revisions show, some writers work from the general to the specific. Early drafts may be a kind of summary, without much detail and with more exposition than drama. If you find that's the case with your work, when you're revising, ask yourself: What would readers want from this passage that I'm not giving them? What does the character look like or sound like? Where does the scene take place, and what exactly happens in it?

- The key here is to be your own toughest critic. Consider all the techniques we've looked at in this course—evoking rather than describing, using setting to create mood, creating character through detail, advancing the plot through dialogue, and so on—and apply them to your draft.

- If you're interested in lean prose, another technique you might try is to see how much you can cut out of a paragraph or a sentence without altering its meaning or intent. For example, see if you can get an eight-line paragraph down to two lines. This "Twitter technique" of revision is a useful exercise to prevent passages from inducing boredom.

- Other methods you can try include printing the previous day's work and editing it by hand or reading sections or chapters out loud. Reading your work aloud slows you down, so you're more likely to catch grammatical errors and repeated words. It's also a great way to gauge the rhythm and flow of your sentences and decide where paragraph breaks should be. By hearing the words spoken, you catch many missteps that might otherwise slip by you.

Suggested Reading

Ellroy, *L.A. Confidential*.

Gardner, *The Art of Fiction*.

Hynes, *The Lecturer's Tale*.

———, *Publish and Perish*.

1. Reverse the process of writing and revising that you used in the last lecture. If you dashed out something without looking back, sit down with it again and try to fix whatever you think is wrong with it by using some of the techniques in this lecture. If did your revisions as you wrote, try adding something new to the scene—insert a new character, say, or change the setting, or even change the point of view or verb tense.

Revision without Tears
Lecture 22—Transcript

Revision comes to all of us, like death and taxes, and it's just about as much fun. In the earlier stages of composing a work of fiction, you're often caught up in the thrill of discovery. You're creating new situations and characters that no one has ever seen before. Whatever frustrations you may experience in the act of creation are often made up for by the sheer pleasure of making something new. But then, having created this beautiful, lively, imaginative, world-changing draft, you now have to sit down and look for everything you did wrong.

Revision is about confronting your own mistakes—which were usually made with the highest hopes and the best intentions—and fixing them in such a way that the reader never knows there were any mistakes to begin with.

Not only can revision be hard, unpleasant work, it can lead to despair. The novelist John Gardner, our friend who wrote *The Art of Fiction*, was once so frustrated with his novel *Grendel*, which is a retelling of *Beowulf* from the point of view of the monster, that he threw the manuscript into a fire. Luckily his wife retrieved it before it could burn, and when Gardner calmed down, he went back to work and finished it.

Not all of us take such drastic action to avoid having to revise, but at one point or another, we've all felt the same way John Gardner did. When you reach the end of a draft that you've composed in a white heat, you can believe that you're the greatest writer since Shakespeare. Then when you read it over the next morning, you can feel like the worst hack who ever drew breath. It's enough to make you want to give up and go to law school, like your mother wanted you to.

Much of what makes revision difficult is that you have to consider your draft on every level, more or less all at once. It's the one time in the whole process where you cannot avoid having to think about everything. Not only do you have to ask yourself if the entire narrative works as a whole, but you have to ask yourself if all the individual parts do what they're supposed to and if they all pull in the same direction. Is each character complete and believable? Did

I use the right point of view, the right verb tense, the right setting? Does each chapter round off and lead to the next? Does each scene? Are my sentences interesting, elegant, and memorable? Having to think about all of this at once is daunting, to say the least, but there are ways to approach it that can make it less intimidating.

The first step of revision is to start thinking about it from the very beginning of your project. You need to prepare for it from the moment you first start writing. Remember that saying from Nick Lowe that I mentioned in the last lecture—"Bash it out now and tart it up later"? For the longest time, I used to keep that motto on an index card that was taped to the wall over my desk. In the last lecture, I cited it mainly as a reminder that you should forge ahead as energetically and heedlessly as necessary to create your drafts in the first place, that you shouldn't worry too much to begin with about length, consistency, economy, and so on.

But look at that motto again and take note of the fact that it comes in two parts: "bash it out now," and *then* "tart it up later." Both halves are equally important, and that second half serves as a subconscious reminder that even during the honeymoon period when you're making something new, getting the story down is only the beginning of the process. The motto reminds you, even during the heat of composition, that you're going to have to change things later on.

In other words, composing and revising are inextricably linked. How you revise depends in large part on how you composed the draft in the first place. As I explained in the last lecture, there are different ways of composing drafts. You can write a whole draft of the complete narrative without looking back, or you can do individual drafts of each section or chapter before you go on to the next one. By choosing one of these methods over the other, you're necessarily choosing how you're going to revise.

If you write a whole draft without looking back and don't start revising until it's done, then you've got all the revision to do all at once. This may make revision seem grim and joyless, because you're looking at rewriting days or months of previous work. Still, forging ahead without having to worry every day about what you wrote the day before can make writing that first draft easier.

On the other hand, if you work and rework each individual section before you proceed to the next one, you'll be revising as you go. This may make the revision a little less daunting, since you do it in easy stages and not all at once. It becomes part of your daily routine. Of course, revising as you go is no guarantee that when you've reached the end, you still won't have to go back and fix mistakes or even make major changes. Even with the second method, you still reach a point where you have to think about whether the narrative works as a whole, and whether all the individual parts do what they're supposed to do.

Now that I've scared the bejesus out of you, let me suggest some ways of approaching revision so that you don't feel depressed or intimidated. And the best way to do that, I've decided, is to use an example from my own work, and so I beg your indulgence here to inflict some of my prose on you. My excuse is that I have access to my early drafts and I can remember what I was thinking when I revised them, which I don't have and can't do for other writers. With that excuse out of the way, let me talk about how I revised the opening paragraphs of my second novel, *The Lecturer's Tale*.

In 1997, I published a book called *Publish and Perish*, which was a collection of three novellas. Each one of these novellas combined supernatural horror with academic satire. *The Lecturer's Tale* was originally intended to be one of the novellas in *Publish and Perish*, but the more I worked on it, the longer it got, and it ended up as the longest novel I've written so far.

Since I'm talking about the opening paragraphs, you don't need to know much about the book. Suffice it to say it's the story of Nelson Humboldt, a failing academic who, in the first chapter of the book, loses his right index finger in a freak accident on the Quadrangle of the campus where he teaches. The supernatural element in the story comes from the fact that after Nelson's finger is reattached, he discovers that he can make anybody do anything he wants by touching them with his reattached finger. Since this is also an academic satire, he uses this power to save his teaching job and then, as he becomes more corrupt, to work his way up to the top of his university's

English department. It was intended to be a sort of mash-up of *Faust* and the Broadway musical *How to Succeed in Business without Really Trying*.

Here's my original version of the first paragraph, back when I was still thinking it was going to be only a novella and not a novel. Bear with me—this is kind of long, and it's not very good:

> Crossing the Quad at noon on a grey Halloween, Nelson Humboldt's finger was severed in a freak accident. Oddly enough, he hadn't been hurrying as he usually did at this time of day, and anyway, Nelson was a tall fellow, standing a full head taller than many of the young people around him. If anyone could see where he was going, it was Nelson Humboldt. On the other hand, this was the busiest class change of the day, as students entered the Quad from all four corners at once, in a vast, slowly moving press that swirled with complex currents and eddies. Out of the eddies little knots would form, students talking loudly in the brisk, damp autumn air, each with a backpack slung over one shoulder. Even when he was in a hurry to get to his next class, Nelson loved this scene. It was the epitome of what life at university ought to be: bright, good-humored, energetic young people chattering happily about their classes, their lives, their loves, in a hurry to be somewhere else. Unlike many of his colleagues—unlike most of them, truth to tell—Nelson tried to be a fundamentally cheerful man. It seemed to him that all of life should have such heedless momentum, all of life should be so full of hope.

> But today Nelson was unusually distracted, and this, he decided later, was the reason for the accident. He had just come from the cramped office of the undergraduate chair of the English department, where Nelson was a lecturer, and just ten minutes before she had told him compassionately but briskly that the department was being forced by budget necessities to terminate his appointment at the end of the semester. This meant not only that his income would stop on the last day of the year, just after Christmas, and that his academic career had now become well and truly dead in the water, but that his health insurance for himself and his family would end in eight

weeks. Nelson had no savings to speak of and no prospects, the job market being what it was, and now he was about to have to no job, and he moved much more slowly than usual through the press on the Quad, still in shock, his mind elsewhere, letting himself be buffeted by the currents and eddies of passing students. The loss of his finger was just the last straw.

I think you can see what's wrong with this, as I did when I was writing this lecture and looked at it for the first time in nearly 20 years. The passage doesn't really work on any level. It doesn't work on the micro level of sentences and phrases, which tend to pile up without going anywhere, and it also doesn't work on the macro level of the narrative as a whole—or at least what I imagined the complete narrative to be when I started.

A lot of the sentences are just plain clumsy. The very first sentence is a particularly egregious example. Here it is again, in case you fell asleep: "Crossing the Quad at noon on a grey Halloween, Nelson Humboldt's finger was severed in a freak accident." Grammatically, that sentence makes it sound as if it was Nelson's finger crossing the Quad, not Nelson himself.

Another problem is that the very first paragraph doesn't really do what a first paragraph is supposed to do. As you may recall, a first paragraph is supposed to intrigue the reader with a character or a situation, and it is supposed to suggest something about the narrative to come. After telling us that Nelson has lost a finger without telling us how, the first paragraph dives down the rabbit hole into a sentimental, metaphorical description of how students mingle on the Quad at the center of campus.

After that pointless digression, the second paragraph shoehorns in the bare minimum of Nelson's backstory, without giving us any visceral, individual details that bring Nelson and his situation to life. We know he has a wife and kids, but we don't know anything about them. We can't see them at all, and we can only barely see Nelson. The only thing we know about him as a person is that he's tall.

In fact, that's the worst fault of the whole passage: I opened this narrative with nothing but exposition, with nothing but an undramatic summary. The sentences are clumsy and rambling and inelegant, there's no evocative detail, and the passage doesn't really suggest much about what is to come. If it had been somebody else's book, I'd have never finished reading that first paragraph, let alone the rest of the story.

So I tried again. Alas, I regret to say that in the second version, the first paragraph didn't change much, so I won't inflict it on you again. But I began to make more of an effort in the second paragraph. Here it is, version two of the second paragraph:

> But today Nelson had been badly shaken, and perhaps he hadn't been watching where he was going. He had just come from the spartan seventh-floor office of Victoria Victorinix, the undergraduate chair of the English department, where Nelson was a visiting adjunct lecturer. Just five minutes before the accident, Professor Victorinix had told Nelson politely but coolly that the department was being forced by budget necessities to terminate his appointment at the end of the semester. Professor Victorinix was a small, slender, steely woman, with cropped, silvery hair, a penetrating gaze, and the trace of a bemused smile always about her mouth. Nelson appreciated her forthrightness, and the fact that she looked at him as she sacked him; indeed, it was Nelson's glance that roamed all over the white walls and spare, elegant shelves of her office, as he swallowed hard and tried not to cry. The emotion would have been an honest response on Nelson's part, but tears wouldn't have changed anything: Professor Victorinix had suffered twenty-five years of being ignored, condescended to, and worse as a gay woman in academia, and she was unusually immune to the self-pity of wounded young men.

> "You have our gratitude, of course," she said, "for all your efforts on behalf of the department. Though I realize that under the circumstances, that may not mean much to you."

This, if I do say so myself, is an improvement, though it still had a long way to go. The bare, unevocative summary of the first version is gone. You get the rudiments of an actual scene, with two characters who are actually interacting with each other. One of them even speaks.

The second version is better because it's more dramatic. In other words, it's better because I have slowed down and started to show rather than tell. Now, at least the second paragraph of *The Lecturer's Tale* was beginning to do what the opening of a narrative ought to do. It puts the reader in the middle of a situation—*in medias res*—with just enough information to make it intriguing and to suggest what's coming, but without giving everything away. Instead of just telling you what Nelson's problem was, I put him in a room with someone else and showed the situation to you.

And not only does that new second paragraph work better on the macro level of the whole narrative, it works better on the micro level of sentences and evocative details. Instead of the nameless, faceless woman who speaks to Nelson "compassionately but briskly" in the first version, we get a woman who has a name—Professor Victorinix—and she has a physical description—she's small, slender, and steely, with cropped, silvery hair and a penetrating gaze. She also has a history—she's a lesbian who has been an academic for 25 years—and she has a personality—she is polite, but chilly.

In my original conception of the story, this character only served one function. She was intended to fire Nelson in the opening chapter, after which she was never supposed to appear again. And when I was writing this revision of the opening, it still hadn't occurred to me that she might be anything more. I just wanted to make that opening passage more visceral. This meant I had to make it more of a scene, which meant in turn I had to make her more of a character.

Now before I read you the version that appears in the finished book, I want to remind you again that revision often requires you to think about everything at once—from the level of phrases and sentences to the nature and importance of individual characters and all the way up to the shape of the narrative as a whole. *The Lecturer's Tale* was my third book, but only my second novel. As I told you in the last lecture, I wrote it differently than I had written my first novel.

With *The Wild Colonial Boy*, I had written out four complete drafts by hand. With *The Lecturer's Tale*, I first used the method that I still use now. I revised as I went, more or less finishing one section before I moved on to the next, so that by time I got to the end, the book was more or less finished. But the operative phrase here is "more or less," because with *The Lecturer's Tale*, and with every book since, I have found myself having to go back and change something at the beginning of the book because of a discovery I made about the story or the characters later on.

Over the course of writing *The Lecturer's Tale*, I made two discoveries about Professor Victorinix which caused me to go back and change passages that I thought I had already finished. One was that Professor Victorinix was not a minor character, but one of the major characters in the book. For example, she turns out to be one of three major characters who take part in the big, over-the-top climax of the novel.

And in keeping with the supernatural flavor of my satire, I also realized that Professor Victorinix was probably a vampire. I never made this explicit, because the supernatural element in the book was mainly a vehicle for my satire of contemporary literary theory, but I did want to have some fun with the idea.

These two discoveries—that Professor Victorinix was a major character and that she was even scarier than a mere English department chair—forced me to go back to that opening scene when I was nearly done with the whole book and revise it to reflect her new status. Here's the opening scene, as it appears in the finished book:

> Crossing the Quad on a Halloween Friday, as the clock in the library tower tolled thirteen under a windy, dramatic sky, Nelson Humboldt lost his right index finger in a freak accident. Someone called his name three times out of the midday press of students, and as he turned to answer, Nelson stumbled over a young woman stooping to the pavement behind him. Falling backwards, he threw his hand out to catch himself, and his finger was severed by the whirring spokes of a passing bicycle.

Only minutes before, in the shadowy office of Victoria Victorinix, the English Department's undergraduate chair, Nelson had lost his job as a visiting adjunct lecturer. He had sat on the far side of Professor Victorinix's severely rectilinear desk, his hands tightly clutching his knees, while she told him with a cool courtesy that the department was forced by budget necessities to terminate his appointment at the end of the semester, only six weeks away.

"You have our gratitude, of course," she said, folding her slim hands in the icy blue light of her desk lamp, "for all your efforts on behalf of the department."

Professor Victorinix was a small, slender, thin-lipped woman with cropped, silvery hair, and a bloodless manner barely masked by a disinterested politesse. Even during the day she kept the blinds of her office drawn, and today she sat in the shadows just beyond the direct glare of the lamp. The reflected glow off her desktop emphasized the sharpness of her cheekbones, the deep groove between her eyebrows, the smooth skullcap curve of her forehead. She regarded Nelson with a gaze that seemed to him aristocratic, ancient, bored.

"Under the circumstances," she said, "I realize that our gratitude may not mean much to you."

Nelson swallowed hard and tried not to cry. His own gaze, in order to avoid meeting hers, darted all over the office. His blurry glance took in pale grey walls, rigorously ordered books in steel and glass shelves, a muted etching in a silver frame of the Countess Bathory in her bath. Nelson appreciated that Professor Victorinix looked at him as she fired him, but couldn't she turn away, just for a moment?

"I, I'm sorry." Nelson cleared his throat. "Don't worry about me."

Now, you may not think this is necessarily better than the first two versions, but I think you will agree that it's certainly more evocative and dramatic. It's full of visceral physical details and a lot of vivid imagery.

To begin with, I fixed that clumsy opening sentence and made it clear that it was Nelson himself who was crossing the Quad, and not just his forefinger.

And I also added more visceral and ominous detail in the very first sentence, by adding the clause about the clock ringing thirteen under a "windy, dramatic" sky.

The first paragraph is also improved by briefly foreshadowing what's going to happen to Nelson, and by deleting that long description of the students milling about on the Quad.

Both the opening paragraph and the sentences that make it up are shorter, sharper, more detailed, and more focused. It's a more dramatic and more striking opening paragraph.

Then, with the next few paragraphs, the narrative shifts slightly back in time in order to do three things. I introduce Nelson, I briefly explain his situation, and I introduce Professor Victorinix. Nelson's fear of the powerful woman across the desk from him is much clearer in this version, because I evoke his fear with physical details: He clutches his knees, he swallows hard and tries not to cry, his glance darts all over the room.

But even though Nelson is going to be the main character, it's Victorinix who dominates the scene. In fact, looking at it now, years after I finished the book, I'll confess that I rather gleefully trowelled on the vampire detail: Victorinix is slender, thin-lipped, and bloodless. She has silvery hair, sharp cheekbones, and a high forehead like a skull. I also gave her three adjectives—aristocratic, ancient, bored—that might have come straight out of an Anne Rice novel.

Even the setting is designed to suggest "vampire": she keeps her office blinds drawn during the day, and she sits just out of the cone of "icy blue" light from her lamp. And again, as in the first paragraph, the sentences are shorter, sharper, and full of evocative and suggestive detail: the glare of her lamp, her rectilinear desk, the steel and glass shelves, the antique etching in a silver frame. Even the subject of the etching, the legendary Countess Bathory, who reputedly drained young women of their blood, is another vampire reference.

All of this, and some further detail that comes in the next few paragraphs, is intended to reinforce the professor's power and menace, and to suggest that she is going to be important later on.

But it's all told from Nelson's point of view, which reinforces the fact that he's the main character of the book. We see Victorinix and her office from his point of view, and we participate only in his physical and emotional responses: He swallows hard and tries not to cry; he avoids meeting her gaze; he wishes she wouldn't look at him; he has to clear his throat before he is able to speak. Nelson may not get much of a physical description in these first paragraphs, but we get a vivid sense of him as a nervous person. And as soon as he leaves her office, I spend the rest of the chapter showing his accident and filling in his backstory in much more detail.

As I was making these revisions, I was thinking about two things at once. I was thinking about both the book as a whole and the needs of the individual scene. And the way I dealt with every level of revision was by adding more detail. I served the larger narrative by introducing Nelson's point of view and by producing a more vivid introduction to Professor Victorinix. I served the chapter by starting with a brief description of the accident and then backtracking a bit to show what happened just before, implying that the rest of the chapter was going to show the accident in more detail. I served the scene itself by providing more action and dialogue, to evoke the situation rather than just describing it. And I served the prose by making the sentences clearer and more dynamic.

However, adding more evocative detail doesn't necessarily mean adding more words. The published opening of *The Lecturer's Tale* that I've quoted to you is 377 words long, while that lamentable first draft was 406 words, and it wasn't nearly as memorable or detailed. I used more words in the first version to say less than I did in the final version with fewer words.

So what did I learn or gain through these revisions? I learned that, in my work, anyway, I often work from the general to the specific. My early drafts tend to be a kind of summary, without much detail. My early drafts are often more expository than dramatic. Then, when I look at them again, I ask myself, what would a reader want from this passage that I'm not giving her?

For example, what do the characters look like? Where is this scene taking place? What exactly happens in the scene? What do the characters say to each other, and how do they say it?

In other words, when you're revising, you need to be your own toughest critic. You want take all the techniques we've talked about in these lectures up until now—about evoking rather than describing; about using setting to evoke mood; about creating character through detail; about advancing the plot through dialogue; about letting a character's point of view guide the reader through a scene, and so on—and apply them to your draft. However, I hasten to add that not every writer revises the way I do.

James Joyce, for example, is said to have added nearly a third of the finished version of *Ulysses* in the galley proofs, or the sample pages that the printers had already set in type. If you've ever read *Ulysses*, or tried to, you'll realize that Joyce was not a writer interested in economy and concision.

On the other hand, the American crime novelist James Ellroy developed an aggressively telegraphic style for his later books almost by accident. When his editor told him that he needed to cut a hundred pages from the manuscript of his novel *L.A. Confidential*, Ellroy took an unusual approach. Most writers would have cut whole scenes and characters, but Ellroy kept all his scenes and characters, and instead cut what he called the "unnecessary words" from each sentence. Not only did he significantly shorten the book, he in effect invented a new, telegraphic prose style for himself.

I've attempted this myself in my own work, trying to see how much I can cut out of a paragraph or a sentence without altering the meaning of it, though not as aggressively as James Ellroy. Sometimes, if I'm editing something on my laptop, I play a little game with myself: if a particular paragraph, for example, has 10 lines, I'll try to see if I can get it down to eight lines. I don't necessarily recommend this technique to everybody. Some writers just aren't interested in lean prose. But if you're going for economy, or just trying to keep a passage from being boring, it's a useful exercise. You might even call it the "Twitter technique" of revision, since it's very similar to the effort it takes to make a wisecrack or a pithy epigram in less than 140 characters.

And, because I am old and I can remember what life and writing were like before spellcheck and search-and-replace, I still usually do my revision and line-editing by hand, with a pen, on paper. I do 99 percent of my composition on a keyboard, but I start each workday by printing out yesterday's work and marking up the text with a pen as I read through it. After that, I enter the changes on the computer file.

If I'm pressed for time or feeling unusually contemporary, I might occasionally revise something directly on my laptop without printing it out. But there's still something about working with a pen and a printout that helps me think. Perhaps it's the last vestige of the muscle memory I gained from those four handwritten drafts of my first novel. I still have the callus on my middle finger of my right hand from having gripped the pen so tightly all those years ago. I guess I'm afraid that if it ever goes away, my career as a writer is over.

Another technique I have found very helpful is to read each draft of a section or a chapter aloud. Many writers do this, and it's an excellent way to pay particular attention to your prose. For one thing, reading aloud is necessarily slower, so you're more likely to catch things like grammatical errors or repeated words. For another, it's a great way to gauge the rhythm and flow of the sentences and to figure out where the paragraph breaks should be.

Please note that I'm not saying that the best prose is that which reads well out loud. There are some very great books, such as *Mrs. Dalloway*, which would be rather tricky to read out loud. But by reading aloud through the text at least once, by hearing the words spoken rather than just scanning them, you can catch a lot of things that might otherwise slip by you.

As an exercise, take the exercise you did for the last lecture, where you tried writing a draft all at once or revising as you go, and reverse the process. For example, if you dashed out something without looking back, sit down with it again and try to figure out whatever you think is wrong with it by using some of the techniques in this lecture—you could read it aloud, for example. And if you rewrote as you went, you might take the same scene and try to add something new to it—insert a new character, say, or change the setting, or even change the point of view or verb tense.

Next time, I'll be talking about how fiction writers do research, and I'll be talking about Hillary Mantel and her research for her historical novels *Wolf Hall* and *Bring up the Bodies*, as well the author Jim Crace, who has a unique approach to doing research for his books.

Approaches to Researching Fiction
Lecture 23

The amount of research required for a work of fiction depends on the sort of story you're telling. If your story is about a police detective who falls in love, then you might be able to get away with parroting a bit of cop slang to establish your character's identity. But if your story is about the detective investigating a murder, then you need to learn enough about police work to make the character seem realistic. To put it simply, the more research matters to your narrative, the more research you have to do. As we'll see in this lecture, it's also important to strike a balance between factual accuracy and the exercise of your imagination.

Varying Approaches to Research

- One pitfall of writing a story that requires research is that the research sometimes overwhelms the story; in those cases, writers lean too hard on the research and not enough on their imaginations. In fact, the necessity of being completely faithful to the facts is not universally accepted among all writers. Two contemporary writers who personify differing opinions on this issue are Hilary Mantel and Jim Crace.

- Mantel is best known for her historical novels about Thomas Cromwell, who was a Lord Chancellor of the Tudor king Henry VIII. The first two books, *Wolf Hall* and *Bring up the Bodies*, each won the Man Booker Prize, and Mantel has often talked about how much research went into them. In more than one interview, she has stated that historical novelists have a moral responsibility to get their facts straight.

- Jim Crace is another celebrated British author whose novels are often set in the distant past, yet Crace declines to call such books as *The Gift of Stones* (set in prehistoric Britain) and *Quarantine* (about Christ's 40 days in the wilderness) historical novels. He prefers to think of each of them as being set in a sort of alternative, imaginative world.
    - Crace does some research for his books, but he makes up many of the details. In part, this is because he's not interested in the

actual history so much as he is in using a particular historical period as a metaphor for contemporary concerns. The impulse behind *The Gift of Stones*, for example, was the industrial decline of the British city of Birmingham.

- If you read *The Gift of Stones* without knowing that it was originally intended to be a metaphor for the decline of British manufacturing, it reads as a powerful account of an ancient, alien way of life. Whether it's historically accurate is more or less irrelevant to the literary merit of the book or to the truths the book speaks about human nature and the effects of technological change on everyday life.

- Rather than relying on exhaustive research to underpin his narratives, Crace pays close attention to his language, using careful word choices to construct fictional details that seem utterly convincing even if they aren't as scrupulously researched as the details in Mantel's books. In fact, Crace insisted in an interview that if you pick the right words, you don't need to get the facts right. For him, a simple bit of vocabulary can make a fictional world come alive.

- There's an obvious difference in intent between Crace and Mantel. Crace doesn't claim that his novels are accurate; in fact, he tries to subvert the idea of accuracy in fiction and insist on the primacy of storytelling. For Mantel, fidelity to what actually happened matters a great deal.
  - It's also true, however, that Mantel is not slavishly dedicated to absolute historical accuracy in all instances. Shrewdly, she has her characters speak in a modern-sounding idiom that makes them seem real to 21st-century readers without also making them sound anachronistic.

  - The research Mantel did for *Wolf Hall* is evident on nearly every page, but what makes the novel soar is the way her imagination inhabits the mind of Thomas Cromwell and the way her muscular and modern prose evokes his world.

o In contrast, Crace's novel *Harvest* is set in the same period of English history as Mantel's novels, but Crace never mentions the year, nor does he include any reference to real historical figures or situations. Instead, he provides a detailed and intimate account of village life. His work has a contemporary immediacy, but Crace evokes the feeling of a distant time and place mainly by using bits of archaic vocabulary.

A Middle Ground

- *Gerontius* is a work by another British novelist, James Hamilton-Paterson, loosely based on the life of the composer Sir Edward Elgar. In the author's note at the beginning of the book, Hamilton-Paterson talks briefly about his research for the book, explaining that he deliberately changed some of the details of Elgar's life, and at the end of the note, he says, "For the rest, I tried to be as factually correct as was interesting."

- This improvisatory, ad hoc attitude to using research seems a sensible approach because it puts the story first. As Gardner said, the primary purpose of a work of fiction is to create a vivid and continuous dream in the mind of the reader, and the two main requirements of any fictional narrative are to be both believable and interesting.

© IPGGutenbergUKLtd/iStock/Thinkstock.

Even the most mainstream novel may often require a few hours of research so that the writer doesn't distract the reader with unnecessary errors of fact.

o For this reason, it's important to get the facts right because doing so will make the narrative more interesting and believable. At the very least, you don't want to distract the reader with obvious, easily preventable mistakes. If your reader must stop to think about something that doesn't seem right, you've broken the surface tension of the dream.

- At the same time, you don't want to be boring. Even Mantel has warned aspiring historical novelists not to inundate the reader with everything you've learned. "Don't show off," she says. "Your reader only needs to know about one tenth of what you know. Depth of knowledge gives the writer confidence and suppleness, but doesn't need to be demonstrated on every page."

- Knowing when to back off from the research is also important to the process of writing itself. A work may be backed by extensive research, but it still needs vividly imagined scenes and character. If it is filled only with useless detail at the expense of the story, it will be monumentally dull.

- If you're writing a research-intensive narrative, the research and the writing should be inseparable. In practice, this means that you need to do the writing and the research at the same time, and this, in turn, means that to begin with, you will be writing scenes without having much of an idea of what you're talking about.

Case Study: Using Research Productively

- Let's consider a scene from an incomplete and unpublished historical novel about an 18th-century Dutch explorer named Jacob Roggeveen, who was the European discoverer of Easter Island. In this scene, Jacob travels from his home in the small Dutch city of Middelburg to the much larger and more cosmopolitan city of Amsterdam, where he hoped to win financial support for his expedition to the South Pacific from the Dutch West India Company.

- Early research revealed that Jacob was a notary, which was a kind of lawyer; that he had never married or had children; and that he was a member of a heretical Calvinist sect. Other than that, the first draft of the scene was written without much research into what Amsterdam was like at the time of Jacob's visit. After the rough version of the scene was written, the additional facts that needed to be researched became clear: What would Jacob have seen and heard in the streets of Amsterdam in the year 1719, and how would his fringe religious beliefs have affected his reaction to the vibrant street life of a large city?

- The answers to these and other questions made the scene come alive in the final version.

  o For example, one important discovery was that the headquarters building of the Dutch West India Company was just off a street near the docks called Haarlemmerstraat. The street was mostly lined with taverns and brothels that catered to sailors.

  o Another important finding was that the members of Jacob's religious sect did not believe in the idea of sin in the traditional sense. Instead, they saw what others called sinful behavior as ignorance of humanity's oneness with God, who controlled everything people did.

- Here's an excerpt from the scene that attempts to capture what Jacob might have seen and heard on a night in Amsterdam in 1719 and how he might have reacted to it:

  After a meal of bread and cheese and beer in the smoky kitchen of the inn, Jacob ascended to his hot, airless room up under the eaves. The little window in his room was high—he had to stand to see out of it—and he pushed it open and looked down the steep slope of the roof. Twilight filled the square below, punctuated by fans of lamplight falling out of tavern doorways. He took off his shoes and his waistcoat and tried to sleep on the swaybacked bed, but he only tossed and turned in the breathless heat, kept awake by the nightly riot below. Woven through the roar of the crowd were the whine of fiddles and the wheeze of hurdy gurdys, playing songs Jacob remembered from childhood, rollicking dance tunes accompanied by the clatter of boots against cobbles as sailors and whores danced in the square. Sudden, violent squalls rose above the general racket: the harsh voices of drunken men braying the words of "The Cuckoo's Nest." The shattering screams of women dissolving into cackling laughter. Bottles breaking. The wordless shouting of men in a fight, the loser's howl as a blade pierced him. More cackling laughter. And as the racket finally receded near dawn into a lone sailor singing

Lecture 23: Approaches to Researching Fiction

tunelessly to himself as he staggered along, Jacob heard carnal groans coming from an entryway just below his window. It was all what his mother used to call wickedness, but Jacob, in his sweaty clothes and tangled sheets, struggled to convince himself that there was no such thing as sin, only ignorance and error, that the poor souls cutting each other in the street or rutting in the doorway were simply stuck in their own flesh like ships run aground in the mud.

- This scene worked because research and imagination played off each other powerfully. Research revealed what a night in the Haarlemmerstraat would have been like, and imagination enabled that experience to be filtered through the consciousness of a single character.

- In the end, the lesson to learn from this case study is that you need to put the story and the characters first. Using your imagination is every bit as important as getting your facts straight. Indeed, we might say that research is just another tool in the service of the imagination. It serves the same function in fiction that plotting, character, and dialogue do: It helps to suggest, to evoke, to put readers in a time and place they might otherwise never experience.

Suggested Reading

Crace, "The Art of Fiction No. 179."

———, *The Gift of Stones*.

———, *Harvest*.

———, *Quarantine*.

Hamilton-Paterson, *Gerontius*.

MacFarquhar, "The Dead Are Real."

Mantel, *Bring up the Bodies*.

———, "Hilary Mantel on Teaching a Historical Fiction Masterclass."

————, *Wolf Hall.*

Wilson, "*Bring up the Bodies* by Hilary Mantel."

1. Pick a historical character who interests you, such as Abraham Lincoln or Margaret Thatcher, and write just a single scene about that person doing something ordinary and private, such as playing with his or her children or fixing something to eat, but at an important historical moment. Abraham Lincoln might be thinking about the Emancipation Proclamation, for example, as he plays checkers with his son, or Margaret Thatcher might be making herself a pot of tea late one night at the start of the Falklands War. Try to make the scene personal and intimate without letting the historical events dominate. Remember that research serves the same function in fiction that plotting, character, and dialogue do: to suggest, to evoke, to put readers in a time and place they might otherwise never experience.

Approaches to Researching Fiction
Lecture 23—Transcript

I can't imagine a work of fiction that doesn't involve at least a little bit of research. Some narratives are obviously research-intensive. Historical novels, certain types of science fiction, thrillers that center around a profession such as the law or medicine or espionage—these and other types of genre fiction require that the author have some knowledge about a particular subject. Even the most mainstream, middlebrow literary novel may often require a few hours of research so that the writer doesn't distract the reader with unnecessary errors of fact.

Years ago, a friend of mine wrote a scene in which two people sat on a California beach on a summer evening and watched the constellation Orion rise over the ocean. Now, I'm no astronomer, but I did know enough to point out to my friend that a) most beaches in California face west; b) constellations always rise in the east; and c) Orion is visible in the evening only during the winter months. After being peeved at me for being a know-it-all, my friend changed the scene. Even though what was happening in the sky wasn't important to the story, it was easier for him to get it right than to risk annoying the rare reader who might have noticed the mistake.

I've been on both ends of this particular continuum, and several places in between. My first novel, *The Wild Colonial Boy*, was about the violent politics of Northern Ireland in the 1980s. I read a lot of books on Irish history, politics, and culture, and I spent a few very nervous days walking the streets of Belfast, taking notes. I would never call myself an expert, but at the time I wrote the novel back in the late 1980s, I had acquired a basic understanding of Irish history and the British law on terrorism, as well as a rough grasp of the sort of slang an IRA bomber might use.

At the other end of the spectrum, my novel *Next* takes place in the present day, and much of it is set in the city where I live, Austin, Texas. That doesn't mean I didn't do any research. It just means that the research was easier and less time-consuming than my research for *The Wild Colonial Boy*.

461

For example, when I wanted to set a scene on a certain stretch of Sixth Street in Austin, I just walked those few blocks and took notes about everything that might stand out for my character. And when I set a scene in a fictional coffee bar downtown, I spent a few hours one morning in a real coffee bar. I took note of the menu, the décor, the patrons, and the music the baristas played on the stereo. Many of these details ended up in the book.

Even when I've written scenes that are pure fantasy, I've found myself performing a little bit of due diligence. Part of the climactic sequence of my novel *Kings of Infinite Space* features ritual human sacrifice in a cave— just roll with me on this. And even though it's a patently ridiculous scene, I wanted the details of the cave to at least feel realistic, so I spent a few days visiting several publicly accessible caves in the Austin area.

As you can see from these examples, the type and the amount of research you do for a work of fiction depends on the sort of story you're trying to tell. For example, say your story is about a police detective and a thoracic surgeon who fall in love. The point of the story is the love affair and not what they do for a living, so you might be able to get away with parroting a little bit of cop slang and some surgical jargon in order to establish your characters' authenticity. On the other hand, say your story is about the detective investigating a murder, or about the surgeon facing a particularly tricky procedure. In that case, you're going to need to learn enough about police work or surgery to make it look as though your characters know what they're doing. So, obviously, if your narrative depends on research, the more research you have to do.

But even when research is important to your work, you still need to find the balance between factual accuracy on the one hand and the exercise of your imagination on the other. Without naming names, I can think of a number of novels I've read over the years which were more interesting for their research than they were as fiction. If the research overwhelms the story, then you're leaning too hard on the research and not enough on your imagination.

In fact, the necessity of being completely faithful to the facts is not universally accepted among all writers. Some writers make their dedication to accuracy a point of pride and even a selling point for their work, while others are equally proud of their ability to invent a reality that may read as if it's factually accurate, but isn't necessarily. Two great contemporary writers who personify this divide are the English novelists Hilary Mantel and Jim Crace. Each of these wonderful writers have written novels that seem to require a fair amount of research, but they each take very different approaches to it.

Hilary Mantel is best known for her historical novels about Thomas Cromwell, who was a Lord Chancellor of the Tudor king Henry VIII. The first two books, *Wolf Hall* and *Bring up the Bodies*, each won the Man Booker Prize, Britain's most prestigious literary award. Mantel has often talked about how much research went into these two books, which was probably as much as would be required for an academic degree. In more than one interview, Mantel has stated that historical novelists actually have a moral responsibility to get the facts straight. She was especially vehement in a *New Yorker* profile, where she said, "I cannot describe to you what revulsion it inspires in me when people play around with the facts. If I was to distort something just to make it more convenient or dramatic, I would feel I'd failed as a writer."

And here she is in another interview, talking less prescriptively about how she enjoys crafting a compelling fictional version out of historical reality:

> I have a general faith that true stories surpass invention, in their twists and turns. I enjoy the research, and being ingenious in what I do with it. I like to see what can be made from a little scrap of evidence, without distorting it. … I actually like the constraints, enjoy solving the narrative problems that arise when you have strict guidelines of fact. One problem is that real life does not have a neat dramatic shape, so you have to find it. There are techniques: you can't falsify the order of events, but you can control the order in which you report them, and the emphasis you give them. You can't change the facts of an incident, but you can change its whole feel and meaning by the angle from which you report it.

Now, compare this approach with that of Jim Crace, another celebrated and award-winning British author whose novels are often set in the distant past. His book *The Gift of Stones* is set in prehistoric Britain, when people were making the transition from stone tools to bronze ones, and his novel *Quarantine* is about Christ's 40 days in the wilderness, told from the point of view of some of the other residents of the Judean desert at the time.

Crace, however, declines to call either of these books historical novels. He prefers to think of each of them as being set in a sort of alternate, imaginary world that some of his readers have called "Craceland." He does some research for these books, but a lot of the details he just makes up. In part, this is because he's not interested in the actual history as much as he is interested in using a particular historical period as a metaphor for contemporary concerns.

For example, the impulse behind his novel *The Gift of Stones* was the industrial decline of the British city of Birmingham, where he lived for many years. Here's Crace talking about the book in an interview in the *Paris Review*:

> I could have written a realist novel, set in Birmingham, about the collapse of the motorcar industry—which is roughly the political impulse of the book. A realist writer would do that, but a nonrealist writer such as me has to find a way to dislocate the subject rather than to locate the subject in a familiar world. I was searching for a parallel moment and I found it at the end of the Stone Age: you can sneer at our terrible village accent and our ugly village center, but the world will always want stone bashers to make the cutters and the scrapers and the arrows and the axes, they would have thought. How could anyone have imagined that something would come along that was sharper, harder, and lighter than stone? And then along comes bronze.

And yet, if you read *The Gift of Stones*, as I did, without knowing that it was originally intended to be a metaphor for the decline of British manufacturing, it reads as a powerful account of an ancient, alien way of life. Whether it's historically accurate or not is more or less irrelevant to the literary merit of the book, or to the truths the book speaks about human nature and the effects of technological change on everyday life.

Rather than rely on exhaustive research to underpin his narratives, Crace instead pays especially close attention to his language. He makes very careful word choices to construct fictional details that seem utterly convincing even if they aren't as scrupulously researched as the details in Hilary Mantel's books.

In fact, later in the same *Paris Review* interview, Crace insists that if you pick the right words, you don't need to get the facts right. Here's how he puts it:

> My wife and my editor think I do lots of research. And I encourage them in their delusion as it makes me seem hardworking. But actually I don't research. I oppose research. What I do is a bit of background reading in order to work out how to tell my lies. I don't look for information, I look for vocabulary and for the odd little emotional idea that will give some oxygen to my imagination. Vocabulary is the Trojan horse that smuggles the lie. Facts don't help. If you're not a persuasive talker at a party, no one's going to believe you, even if everything you say is true. But if you're a persuasive liar then everyone is fooled.

Crace then gives an example of how a simple bit of vocabulary can make a fictional world come alive, by talking about a trip he took to the Judean desert before he started writing *Quarantine*, his book about Christ in the wilderness:

> Me and Izzat, my Bedouin guide, had been sleeping out in the desert under his jeep. It was the perfect morning. No one around, the bluest sky, and just baked landscape stretching away forever. Izzat asked, How did you sleep? He spoke impeccable English and Arabic. I said, Me? I slept like a log. And, as I said it, I saw his eyes narrow and I looked over his shoulder into the desert. Not a single log! All I could see, maybe a kilometer away, was an old tumbled thornbush. I understood immediately that even though Izzat and I had language in common, this metaphor didn't travel. The metaphor couldn't cross the Mediterranean. Logs don't sleep in Judea. So I said to him, How did you sleep? He said, I slept like a dead donkey.

If you'd have kicked me, I wouldn't have woken. I borrowed that phrase for the book. What it told me was that plain facts weren't going to help me convince people that I knew about the Judean desert two thousand years ago, but that vocabulary would do it. The trick of fiction was to remember to turn all my logs into donkeys.

Now, Crace is being a little disingenuous here, of course. He says he opposes research, but he did book a trip to the same desert where Jesus reputedly spent his 40 days. And he did learn a vivid metaphor from his Bedouin guide that he would never have dreamed up on his own just sitting at his desk in Birmingham. But even so, while Hilary Mantel can talk about Tudor England as knowledgeably as a history professor, Jim Crace by his own admission has no expertise or even any special interest in the history of Judea in the time of Christ. And yet he's created a compelling and believable narrative set in something like that world.

There's an obvious difference in intent here: Jim Crace isn't claiming that his novels are accurate. In fact, he's trying to subvert the idea of accuracy in fiction and insist on the primacy of storytelling. On the other hand, fidelity to what actually happened matters a great deal to Hilary Mantel.

Still, I think Mantel is being a little bit disingenuous, too. A writer who was slavishly dedicated to absolute historical accuracy would have her Tudor characters speaking in some approximation of 16th-century dialect, with lots of "thees" and "thous" and "methinks." But in *Wolf Hall* and *Bring up the Bodies*, Mantel very shrewdly has her characters speak in a modern sounding idiom that makes them seem more real to a 21st-century reader, but without making them sound anachronistic.

The research she did for *Wolf Hall* is evident on nearly every page, but what makes the novel soar is the way her imagination inhabits the mind of Thomas Cromwell, and the way her muscular and very modern prose evokes his world.

Here's a passage from early in the book, when Cromwell is thinking about his role in London society as a sort of fixer for international clients:

His house is full of people every day, people who want to be taken to [Cardinal Wolsey]. There are artists looking for a subject. There are solemn Dutch scholars with books under their arms, and Lubeck merchants unwinding at length solemn Germanic jokes; there are musicians in transit tuning up strange instruments, and noisy conclaves of agents for the Italian banks; there are alchemists offering recipes and astrologers offering favorable rates, and lonely Polish fur traders who've wandered by to see if someone speaks their language; there are printers, engravers, translators and cipherers; and poets, garden designers, cabalists and geometricians. Where are they tonight?

"Hush," [his wife] says. "Listen to the house."

At first, there is no sound. Then the timbers creak, breathe. In the chimneys, nesting birds shuffle. A breeze blows from the river, faintly shivering the tops of the trees. They hear the sleeping breath of children, imagined from other rooms. "Come to bed," he says.

This vivid catalogue of businesspeople and artists that begins this excerpt comes from Mantel's deep and intimate knowledge of the economic and social life of early modern Europe. But what makes this great fiction is the rhythm of the prose, the way it builds to the moment where Cromwell's thoughts shift seamlessly from his business to a moment of intimacy with his wife.

No modern reader would mistake this world for the 21st century, but by the same token, no modern reader would mistake this prose for a 16th-century text. The tension between Mantel's research and her imagination is heightened by the tension between the 16th-century experience of Thomas Cromwell and Mantel's 21st-century translation of it.

Now compare this with an excerpt from Jim Crace's book *Harvest*. This exquisitely written novel is about what historians call the Tudor Enclosures, when rural peasants in Britain were driven off the land so that powerful absentee landlords could raise sheep, because sheep were more profitable than rent from tenant farmers.

467

Set in the same period of English history as Mantel's novels, Crace's book never mentions what year it is, nor does it include any reference to any real historical figures or situations, the way Mantel's novels do. Instead, it's a detailed intimate account of a remote, rural village that is being challenged by a new economic reality, as narrated by one of the villagers.

Here are the first couple of paragraphs of the book's last chapter, as the narrator is leaving the village for the last time:

> So I have reached our village bounds. On this main lane, our outer limits are marked on one side by a merestone, about waist high and vivid with its orange overcoat of lichen. It is dressed for traveling. I've not been this close to the edge for several years. It has always seemed too precarious a place; on our side of the stone there can be no trespassing, as Master Kent has told us many times: "If we stay within the bounds, there are no bounds to stay us." One further step beyond, however, and everything you have is left behind.
>
> I snap off a stalk of grass from our side of the limits, tasting our own fodder with an ox's mouth. I grasp the merestone in both hands and bump my head against it, beating in the bounds just as we have beaten the bounds into every village child as soon as they were big enough to stray. I am that boy who needs reminding where he does and does not fit. I bump the stone three times, just hard enough to break the skin and lay the groundings of a bruise, just hard enough to make me admit to pain.

This has a contemporary immediacy, but as he promised in his interview, Crace evokes the feeling of a distant time and place mainly by using two bits of archaic vocabulary. One is "merestone," which is the Old English word that simply means "boundary stone." The other is the expression "beating the bounds," another archaic bit of English culture. "Beating the bounds" is a ceremony marking the boundaries of a village or a parish by bumping the heads of village boys against a boundary stone, to make sure they remember it.

Neither "merestone" nor "beating the bounds" is explained or put in any historical context. Given the antiquity of the two terms, this scene could have taken place anytime from the 10th century to the 21st. But even if you don't know the history behind them, they evoke a different world from our own.

These are real words from English history—I did say that Crace is a bit disingenuous about never doing research—but their use here represents the use of research at its most subtle and effective. Rather than overburdening the story with a lengthy and momentum-killing explanation of English folk tradition, Crace just tilts the camera, as it were, altering the reader's perception just enough to make the scene feel both vivid and strange.

My own belief about research falls somewhere between Jim Crace's and Hilary Mantel's. I don't have Crace's powers of linguistic invention, but I also don't have Hilary Mantel's ability to master a subject entirely before I write about it. To put it another way, I'm a bit more concerned than Crace seems to be about learning the history, but I'm less convinced than Hilary Mantel that the author has a moral responsibility to be absolutely faithful to the facts.

There's another fine British novelist named James Hamilton-Paterson, whose novel *Gerontius* is loosely based on the life of the composer Sir Edward Elgar. In the author's note at the beginning of the book, Hamilton-Paterson talks briefly about his research, explaining how he deliberately changed some of the details of Elgar's life. And at the end of the note he says, "For the rest, I tried to be as factually correct as was interesting."

This has become my motto for doing research. This improvisatory, ad hoc attitude to using research seems the most sensible approach to me, because it puts the story first. The primary purpose of a work of fiction is to create, in the words of John Gardner, a vivid and continuous dream in the mind of the reader. The two main requirements of any fictional narrative are to be both believable and interesting.

So, as far as research goes, you want to use common sense. You want to get your facts right, because it will make the narrative both more interesting and believable. At the very least, you don't want to distract the reader with obvious, easily preventable mistakes, the way my friend did by having the constellation Orion rise in the wrong part of the sky at the wrong time of year. If your reader is stopping to think, "Hey, that's not right," then you've broken the surface tension of the dream.

On the other hand, you don't want to be boring. Even Hilary Mantel has warned aspiring historical novelists not to inundate the reader with everything they've learned. "Don't show off," she says. "Your reader only needs to know about one tenth of what you know. Depth of knowledge gives the writer confidence and suppleness, but doesn't need to be demonstrated on every page."

Knowing when to back off from the research is also important to the process of writing itself. Years ago, I devoted several years of my life to an ambitious historical novel about an 18th-century Dutch explorer named Jacob Roggeveen, who was the European discoverer of Easter Island.

I eventually abandoned the novel for a variety of reasons. But one of those reasons is that I let my research overwhelm the narrative at the expense of the story and the characters. I accumulated enough books about the history and culture of the Netherlands and Polynesia to fill a six-foot bookcase. I filled up notebook after notebook with all sorts of historical arcana. I spent two weeks in the Netherlands and another three weeks camping on Easter Island. I wrote draft after draft after draft, trying to work in as much of this detail as I could. The result was that after three or four years of work, I had only 200 pages of the novel, and I was nowhere near the end of it.

Looking back on those pages now, I can see that they are impressively well-researched and that they have some vividly imagined scenes and characters. But for the most part they have no forward momentum. In places, in fact, this unfinished book is monumentally dull, because I lost sight of the character and the story, and instead, I filled my pages with tons of dramatically useless detail about clothing and houses and ships and landscape.

I wasn't writing a novel anymore. I was just mounting my research on the wall like a big game hunter. I hadn't yet learned Hilary Mantel's lesson not to show off, and I hadn't learned Jim Crace's trick of letting a word stand in for a world.

But I did learn some valuable lessons from that experience, which I have applied productively to my subsequent books. The most important lesson I learned is that, if you're writing a research-intensive narrative, the research and the writing should be inseparable. In practice, this means that you need to do the writing and the research at the same time, and this in turn means that to begin with, you'll be writing scenes without having any idea of what you're talking about.

Yet this is the best way to do it, I think. With any research-intensive work of fiction, you don't know what you need to know until you actually start writing. I learned this the hard way: The dullest passages in my Dutch novel are the ones where I did all the research first and then went back and tried to create a story out of it. On the other hand, the passages that did work were drafted both before and during the research, so that my imagination and the research played off each other.

For example, one of the more successful passages was a scene in which Jacob Roggeveen travels from his home in the small Dutch city of Middelburg to the much larger and more cosmopolitan city of Amsterdam, where he was hoping to win the financial support for his South Pacific expedition from the Dutch West India Company. I knew from my reading that Jacob was a notary, which was a kind of lawyer, and that he had never married or had children, and that he was a member of a heretical Calvinist sect.

But to begin with, I didn't know much about what Amsterdam was like at the time of Jacob's visit. And so my first draft was a barebones account of his trip and reactions, which I imagined were analogous to those of a small businessman from, say, Grand Rapids, Michigan, visiting Chicago in order to seek investors for some scheme. It was only after I had drafted a rough version of the scene that I realized that I needed to know much more about what Jacob would have seen and heard in the streets of Amsterdam in the year 1719. I also needed to know how Jacob's fringe religious beliefs would affect his reaction to the vibrant street life of a big city.

In part, I filled in these gaps by visiting modern-day Amsterdam myself. The old headquarters building of the Dutch West India Company still stands, on a little square off a street called the Haarlemmerstraat, and I walked up and down the street the way Jacob might have, taking copious notes. When I came home, I read several cultural histories about Amsterdam, one of which gave a wonderfully detailed account of the Haarlemmerstraat. Back then, I learned, the street was near the docks, and it was mostly lined with taverns and brothels that catered to sailors who had just come back from long sea voyages, and that after dark, it could be a noisy, gaudy, and dangerous place.

I also read more about the specific beliefs of Jacob's sect, and I learned that its members did not believe in the idea of sin in the traditional sense, but that what people called sinful behavior was just ignorance of their oneness with God, who controlled everything they did.

But what really made the scene come alive in my imagination was the fact that one of the hotels I stayed in during my trip to Amsterdam was on the Rembrandtplein, one of the central squares of the city. What I didn't know when I booked the room was that the Rembrandtplein is lined with nightclubs that draw huge crowds of young people from around the world, who party in the square every night until dawn. My room was up under the eaves of the old hotel, on the third or fourth floor. It was summertime and there was no air conditioning, so I was forced to leave the window open all night. As a result, I didn't get any sleep at all, but tossed and turned all night and listened to the thumping bass of Europop pouring out of the nightclubs, and the shouts and laughter of the kids in the street below.

In the end, I rewrote the scene about Jacob's visit to Amsterdam, bringing together all the things I had learned from my research and from my own visit to the city. Here's a paragraph from that scene:

After a meal of bread and cheese and beer in the smoky kitchen of the inn, Jacob ascended to his hot, airless room up under the eaves. The little window in his room was high—he had to stand to see out of it—and he pushed it open and looked down the steep slope of the roof. Twilight filled the square below, punctuated by fans of lamplight falling out of tavern doorways. He took off his shoes and his waistcoat and tried to sleep on the swaybacked bed, but he only tossed and turned in the breathless heat, kept awake by the nightly riot below. Woven through the roar of the crowd were the whine of fiddles and the wheeze of hurdy gurdys, playing songs Jacob remembered from childhood, rollicking dance tunes accompanied by the clatter of boots against cobbles as sailors and whores danced in the square. Sudden, violent squalls rose above the general racket: the harsh voices of drunken men braying the words of "The Cuckoo's Nest." The shattering screams of women dissolving into cackling laughter. Bottles breaking. The wordless shouting of men in a fight, the loser's howl as a blade pierced him. More cackling laughter. And as the racket finally receded near dawn into a lone sailor singing tunelessly to himself as he staggered along, Jacob heard carnal groans coming from an entryway just below his window. It was all what his mother used to call wickedness, but Jacob, in his sweaty clothes and tangled sheets, struggled to convince himself that there was no such thing as sin, only ignorance and error, that the poor souls cutting each other in the street or rutting in the doorway were simply stuck in their own flesh like ships run aground in the mud.

If I do say so myself, I think this works at least a little better than many of the passages in the novel, largely because I was able to model Jacob's restless night in Amsterdam after my own restless night in Amsterdam: two lonely out-of-towners, centuries apart, trying sleep while hundreds of other people were having noisy fun. My research into the city's history told me what sort of music the taverns would have played, and my reading about Jacob's religious beliefs told me that he would have been conflicted about what he heard. As for the rest, I just used my imagination to recreate what drunken sailors, tavern musicians, and prostitutes would likely have gotten up to on a typical night in the Haarlemmerstraat in 1719.

All of these elements came together to help me create a scene that was reasonably accurate, dramatically satisfying, and consistent with my conception of the character. But the seed for it was the rough draft I wrote before I knew anything about the history of the Haarlemmerstraat, or before I spent a sleepless night in Amsterdam. I needed to be writing even as I was doing the research. As a result, my research, my experience, and my imagination all sparked off each other in a dramatically productive way.

The experience of writing this scene taught me that research is important, but you need to put the story and characters first. It was my research that showed me what a night in the Haarlemmerstraat would have been like, but it was my imagination that enabled me to filter that experience through the consciousness of a single character. Using your imagination is every bit as important as getting your facts straight. I'd even say that research is just another tool in the service of your imagination. It serves the same function in fiction that plotting and character and dialogue do: It helps to suggest, to evoke, to put the reader in a time or place she might otherwise never experience.

Here's a very simple exercise that will help you think about doing research and using it in fiction. Pick an historical character who interests you—Abraham Lincoln, say, or Margaret Thatcher. Then write just a single scene about them doing something ordinary and private, like playing with their kids or making a sandwich, but at a time when something historic is going on that they might be thinking about.

Abraham Lincoln might be thinking about the Emancipation Proclamation, for example, as he plays checkers with his son, or Margaret Thatcher might be making herself a pot of tea late one night at the start of the Falklands War. Try to make it personal and intimate without letting the historical events dominate the scene.

We're coming at last to the end of our journey together, so, in my next and final lecture, I'm going to talk a little bit more personally about what it's like to make a life as a writer.

Making a Life as a Fiction Writer
Lecture 24

Imf you want to be a fiction writer, especially a published fiction writer, you need to learn to be two different people. One is the artist, the blinkered and driven obsessive who creates the work in the first place. By necessity, you must be solitary and self-critical, but you may also be moody, self-involved, and distracted. The other is the businessperson, whose responsibility it is to market and sell the work after it has been created. In this role, you need to be confident, good-humored, and gregarious. In other words, you need to be both the lonely genius in a garret and the glad-handing salesperson. In this final lecture, we'll explore these two halves of a writer's life.

The Business of Writing

- Aspiring writers usually want to know two things from published writers: (1) How do I get published, and (2) how do I make a living as a fiction writer? The answer to the second question is: You probably won't. Most writers have to earn a living doing something else and make time to write when they can. To put it bluntly, unless you're a very lucky fiction writer, you shouldn't quit your day job.

- The answer to the first question—how do I get published?—has always been difficult, but it used to be a fairly straightforward process. A writer either got the attention of an agent or a publisher or paid a vanity press to publish his or her work.

    o Many writers sold a story to a literary or genre magazine, which might lead to interest from an agent or a book publisher.

    o Some writers might find their own agents, who would market their work to commercial publishers in New York. The publisher would buy a writer's book and pay an advance against royalties, out of which the agent would take 10 or 15 percent. Then, the writer would go through the process of editing, copyediting, and printing, and between eight months and a year later, the book would come out.

o Depending on how much money the publisher paid for the book, the writer might be sent on a tour of bookstores, and a publicist might arrange interviews. Lucky writers might have their work reviewed in newspapers and magazines. Most published writers, however, were lucky if they sold enough copies to earn back their advances, which meant that publishers would at least take a look at their next books.

o There were a handful of writers who got rich off their books and a slightly larger handful, mostly writers of genre fiction, who were able to live off their royalties, but the vast majority of writers considered themselves lucky to be in print, to make a little money on the side, and to be able to write fiction while holding down a day job.

• This process is still the main way that many writers get published, and it's still the way most writers would probably prefer to be published. But in the past 30 years, the publishing industry has gone through enormous changes.

o First, there are essentially only five large commercial publishers of English-language fiction, each of which is only one division of a much larger corporation. These publishers are looking for market blockbusters that will appeal to a large and diverse readership or books that can be marketed to a particular niche. The *midlist writers* today earn smaller advances and get less attention from editors or do not get published at all.

o Second, there are now a large number of small, independent presses that publish the authors the Big Five are no longer willing to publish or promote. These don't pay much, and their books don't usually get much attention from the mainstream press, but their editors devote much more attention to the books they publish, they treat their authors with respect, and they are more likely to keep the books in print for a longer time.

o The third change—and the one that has driven the first two—is the rise of the Internet, the digital revolution, and the success of online retailers. These factors have irrevocably changed the way books are published, marketed, reviewed, purchased, and read.

The New Order versus the Old

- As a result of these changes—the corporatization of commercial publishing, the rise of online bookselling and the e-book, and the consequent decline of brick-and-mortar bookstores—the traditional agents and publishers don't have nearly as much power as they used to.
  - Today, there are essentially no barriers to getting published; anyone with a broadband connection can publish a manuscript online through any number of self-publishing platforms, and for a little more money, a writer can even provide readers with physical books through print-on-demand services.

  - Self-publishing is much more widely accepted, even by authors who have previously published in the traditional way. In certain genres, such as romance fiction, for example, many writers sell their work via the Internet directly to readers, who can download e-books in the space of a minute or two.

- There are also downsides to this new, more democratic order. The main drawback is that getting the attention of readers can be difficult. Breaking into the traditional system is hard, but once you're in, you can at least count on your publisher to send out review copies and possibly even to arrange interviews and appearances. Further, most readers understand that a traditionally published book has at least been edited for spelling and grammar. Self-published writers have to do all their own editing, proofreading, design, marketing, and publicity, or they have to pay people to perform these services.

- On the whole, it seems that the odds of success in the new system aren't all that different from the odds of success in the traditional system. The midlist writer who publishes in the traditional way is not likely to get much more attention than someone who self-publishes an e-book. In both the old and new orders, there are a handful of very successful authors; a large number who sell books only to their friends and loved ones; and a group of midlisters, who write the best books they can, do something else to make a living, and promote their work through social media.

Marketing Your Work

- As much as possible, you should write what you want to write—without trying to tailor your work to appeal to the market—and try to keep business out of the creative process. At the same time, the glad-handing salesperson in you should at least be thinking about how to market your book to the public even as you're working on it.

- If you plan to publish by the traditional route, do research online to find agents who have worked with writers you admire and publishers that have published the sort of work

Professionalism and networking are the keys to attracting the attention of agents and editors or readers in an online community.

you're trying to write. If you plan to self-publish, become part of an online community of writers and readers who enjoy reading the sort of thing you're writing.

- The key to attracting the attention of agents and editors or an online community of readers is to be professional. If you approach an agent, for example, write a brief cover letter pitching your novel and say a few words about yourself that make you sound knowledgeable and easy to work with. Mention any previous publications or awards you have received. In an online environment, be respectful, friendly, and brief. Praise the work of others that you genuinely admire and be honest but polite about work you don't like.

© Flying Colours Ltd/Photodisc/Thinkstock.

Why Write Fiction?

- In 1946, George Orwell published an essay, "Why I Write," in which he listed his four reasons: (1) sheer egoism, (2) aesthetic enthusiasm, (3) historical impulse, and (4) political purpose.

- The first two of these reasons probably hold true for most writers. No writer can function without ambition, but most would likely admit that egoism can be dangerous. Aesthetic enthusiasm is a much more benign and honorable motivation and probably also drives most writers.

- Akin to Orwell's "historical impulse" as a reason for writing is intellectual curiosity about a particular topic or even curiosity about one's own life. A novel is a way of thinking out loud to help writers understand certain issues or to explain their own lives to themselves.
  - As we've seen throughout this course, fiction writing can show you the unmediated consciousness of another person, revealing, as E. M. Forster put it, "the hidden life at its source."

  - This is an essential motivation for all fiction writers, but like any other motivation, it comes with consequences. One is the risk of narcissism, the temptation to believe that everything in your life is as interesting to a reader as it might be to you. The other is the hurt it might cause your family and friends.

- One final reason to write is to erase oneself in the creative act. Writers are achingly self-conscious creatures, and our live-wire awareness of everything around us and the constant hum of our own imaginations cause us to crave some sort of peace. Writing itself is an intensely self-conscious act, as you find yourself inhabiting the minds of your characters and forcing yourself to think about things that most people never think about at all. The paradox is that most writers find respite from this acute self-consciousness in the act of writing itself.
  - This motivation is tied to the desire to re-create the pleasure you gain by reading books you admire, a pleasure that takes you completely out of your own experience or even out of your own self-awareness. This is not the same thing as reading for escape, where your mind switches off and lets the narrative play

as if on a screen. Rather, it's the experience of fully inhabiting another life or world, where your mind is fully engaged—but not as yourself.

- o Another way to express this reason is to say that the most sublime experience in writing comes when you feel as if you are remembering the book, not creating it. It is as if the book is out there in the ether someplace, and you are simply recording what you have heard. When you're finished, you feel relief that what's on the page at last matches the melody in your head, the one only you can hear.

- For Orwell, the motive he valued above all others was politics; for many writers, it's more personal. What it might be for you is something only you can find out for yourself. But whatever your motivation turns out to be and whatever struggles and triumphs you have with writing and publishing, the act of creation itself will provide a great deal of meaning and satisfaction in your life.

Suggested Reading

Lamott, *Bird by Bird*.

Orwell, "Why I Write."

Woolf, *A Room of One's Own*.

Making a Life as a Fiction Writer
Lecture 24—Transcript

If you want to be a fiction writer, especially if you want to be a published fiction writer, you need to learn to be at least two different people. One of those people is the artist, the blinkered and driven obsessive who creates the work in the first place. By necessity, you must be solitary and self-critical, but you may also turn out to be moody, self-involved, and distracted.

The other person that a writer needs to be, however, is the businessperson. And the businessperson's responsibility is to market and sell the work after it has been created. In this role, you need to be confident, good-humored, and gregarious.

In other words, you need to be both the lonely genius in a garret and the glad-handing salesperson. You may drive yourself and everyone around you crazy while you create the work, but then you will have to charm other people who aren't actually related to you by blood, marriage, or friendship to read it and—who knows?—maybe even pay for it. I'm not sure which if these personas is Jekyll and which is Hyde, but you need to learn to balance them with each other.

As the great French novelist Gustave Flaubert put it, "Be steady and well-ordered in your life so that you can be fierce and original in your work."

In this final lecture, I'm going to talk about these two halves of a writer's life. Please bear in mind that nearly all of what I'm about to tell you is only my own opinion, even more than the previous lectures have been. What I have to say is based mostly on what's happened to me or other writers I know, and on what I've observed over the years about the publishing business. Another writer might tell you something completely different on these same topics, and at different stages in my career, I'd have told you something different from what I'll be telling you today. This lecture is going to be part jeremiad, part pep talk, and part sermonette.

Let's start with the business end of it. Aspiring writers often want to know two things from published writers: one is, "How do I get published?" and the other is, "How do I make a living as a fiction writer?" If I had been giving this lecture 20 years ago, the first question would have been easier to answer than it is now, while the answer to the second question—"How do I make a living as a fiction writer?"—has been the same for generations: You probably won't.

In her famous 1929 book about women and writing, *A Room of One's Own*, Virginia Woolf said that in order for a woman to have the same freedom to write that a man has, she needs a room of her own in which to work and a guaranteed income of 500 pounds a year, which would buy her the time to do nothing but write. Adjusted for inflation, 500 pounds in 1929 is about 25,000 pounds in 2012, or about $40,000.

Virginia Woolf was lucky enough to have 500 pounds a year, as the result of a bequest from an aunt. But before that she'd struggled to get by on the miserable sort of jobs available to women in the early 20th century, so she realized how lucky she was. Even today, most women writers, and most men, for that matter, don't make that kind of money writing fiction. They have to earn their living doing something else and make the time to write as best they can. To put it bluntly, unless you're a very lucky fiction writer, you should keep your day job.

Now let's turn to the subject of getting published. When I was starting out as a fiction writer back in the Pleistocene, by which I mean the 1980s, getting published was a difficult but fairly straightforward process. Back then, there were basically only two ways to get published. One way was to get the attention of an agent or a publisher. The other was to pay a vanity press to publish your work.

The less said about vanity presses, the better, but the more reputable route required that you persuade an editor at a literary magazine like *Ploughshares* or at a genre magazine like *The Magazine of Fantasy and Science Fiction* to buy one of your short stories. This in turn might lead to interest from an agent or a book publisher.

Or you might find yourself an agent on your own, who would market your book-length manuscript to commercial publishers in New York. The publisher would buy the book and pay you an advance against royalties, out of which your agent would take 10 or 15 percent. Then you'd go through the publication process of editing, copyediting, and printing, and between eight months and a year later, the book would come out.

The higher the advance a publisher pays you, the more effort they expend on your behalf. And so, depending on how much money the publisher paid for the book, you might be sent on a tour of bookstores, and a publicist might arrange interviews for you. If you were lucky, your book was widely reviewed in newspapers and magazines. If you were really lucky, you might have a bestseller, which means the advance for your next book would be even larger. However, most published writers were lucky if they just sold enough copies to earn back their advance. This meant that publishers would at least take a look at their next book.

Then, as now, and as it has ever been, there were a handful of writers who got rich off their books and a slightly larger handful, mostly writers of genre fiction, who were able to live off their royalties without getting rich. The vast majority of published fiction writers don't make a living off their work. They consider themselves lucky to be in print, to make a little money on the side, and to be able to write fiction while holding down a day job.

Now, at the time I'm giving this lecture, this is still the main way that many writers get published, and it's still the way that most writers, I think, would prefer to be published. Writers of all levels of experience love to rail against the imperious gatekeepers, namely the agents, editors, and reviewers of the mainstream publishing industry. But as in any unequal and dysfunctional relationship, we also crave their attention and want to be inside the club.

More importantly, we like to be paid for what we do.

But, in the 30 years since I started work on my first published novel and started publishing articles and book reviews in newspapers and magazines, the publishing industry has gone through enormous changes. These changes are very similar to the changes that have happened and continue to happen in the film and music industries. This is a vast topic, too big for me to go into detail, but here are the main points.

First, there are, at the time I'm giving this lecture, essentially only five large commercial publishers of English-language fiction, and each one of these publishers is only one division of a much larger corporation. On the whole, these publishers are still run by people who love good books, but they are under tremendous pressure from the corporations they work for to meet profit projections.

This business model means that publishers need to find and market blockbusters that will appeal to a large and diverse readership, or books that can be successfully marketed to a particular niche. This second type of book is often written by someone who is not necessarily a writer, but who is already famous for other reasons, such as an actor or a politician or an expert in a particular topic. Meanwhile the majority of fiction writers, the sort known as midlist writers, find ourselves earning smaller advances, getting less attention from editors than more profitable authors do, or just not getting published at all.

Second, there are now a number of small, independent presses who are publishing the authors that the Big Five are no longer willing to publish or promote. On the one hand, these indie presses don't pay much, and their books don't often get the attention from the mainstream media that books from the Big Five get. On the other hand, the editors at indie presses devote more attention to the books they do publish. They often treat their authors with a great deal of respect, and they are more likely to keep the books in print for a longer time.

Third—and this is the biggest change, the one that has driven the two I've already mentioned—the rise of the internet, the digital revolution, and the overwhelming success of online retailers, by which I mean Amazon, have irrevocably changed the way books are published, marketed, reviewed, purchased, and read.

Some of these changes are frightening to those of us who came up under the old way of doing things. For example, every medium-sized newspaper in America used to publish book reviews, but now there are fewer newspapers than there used to be. And of the newspapers that still exist, only a handful of the largest papers, such as the *New York Times*, the *Washington Post*, and the *Los Angeles Times*, publish book reviews at all.

This means that the sort of books that would have received at least a few reviews under the old regime now don't get reviewed at all, and the shrinking number of books that do get reviewed get fewer reviews than they used to. And even these reviews have less authority than they once did. The influence of professional book reviews is now rivaled, if not actually surpassed, by reader reviews online.

But the new order is not all bad news. As a result of these changes—the corporatization of commercial publishing, the rise of online bookselling and the e-book, and the consequent decline of brick-and-mortar bookstores—the power of the traditional gatekeepers has been greatly reduced. The answer to the question, "How do I get published?" used to involve laying siege to agents and editors and hoping you'd get noticed. If you couldn't get a commercial publisher to publish your book, you could get a vanity press to produce as many copies of your book as you were willing to pay for, but then no bookstore would carry it and no professional reviewer would review it.

Now, there are essentially no barriers to getting published. Anybody with a broadband connection can publish a manuscript online in a matter of minutes through any number of self-publishing platforms. For a little more money, you can even provide your readers with actual, physical books through print-on-demand services.

And today self-publishing is much more widely accepted than vanity publishing used to be, even by authors who have previously published in the traditional manner. In certain genres, such as romance fiction, for example, a lot of writers simply leap past the gatekeepers of traditional publishing and sell their work directly to readers via the internet, sometimes with considerable success.

In principle, self-published work is instantly available to the whole world. It used to be that if you read a review of a book that sounded interesting, you had to trek to a bookstore, assuming there was one nearby, and hope the store had a copy in stock. Now you can download an e-book while you're still reading the review, and be reading the book itself 90 seconds later.

Another benefit of this democratization of fiction publishing is that the arbitrary barriers between genres have begun to break down. During my first week as a student at the Iowa Writers Workshop in the fall of 1987, I was solemnly informed by two well-meaning second-year students that I should keep my love of genre fiction to myself. But when I went back to teach at Iowa in the winter of 2005, I was astounded and enormously pleased to discover that the students there, who were a generation younger than me, no longer cared much about genre distinctions.

Two of my best students, in fact, were enthusiastic and unapologetic fans, as I am, of Joss Whedon's great television show, *Buffy the Vampire Slayer*. And you can see this change not just with the students I knew at Iowa, but as a general trend in literary life. For example, Colson Whitehead and Karen Russell are both considered literary writers, and yet Whitehead has published a terrific zombie apocalypse novel, called *Zone One*, and Russell is the author of a creepy science fiction novella called *Sleep Donation*, about a plague of insomnia.

And coming from the other direction, great genre writers such Elmore Leonard, Denise Mina, George Pelecanos, Dennis Lehane, and Laura Lippman have garnered serious readers and mainstream respect for their consummate skill at storytelling, creating character, and crafting distinctive prose.

I've felt this welcome change in my own career as a writer. I have published entertaining but seriously intended works that feature sex, violence, ghosts, and zombies. As a reader, I find that I no longer get condescending looks when I say that both George Eliot's *Middlemarch* and Tolkien's *Lord of the Rings* are two of the greatest books ever written.

To be sure, there are also downsides to this new, more democratic order. Certainly the traditional system of gatekeepers could be, and often still is, conservative or crassly commercial or elitist. And there are certainly many famous stories of agents and editors turning down books that went on to become bestsellers or to be considered masterpieces. But those gatekeepers also serve a useful function by wading through piles of dreck so that the reader and prospective book-buyer don't have to. As a friend of mine once put it, the best thing about contemporary publishing is that anybody can publish a novel. On the other hand, the worst thing about the contemporary literary scene is that … anybody can publish a novel.

This fact is a particular drawback for writers. Even if you're one of the good ones, getting the attention of readers for your self-published work can be difficult, at best. Getting into the traditional system is hard, but once you're in, you can at least count on your publisher to send out review copies, and possibly even to arrange interviews with book bloggers and appearances at bookstores or with book clubs. Most readers understand that a traditionally published book has been selected by someone with a little discernment who read the manuscript and at least corrected the spelling and the grammar. Self-published writers do all their own editing, copyediting, proofreading, design, marketing, and publicity themselves, or they have to pay people out of their own pocket to perform these services, with very little chance of ever making that money back.

But this difficulty in getting the world's attention isn't really all that new. For the majority of fiction writers, the odds of success in the new system aren't really all that different from the odds of success in the traditional system.

Even in the old system, many writers were, and continue to be, ignored. Most of the review attention goes to a handful of literary novels, and the vast majority of sales go to brand name genre writers. The midlist writer who publishes in the traditional way is not likely to get much more attention than someone who self-publishes an e-book.

In both the old and new orders, there are going to be a handful of very successful authors who sell a lot of copies, get a lot of attention, and make a lot of money. And then there are going to be a huge number of others who will sell a few copies to their friends and loved ones.

In the middle, as always, are the rest of us, the midlisters, who write the best books we can under the circumstances, do something else to make a living, and somehow manage to find the time and energy to promote our own work through social media.

Now, some writers will tell you that you should study the market, see what sells, and tailor your work to appeal to that market. I'm not one of those people, but then, I'm not a particularly successful writer either, so maybe you shouldn't listen to me.

I still have a romantic and possibly naïve idea that you should write what you want, and keep the business part of it out of the creative process as much as possible. There's already a lot of pandering and cynical calculation in the culture, there's no need for fiction writers to add to it.

That said, the glad-handing salesman part of you should at least be thinking about how to market your book to the public even as you're working on it. If you're publishing by the traditional route, you want to do your research online and find out which agents and publishers have worked with the writers you admire or have sold or published the sort of work you're trying to write.

And while it's true that genre boundaries are breaking down, they still haven't vanished entirely. If you're writing a genre novel, don't waste your time trying to attract the attention of an agent who only does literary fiction, or vice versa.

If you decide to publish your work yourself as an e-book or a print-on-demand book, you want to become part of an online community of writers and readers who enjoy reading the sort of thing you're writing. If you're writing a work that appeals to a particular niche of readers, then become part of that community and make yourself known to them. But bear in mind that you don't want turn this activity into the substitute for actually writing the book. As I said in the very first lecture, writers are, by nature, expert procrastinators, so you don't want to encourage that in yourself. And either way, whether you're trying to attract the attention of agents or editors, or you're cultivating the fellowship of a community of readers with a shared interest, you want to be, above all, professional.

If you're approaching an agent, for example, you want your cover letter to be brief, no more than two pages and probably only one, and you want to put your best foot forward. Pitch the novel in as few words as possible, as attractively as possible, and say a few words about yourself that make you sound knowledgeable, interesting, and easy to work with. If you've published something already, tell the agent what and where, along with any awards or professional recognition you might have received.

The same goes for dealing with an online community. Be respectful, friendly, and brief. Engage actively in the conversation, but don't be overbearing or longwinded. Praise the work of others if you genuinely admire it, be honest but polite about the work you don't like, and, in general, just be a good neighbor. It's all about networking, in other words. The people you praise and befriend are much more likely to praise your work when you publish it.

Most of us write to be published. You want other people to read your work. But, as Anne Lamott puts it in her book *Bird by Bird*, "Publication is not going to change your life or solve your problems. Publication will not make you more confident or more beautiful, and it will probably not make you any richer."

So, given the difficulty of earning a living, finding time to write, and just getting into print—not to mention the unlikelihood of making money or getting famous—why write fiction at all?

One of the most famous answers to this question, and one that has been particularly influential in my life as a writer, is George Orwell's famous 1946 essay, "Why I Write." Orwell was a born writer, but he had no illusions about how hard it could be. In the essay's final paragraph, he writes:

All writers are vain, selfish and lazy, and at the very bottom of their motives there lies a mystery. Writing a book is a horrible, exhausting struggle, like a long bout of some painful illness. One would never undertake such a thing if one were not driven on by some demon whom one can neither resist nor understand.

Now, this is laying it on a bit thick. Like a lot of writers on the subject of writing, Orwell is rather narcissistically generalizing from his own experience to that of all writers. Not everybody finds writing as painful as he did, or at least, not all the time. And yet, as hard as he found it, Orwell dedicated his life to writing, and he gave four famous reasons why:

> Sheer egoism. Desire to seem clever, to be talked about, to be remembered after death, to get your own back on the grown-ups who snubbed you in childhood, etc., etc. ...

> Aesthetic enthusiasm. Perception of beauty in the external world, or, on the other hand, in words and their right arrangement. ...

> Historical impulse. Desire to see things as they are, to find out true facts and to store them up for the use of posterity.

> Political purpose. ... Desire to push the world in a certain direction, to alter other people's idea of the kind of society they should strive after.

I first read this essay in my early 20s, which is a very impressionable age for a writer, and for a time, I adopted Orwell's reasons for writing as my own. But as I got older and started to find my own way a writer, and as I came out from under the spell of George Orwell and the other writers I hero-worshipped, I realized that my own reasons for writing fiction were somewhat different.

The first two reasons still hold true for me, and, I suspect, for most writers. At the risk of overgeneralizing in the fashion of Orwell, I think it's safe to say that writers, on the whole, are demonstrably more egotistical and narcissistic than most people.

And a little egoism is not necessarily a bad thing. No writer can function without it. Genuinely meek, self-effacing people tend not to write novels. But I think most writers would admit that egoism is as dangerous as it is necessary, especially in an age and a culture that seems to worship success, money, and celebrity more than anything else.

As I explained rather bluntly earlier in this lecture, most of us are never going to be famous. Even those writers who do become famous never achieve fame at the level of movie stars, athletes, or musicians. There's no denying the power of egoism to keep you at your keyboard, but if you're not careful, the desire for fame can scorch your life and ruin your work.

Orwell's second reason, aesthetic enthusiasm, is a much more benign and honorable motivation, and I think it's something that drives most writers, even those who claim it doesn't. Some authors, such as Vladimir Nabokov and Eudora Welty, are celebrated for the beauty of their prose. But even the most unpretentious and workmanlike genre writer, who's just trying to get his characters from point A to point B and tell a compelling story, will take at least some secret pleasure in a well-turned phrase, an evocative metaphor, some pungent dialogue, or even an efficient passage of exposition.

And for many writers, much of the impulse to create something elegant or beautiful arises from our desire to reproduce the pleasure we have derived as readers from the books and authors we admire.

This is especially true when we are starting out. My first novel, *The Wild Colonial Boy*, was written partly to explore revolutionary politics in Northern Ireland. But it was also written to reproduce the thrills and excitement I got from reading such writers as Joseph Conrad, Graham Greene, John le Carré, and Robert Stone.

And while I think—or at least, I hope—I have become less imitative of other writers and more confident in my own voice, I still often feel inspired and more than a little competitive when I read a book I admire by another writer. This has happened to me with canonical masterpieces from the 19th century, but it also happens to me sometimes with some new book by some hot young writer who is 30 years younger than I am. The mix I feel of admiration and envy plays an important part in keeping me at my keyboard.

But for me, a more important reason for writing is intellectual curiosity about a particular topic, or even just curiosity about my own life. This is similar to Orwell's "historical impulse," the desire to explain to the world

491

"true facts" and "things as they are." In my case, however, the impulse is a little more personal.

We live in an age that is less certain of "things as they are" than Orwell's age was, or maybe it's just me who's uncertain. Either way, I have written novels on large, complicated subjects, such as terrorism in Northern Ireland or the role of postmodern literary theory in modern academia. But I didn't write these books because I think I have the last word on these subjects, I wrote them so that I could explain these issues to myself.

A novel is my way of thinking out loud. When I wanted to understand the violence in Northern Ireland in the 1980s, I created a story about it. I put characters inside the situation just to see what would happen, to help me understand where that kind of political violence came from and how it affected people's lives.

But this particular motivation, as I've said, doesn't just encompass history and politics; many writers use the writing of fiction for a more intimate purpose, to explain their own lives to themselves.

In *Bird by Bird*, Anne Lamott talks about writing books in order to fill a need in her own life that no other books can fill. This can be even more difficult and scary than taking on a large subject outside yourself like terrorism, because you may reveal things to yourself or to your loved ones that most people would leave unsaid.

As Lamott puts it,

> We write to expose the unexposed. If there is one door in the castle you have been told not to go through, you must. Otherwise, you'll just be rearranging furniture in rooms you've already been in. Most human beings are dedicated to keeping that one door shut. But the writer's job is to see what's behind it, to see the bleak unspeakable stuff, and to turn the unspeakable into words—not just any words but if we can, into rhythm and blues.

This is a very eloquent way of saying what I talked about in my lectures on character, that fiction writing can show you the unmediated consciousness of another person, that it reveals, as E. M. Forster put it, "the hidden life at its source."

This is an essential motivation for all fiction writers, but like any motivations, it comes with consequences. One is the risk of narcissism, the temptation to believe that every little thing in your life is as interesting to a reader as it might be to you. The other risk is the hurt it might cause your family and friends, who may not see the moral imperative of opening that particular door in the castle.

A writer's obsessive need to tell secrets is itself an uncomfortable secret that is badly kept by all fiction writers. "Writers are always selling somebody out," said the American writer Joan Didion, and the novelist Graham Greene said, "There is a splinter of ice in the heart of a writer." Anne Lamott turns this sentiment into a witty imperative: "Write as if your parents are dead."

The best you can hope for is that telling the truth is worth the pain it might occasionally cause other people. I won't go into detail, but I've had some uncomfortable conversations over the years because of things I've written. I've felt regret for the pain I've caused, but—and here's my own sliver of ice, on full display—I don't regret anything I've written. Or not much of it, anyway.

But there's one last reason to write that I think is pretty common among writers, if not universal. And for me, it runs deeper and drives me more urgently than any of the other reasons I've talked about so far. And that reason is this: I write to erase myself in the creative act.

Writers are achingly self-conscious creatures, and our live-wire awareness of everything around us and the constant hum of our own imaginations cause us to crave some sort of peace.

Writing itself is an intensely self-conscious act. On a daily basis, you find yourself inhabiting the minds of your characters and forcing yourself to think explicitly about the things that most people, in their day-to-day lives, never think about at all.

The paradox is that most writers find respite from this acute self-consciousness in the act of writing itself. This motivation is closely tied to the desire to recreate the pleasure you gained by reading the books you admire. That pleasure can take you completely out of your own experience, or even out of your own self-awareness. It can make you feel as if you're living in the story the way the characters do.

This is not the same thing as reading for escape, where your mind just switches off and lets the narrative play as if upon a screen. Rather, it's the experience of fully inhabiting another life or world, where your mind is fully engaged—but not as yourself.

Another way to put it is say that the most sublime experience in writing comes when you feel as if you are remembering the book, not creating it. It's as if the book is out there in the ether someplace, and you're simply recording what you've heard. This is what a writer means when she says, after multiple, agonizing drafts, "This is it." It's the relief you feel when what's on the page at last matches the melody in your head, the one only you can hear.

This spiritual release is not unique to me. Countless writers have talked about this feeling over the years. Stephen King has talked about "the boys in the basement" who write his books, and he even quotes the great editor Maxwell Perkins, talking about the writer Thomas Wolfe: "The wind blew through him and he just rattled."

I know that this smacks of vulgar Platonism or New Agey channeling, but I don't know how else to say it. The most vivid and transcendent moments of my life, the moments when I completely forget where and who I am, have come when I was writing fiction.

I know this sounds kind of crazy, but I can't think of a better way to express the feeling I get when I'm writing well. I can't even say for sure that the writing that results from this release of self is even my best work. I only know that the pleasure I take in it is so similar to the pleasure I take from reading someone else's best work that I can only conclude that the two pleasures come from the same place.

This conclusion brings me full circle back to the original question—"Why write fiction?" It also threatens to unravel the tapestry of answers I've stitched together. If I get the same pleasure from reading as I get from creating, why endure rejection, shredded nerves, bad reviews, the world's indifference, and all the rest? Why write at all?

Maybe all literary achievement comes from sheer egoism. Maybe I write my own work because there is more pleasure to be derived from erasing myself than from letting somebody else do it for me. Perhaps each writer is his own ouroboros, eagerly opening his ego wide to devour himself, and vanishing in a little flash of creation that leaves a story or a novel behind. Whatever it is, this mysterious alchemy of self-effacement on the one hand and self-aggrandizement on the other, is what keeps me coming back to writing, no matter what the success or failure of my work in the world.

Since I've come full circle, I'll return to Orwell:

> For all one knows that demon [that makes one write] is simply the same instinct that makes a baby squall for attention. And yet it is also true that one can write nothing readable unless one constantly struggles to efface one's own personality. Good prose is like a window pane. I cannot say with certainty which of my motives are the strongest, but I know which of them deserve to be followed.

For Orwell, the motive he valued above all others was politics. For me, it's more personal. What it might be for you is something only you can find out for yourself. But whatever your motivation turns out to be, and whatever struggles and triumphs you have with writing and publishing, I hope the act of creation provides as much meaning in your life as it has in mine, and that the art of fiction gives you as much satisfaction as it has given me over the years. Good luck!

Appendix: Punctuating Dialogue

Most of what you need to know about the mechanics of writing dialogue can be summed up in a few rules. The vast majority of fiction published since the 18th century has followed these rules, although some great writers, including William Faulkner and Cormac McCarthy, have violated them. In the following paragraphs, Mr. Faulkner and Mr. McCarthy will help us review dialogue rules.

The first rule is that all direct quotations, namely, the exact words of a character, should be set apart from the rest of the text by quotation marks. The second rule is that every time a new character speaks or the speaker changes, his or her first line of dialogue should be set apart with a paragraph break. Also, the first word of a direct quotation always starts with a capital letter. Here's an example that illustrates these rules:

> "Do you think quotation marks are necessary?" asked Mr. Faulkner. "Some people say yes; some people say no."

> "I don't use quotation marks myself," said Mr. McCarthy. "I think they just clutter up a page."

Remember that these rules of punctuation serve two purposes: to set dialogue apart from the rest of the narrative and to identify who is speaking at any given time. The quotation marks and the paragraph breaks serve the first purpose, and the second purpose is served by identifying each speaker with a *dialogue tag*, which in its most basic form is simply the name of the character or a pronoun standing in for the name plus some variation on the verb *said*. In the exchange above, *asked Mr. Faulkner* and *said Mr. McCarthy* are dialogue tags; other common tags include *he said*, *she said*, *he replied*, *she shouted*, and so on.

The rules for punctuating dialogue tags get a little tricky. The first rule is that the dialogue tag is not part of the actual quotation; thus, it should never be included within the quotation marks. The following example is incorrect:

"Do you think this fellow Hynes, said Mr. McCarthy, has any idea what he's talking about?"

The reason it's incorrect is that there are only two sets of quotation marks, one at the beginning of the quotation and one at the end, when there should be four sets of quotation marks: one at the beginning, a second one just before the dialogue tag, a third one right after the dialogue tag, and a fourth at the end, as shown below:

"Do you think this fellow Hynes," said Mr. McCarthy, "has any idea what he's talking about?"

Sometimes a dialogue tag comes in the middle of the quoted sentence; in those cases, the first half of the quotation is set off by a comma and a quotation mark, the dialogue tag is followed by a comma, and the second half of the sentence begins with a quotation mark and a lowercase letter, as shown below:

"I have a feeling," said Mr. Faulkner, "that this fellow Hynes is not paying any attention to us."

However, if a dialogue tag appears between two *complete* sentences, then it is followed by a period, and the second sentence starts with a capital letter:

"There's no reason for him to listen to us," said Mr. McCarthy. "You've been dead for fifty years, and I'm famously reclusive."

There are a couple of additional rules for dialogue: Punctuation always appears inside the quotation marks, and when the dialogue tag appears after the quotation or after the first half of the quotation, the quote can be separated from the tag with a comma, a question mark, or an exclamation point but never with a period. Thus, the following quotations are punctuated correctly:

"That's no excuse," said Mr. Faulkner.

"What can you do with a young fellow like that?" said Mr. McCarthy.

"Kids today!" said Mr. Faulkner.

But the one below is not:

"As far as I'm concerned, there are no rules in creative writing." said Mr. McCarthy.

Let's look at the whole dialogue, this time, punctuated correctly:

"Do you think quotation marks are necessary?" asked Mr. Faulkner. "Some people say yes; some people say no."

"I don't use quotation marks myself," said Mr. McCarthy. "I think they just clutter up a page."

"Do you think this fellow Hynes," said Mr. McCarthy, "has any idea what he's talking about?"

"I have a feeling," said Mr. Faulkner, "that this fellow Hynes is not paying any attention to us."

"There's no reason for him to listen to us," said Mr. McCarthy. "You've been dead for fifty years, and I'm famously reclusive."

"That's no excuse," said Mr. Faulkner.

"What can you do with a young fellow like that?" said Mr. McCarthy.

"Kids today!" said Mr. Faulkner.

"As far as I'm concerned, there are no rules in creative writing," said Mr. McCarthy.

Remember, any good grammar guide will explain these rules in more detail, but an even better way to learn them is simply to model what you do after what your favorite writer does—assuming your favorite writer isn't Cormac McCarthy.

Bibliography

Ackroyd, Peter. *Dickens*. New York: HarperCollins, 1990.

Alvarez, Julia. *How the Garcia Girls Lost Their Accents*. London: Bloomsbury, 2004.

Aristotle. *Poetics*. Translated by Malcolm Heath. London: Penguin Books, 1996.

Atkinson, Kate. *Life after Life*. New York: Little, Brown, 2013.

Austen, Jane. *Emma*. Oxford: Oxford University Press, 1971.

―――. *Pride and Prejudice*. London: Penguin Books, 1996.

Baldwin, James. *Giovanni's Room*. New York: Penguin Books, 2001.

Banville, John. *Doctor Copernicus*. New York: Vintage, 1993.

Barker, Nicola. *Darkmans*. New York: Harper, 2007.

Barker, Pat. *The Eye in the Door*. New York: Plume, 1995.

―――. *The Ghost Road*. New York: Plume, 1996.

―――. *Regeneration*. New York: Plume, 1993.

Bellow, Saul. *The Adventures of Augie March*. New York: Penguin Books, 1999.

Beowulf. Translated by Seamus Heaney. New York: Farrar, Straus and Giroux, 2000.

Berger, Thomas. *Little Big Man*. New York: Dial Press, 1989.

Bernays, Anne, and Pamela Painter. *What If? Writing Exercises for Fiction Writers*. 3ʳᵈ ed. New York: Longman, 2009.

Borges, Jorge Luis. "Epilogue." In *Dreamtigers*. Translated by Mildred Boyer and Harold Morland. Austin, TX: University of Texas Press, 1964.

Boylan, Roger. *Killoyle*. Normal, IL: Dalkey Archive, 1997.

Brontë, Charlotte. *Jane Eyre*. London: Penguin Books, 2006.

Burroway, Janet. *Writing Fiction: A Guide to Narrative Craft*. 7ᵗʰ ed. New York: Pearson Longman, 2007.

Byatt, A. S. *Possession*. New York: Vintage Books, 1991.

Catton, Eleanor. *The Luminaries*. New York: Little, Brown, 2013.

Chandler, Raymond. *The Big Sleep*. New York: Vintage Books, 1988.

———. *The Long Goodbye*. New York: Vintage Books, 1988.

Chekhov, Anton. "The Darling." In *The Darling and Other Stories*. Translated by Constance Garnett. New York: The Ecco Press, 1984.

———. "The Kiss." In *The Party and Other Stories*. Translated by Constance Garnett. New York: The Ecco Press, 1984.

Chopin, Kate. *The Awakening*. In *Complete Novels and Stories*. New York: Library of America, 2002.

Christensen, Kate. *The Epicure's Lament*. New York: Anchor Books, 2005.

Conan Doyle, Arthur. *The Hound of the Baskervilles*. New York: Barnes and Noble, 2009.

Conrad, Joseph. *Lord Jim*. London: Penguin Books, 2000.

———. *Nostromo*. Oxford: Oxford University Press, 2007.

Crace, Jim. "The Art of Fiction No. 179." *The Paris Review*. http://www.theparisreview.org/interviews/122/the-art-of-fiction-no-179-jim-crace.

———. *The Gift of Stones*. New York: The Ecco Press, 1988.

———. *Harvest*. New York: Vintage Books, 2013.

———. *Quarantine*. New York: Picador, 1998.

Dickens, Charles. *Bleak House*. London: Penguin Books, 2003.

———. *David Copperfield*. London: Penguin Books, 2004.

———. *Great Expectations*. London: Penguin Books, 2002.

———. *Oliver Twist*. London: Penguin Books, 2003.

Dreiser, Theodore. *Sister Carrie*. New York: Penguin Books, 1994.

Egan, Jennifer. *A Visit from the Goon Squad*. New York: Anchor, 2011.

Eliot, George. *Middlemarch*. London: Penguin Books, 1994.

Ellroy, James. *L.A. Confidential*. New York: Grand Central, 1990.

Farrell, J. G. *Troubles*. New York: NYRB Classics, 2002.

Faulkner, William. "A Rose for Emily." In *Collected Stories*. New York: Vintage Books, 1995.

———. *As I Lay Dying*. New York: Vintage Books, 1990.

———. *Light in August*. New York: Vintage Books, 1991.

———. *The Sound and the Fury*. New York: Vintage Books, 1990.

Ferris, Joshua. *Then We Came to the End*. New York: Back Bay Books, 2008.

Fielding, Henry. *The History of Tom Jones, A Foundling*. London: Penguin Books, 2005.

Figes, Eva. *Light: With Monet at Giverny*. London: Pallas Athene, 2007.

Fitzgerald, F. Scott. *The Great Gatsby*. New York: Scribner, 2004.

———. *The Last Tycoon*. New York: Scribner, 1941.

Flaubert, Gustave. *Madame Bovary*. Translated by Geoffrey Wall. London: Penguin Books, 2002.

Forster, E. M. *Aspects of the Novel*. New York: Harcourt Brace Jovanovich, 1955.

Franzen, Jonathan. *The Corrections*. New York: Farrar, Straus and Giroux, 2001.

Gaddis, William. *The Recognitions*. Champaign, IL: Dalkey Archive, 2012.

Gardner, John. *The Art of Fiction: Notes on Craft for Young Writers*. New York: Vintage Books, 1991.

———. *Grendel*. New York: Vintage Books, 1989.

Gibson, William. *Neuromancer*. New York: Ace Books, 1984.

Graves, Robert. *I, Claudius*. New York: Vintage Books, 1989.

Gwynn, Frederick L., and Joseph Blotner. *Faulkner in the University*. Charlottesville, VA: University of Virginia Press, 1959.

Hamid, Mohsin. *The Reluctant Fundamentalist*. New York: Mariner Books, 2008.

Hamilton-Paterson, James. *Gerontius*. New York: Soho Press, 1989.

Hammett, Dashiell. *The Maltese Falcon*. New York: Vintage Books, 1989.

Hawkes, Judith. *Julian's House*. New York: Signet, 2001.

Heller, Joseph. *Catch-22*. New York: Everyman's Library, 1995.

Higgins, George V. *The Friends of Eddie Coyle*. New York: Picador, 2010.

Homer. *The Iliad*. Translated by Robert Fagles. London: Penguin Books, 1990.

———. *The Odyssey*. Translated by Robert Fagles. London: Penguin Books, 1997.

Hornby, Nick. *About a Boy*. New York: Riverhead Books, 1999.

———. *How to Be Good*. New York: Riverhead Books, 2002.

Hurston, Zora Neale. *Their Eyes Were Watching God*. New York: HarperCollins, 2000.

Hynes, James. *Kings of Infinite Space*. New York: St. Martin's Press, 2004.

———. *The Lecturer's Tale*. New York: Picador, 2001.

———. *Next*. New York: Little, Brown, 2011.

———. *Publish and Perish*. New York: Picador, 1998.

———. *The Wild Colonial Boy*. New York: Picador, 1990.

Jackson, Shirley. "The Lottery." In *The Lottery and Other Stories*. New York: Farrar, Straus and Giroux, 2005.

James, Henry. *The Turn of the Screw and The Aspern Papers*. London: Penguin Books, 2003.

James, M. R. "Casting the Runes." In *Count Magnus and Other Ghost Stories*. New York: Penguin Books, 2005.

Joyce, James. "The Dead." In *Dubliners*. London: Penguin Books, 1993.

———. *Ulysses*. New York: Everyman's Library, 1992.

Kafka, Franz. "Metamorphosis." In *Metamorphosis and Other Stories*. Translated by Michael Hoffman. London: Penguin Books, 2007.

King, Stephen. *'Salem's Lot*. New York: Pocket Books, 1999.

Kundera, Milan. *The Unbearable Lightness of Being*. New York: Perennial Classics, 1999.

Lamott, Anne. *Bird by Bird: Some Instructions on Writing and Life*. New York: Anchor Books, 1995.

Le Carré, John. *Tinker, Tailor, Soldier, Spy*. London: Penguin Books, 2011.

Lee, Harper. *To Kill a Mockingbird*. New York: Grand Central Publishing, 1982.

Leonard, Elmore. *Cuba Libre*. New York: William Morrow, 2012.

Lowry, Malcolm. *Under the Volcano*. New York: Harper Perennial Modern Classics, 2007.

MacFarquhar, Larissa. "The Dead Are Real: Hilary Mantel's Imagination." *The New Yorker*, October 12, 2012.

Mansfield, Katherine. "Miss Brill." In *Stories*. New York: Vintage Books, 1991.

Mantel, Hilary. *Bring up the Bodies*. New York: Picador, 2012.

———. "Hilary Mantel on Teaching a Historical Fiction Masterclass." *Fiction at Its Finest*. http://www.themanbookerprize.com/feature/hilary-mantel-teaching-historical-fiction-masterclass.

———. *Wolf Hall*. New York: Picador, 2009.

Marks, John. *Fangland*. New York: Penguin Books, 2007.

Marshall, Paule. *The Chosen Place, the Timeless People*. New York: Vintage Books, 1984.

Martin, George R. R. *A Song of Ice and Fire: A Game of Thrones*, *A Clash of Kings*, *A Storm of Swords*, *A Feast for Crows*, and *A Dance with Dragons*. New York: Bantam Books, 1996, 1999, 2000, 2005, and 2011.

Martin, Valerie. *Mary Reilly*. New York: Vintage Books, 2001.

McCarthy, Cormac. *Blood Meridian*. New York: Vintage Books, 1992.

———. *The Road*. New York: Vintage Books, 2006.

Melville, Herman. *Moby-Dick*. New York: Penguin Books, 2001.

Mina, Denise. *Field of Blood*. New York: Little, Brown, 2005.

Mitchell, Margaret. *Gone with the Wind*. New York: Pocket Books, 2008.

Morrison, Toni. *Beloved*. New York: Vintage Books, 2004.

Munro, Alice. *The Beggar Maid: Stories of Flo and Rose*. New York: Vintage Books, 1991.

———. "Walker Brothers Cowboy." In *Dance of the Happy Shades and Other Stories*. New York: Vintage Books, 1998.

Nabokov, Vladimir. "The Art of Fiction No. 40." *The Paris Review.* http://www.theparisreview.org/interviews/4310/the-art-of-fiction-no-40-vladimir-nabokov.

————. *Lolita*. New York: Vintage Books, 1997.

Némirovsky, Irène. *Suite Française*. Translated by Sandra Smith. New York: Vintage Books, 2007.

O'Connor, Flannery. "A Good Man Is Hard to Find." In *The Complete Stories*. New York: Farrar, Straus and Giroux, 1971.

Orwell, George. "Why I Write." In *Essays*. New York: Everyman's Library, 2002.

Pelecanos, George. *The Cut*. New York: Little, Brown, 2011.

Pinter, Harold. *Betrayal*. London: Faber and Faber, 2013.

Randall, Alice. *The Wind Done Gone*. New York: Mariner Books, 2002.

Rhys, Jean. *Wide Sargasso Sea*. New York: W. W. Norton, 1992.

Robinson, Marilynne. *Housekeeping*. New York: Picador, 1980.

Rowling, J. K. *Harry Potter and the Sorcerer's Stone*. New York: Scholastic, 1997.

Rushdie, Salman. *Midnight's Children*. New York: Random House, 2006.

Russell, Karen. *Sleep Donation*. New York: Atavist Books, 2014.

Schwartz, John Burnham. *Reservation Road*. New York: Vintage Books, 2008.

Sebold, Alice. *The Lovely Bones*. New York: Back Bay Books, 2004.

Shakespeare, William. *Hamlet, Prince of Denmark*. London: Penguin Books, 1970.

———. *King Lear*. London: Penguin Books, 1970.

Smiley, Jane. *A Thousand Acres*. New York: Anchor Books, 2003.

Spencer, Scott. *Endless Love*. New York: The Ecco Press, 2010.

St. Aubyn, Edward. *The Patrick Melrose Novels: Never Mind, Bad News, Some Hope, and Mother's Milk*. New York: Picador, 2012.

Stead, Cristina. *The Man Who Loved Children*. New York: Picador, 2001.

Stevenson, Robert Louis. *Dr. Jekyll and Mr. Hyde and Other Tales of Terror*. London: Penguin Books, 2002.

Stoker, Bram. *Dracula*. New York: Barnes and Noble, 2012.

Stone, Robert. *A Flag for Sunrise*. New York: Vintage Books, 1992.

Sutcliff, Rosemary. *The Eagle of the Ninth*. New York: Farrar, Straus and Giroux, 1999.

———. *The Lantern Bearers*. New York: Farrar, Straus and Giroux, 2010.

———. *The Silver Branch*. New York: Farrar, Straus and Giroux, 2000.

Tolkien, J. R. R. *The Hobbit*. New York: Houghton Mifflin Harcourt, 2012.

———. *The Lord of the Rings*. New York: Mariner Books, 2012.

———. *The Two Towers*. New York: Mariner Books, 2012.

Tolstoy, Leo. *Anna Karenina*. Translated by Richard Peavar and Larissa Volokhonsky. New York: Penguin Books, 2002.

———. *The Death of Ivan Ilyich and Master and Man*. Translated by Ann Pasternak Slater. New York: Modern Library, 2003.

Truffaut, François. *Hitchcock*. New York: Simon and Schuster, 2005.

Twain, Mark. *Adventures of Huckleberry Finn*. London: Penguin Books, 2002.

Updike, John. *Rabbit Angstrom: The Four Novels*. New York: Everyman's Library, 1995.

Wallace, David Foster. *Infinite Jest*. New York: Back Bay Books, 2006.

Welty, Eudora. "Why I Live at the P.O." In *The Collected Stories of Eudora Welty*. New York: Harcourt, 1994.

Wharton, Edith. *The House of Mirth*. London: Penguin Books, 1993.

Whitehead, Colson. *Zone One*. New York: Anchor Books, 2011.

Wilson, Leslie. "*Bring up the Bodies* by Hilary Mantel." *The History Girls*. http://the-history-girls.blogspot.com/2012/05/bring-up-bodies-by-hilary-mantel.html.

Woolf, Virginia. *A Room of One's Own*. New York: Mariner Books, 1989.

———. *Mrs. Dalloway*. New York: Everyman's Library, 1993.

Yourcenar, Marguerite. *The Memoirs of Hadrian*. Translated by Grace Frick. New York: Farrar, Straus and Giroux, 1990.

Zola, Emile. *Germinal*. Translated by Roger Pearson. London: Penguin Books, 2004.

Notes

Notes

Notes